Machine Shop Know-How

The Tips & Techniques of Master Machinists

First Edition

Frank M. Marlow, PE

Illustrations by

P. J. Tallman

Metal Arts Press
Huntington Beach

Metal Arts Press
www.MetalArtsPress.com
8461 Valencia Drive
Huntington Beach, CA 92647-6033
USA

Machine Shop Know-How
The Tips & Techniques of Master Machinists
First Edition
ISBN-13 978-0-975-9963-4-8
Copyright © 2010 by
Frank M. Marlow & Pamela J. Tallman
All rights reserved.

Printed and bound in the United States of America.
This book, or any parts thereof, may not be reproduced,
stored in a retrieval system, or transmitted in any form
without the express written permission of the authors.

Cover design by Stephanie Starr

10 9 8 7 6 5 4 3 2 1

To David Randal

for his friendship and his knowledge

Contents

Preface

What This Book Is About

If you've ever wished you could take all of the knowledge of a master machinist and pour it directly into your brain, here is your chance. *Machine Show Know-How* proves that there are no secrets in the machine shop, just information that is rarely documented—until now. This book focuses on manually controlled machine tools, but moves beyond the basics to present the problem-solving insights, shop shortcuts, and clever tips and tricks that normally take years of first-hand shop experience to learn.

Who This Book Is For

This book is for home shop machinists, industrial model and scientific instrument makers, R&D lab technicians, prototype designers, custom motorcycle and car builders, gunsmiths, teachers, students, and anyone who has a fundamental knowledge of machine shop practice and wants to advance to the next level.

How This Book Is Organized

Organized in an easy to understand chapter format, *Machine Shop Know-How* presents hundreds of imaginative shop solutions devised by top industry professionals, including how to *really* organize your shop; how to truly master your lathe, milling machine, bandsaws and grinders; how to fabricate ingenious shop-made tools and modify existing ones; how to make clever and useful jigs and fixtures; and how to use the valuable skill-building lessons learned in this book to solve your own shop problems.

Note From the Author

I hope this book answers your questions, stimulates your creativity, and improves your machine shop projects so you can finally eliminate the *Oh, darn* factor. To this end, the nearly 600 line drawings in this text were developed specifically for this book—no copies of copies of old Army manuals.

I am thankful for the generous help of the many individuals and companies who contributed their time and knowledge to the book. The greatest care has been taken to be precise and accurate, but naturally, I remain responsible for any errors.

Frank Marlow   Huntington Beach, California
                                                                                      February 2010

Acknowledgements

Albrecht, Inc.
David Bishop
Bryce Fastener, Inc.
Chicago-Latrobe/Kennametal
Clausing Industrial, Inc.
Cooper Industries, Inc.
Criterion Machine Works
Prof. Robert J. DeVoe, PE
The Do-All Company
Form Roll Die Corporation
Réne Graf
Grobet USA
Hardinge Inc.
Jacobs Chuck Manufacturing Company
William Johnson
Kent Industrial (USA), Inc.
KEO Cutters
Guy Lautard
Craig Libuse
The James F. Lincoln Welding Foundation
Jon Maki
Joe Martin
Mitee-Bite Products LLC
The M. K. Morse Company
Michael Plankey
Connie Randal
David Randal
Phil Samuels
Sherline Products Inc.
L.S. Starrett Company
Don Tallman
TE-CO Products, LLC
Eddie Torres
Toyota Motor Corporation
Usines Métallurgiques de Vallorbe SA
Bob Wahlstrom
Bernie Wasinger
George Young
Sandrine Zender

Chapter 1

Setting Up Shop

We cannot solve problems by using the same kind
of thinking we used when we created them.
—Albert Einstein

Introduction

Setting up a good working shop does not happen overnight. Gathering the right tools, adapting them to fit your needs and properly storing them comes gradually. Whether you are an experienced machinist or just starting out, this chapter will help speed the process. Many machinists underestimate the value of neat, well organized storage, but the old adage, "If you can't find it, you don't own it," could not be more true than in the machine shop.

Section I – A Place for Everything

Workbenches

The workbench is the most basic piece of equipment in the shop. Figure 1-1 shows a workbench that really works. Besides a rigid surface, this design has lots of handy storage. There are many other excellent workbench designs, but they all have the following features in common:

- *Rigidity* – When hacksawing, filing or tugging on a wrench in the vise, the bench must not wiggle. Also, it must be solid enough for center punching and hammering. A rigid bench usually has bolted or welded joints and robust legs of 4 × 4-inch lumber or 4-inch steel pipe. There are also commercially available steel legs which simplify building a good sturdy bench. Bolting the bench to a wall adds rigidity and is a good idea in earthquake zones.

- *Storage drawers with trays* – Two or three 6-inch deep wood or steel drawers placed under the bench are handy for holding frequently used tools. Sliding shallow trays inside the drawers make small tools easy to find among the larger ones. Ball-bearing drawer slides are inexpensive, simple to install, and can handle heavy loads. See Figure 1-2.

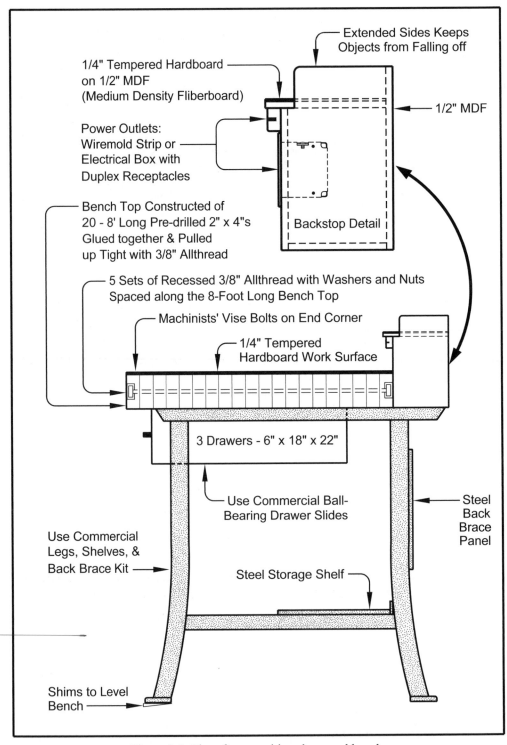

1/4" Tempered Hardboard
on 1/2" MDF
(Medium Density Fliberboard)

Extended Sides Keeps
Objects from Falling off

1/2" MDF

Power Outlets:
Wiremold Strip or
Electrical Box with
Duplex Receptacles

Backstop Detail

Bench Top Constructed of
20 - 8' Long Pre-drilled 2" x 4"s
Glued together & Pulled
up Tight with 3/8" Allthread

5 Sets of Recessed 3/8" Allthread with Washers and Nuts
Spaced along the 8-Foot Long Bench Top

Machinists' Vise Bolts on End Corner

1/4" Tempered
Hardboard Work Surface

3 Drawers - 6" x 18" x 22"

Use Commercial Ball-
Bearing Drawer Slides

Steel
Back
Brace
Panel

Use Commercial
Legs, Shelves, &
Back Brace Kit

Steel Storage Shelf

Shims to Level
Bench

Figure 1-1. Plans for a machine shop workbench.

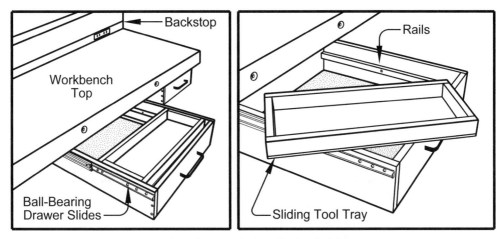

Figure 1-2. Ball-bearing slides make heavily loaded drawers easy to open.
Sliding trays in the drawers make smaller tools easy to find.

- *Backstop with shelf* – The backstop not only prevents small items from falling off the back of the bench, it provides a mount for power receptacles and supports a separate shelf above the workbench surface. On this shelf delicate tools and supplies that could be lost or damaged on the bench are kept handy and safe. Many machinists make this shelf deep enough to hold their Kennedy or Gerstner tool chests. Putting a machinists' chest on a backstop shelf instead of directly on the workbench avoids having to clear the workbench in front of the chest every time the chest drawers must be opened.

- *Smooth, hard work surface* – Tempered hardboard, formerly called Masonite®, is ideal for most workbench surfaces. It is inexpensive and easy to replace when damaged or oil-stained. Plywood is a poor choice because it splinters, but it is fine as a base *underneath* the Masonite.

- *Lower storage shelf* – A shelf below the bench provides ready access to tools and materials and adds weight to the bench, improving its stability.

- *Cross bracing* – Angle iron, steel straps, steel panels or plywood sheets fastened between the back bench legs adds rigidity to the bench.

- *Electrical outlets* – Individual duplex outlets can be installed *inside* the backstop or pre-wired power strips can be secured *to* the backstop. To reduce the chances of electrical shock, mount the outlets a few inches above the bench surface so items on the bench do not poke into the power receptacles.

- *Bench top height* – Workbench heights vary according to the height of the user. Spacers can be placed under bench legs to raise them, or legs can be shortened to fit the user. The optimum height is usually determined by the vise jaws, which should be at the height of the user's elbow to make filing and hacksawing more comfortable. Workbench top height for average individuals runs 28–32 inches, but to avoid stooping, taller people need higher benches.

- *Rounded corners* – Wherever possible, workbenches, worktables and workcarts should have rounded corners because curved corners hurt less when you bump into them. A 5-inch corner radius works well.

- *Shims* – If needed, use shims to level the workbench.

Vises

Vises and workbenches go together. After the workbench, the vise is the second most essential tool in the shop. When selecting a vise, here are some things to look for:

- Jaws that are a minimum of 4 inches wide and open to at least that same width. Also, using shop-made soft jaws of lead, aluminum, copper or leather prevent the jaws from marring workpieces.

- Replaceable jaws which fit against a step in the vise casting. This step adds strength to the vise by absorbing vertical hammering forces. See Figure 1-3.

- Vise screw threads should be concealed within the vise to protect them from damage by chips and other shop debris.

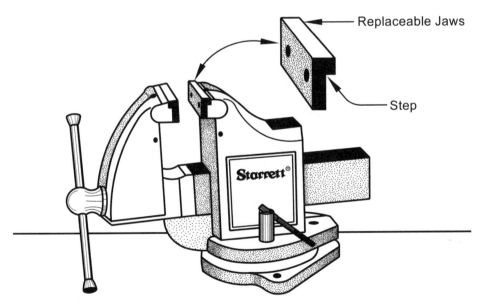

Figure 1-3. A quality machinists' bench vise. Steps in the back of each vise jaw absorb vertical hammering forces instead of the jaw screws which could shear off.

- If the vise has a swivel base, the locking mechanism when tightened must prevent all movement. When the vise is open about one inch, the front jaw should not wiggle more than ⅛-inch.

- Vise handle must be longer than 6 inches for adequate clamping force.

Removable Table-Mounted Vise

When a vise must be made removable from a steel-topped table, such as a welding table, make the vise mounting base shown in Figures 1-4 and 1-5. The mounting base has three parts: The *mounting plate*, the *face bar* and the *capture bar*. The mounting base can be assembled using either wire feed, TIG or stick welding.

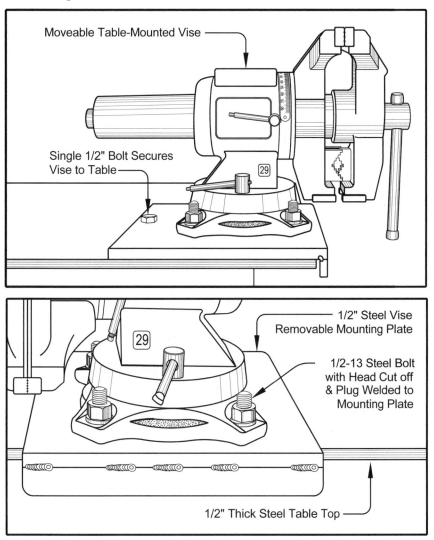

Figure 1-4. Removable vise mounting plate.

The removable table-mounted vise has several design details worth noting:

- The ⅜ × ½-inch steel capture bar, which is welded to the back of the face bar, keeps the vise mounting plate from lifting when subjected to upward forces. The capture bar is clamped in place on the steel table, then welded to the mounting plate for a snug fit.

- Use 4–5 business cards as spacers between the back of the face bar and the table edge, then drill the bolt clearance holes for the ½-inch hold-down bolt that goes through both the vise mounting plate and the steel table top. See Figures 1-4 (top) and 1-5 (top).

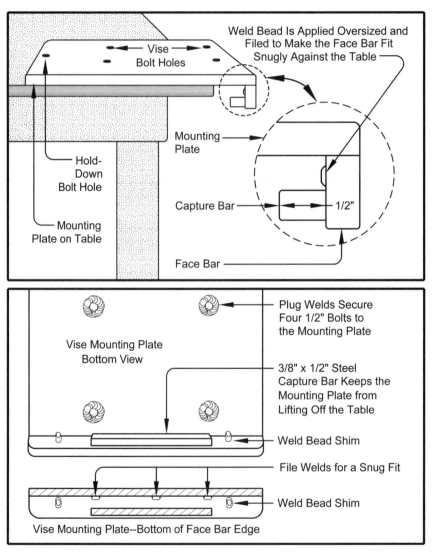

Figure 1-5. Details of the vise mounting base.

- Place two small weld beads on the back of the face bar so the welds bump the edge of the steel table. These will be used as shims as in Figure 1-5 (top and bottom). With a file, adjust the thickness of these weld-bead shims so that the table hold-down bolt just slips into the hole when the vise mounting plate is snugged against the welding table.

- The vise attaches to the mounting plate with four ½-inch bolts. The heads of these bolts are cut off and the remaining threaded bolt shafts are used as threaded studs. Secure the bolts to the mounting plate with plug welds. See Figure 1-5.

- A large welding Vise-Grip® may also be used to hold the mounting base in place instead of a ½-inch bolt.

Speed Vises

Since we're discussing vises, let's throw in the speed vise. While speed vises do not position work as accurately as a milling vise, they are fine for most rough drilling and cutting operations. See Figure 1-6. The advantages of speed vises are:

- They open and close without running the clamping screw the full distance since they have a quick opening and closing feature.

- The three stacks of metal wafers on each side of the jaws can be positioned to securely hold irregular work.

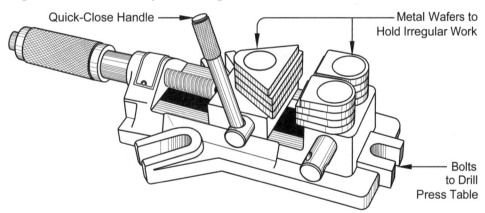

Figure 1-6. A speed vise is good for rough drilling and cutting.

Keeping Tools Close at Hand

You will work more efficiently if your most frequently used tools are stored close to where they are used. Here are some suggestions:

- Keep hammers and hacksaws near the bench vise, since they are often used with it. Storing them in overhead racks above the vise works well as it saves drawer space and you have only to reach up to grab a hammer.

- Store layout tools—steel rule, combination machinists' square, prick punch, center punch, layout dye and scriber—in a bench drawer tray.

- Other small tools that should be stored in a workbench drawer tray are extra safety glasses, a tapered repairmens' reamer, utility or mat knife, Xacto®-style knife, deburring scraper and reamer, scissors and assorted miniature screwdrivers.

- Many machinists store pliers and screwdrivers in racks secured to the ends of their workbenches. Commercial wire racks are so inexpensive it usually makes more sense to purchase them rather than make your own. Small frequently-used files should also be stored near the vise, usually in racks, on the end of the bench. The main file assortment belongs in a wall rack, not in a drawer where they will knock around and damage one another.

- Assorted pencils, markers, small cans of oils, solvents, lubricants and cutting fluids, as well as duct tape and Scotch blue tape can be stored on a shelf behind or over the workbench. Also, keep wooden stir sticks, acid brushes, sketch paper and paper towels within easy reach.

Hammer Storage

By storing the four most-used hammers in a rack over the bench vise, they are right at hand and ready for immediate use without stepping away from the vise to search in a drawer. See Figure 1-7.

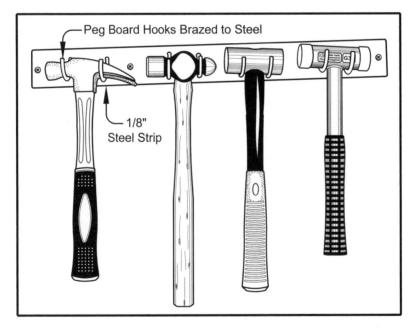

Figure 1-7. Shop-made hammer rack uses peg-board wire hooks silver-brazed into holes drilled into a ⅛-inch thick steel strip.

File Storage

The most frequently used files should be stored close to the vise. As stated before, files should be in a rack, as in Figure 1-8, not a drawer, because in drawers they bang into each other, damaging their teeth. A simple storage rack can be made of steel or aluminum angle with slots milled into it.

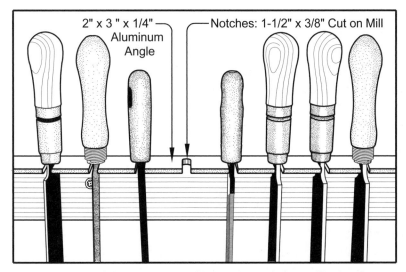

Figure 1-8. Aluminum angle file storage racks keep files handy.

Hand-Held Grinder Storage

Bent steel wire racks keep grinders within reach, but out of the way as in Figure 1-9. For convenience and to save time, the grinders are left plugged in. By having several grinders, the time-consuming process of changing abrasive wheels and grinding discs can be avoided.

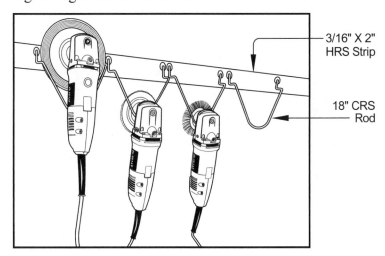

Figure 1-9. Simple-to-make bent wire rack for storing hand-held grinders.

Holders for R8 Collets, End Mills, Tool Holders & Drill Chucks

Instead of allowing milling machine and lathe tooling to roll around in a drawer, drill a few holes in a piece of 4×4-inch lumber to get them organized. See Figure 1-10. Some machinists drill these holes all the way through the wood and add a piece of ¼-inch plywood on the base. Others drill blind holes.

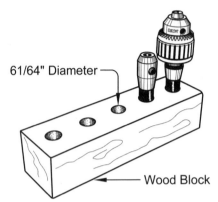

61/64" Diameter

Wood Block

Figure 1-10. A shop-made rack for R8 collets, end mill tool holders and drill chucks. Similar racks work for Silver & Deming drills, MT-shank drills and end mills.

Tray Storage for Small End Mills, Drills & Taps

Cutting a series of grooves in wood or plastic keeps small tools from banging into each other and makes finding the right tool easy. Figure 1-11 shows a grooved tray for holding end mills and drills made from kitchen counter top material that was cut out when a sink was installed and became scrap. By making a second milling pass about 0.050-inch wider than the initial cut, tools stored in these grooves are easier to remove.

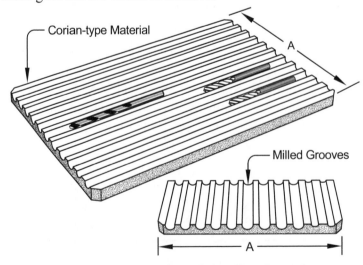

Corian-type Material

A

Milled Grooves

A

Figure 1-11. Grooved tray for small cutting tools.

Rod Goods Storage

White 1½-inch PVC pipe, capped at both ends, makes excellent and inexpensive storage containers for drill rod, steel, brass and aluminum rods, welding and brazing rods and all-thread. Tucked inside the PVC pipe, the rods are kept clean, straight, dry and protected from rust. One of the end caps is secured in place with purple primer and PVC cement. The primer leaves a visual indication of the sealed end so you can pick up the pipe without dumping the contents. Friction holds the other uncemented cap in place. These containers may be stored either vertically or horizontally in ceiling rafters as in Figure 1-12. Use a water-proof felt-tip marker to label the contents of the PVC pipes.

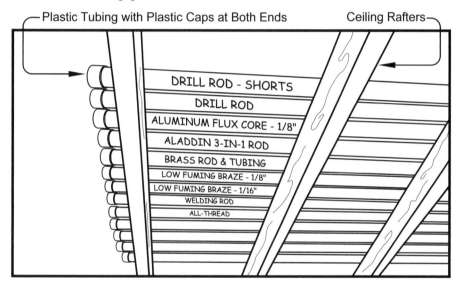

Figure 1-12. Storing rods in 1½-inch PVC pipe keeps rods clean, straight and organized.

Plans for Storage Shelves

Heavy-duty storage shelves are needed for chucks, angle plates, rotary tables, steady-rests and metal stock. Figure 1-13 shows one design which uses home improvement store lumber, Simpson Strong-Tie A23 steel angles and #8 × 1¼-inch drywall screws. (Simpson SD8 Strong-Drive screws are an even better choice than drywall screws because of the integral washers under their heads.) These storage shelves are rock solid and will not wiggle under a heavy load.

Horizontal 2″ × 4″s are supported and fastened to vertical 2″ × 4″s with Simpson A23 angles. This arrangement makes it easy to either change shelf heights, take the shelves apart for moving, or for re-using the lumber later. With a table saw and a chop saw, it takes less than three hours to cut and assemble these shelves.

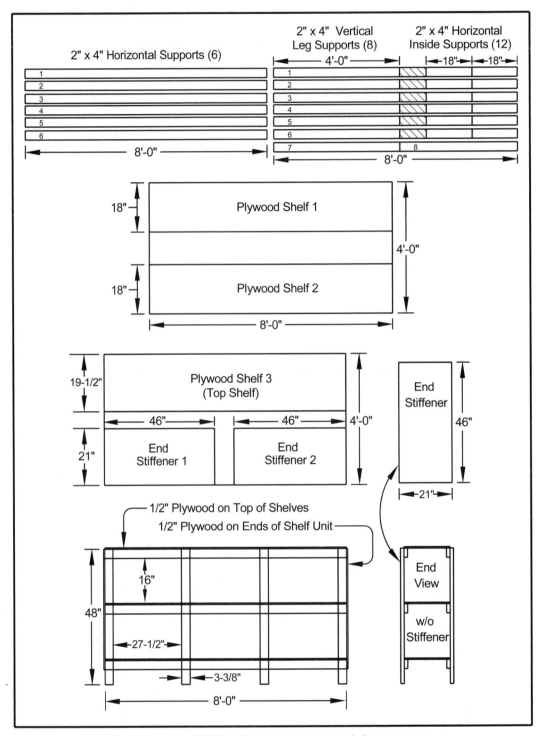

Figure 1-13. Plans for wooden storage shelves.

Metal Stock Storage

Metal stored horizontally on the shop floor, besides being a tripping hazard, rusts quickly, especially those pieces closest to the floor. The solution is the shop-made holders for metal rod and bar stock shown in Figure 1-14. Storing metal vertically instead of piling it on the floor not only reduces rust, it makes finding the right piece easy. The holders are made of 4½-inch electrical conduit with an HRS tab tack-welded onto each end. Drywall screws through the tabs secure the holders to the end of a set of wooden shelves as in Figure 1-13.

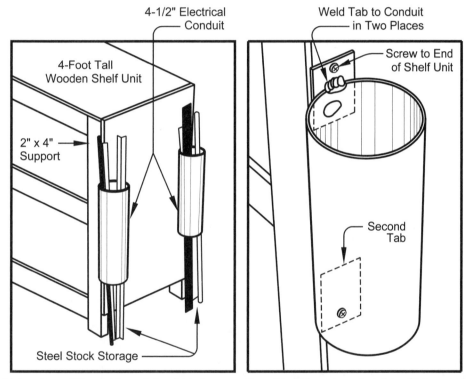

Figure 1-14. Electrical conduit with tabs on each end holds steel stock safely. This storage solution makes finding the right piece easy and keeps stock off the floor, reducing rust.

Section II – Human Factors

Machine Tool Height

As with your workbench and vise, the height of your mill, lathe and grinder should be adjusted to *your* height, not the height of an average person. Many tall machinists raise their lathes and mills to a comfortable height by placing steel or wooden spacers under the bases of their machines. This eliminates stooping and helps prevent fatigue, and, when painted to match the machine tools, these spacers are hardly noticeable.

Work Area Lighting

To work with precision you must be able to see what you are doing. Low-cost flexible-goose-neck incandescent lamps with magnetic bases are available from industrial tool suppliers and are perfect for lighting drill presses and grinding wheels, as well as belt and disc grinders. Installing one of these lamps is easy—place it on the machine and turn on the magnet in the base of the lamp.

For even better visibility on lathes and milling machines, try a low-voltage high-intensity lamp on a hinged boom. On a full-sized mill, a high-intensity lamp on each side of the spindle is even better, but angle brackets are needed to fasten the lights to the machine's casting. This is not a problem since most machine tool castings are relatively soft, and are easy to drill and tap. See Figure 1-15. On mini-lathes and mini-mills, Luxo-style lamps, which have both an incandescent bulb and a fluorescent ring, work well. Also, don't forget to provide high illumination levels on the layout, height-gage and center-punching areas.

Many lamps designed for machine tools are supplied with 220-volt to 110-volt step-down transformers because most 220-volt-powered machine tools do not have 110-volts available in their power box.

Multiple light sources are always better than a single source because they leave fewer areas in shadow. Install good lighting and you'll be surprised how much your work improves.

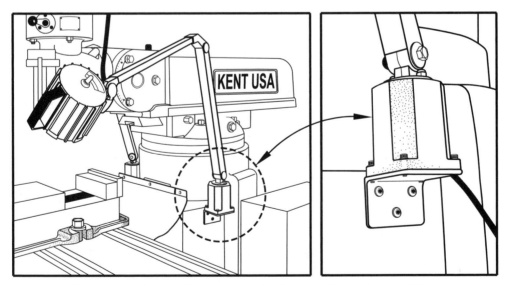

Figure 1-15. Shop-made lamp mounting brackets fastened to a milling machine casting using three #10-32 button-head machine screws.

Eye Glasses

If you're now wearing bifocal lenses, you should know that Varilux-type progressive lenses are a big improvement over traditional bifocals. When the wearer looks straight ahead, these lenses focus at long distances, and when the wearer looks down at an angle, the lenses focus at a normal distance for reading. This arrangement works well for most situations, but for some shop projects—layout work and welding are good examples—the wearer needs to see close work at a *straight-ahead* angle. In this case, the lenses are set for a long-distance focus and the work is blurry. For most people the solution is to purchase a pair of inexpensive, drug-store reading glasses for close work.

Shop Carts

Lathe and mill work requires a flat surface near the machine being used for holding T-wrenches, chuck keys, workpieces, cutters, measuring tools and prints.

Many machinists use a rolling metal table, as in Figure 1-16, positioned on the right-hand side of the machine for right-handed people and on the left for lefties. This table provides a large and secure work surface that can be reached without stepping away from the machine. And, since the table is not part of the machine tool, it does not vibrate, so parts will not walk off.

The ½-inch steel plate top can also be used for hammering metals flat and for bending metal. Also, since the steel top does not flex when struck like a Masonite workbench top, it is ideal for center punching because the rigid top will not allow the workpiece to dish under the force of the center punch. Even with rubber-rimmed wheels, the rolling table is much more solid than the usual workbench top. Shop carts should have wheel locks to keep them in place while working and to prevent them from rolling on sloping floors.

Work can be securely clamped and positioned to this steel table for welding, brazing, heavy grinding and wire brushing. Grounding the steel table top to the welding machine is usually adequate, so the electrical ground does not have to be fastened to the workpiece itself. A table with a welded $2 \times 2 \times \frac{1}{4}$-inch angle iron frame will easily hold a 300-pound workpiece and can safely be moved about under this load.

The shelf under the table provides more storage for heavy machine tool accessories like chucks, vises and rotary tables. An additional table top cover made of white laminate on a flakeboard base can be placed over the steel top to provide a removable light-colored table top for clean work. And, unless you like bruises, remember to round all table-top corners.

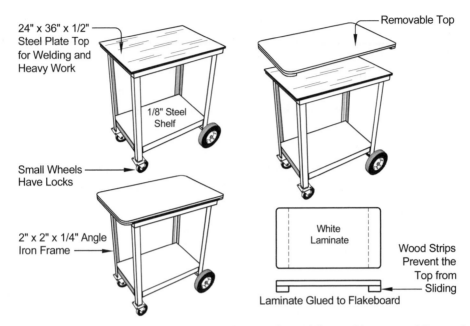

Figure 1-16. Shop cart with a ½-inch steel plate top for welding and heavy machine work and with a removable top of white laminate over flakeboard for clean work.

Section III – Tools for a Basic Machine Shop

Essential Machine Tools

The following three machines, each of which has a chapter of its own later in this book, form the basis of all machine shops:

- *Drill press* – Including drills (Sizes 1–60, A–Z and inch-fractionals), a drill press vise and Vise-Grip-style hold-down clamps.

- *Lathe* – Including a three-jaw chuck, four-jaw chuck, drill chuck, dead centers, live center, steady-rest, follower-rest, faceplate, driveplate, collet set, collet closer, QCTP plus tool holders and cutting tools.

- *Milling machine* – Including a mill clamping set, milling vise, R8 collets and R8 tool holders, rotary table, boring head, flycutters and end mills.

The size and accuracy of the work handled by these machines should be similar. If not, the smallest, least accurate machine is the limiting factor.

Bandsaws

Most machinists consider a bandsaw the number four item in the list of essential tools. Although every well-equipped shop has a bandsaw, if you're strong and willing, you can instead use a hacksaw or a portable bandsaw. This work-around exacts a big penalty in time and effort, and making curved cuts will be difficult, requiring a series of straight cuts blended with a file.

Horizontal bandsaws cut metal stock into lengths suitable for machining. Horizontals are much more convenient than a hand-held bandsaw or a Sawzall-type saw because they cut faster, make accurate square cuts, and once set up, can run unattended. When finished cutting, horizontal bandsaws shut off automatically. Industrial-grade horizontal bandsaws continuously pump cutting fluid onto the blade for faster cuts and longer blade life.

Vertical bandsaws remove large sections of metal quickly without wasting the machine time and electricity needed to remove the metal by turning it into chips. As a bonus, the cut-out sections of metal can be used in other jobs. To remove material from internal islands, you need a vertical bandsaw.

Inexpensive combination horizontal-vertical bandsaws are available today. They can do *some* bandsaw stock removal operations as well as cutting stock to length. They are a good compromise when space and cost prevent having a full-sized vertical bandsaw. For more on bandsaws, see Chapter 6.

Bench or Pedestal Grinders

Grinders allow the machinist to make, sharpen and modify HSS tools himself. This provides the flexibility to alter cutting tools for specific tasks. Without a grinder, HSS tools such as lathe cutters, drills and milling machine flycutters cannot be sharpened or modified. Additional grinders with green and diamond wheels allow sharpening and modification of carbide cutters.

Because grinders cost so little in comparison with other machine tools, a well-equipped shop may have 10–12 grinders, each dedicated to a specific task, with abrasive cutoff blades, stainless steel wire brushes, flap wheels, 3M Scotch-Brite™ deburring and polishing wheels and cloth polishing wheels. For more on grinding, see Chapter 4.

Other Important Tools

- *12-inch disc* and *6-inch belt grinder* – Either separate or combined on one machine, they are ideal for squaring up stock, removing burrs on all metals, dressing cut thread ends, and grinding non-ferrous metals which would quickly clog the pores of a grinding wheel.

- *1-inch* or *2-inch belt grinder* – This is a good tool for adding the finishing touches to a job and giving it smooth corners. Many belt grinders can grind work against an unsupported length of the belt, providing more gentle curves and transitions. These grinders are preferred by knifemakers and gunsmiths.

- *Air compressor* – This is needed for air-driven tools, paint sprayers, sand and glass bead blasting, chip removal and also for operating air-over-oil arbor presses. All air compressors should have in-line particle filters.

- *Vacuum cleaner* – For general shop cleaning, but vacuum cleaners can also be used for chip removal on lathes and mills instead of compressed air. This method is much safer than using compressed air.

- *Arbor press* – Useful for repairing chucks, removing MT and JT arbors, pressing out bushings and bearings and for broaching keyways. An arbor press is also useful for hydraulic metal forming and bending.

- *Hand-held electric-* or *air-powered grinders* – These are good for marking, smoothing and deburring.

Nice-to-Have Tools

- *Sheet metal brakes* and *shears* – For bending and cutting sheet metal.

- *Rolling mills* – For forming metal into curves and rings.

- *MIG* and *TIG welders* – A rapid way to join metals with strong joints.

- *Plasma cutting torch* – A fast, smooth and accurate way to cut steel up to ½-inch thick.

- *Bernz-O-Matic-style MAPP gas torch, oxyacetylene torch, regulators, goggles* and *compressed gas cylinders* – These can be used for welding, but they are used mainly for brazing, silver brazing and bending.

- *Welding bench* – Great for putting welding work at a comfortable height and for providing a place for clamping welding parts into position.

Section IV – Marking, Measuring & Layout

Digital Calipers

Though the design and simplicity of traditional machine shop measuring instruments—micrometers and vernier calipers—assure the long-term accuracy and stability of their measurements, over the last decade, electronic digital slide calipers have taken over many measuring tasks and limited the use of micrometers and vernier calipers to high-precision work and when checking the accuracy of digital calipers.

Still, for many tasks the digital calipers' slight reduction in fourth-place decimal accuracy is more than made up for by their advantages, which are:

- Ease and speed of reading reduces the chance of error.

- The ability to zero the display at any point simplifies many jobs by directly showing the *distance-to-go* on the readout.

- The versatility of combining inside, outside and depth measurement in one instrument.

Figures 1-17 through 1-19 show several ways to use digital calipers.

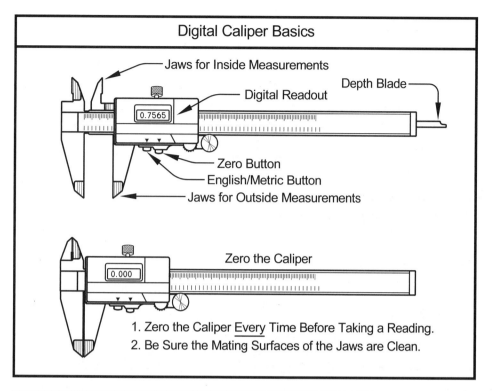

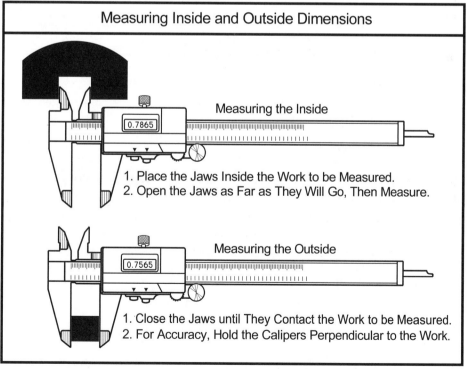

Figure 1-17. Digital caliper basics and inside/outside measurement.

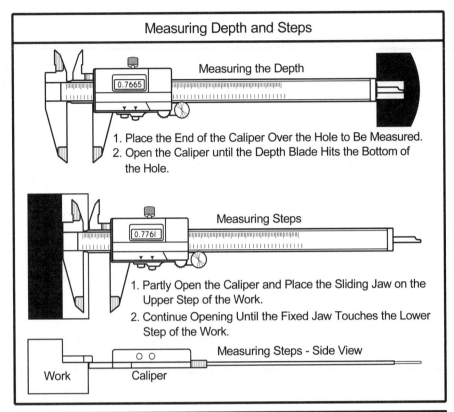

Measuring Depth and Steps

Measuring the Depth

0.7665

1. Place the End of the Caliper Over the Hole to Be Measured.
2. Open the Caliper until the Depth Blade Hits the Bottom of the Hole.

Measuring Steps

0.7761

1. Partly Open the Caliper and Place the Sliding Jaw on the Upper Step of the Work.
2. Continue Opening Until the Fixed Jaw Touches the Lower Step of the Work.

Measuring Steps - Side View

Work   Caliper

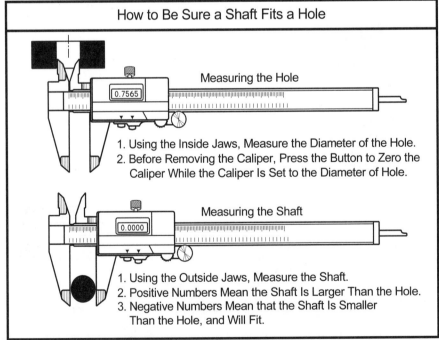

How to Be Sure a Shaft Fits a Hole

Measuring the Hole

0.7565

1. Using the Inside Jaws, Measure the Diameter of the Hole.
2. Before Removing the Caliper, Press the Button to Zero the Caliper While the Caliper Is Set to the Diameter of Hole.

Measuring the Shaft

0.0000

1. Using the Outside Jaws, Measure the Shaft.
2. Positive Numbers Mean the Shaft Is Larger Than the Hole.
3. Negative Numbers Mean that the Shaft Is Smaller Than the Hole, and Will Fit.

Figure 1-18. Measuring depths, steps and shafts with digital calipers.

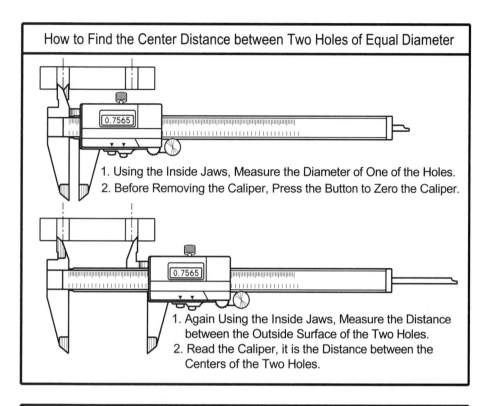

How to Find the Center Distance between Two Holes of Equal Diameter

1. Using the Inside Jaws, Measure the Diameter of One of the Holes.
2. Before Removing the Caliper, Press the Button to Zero the Caliper.

1. Again Using the Inside Jaws, Measure the Distance between the Outside Surface of the Two Holes.
2. Read the Caliper, it is the Distance between the Centers of the Two Holes.

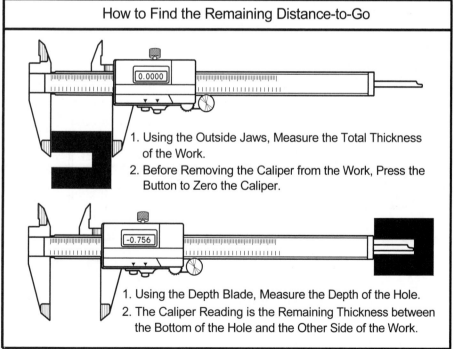

How to Find the Remaining Distance-to-Go

1. Using the Outside Jaws, Measure the Total Thickness of the Work.
2. Before Removing the Caliper from the Work, Press the Button to Zero the Caliper.

1. Using the Depth Blade, Measure the Depth of the Hole.
2. The Caliper Reading is the Remaining Thickness between the Bottom of the Hole and the Other Side of the Work.

Figure 1-19. Finding the distance between holes and the remaining distance-to-go.

Caliper Accessories

There are several accessories that can further extend the tasks that a digital caliper can perform. Attaching two steel bars with set screws to the caliper jaws, as in Figure 1-20, allows a caliper to hold a pair of round pins. These pins add three more functions; the caliper can now measure:

- Inside dimensions of holes larger than 0.400 inches, using the round pins.

- Distances between center-punch marks, using a pair of the pointed pins.

- Distances between two holes.

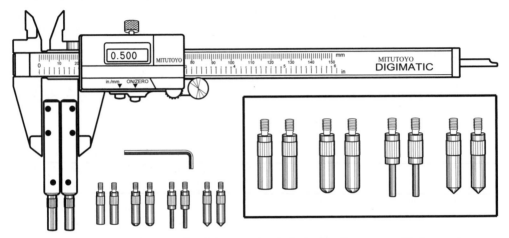

Figure 1-20. Caliper accessories for measuring hole inside diameter and hole spacing.

Although a depth measurement rod is an integral part of most slide calipers, adding a clamp-on base, called a *caliper depth attachment*, to the depth blade end of the digital calipers insures that the calipers are truly vertical when the measurement is taken. This greatly increases accuracy. See Figure 1-21.

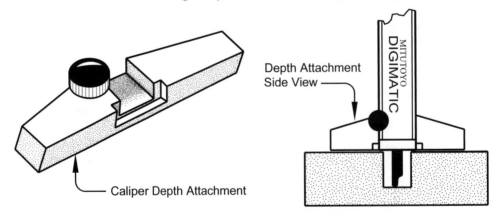

Figure 1-21. A caliper depth attachment fastens to the right end of a digital caliper and holds it perpendicular to the work.

Height Gages

There are many uses for height gages:

- For layout work they are used for scribing lines on parts at a precise distance above the layout plate or at a precise incremental distance from a reference point.

- To measure the distance from the layout plate to a point on a part, or between points on a part.

- For measuring hole locations – If the scriber on the height gage is replaced with a gage pin or a piece of drill rod, the height gage can measure hole locations. The diameter of the gage pin must be smaller than the diameter of the hole being measured so that the pin will fit inside.

- Holding a dial test indicator (DTI) for part inspection – When a group of similar parts must be inspected, a dial test indicator can replace the scriber by being set to the nominal dimension. Then, any part measured will show its *deviation* from nominal on the dial indicator.

The digital height gage in Figure 1-22 (right) has a tungsten carbide scriber installed with the scriber positioned on the bottom face. This configuration is used for most work. The dial height gage in Figure 1-22 (left) has the scriber inverted, the position used when measuring up to the bottom of a step on the work or for when picking up an existing line on the work. This inverted scriber position makes it easier to match an existing line to the scriber.

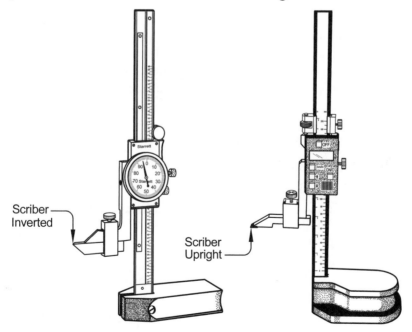

Figure 1-22. Dial height gage (left) and digital height gage (right).

With 1-2-3 blocks, the reach of a height gage can be expanded to measure the interior height of a part as in Figure 1-23.

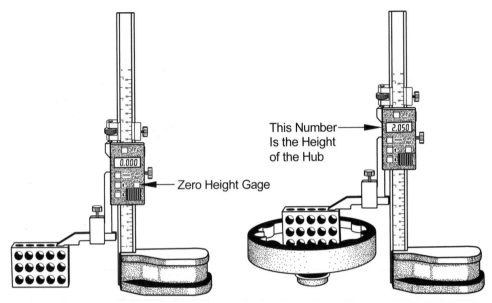

Figure 1-23. Height gage measuring the hub height of a part by using a 1-2-3 block. Without the block, the face of the hub would be inaccessible.

Granite Plates

Traditionally, cast iron layout plates were used in machine shops, but granite plates have replaced them for two reasons: first, granite plates are much less expensive—often their shipping cost is more than their purchase price—and second, granite is much less compromised when damaged. Every ding on a cast iron plate leaves both a crater *and* a surrounding ring of raised metal. When a granite plate is damaged, it too gets a crater, but the crater material is removed from the granite block as chips or powder and not raised. Therefore, a granite plate can sustain a lot of damage before it becomes unusable.

Layout plates, whether granite or cast iron, should be covered when not in use as in Figure 1-24. A simple shop-made wooden tray with raised edges to hold the tray in position, not only protects the granite, it makes a convenient storage place for your height gage. Strips of industrial felt on the bottom of the tray protect the plate from wear.

Before using a granite plate, wipe off its surface with your hand to remove any dirt that would reduce its accuracy. Your hand works better than a cloth because it can feel any remaining grit. Also, wipe off the base of the height gage. Dirt and grit on the base of the gage can reduce accuracy. Do not perform center punching on a layout plate or the surface will be dinged.

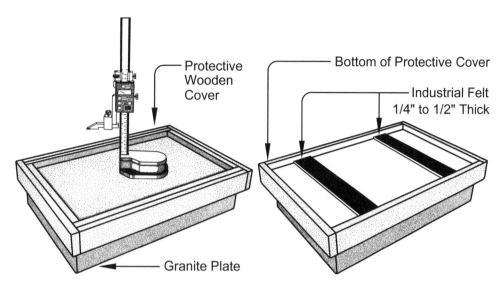

Figure 1-24. Shop-made wooden covers can hold height gages and related accessories.

Cheap vs. Expensive Dial Indicators

Dial indicators, also called *dial test indicators (DTIs)*, are used for centering work in chucks, aligning milling vises with their tables, comparing heights, and for centering round work under the milling machine spindle. DTIs can be expensive or cheap. The expensive ones cost 8–12 times more than similar budget Asian imports. Included in the better brands are Starrett Last Word, Brown & Sharp BesTest, GEM, Interapid, Compac, Mitutoyo, Tesa Tesatast, and Fowler. See Figure 1-25. While the low-cost DTIs are satisfactory for most shop work, the expensive ones have:

- *Jeweled movements* – These require less force to actuate, have less backlash and provide longer service.

- *Better linearity* – This provides equal deflection across their entire range. In other words, an increment of 0.001 inches on the leg produces the same dial deflection anywhere within the range of the DTI. This is important when indicators are used for inspection rather than centering.

- *Finer measurement increments* – More expensive dial test indicators have finer scale divisions and shorter measurement ranges. For most work, indicators with scale divisions of 0.001 inches are best. Typical ranges and scale divisions are:

  - 0.030-inch range with 0.001-inch scale divisions.

  - 0.020-inch range with 0.0005-inch scale divisions.

  - 0.008-inch range with 0.0001-inch scale divisions.

- *Automatic reversal* – The initial deflection direction of the measuring foot determines positive, or clockwise rotation, of the dial needle.

- *Interchangeable measuring foot* – This permits replacement when the foot becomes worn.

- *Choice of tip sizes* – Larger tips are used on rougher surfaces because smaller tips would be more sensitive to surface imperfections. In a way, a larger tip *averages* the surface height.

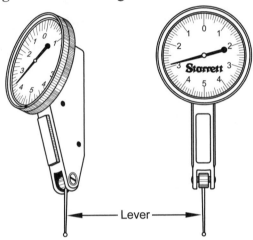

Figure 1-25. A good quality dial test indicator.

Scribers

Many double-ended scribers have a point turned 90° from the handle as in Figure 1-26 (top). While this hooked end is useful for scribing in tight spaces and removing O-rings, it will eventually hook into your hand. A good solution is to cut off this hooked end and use it to make a single-ended scriber with a shop-made handle, as shown in Figure 1-26 (bottom).

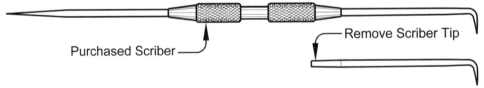

For Steel, Make the Hole 0.001 Inch Larger than the Scriber Diameter.
For Aluminum, Make the Hole 0.002 Inch Larger than the Scriber Diameter.

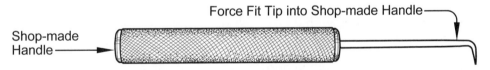

Figure 1-26. To avoid injury, remove the hooked end of a double-ended scriber to make another single-ended scriber.

Ball-End Dividers

When a circle must be scribed around a hole, or the distance from the center of a hole must be found, *ball-end dividers* are the tool for the job. Although not a high-precision instrument, a ball-end divider is fine for most layout and repair work. Commercial ball-end dividers are available, but many machinists make their own by silver soldering or silver brazing a ball bearing to a pair of dividers. See Figure 1-27 (left).

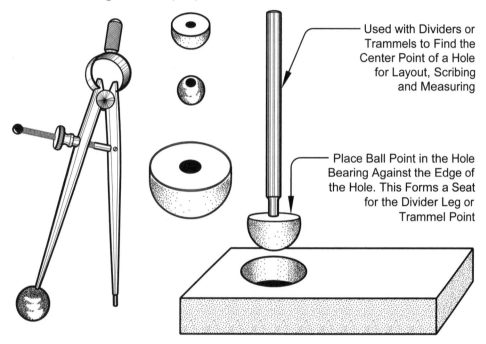

Used with Dividers or Trammels to Find the Center Point of a Hole for Layout, Scribing and Measuring

Place Ball Point in the Hole Bearing Against the Edge of the Hole. This Forms a Seat for the Divider Leg or Trammel Point

Figure 1-27. Ball-end dividers (left) and Starrett № 88 ball centers for larger dividers and trammels (right).

Starrett offers its № 88 *divider ball centers* with a holder for use with its larger dividers and trammels, Figure 1-27 (right). The holder fits where a pencil or large divider point usually goes. This set covers a hole diameter range from ½–7½ inches. For larger diameter holes, shop-made plugs turned on a lathe will do the job.

Center Punches

Accurate center punching is critical to machining accurate work. Keep prick punches and center punches sharp and regard them as consumables. See Figure 1-28. Sharpen punches on a grinder by holding them parallel to the plane of the grinder wheel's rotation and twirl them in your fingers as in Figure 1-29. This places the abrasive scratches *along* the punch's cone and in the direction of punching action instead of across it, making for a smoother entrance for the punch tip. Here is how to center punch:

1. Apply layout fluid to make scribed lines stand out.

2. Mark the location with a scriber.

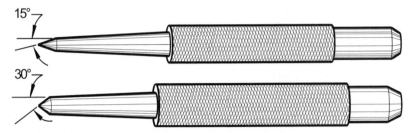

Figure 1-28. Prick punch (upper) and center punch (lower).

3. Using a prick punch, find the center-punch location by feeling for the intersection of the scribe lines. Place the prick punch point at this intersection and hold it perpendicular to the work. Strike the punch *once* with a 2 oz. ball-peen hammer. Using a larger ball-peen hammer with a prick punch will degrade your positional accuracy. Check for the proper punch-mark location. If the mark must be moved slightly, angle the punch in the direction of the correction.

4. When you are satisfied that the prick-punch mark is correct, follow up with a center punch using a 6- or 8-oz. ball-peen hammer. Several strikes may be needed to create a depression large enough for a center drill or twist drill to easily follow. An experienced machinist can place his punch marks with an accuracy within a few thousandths of an inch. Mastering this technique takes practice.

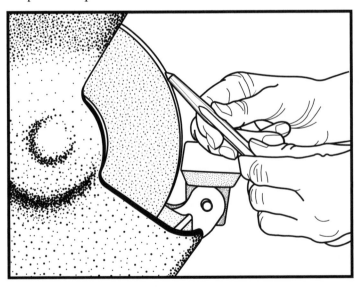

Figure 1-29. Grinding a punch tangential to the grinding wheel produces better punch marks.

Witness Marks

Witness Marks are the marks placed opposite one another on two mating mechanical parts to indicate their correct positioning or alignment. Proper positioning is especially important when the parts can fit together incorrectly. Whenever making or disassembling a device with more than one way to be reassembled, place witness marks *before* disassembling it. There are many ways to make witness marks:

- *Center-punch marks* – On plates and hatch covers, pairs of center-punch marks are often used, one mark on each component as in Figure 1-30 (top left). When there are multiple plates or covers which may become swapped, machinists often use a series of punch marks to distinguish each pair as shown in Figure 1-30 (top right).

- *Chisel strikes* and *scribe lines* – Sometimes called *clocking*, these are placed on two cylindrical parts to indicate their proper orientation. Chisel strikes are usually made on both components at the same time as in Figure 1-30 (bottom row). Scribed lines are usually more accurate than chisel strikes and are used on finer work.

- *Steel letter* or *number stamps* – These stamps are commercially available and look nice, but are not always at hand.

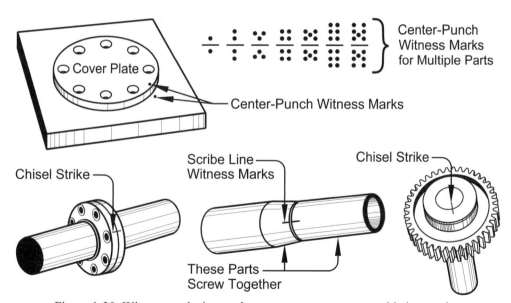

Figure 1-30. Witness marks insure that components are reassembled properly.

- *Other marks* – Parts can also be marked for proper clocking by using U-shaped notches cut into the side of the part or by drilling shallow holes, usually less than ⅛-inch deep.

- *Digital cameras* – These are useful for making a record of equipment not only *before* disassembly, but as each major part is removed. This visual record will remove the mystery of how to put a device back together.

Deburring & Edge & Corner Breaking

Cutting, drilling or machining metal raises dangerous burrs which need to be removed. Taking this extra step not only prevents cutting your fingers, it allows the work to lie flat, prevents scratches on layout plates and prevents damage to your milling tables and faceplates. Be sure to remove the burrs from the metal stock being returned to storage too. To remove a burr raised by drilling, use a hand deburring reamer or a large twist drill. See Figure 1-31.

All edges of machined parts should be *broken*, which means applying a chamfer, or a small flat edge of as little as 0.005 inches. This chamfer will prevent cuts and allow the parts to lie flat. Corners where three or more edges meet should be blunted with a file, disc or belt sander, or abrasive paper. Wire wheels and Scotch-Brite abrasive wheels also work well for this task.

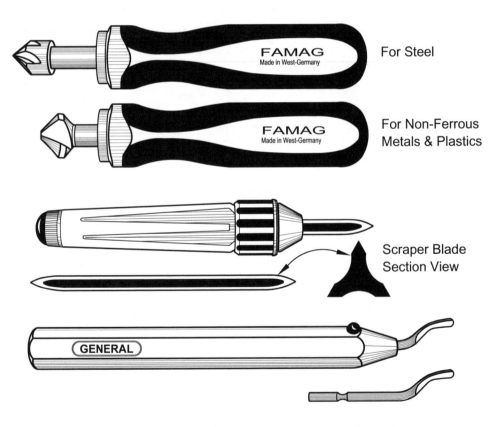

Figure 1-31. Hand reamers (top) and scrapers (bottom)
quickly remove burrs from workpieces.

Section V – Safety

Shop Safety Equipment

Here is the safety equipment every shop must have on hand to avoid injuries:

- *Wrap-around plastic safety glasses* – Wear these at all times unless wearing prescription glasses with side shields. Prescription glasses sold in the US with plastic lenses meet ANSI Standard Z87.1 for safety.

- *Goggles with a one-piece plastic lens that fits over glasses* – Used when handling solvents and when flying chips are a hazard, particularly when using compressed air.

- *Full-face safety shield for wire-brushing and grinding with a hand-held grinder* – Wire brushes throw off bits of wire with considerable force. This shield prevents them from lodging in your skin. Safety glasses should be worn underneath full-face safety shields.

- *Fire extinguishers* – Place in several locations in the shop.

- *Safety trash can* – To reduce the chances of spontaneous combustion of paper, rags and metal chips soaked with oil, use a safety trash can. See Figure 1-32. The best practice is to empty trash cans every night.

Figure 1-32. Safety trash cans help prevent spontaneous combustion fires.

Shop-Wide Safety Hazards

- All rotating machinery presents a major hazard to humans. Keep your hands away from their moving parts. Years ago apprentice machinists were taught to keep their left hands at their sides or behind their backs to discourage them from using their free hand to stop spinning lathe chucks. This is still a good idea.

- Always wear safety glasses. This cannot be repeated enough. In addition to the hazards of moving machinery and cutting tools, compressed air, springs, parts in arbors and in hydraulic presses can also become eye hazards.

- On milling machines, transparent plastic shields on magnetic bases protect your eyes from flying chips and fractured cutting tool fragments, yet permit close observation of the cutting process. They also simplify clean-up. Chip shields for lathes are also available, but not as effective as those used on milling machines. Chip shields are covered in Chapter 8 – Milling Machines, Section XI.

- Remove loose clothing and all jewelry so these items are not caught by machinery and pull you into it. This also means wedding rings, which, if caught by a spinning machine, can pull off your finger.

- Use only low-pressure compressed air (< 30 psi) around mills and lathes to prevent eye injuries and to prevent driving chips under the machines' ways. Do not take personal compressed air baths; the force of the air can drive chips into your skin and eyes.

- Break all corners on metal – For both safety and appearance, remove the sharp edges and burrs from work and holes so that you will not be cut and the work will not scratch other surfaces. Also, blunt all corner points where three surfaces meet. Usually a chamfer of just 0.005 inches is all that is needed. Remove the burrs on stock being returned to storage after the needed metal has been cut off.

- Remove all chips with a chip hook, brush, or removal special tool, not with your fingers. Chips may be razor sharp or red hot.

- Stop machines before taking measurements.

- Never leave a running machine tool unattended.

- Never allow a machine tool to be operated by more than one person at a time.

- Table saws are a hazard to hands and fingers, but also can throw work back at the operator with great force. Always push work *completely* through the blade and past it because work can be trapped between the rip fence and the blade, causing the work to jam sideways and be thrown back at the operator. Always stand to one side so you are not in a direct line with the blade and its plane of rotation.

- Never work in the shop when tired, angry, rushed, or under the influence of alcohol or drugs.

Chapter 2

Metals, Alloys, Oils & Hardness Testing

Prediction is difficult—particularly when it involves the future.

—Mark Twain

Introduction

This chapter covers common sizes and shapes of steel products, common steel finishes, steel and aluminum numbering systems, steel categories, pipes and tubing, special steel products including stainless steel, rust prevention, metal hardness testing, metal hardening and the importance of metal grain direction.

Section I – Common Carbon Steel Sizes & Shapes

Carbon Steel Plate & Bar Sizes

Steel is available in the standard dimensions listed in Table 2-1.

Product	Maximum Thickness (inches)	Width or Diameter (inches)	Incremental Dimensions (inches)
Sheet Steel	$> {}^3/_{16}$	36–84	Even-numbered gages are most common; odd-numbered gages are special order.
Plate Steel	$\leq {}^3/_{16}$	> 8–60	${}^1/_{32} - {}^1/_2$ thickness, then ${}^1/_{16} - 1$ thickness, then ${}^1/_8 - 3$ thickness, and ${}^1/_4$ above 3 thickness.
Rectangular Bars	–	≥ 8	Thickness: ${}^1/_{16}$ increments, but usually ${}^1/_8$ increments. Width: ${}^1/_4$ increments.
Round Bars	–	≥ 8	Diameter: ${}^1/_8$ increments.

Table 2-1. Product size, shape and increment availability of carbon steel.

Carbon Steel Products

Figure 2-1 shows many of the available carbon steel product that will work for most any project. A lot of the structural shapes—bar stock, plate, sheet and tubing—are also available in alloy steels, stainless steel, aluminum and brass.

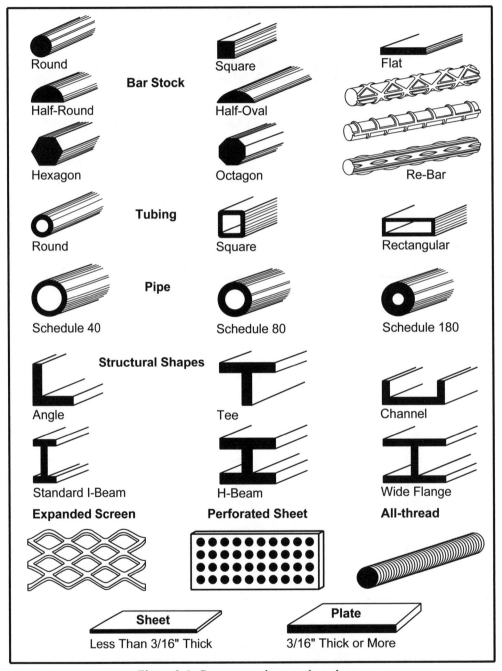

Figure 2-1. Common carbon steel products.

Differences between Stock, Standard & Special

There are three terms you are likely to hear at a metal supply house—terms which suppliers are likely to redefine for their convenience and profit:

- *Stock* – Metal the supply house has on hand.

- *Standard* – Metal in a particular shape, size or alloy that is regularly produced by the industry. This material may or may not be in the steel seller's inventory.

- *Special* – Metal forms, shapes, sizes and alloys not regularly produced. They are made for a specific customer.

Problems arise when standard products not in current stock are described as "special products" and are sold for a premium price. Do not tolerate this. Check the internet, other possible suppliers, or revise your design before accepting this answer and the high price that goes with it.

Section II – Carbon Steel Finishes

Finish vs. Alloy

The final process steel receives before leaving the mill determines its *finish*. Although some alloys and shapes are frequently made in a particular finish, the finish and *alloy* of a steel product—carbon content in the case of low-carbon steel—are two different, independent things. Alloy affects the physical and chemical properties of the steel—hardness, strength, rust resistance—while finish affects the steel's surface finish or smoothness, how it accepts paint, and its ability to be bent without fracturing. In the case of cold-rolled steel, its finishing process increases its surface hardness. The three most common steel finishes are:

- Hot rolled

- Cold rolled

- Pickled and oiled

Hot-Rolled Steel (HRS)

After steel is produced in a basic oxygen, blast, or electric furnace, it is poured into ingots where it solidifies, but remains in a red-hot, plastic state. In the next step, these ingots are placed in a rolling mill and rolled back and forth through a series of shaped rollers that form the steel into a particular profile. Since the steel is relatively soft, intricate shapes may be formed. Because all rolling is performed in the plastic state, *hot-rolled steel* has little residual stress when cooled and is essentially in the annealed state. Hot-rolled stock tends to have rounded corners and edges.

When the hot steel is exposed to the atmosphere during rolling, a thick, tough, blue-gray oxide scale forms on its surface. This coloring is not uniform across a single product, nor uniform from piece to piece. No attempt is made to control its appearance. This characteristic scale is virtually inert and takes paint well, but should be removed before welding. Since it has a low carbon content, hot-rolled steel cannot be hardened by heat treatment, but can be case hardened.

Hot-rolled steel is readily bent, drilled and formed. With 25 standards forms, hot-rolled steel is available in sheet, plates, rods, tubes, welded-seam pipe and shapes. Products can be purchased in 12-foot, 20-foot and 40-foot lengths. While this material is readily machined, aside from structural applications, it finds little use in the machine shop.

Cold-Rolled Steel (CRS)

Cold-rolled steel differs from hot-rolled steel because its final rolling takes place at room temperature in an oil bath. Because its scale is removed before the cold-rolling step, the final product surface is the unoxidized gray of the steel itself. This final cold-rolling step induces surface stresses in the finished product. Although this makes the product stiffer than the same size or shape of hot-rolled steel, machining that removes material from just one side of the material often leads to warpage as the surface stresses produced by cold rolling become unbalanced. In general, except for the cold-rolling induced surface stresses, the inside structure of hot- and cold-rolled steel is the same. Thinner shapes tend to have the rolling-induced hardening all the way through, but with larger shapes only their outer shell is affected by rolling-induced hardening.

There are eight regularly available forms of cold-rolled steel: round bar, TGP (turned, ground and polished), square bar, hexagonal bar, flat bar, hydraulic tubing, coil and threaded rod with both National and Acme Threads.

Hot-Rolled vs. Cold-Rolled Steel

There are more hot-rolled steel forms than cold-rolled because rolling steel in the red-hot plastic condition permits intricate shapes to be formed that cold-rolling does not. Only simple shapes such as flats, hexes and rounds are available cold-rolled. Like hot-rolled steel, cold-rolled steel may be welded and case-hardened, but neither material can be hardened by heat treating. In general, using cold-rolled steel is a better starting point for machine parts than hot-rolled steel, which should be reserved for structures and reinforcement.

The advantages of cold-rolled steels:

- Stiffer and harder than hot-rolled steel of the same size.
- A surface finish free of oxidation.

- Sharper, better defined corners.
- Smoother surfaces.
- More accurate and consistent dimensions.
- No need to remove oxide before welding as with hot-rolled steel.

Some disadvantages of cold-rolled steels:

- More expensive than hot-rolled steel of the same size and shape.
- Fewer shapes to choose from.
- Rolling stresses imparted during cold-finishing can cause distortion if metal is removed from just one side of a part and stresses become unbalanced.

Pickled & Oiled Steel (P&O or HRP&O)

This is hot-rolled steel that has been:

- Pickled in hydrochloric acid to remove surface scale.
- Water rinsed and air dried.
- Slit on its edges to improve its width uniformity; an important feature in stamping and forming operations.
- Oiled to prevent rust before further processing.

Because these steels retain their hot-rolled properties, they bend without cracking, have better flatness than common hot-rolled steel, a better surface smoothness, paint adhesion and thickness uniformity. Steel with this finish goes into making appliances, steel pipe and tubing, auto parts, racking systems and containers.

Section III – Steel Numbering Systems

Identifying Steel

Because there are several hundred different alloys, at least six systems have been devised to assign each alloy an identifying number or code. In some cases the numbering system indicates the percentage of carbon and the principal alloying element, while other systems are just a series of numbers and letters with no relation to the percentage of carbon.

A word of caution is in order here. The numerical code for an alloy may or may not have a corresponding *specification*—a detailed statement of the technical and commercial requirements the product must meet. Just calling out a code number to a steel supplier may not be adequate to get the proper product and may be legally deficient in government contracting and in the aerospace and aviation industries to name a few.

Here are the three most important steel numbering systems:

- *AISI (American Iron and Steel Institute)* and *SAE (Society of Automotive Engineers)* jointly devised and coordinated almost identical systems for carbon steel and alloy steels.

- *UNS (Unified Numbering System)* is a joint effort of SAE and ASTM to assign a unique number to each steel to avoid the confusion that may result from having two different numbers assigned to the same steel alloy by each of these organizations.

- *ASTM (American Society of Testing Materials).*

AISI/SAE Steel Designation System

This four-digit classification system for steel and its alloys is by far the most common and works this way:

- The first digit classifies the steel into one of about ten groups.
- The second digit indicates the approximate percentage of the alloying element. For alloys with several alloying elements, the one with the highest content determines the second digit.
- The last two digits indicate the approximate carbon content in hundredths of a percent or *points*.

For example, AISI/SAE 1018 is carbon steel containing zero alloying elements and with 18 points of carbon (0.18% carbon). *Machinery's Handbook* tables show the typical composition of more than a hundred steels as well as their AISI/SAE to UNS equivalents.

Section IV – Principal Steel Categories

Main Categories

There are four main categories into which we can divide steels:

- *Carbon steels* – Are divided into low-, medium- and high-carbon steels.
- *Free-machining steels* – Really a special class of carbon steels modified to produce a smooth surface finish at high cutting speeds.
- *Alloy steels* – Usually carbon steels with a few percent of additional elements to improve one or more physical or chemical properties.
- *Tool steels* – These have alloying elements added to improve the steel's hardness, hot hardness, heat treatability and shock resistance.

Low-Carbon Steels

Low-carbon steels, also called *mild steel* or *machine steel*, contain less than 0.30% carbon, not enough to harden with heat treatment. They are easy to machine and weld and may be case hardened. Low-carbon steels are used for nuts, bolts, screws, shafts, tie rods, hydraulic cylinders, machine parts and for structural steel beams and columns.

Common Low-Carbon Steel Products

Most commonly, *hot-rolled steel* refers to ASTM A36 steel and *cold-rolled steel* refers to 1018 (ASTM 1018) steel. These two products are the ones you are likely to see at a metal supply house. However, hot rolling and cold-rolling are finishing processes, not particular steels. Many steels in addition to A36 and 1018 are available hot rolled or cold rolled, but ASTM A36 and ASTM 1018 steels are by far the most common grades of low-carbon steel products.

Starrett № 498 Low-Carbon Steel

This is *precision-ground, low-carbon flat stock* that is much more expensive than ordinary hot-rolled, low-carbon steel, yet less expensive than tool steels. Here are its particulars:

- Similar to AISI 1018 steel.

- Contains 0.2% carbon, so it cannot be hardened using heat treatment, but can be case hardened.

- Supplied in 24-inch lengths in over 100 sizes with thicknesses from $^1/_{16}$–3 inches and widths from $^1/_2$–$2^1/_2$ inches.

- Supplied soft, it has little residual stress from rolling and is dimensionally stable, so removing material from one area will not cause warpage.

- Marked *LC* for low carbon in alternating large and small letters along its length.

- Used for jigs, fixtures, machine and component parts and templates.

- Readily available at most industrial tool and hardware distributors and has stable, known properties.

- Supplied in individual pieces in paper wrappers.

Although similar in chemistry and hardness to hot-rolled steel, Starrett's precision-ground low-carbon steel has the following advantages:

- Grinding time is saved because Starrett № 498 is already ground flat and parallel on four sides, making it an ideal starting point for many parts that do not require heat treatment. This factory grinding is especially helpful if your shop lacks a surface grinder.

- Savings of up to 60% over hardenable tool steel flat stock.

Hardenable tool steel flat stock costs dramatically more than hot-rolled low-carbon steel, a metallurgically similar material, because it has very predictable properties, is stress relieved, and is ground flat and square. Despite its higher cost, hardenable tool steel is often the better choice.

Free-Machining Steels

Free-machining steels are usually hot-rolled steels containing additives—lead, sulfur or phosphorous—to improve their machinablity. Because these additives form inclusions, they produce small broken chips when machined. This reduces power consumption, results in a better surface finish and lengthens tool life. Although these steels usually cost more than their carbon-steel cousins, they may still be a better choice because of their higher machining speeds. For example, the most common of these alloys, 12L14, machines at twice the speed of 1018. Improved machinablity, though, comes at the cost of degradation in other physical properties and prevents welding, but in many workpieces, this degradation is not important.

Elements for Alloy Steels

Adding additional elements to carbon steel, results in *alloy steel,* with one or more improved properties. These added elements increase the cost of alloy steels, but the improvement in properties and performance in manufacturing or use justifies the increase. Refer to Table 2-2 for the most common alloying elements and the effects they have on steel properties. Alloys can be tailored for specific applications. In order to meet cost, performance and processing goals, hundreds of alloys have been developed. The two most common alloy steels available at a metal supply house are:

- AISI/SAE 4130 steel, which is not heat treatable.

- AISI/SAE 4141 steel, which is heat treatable.

Alloying Element	Effect on Steel Alloy
Carbon	Hardness, strength, wear
Chromium	Corrosion resistance, hardenability
Lead	Machinablity
Manganese	Strength, hardenability, more responsive to heat treatment
Aluminum	Deoxidation
Nickel	Toughness, strength
Silicon	Deoxidation, hardenability
Tungsten	High temperature strength, wear
Molybdenum	High temperature strength, hardenability
Sulfur	Machinablity
Vanadium	Fine grain, toughness
Boron	Hardenability
Copper	Corrosion resistance, strength
Columbium	Elimination of carbide precipitation
Phosphorus	Strength
Tellurium	Machinablity
Cobalt	Hardness, wear

Table 2-2. Effect of alloying elements on steel.

These two alloy steels will meet the needs of most applications. For more demanding and critical applications, a metallurgical engineer must be consulted to bring more knowledge and insight to the selection process.

Tool Steels

Tool steel is a *working steel* that does drilling, cutting, reaming, broaching, sawing, forming, bending, forging, punching and molding. Whenever steel is being modified, subjected to impact, heat or high wear, you will find tool steel doing the job. Tool steels are a special, more expensive class of alloy steels with one or more of the following metals: chromium, manganese, vanadium, molybdenum, or tungsten. Just a few percent of these alloying elements dramatically changes the properties of carbon steel. Not only can tool steels be hardened with heat treatment, their hardness *after* heat treatment, *hot hardness* (hardness at high temperatures) and shock resistance allow these steels to perform where other steels would immediately fail. Today, tool steel represents only 2% of the steel used by weight, but 20% by dollar volume.

There are many tool steels to choose from, but unless you are making parts for very demanding applications, you are better off sticking with O-1, an oil-hardening steel. Although Starrett recommends one-hour tempering, which would require a furnace, smaller parts of O-1 can be successfully hardened and tempered using only an oxyacetylene torch. This property makes O-1 an ideal tool steel for shops without a metallurgical furnace and temperature controls.

But, there are two issues to remember:

- If a tool steel alloy requires several hours of tempering, it cannot be done with an acetylene torch because of the prohibitive cost and the unevenness of the heat, so a heat-treat furnace is needed.

- Finished tool steel parts are often made to tolerances measured in the tenths of thousandths of an inch, and when subjected to oxyacetylene torch heat, they develop scale and shed surface metal as an oxide, altering their precise dimensions. Putting these parts in a stainless steel foil bag to keep the air from the surface of the parts and placing the bag in a furnace solves the scaling problem.

During WWII, Germany and the US were forced into different alloying approaches for making tool steels. The US had plentiful domestic supplies of molybdenum, and no sources of tungsten, while Germany had tungsten and no molybdenum. As it turned out, both alloying methods worked well and, because of familiarity and sourcing, European tool steels still tend to emphasize tungsten alloys, while American tool steels emphasize molybdenum.

With the advent of modern analytical instruments, there are no longer any secret alloys. However, tool steel suppliers tend to make slightly different alloys with slightly different properties. And yet, despite the differences, they still claim that their product is *like* a recognized industry standard alloy— just better. When you become familiar with a particular steelmaker's alloy and how it behaves in your shop, staying with the same supplier can avoid problems. The really tricky part comes when a supplier modifies his alloy or its source. Most times the supplier will not tell you about these changes and will not admit it until you have a problem and have paid to run an elemental lab analysis.

Starrett № 496 Oil-Hardening Flat Stock & № 480 Oil-Hardening Drill Rod (O-1 Tool Steel)

These materials are so useful that some of them should be on hand in the shop at all times. Oil-hardening steel meets the following specifications:

- Fully annealed and dimensionally stable.

- Responds well to heat treatment:

  - Heat to 1450–1500°F.

  - Quench in oil at 120–140°F for R_c of 63–65.

- Machines freely before hardening.

- Flat stock comes in 18- and 36-inch lengths and drill rod in 3-foot lengths.

- Drill rod comes in fractional-inch, letter, number and metric diameters.

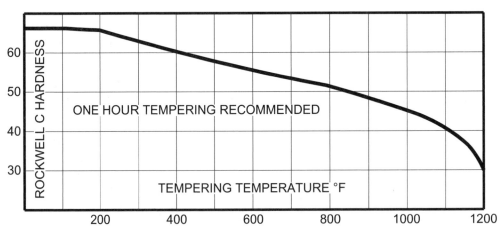

Graph 2-1. Hardness vs. tempering temperature for
Starrett № 496 and № 480, oil-hardening steel, AISI 0-1.

- Graph 2-1 above shows the recommended tempering temperatures for Starrett № 496 and № 480 oil-hardening steels, but tempering (oxide) colors may also be used as a guide:

- Cutting tools – 300 to 350°F (Light Straw).
- Solid punches and dies – 400 to 450°F (Straw).
- Spring temper – 750 to 800°F (Blue).

Section V – Pipes vs. Tubes

Definitions

In general, a *pipe* is a vessel used to carry fluid. It is measured by its *nominal pipe size (NPS)*, roughly based on its OD in inches, and its *schedule,* which relates to its wall thickness. For NPS ¼–12 inches, the actual OD is slightly larger than its NPS. For example, NPS 8 pipe has an OD of 8.625 inches. Figure 2-2 shows how its OD remains the same, but its wall thickness varies with the pipe's schedule. The most common wall thickness is Schedule 40, also called *Standard*.

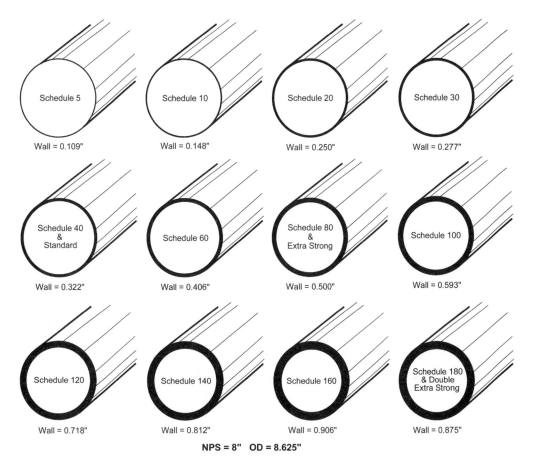

NPS = 8"   OD = 8.625"

Figure 2-2. Pipe wall thickness comparisons based on schedule number.
Note that all these pipes have the same OD of 8.625 inches, but varying ID with its schedule.

The men writing the original pipe standards had hoped that each schedule would relate to a specific pressure rating, but this did not work out and we are left with the workable, but peculiar system we have today, based on nominal diameter and schedule.

A *tube* is a structural member and is measured by its outside dimension, though this definition is not universally applicable. For example, hydraulic tubing and copper tubing carry fluids, not structures, and pipes which normally carry fluids are frequently used for supports, table legs and braces.

Pipe & Tubing Manufacturing Processes

The two most common methods for making steel pipe and tubing are:

- *Welded seam* – This process begins with flat strip steel coils. Heat and a series of rollers form the strip into a cylinder, and electrical welding closes the seam. After being cut into lengths, a scraper is pulled through the pipe or tubing interior to smooth and reduce the height of the weld bead. See Figure 2-3 (left).

- *Seamless* – This process starts as a red-hot billet. The billet is then spun between rollers while a water-cooled lance pierces it to form tubing. See Figure 2-3 (right).

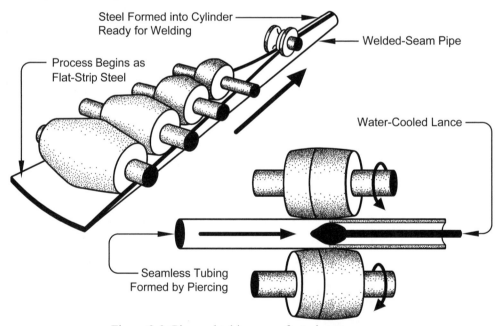

Figure 2-3. Pipe and tubing manufacturing processes.

Tubular Products Overview

Figure 2-4 shows an overview of the common types of pipe and tubing by application and by name.

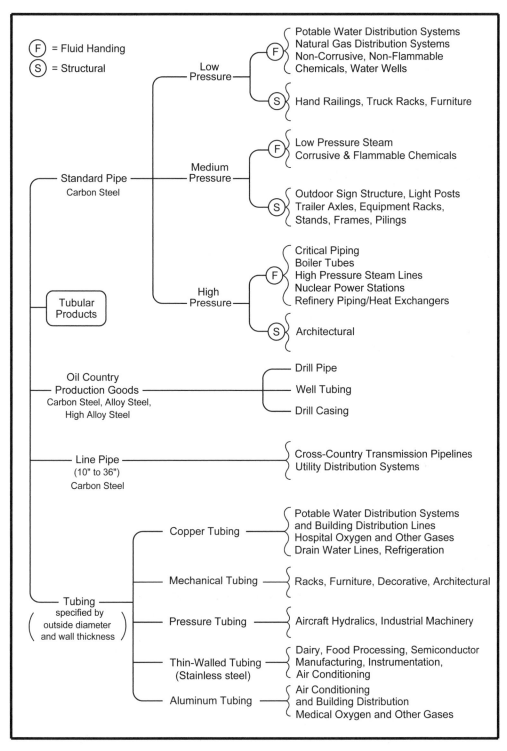

Figure 2-4. Common types of pipe and tubing.

Section VI – Special Steel Products

Key Stock

Key stock fits into keyways on shafts, locking pulleys and gears. Keys are much stronger than set screws and transfer much greater torque. Key stock is most often square in cross section, but larger sizes may be rectangular as well. This material is sold in 2- and 3-foot lengths, as well as precut keys ready for use. Smaller key stock sizes come in $1/32$-inch increments starting with $1/16$-inch squares, and larger sizes come in $1/16$-inch increments. In general, key stock is more accurately dimensioned than cold-rolled stock and comes in a greater assortment of sizes. Because of its uniform dimensions, key stock makes excellent spacers for both machining and welding, and also, since this stock is high-strength, it makes a good starting point for many machine parts. Key stock comes in alloy steel, high-carbon steel, plain steel, zinc-plated steel, stainless steel, brass and aluminum.

Piano Wire

Piano wire, also known as *music wire* and *spring steel*, is a tempered, high-carbon steel used in musical instruments, spring making, food processing equipment and machinery. It is sold by weight, usually in small coils, but assortments of straightened one-foot lengths are also available. Because of its hardness, piano wire must be cut with the special cutters shown in Figure 2-5, or with an abrasive wheel. Both inch and metric diameters from 0.006–0.192-inch diameter are available.

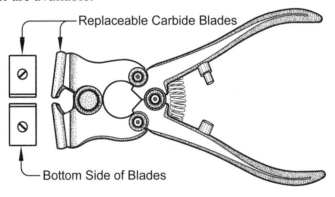

Figure 2-5. Starrett nippers for piano wire.

Section VII – Stainless Steels

Common Alloys

For stainless steels, the AISI three-digit numbering system is more widely used than the five-digit SAE system. All stainless steel alloys contain chromium and nickel and sometimes manganese, but it is the chromium which inhibits corrosion. There are hundreds of stainless steel alloys, but the most common are in the AISI 300 Series, commonly called *Type 300* or *Grade 300*. The following two alloys are likely to meet all your requirements:

- *Grade 304* – Of all the 300 Series alloys, this is the most used, least expensive, and comes in the widest variety of forms and finishes. It may be brake-formed or roll-formed, and it welds easily, but in thick sections it requires post-weld annealing. Grade 304 is also called $^{18}/_8$ because of its chromium and nickel percentages: 18% chromium and 8% nickel.

- *Grade 316* – In this chromium-nickel-molybdenum alloy, molybdenum provides additional corrosion resistance to seawater and chlorides. You are likely to find this grade of stainless steel used in chemical and desalination plants, and in ships and submarines.

Stainless Steel Advertising Claims

Although the words *Swedish steel* and *surgical steel* often appear in advertisements, these terms do not describe a particular alloy and are entirely the creations of advertising agencies.

Firearms often suffer from this advertising-speak. Many quality firearms sold as "stainless steel" do have stainless steel frames, receivers and barrels, but have carbon steel hammer springs and firing pins. Stainless steel hammer springs and firing pins would likely fail because they do not have the hardness and spring properties needed for these critical, life-and-death applications. Carbon steel is used for reliability, not to lower costs. And, because carbon steel is used for some firearm parts, never assume that a stainless steel firearm will not suffer from rust. These guns must be inspected, lubricated, and maintained like any steel firearm. A rust-free improvement on carbon-steel springs in stainless steel firearms would be to nickel plate the carbon-steel hammer springs and firing pins.

Section VIII – Aluminum

Identifying Aluminum

The *Aluminum Association Designation System*, is a four-digit alloy code plus a temper code that indicates the alloy and its temper, or hardness. If you are in aerospace manufacturing, you are likely to use many special alloys because critical applications justify their additional cost. Some, but not all, of these special alloys may be welded, heat treated and easily machined. There are dozens of aluminum alloys, but the most important and popular ones are:

- *1100 Series* – This is nearly pure aluminum. It is very soft, malleable and weldable.

- *6061-T6* – This is the most common and highest strength alloy. Fine finishes are possible in this alloy using sharp tools and heavier cuts. It is weldable, but welding heat destroys the T6 temper and leaves it soft.

- *7075-T6* – This aluminum alloy machines very well and is used for fixtures, but it *cannot* be welded.

Aluminum Shapes

Because aluminum rounds and shapes are extruded in a plastic state onto a cooling table then straightened, they do not have the dimensional symmetry and precision of cold-rolled steel products. Small variances are to be expected. Rounds are not really round and squares not really square.

Engine Turning

The cowling of the *Spirit of St. Louis* was fabricated of 1100 Series aluminum, or nearly pure aluminum, because it was light, attractive, and easy to weld and form. It was oxyacetylene-torch welded with strips of its own 1100 alloy used as welding rod. Beside being decorative, the cowling's surface swirls, called *engine-turning*—created by running maple dowels in a drill press to make an overlapping pattern on the metal—added stress to the metal, increasing its hardness and stiffness.

Section IX – Preventing & Removing Rust

Rusting of Iron & Steel

Rusting is a complex electrochemical process that converts iron into several forms of iron oxide. For rusting to occur, three things are required: iron (including the iron within steel), oxygen and water.

After an exchange of electrons, iron and oxygen combine to form iron oxides, or rust. The water provides the conduction path needed so that the electrons can move around and form new compounds. When water—dew or water vapor—lands on iron, it combines with the carbon dioxide in the atmosphere to form a weak carbonic acid which makes the water an electrolyte, a liquid that allows electrons and ions to move through it. The water becomes a conductor of electric current. As the carbonic acid is formed, it breaks some of the water into its components: hydrogen and oxygen. The free oxygen in the water and the dissolved iron combine to form iron oxide, or rust.

Chemicals, like those found in acid rain, seawater and salt spray from salted highways, make the water an even better electrolyte and speed up the rusting process. Iron oxide occupies a greater volume than the iron which formed it, and when iron oxide becomes thick enough, it falls away from the parent metal, reducing its mass and weakening the metal.

Preventing Rust

There are several ways to prevent rust:

- Iron and steel can be painted, plated or coated with grease, oil or a preservative to keep oxygen and water from reaching it.

- Maintaining the temperature of the iron above the dew point prevents water vapor from condensing on the surface of the iron and halts rusting.

- Lowering the humidity around the iron with dehumidifiers and *dessicants*, chemicals which absorb water from the air and hold onto it, reduces rusting.

- Sealing the iron and steel inside an airtight container keeps away both water vapor and oxygen and halts rusting.

Preventing Rust in a Tool Chest

Unlike machinists' tool chests, roll-aways do little to restrict airflow, allowing condensation to end up on your tools. To prevent this, many machinists install a 40-watt electrical heating element inside the empty, unused hollow space in the base of every steel roll-away tool box. A roll-away with upper and lower drawer sections requires two heaters, one in each section. Heaters are run only in cooler weather when the shop is cool at night and warms up during the day.

Rust occurs when warm air contacts the still cool tools, causing condensation if the temperature of the tools is below the dew point. Keeping the tools inside a roll-away warmer than the dew point prevents condensation and rust.

Covering machine tools with fitted cloth covers prevents warm, moisture-laden air from reaching them and condensing. Tools stored in drawers away from direct air circulation are also less likely to rust. Keeping tools lightly oiled or coated with products like LP-1 also helps retard rust.

Rust Removal

There are a couple techniques for rust removal:

- Using a pedestal or hand grinder with:

    - *Wire brush wheels* – These are very effective for removing light rust without removing any metal, but this may leave brush marks.

    - *Scotch-Brite finishing wheels* – These wheels have abrasive embedded in their nylon matrices so you will see occasional sparks, indicating that metal is being removed. Finishing wheels are slightly more aggressive than wire wheels and leave a distinctive surface pattern.

    - *Flap wheels* – These liberally remove both rust and base metal.

    - *Abrasive grinding discs* – These are the most aggressive grinding media. They rapidly remove rust and some base metal, but leave a pleasing swirl pattern. Grinding discs are mainly used to smooth welds and to remove defective welds.

- *Loosening rust with Liquid Wrench* and *scrubbing the rust off with a brass brush or wheel* – This is a mild, but effective means of removing light rust without damaging the work or leaving evidence of cleaning.

Blackening Processes

These are oxidation processes that put a thin copper-selenium film on the surface of steel. This film holds oil in place and protects the metal from oxygen—and rust. There are several blackening processes based on different chemistries. Some require hot chemical baths, others just warm or cold. In general, the more aggressive the chemicals used to form the film and the higher the process temperatures, the more permanent the film. There are blackening kits available which cost about one dollar per square foot of surface treated.

Bluing Processes

Bluing forms a very thin (0.0001-inch) coating of magnetite, the black oxide of iron (Fe_3O_4) via a *passivation* process. This finishing process is mostly used on firearms for appearance. It offers limited rust protection and should be coated with oil to reduce wetting and galvanic action. The process is named for its blue-black appearance. Unlike Fe_2O_3—the red oxide of iron—the black oxide occupies the same volume as the iron forming it, so it tends to remain in place, but it is eventually worn off by holster wear.

While there are some "cold" touch-up bluing products which can be brushed onto steel from a bottle, they offer little rust protection and are used mainly to hide defects and wear. The true bluing processes require a series of heated, aggressive chemical baths for a permanent treatment, and only the "hot" processes offer any significant rust protection.

Section X – Metal Hardness

Hardening

There are nearly a half-dozen processes and mechanisms which harden steel. Now is a good time to detail some of them because hardening is one of the first principles a machinist must understand.

- *Work hardening* – Rolling, bending and peening—any way the steel has stress introduced—increases its hardness. This is the principal difference between hot-rolled and cold-rolled steel. Cold rolling increases the hardness of the steel on and near the surface, but in thicker cold-rolled stock, the hardness does not extend into the interior metal.

- *Heat treatment* – This term is often a source of confusion because *any* operation which heats and cools steel is a *heat treatment*. There are a good half-dozen heat treating processes. This term is also used to describe the three-step process of heating steel above its austenizing point, quenching it rapidly to reduce its temperature to preserve the austenite at room temperature, and finally, raising its temperature to reduce its brittleness. Only steels with a carbon content of 0.3% or more can be hardened by heat treatment.

- *Case hardening*, also called *carburizing* – This process starts with heating low-carbon steel in a sealed container to exclude air while the steel is in contact with carbon-containing compounds which release carbon monoxide. This carbon monoxide gas diffuses into the outer layers of the steel and raises its carbon content enough to make it hardenable. When sufficient carbon has entered the outer layers of the steel, it is quenched by dumping it into a water bath. This high-carbon outer layer becomes glass-like hard, while the interior steel remains tough. This outer hard shell is called a *case* and the workpiece is said to be *case hardened*. The longer the time and the higher the temperature of the diffusion cycle, the thicker the case. Cases run from a few thousandths of an inch to $\frac{1}{16}$ of an inch. Traditionally, charcoal, bone, walnut shells and leather have been used as the carbon source. Air used to be excluded from the work during the heat soak by placing the work in an air-tight metal or clay container, but today, these containers have been replaced by stainless steel foil. The case hardening process may take a few hours or up to a day to complete.

Importance & Advantages of Hardness Testing

When discussing steels, machinists, engineers and metallurgists frequently speak of *Rockwell* and *Brinell hardness numbers*. These numbers reveal important information about the metal and how it will perform. Hardness often provides an *indication* of how well a part will wear in use, but it is not a perfect indicator; sometimes parts with a lower hardness will outwear ones with a higher hardness.

Because both of these methods test a small spot on the workpiece, the hardness of a particular, and possibly small, but important, area can be measured. For example, a Rockwell hardness test can check the hardness of the slide rails on an automatic pistol, portions of the gun which have been case hardened. Weld beads, critical areas of molds, punches, dies, gears and other machine parts can be checked for proper hardness using either of these two testing methods.

Although hardness tests—and their scales—have been devised for most materials including rubber, plastics and soft metals, the Rockwell C Scale, often written as R_c or RHC, and the Brinell scales are of the most interest to machinists and those who work with steels. The Rockwell B Scale is of interest to those working in softer metals like copper, soft steel, malleable iron, brass and aluminum. Altogether, there are 30 different Rockwell scales that cover nearly all materials.

The Rockwell and Brinell tests differ in detail, but both depend on measuring the penetration of a 10-mm tungsten carbide ball or a cone-shaped diamond indenter, known as a *Brale*, into the sample under a prescribed load. Two advantages of the Rockwell test are its direct hardness readout—no calculations are needed to get an answer—and the relatively low cost of the testing instrument itself. This test is also rapid, reliable, has good resolution, and makes a small indent.

Rockwell testing is more commonly used on hardened steels because the size of the indent left in hardened steels by the Brinell hardness test ball is small and difficult to measure. On softer metals, the indent left by the Brinell ball is so large that the test sample is damaged.

Rockwell Hardness Test Method

Figure 2-6 shows the sequence, Steps 1–7, that Rockwell testing machines use to measure hardness.

1. The indenter—the depth probe—is placed on the sample. Care is required so the indenter diamond is not damaged during sample insertion.
2. The 10 kg pre-load weight is applied to the indenter. A series of weights and levers inside the instrument apply this pre-load and the major load.
3. The depth gage is set to zero.
4. The major 3000 kg load is applied in addition to the pre-load.
5. A short waiting period permits the indenter to reach final penetration. This time delay is built into the testing machine.
6. The major load is removed.
7. The depth of penetration is measured by the testing machine, converted to a Rockwell number, and the number is displayed on its read-out dial.

The Rockwell Formula

Below is the formula that converts Brale depth penetration to a Rockwell C-scale hardness number:

$$R_c = 100 - \frac{D \text{ (in mm)}}{0.002}$$

Note that each 0.002 mm (8 hundred thousandths of an inch) of additional Brale penetration, or depth, adds one point of Rockwell hardness. The higher the Rockwell number, the harder the material.

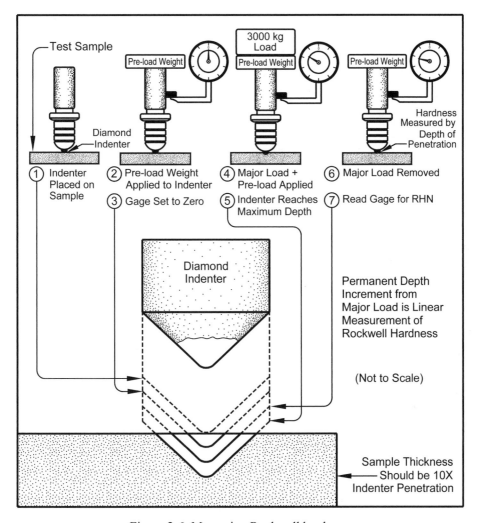

Figure 2-6. Measuring Rockwell hardness.

Typical RHNs

Table 2-3 shows some typical Rockwell C scale hardness figures for common metals and metal products. Both the material and its heat treatment determine its hardness. These numbers are only representative. Rockwell numbers will vary with the individual item and the point of measurement.

Tool steels, like oil-hardening O-1, are very hard as quenched at R_c 60, but are extremely brittle and must be tempered to R_c 50–52 to reduce brittleness, increase their toughness and to become useful tools.

Quality knife blades have R_c hardness in the low 60s, are hard to sharpen, and hold their edges well. Softer blades with lower Rockwell numbers are easier to sharpen, but lose their edges more rapidly.

Material	Rockwell C Scale
Knife Blades	63–50
File	62
Thread Tap	60
Steel – O-1 (Quench only)	60
HSS Drill Point	57
Axe	57
Cold Chisel Point	56
Hedge Shears	53
Steel – O-1 (Straw)	52
Steel – O-1 (Medium Straw)	50
Ball Peen Hammer Face	47
Hatchet	40
SHCS (#10-24 x 1″)	39
Grade 8 Bolt	39–27
Auto Leaf Spring	38
Tool Steel (P20)	32–20
Grade 5 Bolt	31–18
Ductile Cast Iron	25
Brass Hinge	20

Table 2-3. Some common engineering materials and
their typical Rockwell hardness numbers.

Hardness Testing Files

A set of *hardness testing files*, as shown in Figure 2-7, costs about the same as a quality digital micrometer. These files are good for field testing and, within their test range of 40–66 HRC, hardness can be measured to within 2–3 Rockwell points. Though these hardness testing files are not as accurate as a Rockwell tester, they are a quick, portable and inexpensive way to test material hardness.

Some machinists, reserve a specific file for hardness testing. A favorite choice is an 8-inch Nicholson mill bastard file. Machinists often drill a ¼-inch hole in the file to indicate that it is to be used exclusively for hardness testing. Having some test coupons—small steel discs whose Rockwell hardness is known—allows a quick hardness comparison with the unknown sample.

HARDNESS TESTER / FILE SET

This new innovative file set provides a quick, inexpensive and simple way to check material hardness. No need to bring the material to be tested over to a hardness testing machine. Just bring this file set (6 files from 40 to 65 HRC) to the piece to be tested.

Follow these simple steps to test your material:

1. Start with the BLACK handle file (65 HRC) and run the file over the test material. If it marks the material, the material is less than 65 HRC.

2. Try the BLUE handle (60 HRC): If it does not mark the material, the file is softer than the material. In this case the material is between 60 and 65 HRC.

3. If the BLUE handle (60 HRC) did mark the material, simply try the GREEN file (55HRC), LIGHT-GREEN file (50 HRC), and continue until the material is not marked. The approximate hardness of the material is between the file that marks the material and the file that slips over the material.

(Standard) ϕ 4.3 x 175$\frac{m}{m}$

COLOR	INDICATION	FILE HARDNESS	
RED	40 HRC	40-42 HRC	392-412 HV
YELLOW	45 HRC	45-47 HRC	446-471 HV
LIGHT-GREEN	50 HRC	50-52 HRC	513-544 HV
GREEN	55 HRC	55-57 HRC	595-633 HV
BLUE	60 HRC	60-62 HRC	697-746 HV
BLACK	65 HRC	64-66 HRC	800-865 HV

HRC40 TSUBOSAN
HRC45 TSUBOSAN
HRC50 TSUBOSAN
HRC55 TSUBOSAN
HRC60 TSUBOSAN
HRC65 TSUBOSAN

Figure 2-7. Hardness testing files. The file is held differently for different shaped parts. Instructions for using these files are printed on the inside of the lid.

Hardness Testing Complications

A competent Rockwell testing machine operator can obtain consistent and reliable hardness measurements. However, there are many factors that can invalidate test results. Some of these are:

- Measuring dirty, rusted or paint-covered samples.

- Using samples that are not flat or testing on a curved surface.

- Measuring too close to the edge of the part, near a hole, or above a hollow.

- Measuring too close to a previous hardness measurement point can also skew results. The initial indentation and disturbance has already introduced stress on the surface of the metal and this affects the second measurement.

- While some samples may have uniform hardness in all points of its volume, many samples, such as those which are case or work hardened, are likely to be harder on the surface than in their interiors. Special precautions and test techniques are needed for reliable results on case-hardened and thin work.

- Measurements on inside corners and on thin-walled bushings are usually invalid. Also, getting accurate shaft-hardness measurements requires special precautions or they too will be invalid.

- The Rockwell tester must be calibrated to apply the test load at the prescribed rate, if this is not done, the test will be invalid.

Brinell Hardness Testing Method

Brinell testing machines press a 10 mm steel or tungsten carbide ball into the test sample with a 3000 kg force for 10–15 seconds. Then, with the load removed, the diameter of the indent impression is measured with a 20-power microscope. Two diameter measurements 90° apart are taken and averaged. Using the formula in Figure 2-8, the indention diameter is converted to a BHN—Brinell Hardness Number.

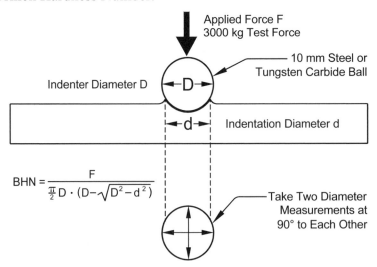

Figure 2-8. Brinell hardness testing method and formula.

Other Rockwell Hardness Testing Devices

Other testing machines, such as the simple ball-drop device in Figure 2-9, depend on the rebound of a ball bearing dropped from a standard height to measure hardness. These ball-drop testers are simple, inexpensive, lend themselves to field use, and produce a Rockwell hardness number. Except for polished surfaces, they do not damage the part because they leave no indent marks. Neither as expensive, nor as accurate as laboratory Rockwell testing machines, these simple ball-drop testers are perfect for both portable use and in-place testing. To use one, observe how high the ball bearing rebounds, and then check the hardness tables.

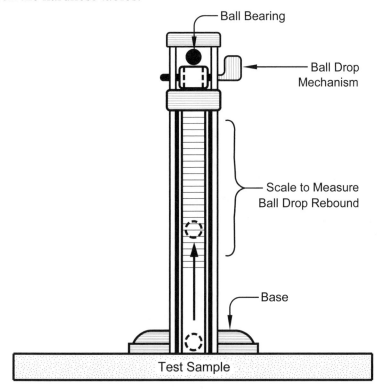

Figure 2-9. A simple ball-bearing drop device can be used in the field without damaging the workpiece, with the exception of polished surfaces, which can be dinged.

Hardness Testing Damage

When hardness testing is performed on a part which will not be discarded and be put into service, you must consider whether the testing process has inflicted damage that can ultimately result in part failure. Deep penetration by the diamond-tipped Brale or carbide ball may become the origin of stress fatigue cracks. The deeper the penetration, the more likely it will cause failure if the part is subject to fluctuating loads. This is particularly true for Brinell tests where the optimum penetration is 4–5 mm, making it a destructive test.

Hardness & Tensile Strength

Hardness is not an intrinsic property of a metal, but developed from a complex combination of deformation and elastic behavior which occurs under the conditions of a particular test method. Put another way, the alloy, test method, tensile strength, yield strength, modulus of elasticity, crystalline structure, work-hardening history and its thermal/heat-treating history all come into play in determining hardness. Tables exist which list the correlation between hardness test numbers and tensile strength, and all of these, including Table 2-4, are determined by experiment. There are four important cautions to take into consideration when applying this information:

Rockwell C Scale	Brinell Hardness	Tensile Strength	Rockwell C Scale	Brinell Hardness	Tensile Strength
150 kg 120° Diamond Brale	3000 kg 10 mm Ball	psi × 1000	150 kg 120° Diamond Brale	3000 kg 10 mm Ball	psi × 1000
45	421	215	59	-	351
44	409	208	58	615	338
42	390	194	57	595	325
40	371	182	56	577	313
38	353	171	55	560	301
36	336	161	54	543	292
34	319	152	53	525	283
32	301	146	52	512	271
30	286	138	51	496	264
28	271	131	50	481	255
26	258	125	49	469	246
24	247	119	48	451	238
22	237	115	47	442	229
20	226	110			

Table 2-4. Rockwell & Brinell hardness vs. tensile strength for steel.

- Tables relating hardness numbers to tensile strength are valid only for a particular metal. You cannot take a hardness number for steel, and using this same table, get the tensile strength for copper from copper's Rockwell hardness number.

- The correlation between hardness number and tensile strength becomes both less accurate and more uncertain as hardness numbers increase.

- Rockwell hardness numbers above 59 indicate a metal so hard and brittle that tensile strength is meaningless. Putting metal this brittle under high tensile load and subjecting it to even a small shock will shatter it. There is no practical use for metal in such a hard, brittle condition.

- These correlation tables cannot be used for tool steels.

Section XI – Lubricating Oils, Motor Oils & Cutting Fluids

Oil Applications

- *Lubricating oils* are formulated to separate surfaces with a very thin film, preventing friction and wear. These oils, which also prevent rust, lubricate bearings, axles, transmissions, slide ways, gears and other moving parts.

- *Motor oils* are intended for use in internal combustion engines and contain anti-foaming agents, acid neutralizers and detergents. The detergents keep metal particles in suspension so they can be trapped and removed by the engine oil filter. Machinery transmission oil should not contain detergents because metal particles do the least damage when they settle out of the oil and remain on the bottom of the gear box where they do not contact gears or bearings.

- *Cutting fluids* have several functions:

  - Cooling the cutting tool and the work is the most important function of cutting fluids. Each cutting tool material has a maximum working temperature. Go above this temperature and the tool will soften and stop cutting.

  - Reducing friction between the cutting tool and the work is the next most important function of cutting fluids. Reducing friction reduces heat generated as well as electrical power consumed by the machine tool.

  - Preventing cut pieces of the work from adhering to the edge of the cutting tool and causing what is called a *built-up edge (BUE)*.

  - Flushing chips out of the work area.

Cutting Fluid Issues

- Because water has greater *specific heat*—the ability to carry heat away from the work—the majority of industrial cutting fluids are emulsions, mixtures of oil *and* water, not just oils. Formulated to remain mixed and not separate into their phases, these mixtures also contain anti-rust and anti-bacterial additives. Anti-bacterials are needed because these cutting fluids contain organic oils which can go rancid. Many shops experience what is known as *Monday morning stink* when cutting fluids sit all weekend and are not properly maintained to reduce bacterial growth.

- Cutting fluids should always be used during cut-off operations in lathes, and always during threading, reaming or broaching operations. Applying cutting fluid directly onto the work from a polyethylene squeeze bottle works well and makes the least mess.

- Thinner cutting fluids usually provide a better surface finish and get into all the nooks and crannies, but thicker, more viscous fluids are needed for heavy machining and hardened steels. These thicker cutting fluids cling to rotating work and perform better under high tool pressures. Some cutting fluids, like Moly-D, will permanently stain workpieces and machine surfaces, but work when no other fluids will do the job.

- Cutting lube sticks are excellent for bandsaw blades and for where cutting fluid on and around the work is undesirable.

- Sherline miniature machine tools use lower cutting pressures than full-size machine tools and do not need cutting fluid during most operations except cutting-off, drilling and tapping.

- There are many cutting fluids and cutting lube sticks available because different properties are needed for different materials and cutting processes. You are likely to need a variety of fluids to meet all shop needs.

- Although most production set-ups apply cutting fluid continuously and often at high flow rates, this is an inherently messy process which requires the cutting fluid to be monitored and replenished regularly. The payoff for this effort and mess is that cutting speeds may be increased by as much as 30% over working without fluid. In the interest of keeping a clean work area, many model shops choose to apply cutting fluids only on an as-needed basis during cutting-off, tapping, reaming, broaching and tough drilling jobs.

Cooling with Cutting Fluids, Vortex Tubes & Compressed Air

There are three methods for applying cutting fluids to the work and to the cutting tool:

- *Continuous coolant flooding* – A motor-driven pump pulls cutting fluid from a tank or sump under the machine, forces it through a hose, and onto the work and cutter. This cools the cutting tool and workpiece. It also flushes chips away from the cutter, preventing the chips from re-entering the work-cutter interface. Flooding is the most effective application method and is necessary and cost effective for production operations.

  However, there are several important drawbacks:

- As stated before, it is messy. With continuous coolant flooding there is no way to avoid splashes and spills. Cutting fluid gets spread over the workpiece, the machine tool and the machinist.

- Cutting fluid must be carefully monitored and replenished with appropriate additives to avoid bacterial growth, odor and rust. As the water evaporates from the cutting fluid with repeated use cycles, the remaining fluid turns into sludge. Just adding new cutting fluid will not stop this process once it has begun. The entire sump system must be emptied and cleaned.

- Machine tools are exposed to the water in the cutting fluid, putting them at increased risk of rusting.

• *Using a mister* or *a sprayer – Misters* use compressed air to apply a very fine *cloud* of cutting fluid to the tool and workpiece, while *sprayers* use compressed air to apply larger fluid particles to the work. Sprayers are slightly less messy than fluid flooding and only about half as effective as flooding in raising cutting speed and increasing tool life. Misters, as in Figure 2-10, are prohibited in the EU because the clouds of cutting fluid that they create float around the shop, posing a breathing risk. Sprayers are less hazardous to the machinist, but slightly less effective. When using either a mister or a sprayer, the rust and maintenance issues of coolant flooding remain because all cutting fluids contain water.

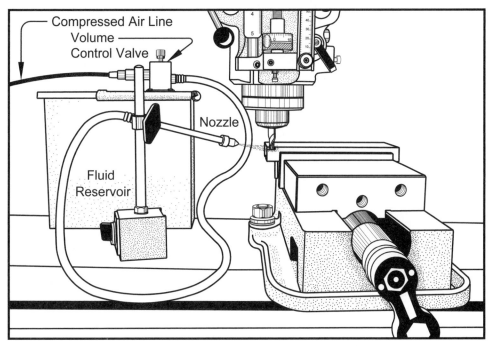

Figure 2-10. Mister with cutting/cooling fluid.

- *Application with a brush* or *squeeze bottle* – This method is a good compromise in non-production operations. It uses cutting fluid when and where it is needed, but not continuously.

There are two methods for cooling and chip removal using compressed air:

- *Cooling with a vortex tube* – These mechanical devices, also called *Ranque-Hilsch vortex tubes*, separate compressed air into hot and cold air streams. Vortex tubes produce temperature differences of as much as 80°F for spot cooling. They use no cutting fluid, do not create a rust or breathing hazard, and are maintenance free. Unfortunately, they are about half as effective as a mister.

- *Cooling with compressed air* – This cooling method, which has none of the health hazards of the misters, is good at removing chips, has no rust or maintenance issues and is relatively inexpensive because it uses shop compressed air. Unfortunately, it is only half as effective as a vortex tube. Besides cooling the cutter and workpiece, compressed air removes chips so they do not re-enter the cutters and damage the workpiece finish.

Section XII – Metal Characteristics

Metal Grain

Both hot- and cold-rolled metal stock have a different grain structure along and across their rolled direction. In cold-rolled steel, when there is a choice, bends should be made at right angles to the rolling direction—across the grain. In thick metal, sharp bends along the grain cause immediate cracking, while more gradual bends which are subject to vibration, may eventually cause fatigue failure.

In aluminum sheet, to determine the grain, or rolling direction, look for the manufacturer's ink stamp. Manufacturers use inked rollers to mark the metal's grade such as "6061-T6" and these markings run parallel to the rolling and grain direction.

Metal grain direction becomes important when multiple parts are cut at the same time with plasma, water jet or oxyacetylene flame. To get the most parts out of a sheet of metal, manufacturers "nest" parts, cutting them out like a jig-saw puzzle. This nesting leads to bend and fold lines being both with and across the grain, a potentially disastrous practice. On critical applications, insure that parts will be oriented perpendicular with the grain of the metal *before* approving the cutting plan.

Chapter 3

Tapers, Dowel Pins, Fasteners & Key Concepts

*The greatest unexplored territory in the world
is the space between the ears.*

—Bill O'Brien

Introduction

This chapter covers a variety of subjects critical to understanding machine shop work: Morse tapers and their repair, 5C and R8 collet dimensions, threaded fasteners, and clearcutting. These subjects may seem basic to some, but they are important concepts and a little review never hurts.

Section I – Tapers

Taper Functions

Most tapers position and hold a tool or workpiece precisely on an axis of rotation, often within a few ten-thousandths of an inch. Because their male-cone-within-a-female-cone design is self-centering, tapers line up on their axial position time after time without an alignment step. This simplifies changing set-ups.

Common Taper Designs

In the machine shop, there are five common taper designs:

- *Morse tapers (MTs)* are used in spindles and tailstocks of the majority of modern lathes. Tapers in spindles usually hold lathe centers, while tailstock tapers can hold not only lathe centers, but drill chuck arbors and large twist drills. Tapers are also used to hold drill chuck arbors in drill press spindles. Many rotary tables have a Morse taper at their centers for holding center points or collets. The shallow taper of the MT cone makes them *self-locking*. This means that once seated by tapping them into place, MTs will hold in place without the need for a drawbar, but to release them, they must be tapped or pressed on their inside ends. Morse tapers come in eight sizes: 0, 1, 2, 3, 4, 5, 6 and 7. All sizes have slightly different tapers of *about* 0.62 inches/foot. There are two ways to identify the taper number of an unknown Morse taper. If the unknown MT is male, measure its taper in inches/inch as shown in Figure 3-1, and then find the matching taper in Table 3-1 (third column from the left). If the taper is female, measure its interior diameter at the end of the socket, and then find the matching diameter in Table 3-1 (far right column).

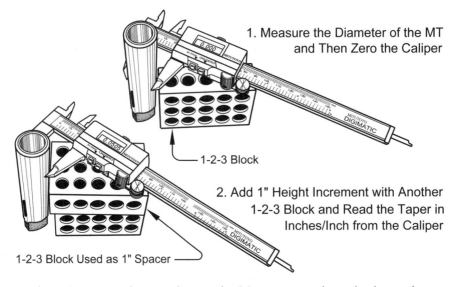

1. Measure the Diameter of the MT and Then Zero the Caliper

1-2-3 Block

2. Add 1" Height Increment with Another 1-2-3 Block and Read the Taper in Inches/Inch from the Caliper

1-2-3 Block Used as 1" Spacer

Figure 3-1. Measuring an unknown size Morse taper to determine its number.

MT Taper Number	Taper (inches/foot)	Taper (inches/inch)	Diameter at End of Socket (inches)
0	0.62460	0.05205	0.3561
1	0.59858	0.04988	0.475
2	0.59941	0.04995	0.700
3	0.60235	0.05019	0.938
4	0.62326	0.05193	1.231
5	0.63151	0.05262	1.748
6	0.62565	0.05213	2.494
7	0.62400	0.05200	3.270

Table 3-1. Morse taper dimensions.

Morse tapers come in three variations:

- *Without tang* – This includes most live and dead lathe centers. See Figure 3-2 (top).

- *With slits and drawbar threads* – These are collets. See Figure 3-2 (middle).

- *With tang* – These are for MT shank drills to prevent them from spinning. See Figure 3-2 (bottom).

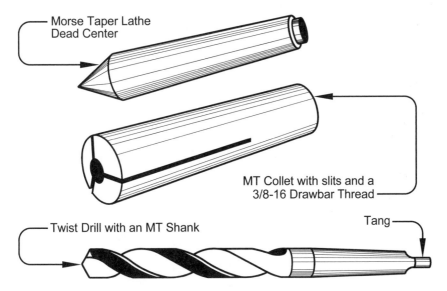

Figure 3-2. The three Morse taper designs. The extended shank on the twist drill prevents the drill from spinning under load and makes it easy to eject from the lathe spindle.

Many older lathes used MT collets directly in their spindles, and Sherline lathes still do. But today, most larger lathes with MT spindle holes have a reducing *adapter* to hold smaller MTs. For example, the Kent 13×40 lathe has an MT 5-sized spindle hole, but with its spindle MT adapter installed, it can hold an MT 3. Besides the cost savings, this is a great advantage as the tailstock also takes the same size center. Another tool today that uses MTs is the rotary table, which has a female MT center hole to accommodate a collet for holding work or center points.

- *Jacobs tapers* (*JTs*) are confined to drill chucks and their arbors. There are nine JT sizes: 0, 1, 2, 2 short, 3, 4, 5, 6 and 33. The 33 is not a typo; it's an odd numbering system. See Table 3-2. Like Morse tapers, JTs are self-locking, but because drill chucks, once placed on their arbors, are infrequently changed, considerable force is needed to secure them so that the chuck and its taper do not come apart under load. See Figure 3-3.

JT Taper Number	Taper (inches/foot)	Small End (inches)	Big End (inches)	Length (inches)
0	0.59145	0.22844	0.2500	0.43750
1	0.92508	0.33341	0.3840	0.62625
2	0.97861	0.48764	0.5590	0.87500
2 Short	0.97861	0.48764	0.5488	0.7500
3	0.63898	0.74610	0.8110	1.21875
4	0.62886	1.0372	1.1240	1.6563
5	0.62010	1.3161	1.4130	1.8750
6	0.62292	0.6241	0.6760	1.0000
33	0.76194	0.5605	0.6240	1.0000

Table 3-2. Jacobs taper dimensions.

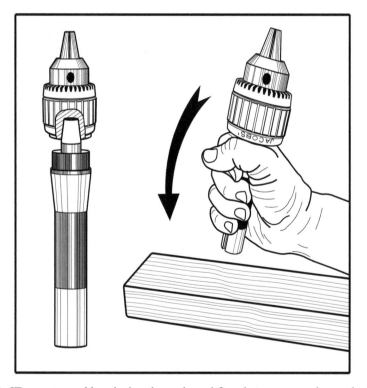

Figure 3-3. JTs are secured by placing the male and female tapers together and striking the opposite end of the arbor on a piece of wood. The inertia of the drill chuck produces large forces when the arbor stops suddenly upon striking the wood and forces the chuck onto the arbor. Do not use an arbor press.

- *5C collets* are the most common collet design, although there are dozens of others. 5C collets are used in medium-sized lathes, indexing heads and in collet blocks. See Figure 3-4 for 5C collet dimensions.

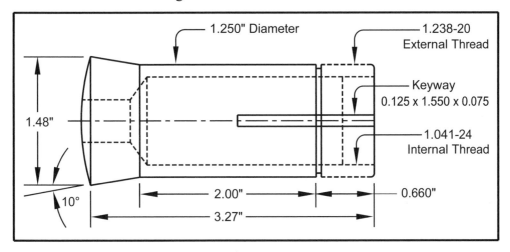

Figure 3-4. 5C collets are the most common of the dozens of collet designs.

- *R8 collets* are widely used on Bridgeport-style milling machines to hold tools in their spindles. See Figure 3-5 for R8 collet dimensions.

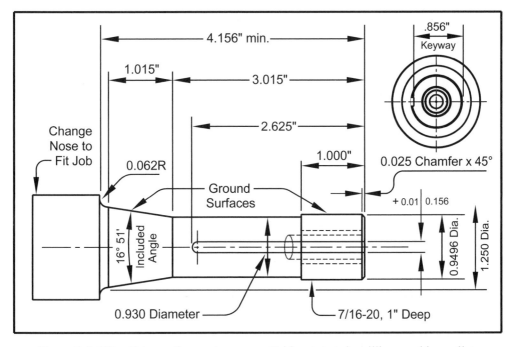

Figure 3-5. R8 collets are the most common Bridgeport-style milling machine collet.

Although R8 tapers are self-locking, additional holding forces are required to secure cutting tools in them and to prevent the tools from spinning. A drawbar provides this extra gripping force by pulling the collet farther up into the spindle. Then the collets' taper causes the collet to collapse, or press inward, along its precut slits, increasing its hold on the cutting tool.

- *NMTB tapers* (for National Machine Tool Builders Association, which is now called the Association for Manufacturing Technology) are also called *NMT tapers*, *NT tapers* and *V-flange mounts*. See Figure 3-6. They are used on CNC milling machines and on some heavy-duty Bridgeport-style manual mills. These tapers come in different sizes: NMTB-25, -30, -35, -40, -45, -50 and -60. All sizes have the same taper of 3.500 inches/foot. The objective of this design is to make machine tool changes quick and easy, so this taper is *self-releasing*. Tools on these tapers release when their drawbar is unscrewed. This facilitates automatic tool changers since the tool holder does not need to be forced out to release it.

Note: Tapers with angles less than 10° are *self-locking*; those with angles steeper than 16° are *self-releasing*. Tapers with angles in the 10–16° transition zone are not predictable, but depend on the properties of the taper metals and the smoothness of the mating surfaces. In general, taper angles in this transition zone are undesirable because either a self-locking or self-releasing taper is needed, not a taper with an unpredictable outcome.

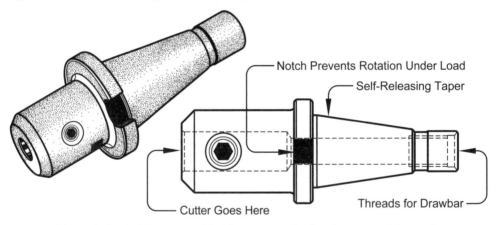

Figure 3-6. NMTB taper tool holders are standard on larger machine tools. Their self-releasing taper design permits them to work with automatic tool changers, essential for NC-machines.

- *Brown & Sharp (B&S) tapers* appear on older model, horizontal milling machines and come in 18 sizes. Their taper is close to 0.5 inches/foot, and like the Morse tapers, they are self-locking. Brown & Sharp tapers closely resemble Morse tapers in appearance, but differ in having a shallower taper. Brown & Sharp tapers remain important for larger, older horizontal mills and for many precision grinders. B&S tapers are not usually seen in smaller shops. Table 3-3 shows a comparison of taper dimensions.

	Taper (inches/foot)	Taper (1:X)	Taper (Degrees)	Self-Locking
Morse Tapers*	0.62	1:20	1.5	Yes
5C Collets	0.5	1:24	20	Yes
Jacobs Tapers	0.59–0.75*	20–16*	1.4–1.8*	Yes
R8 Collets	—	—	16.85	Yes
NMTB Tool Holders	3.5	1:2.9	—	No
B&S Tapers	0.5	1:24	1.2*	Yes

*varies with size.

Table 3-3. Comparison of tapers.

Repairing Morse Taper Shanks

When a ding is inflicted on an MT shank, it results in both a crater and a surrounding raised area. The raised area contains metal previously in the crater. Since this raised metal causes the taper to fail to lock up, the high spots need to be removed. Here are the steps:

1. Clean the MT shank thoroughly using carburetor cleaner or acetone. This will help reveal what is happening on the metal surface.

2. Paint the taper with layout fluid and quickly draw the edge of a paper towel across its wet surface to thin the coating. Thinning will change the surface color from a deep blue to a pale blue and leave a very thin, easily removed coating.

3. Push the MT shank into a socket of the same size and attempt to get it to lock up. Remove the shank from the socket, turn it 180° and attempt to lock it up again, then remove it.

4. Layout fluid on the high spots will be removed as these spots rub the socket walls. The high spots will appear as light colored areas or bare metal. These are the raised problem areas which must be removed with a soft abrasive stone. To do that, rub the stone on each high spot, and then repeat Steps 2 and 3. When all of the high spots are removed, the taper will lock up.

Repairing Morse Taper Sockets

The reason for repairing male MT sockets is the same as for shanks, they will not lock up when lightly tapped in place. Some Morse taper sockets are damaged in use and others were never made correctly at the factory. Damage commonly occurs when debris remains between the MT components, gouging or scraping their surfaces. Factory defects, such as concave or convex tapers, are caused by worn production reamers at the factory and result in poor MT lockup. Many imported drill presses suffer from defective MTs.

MT repair reamers, as shown in Figure 3-7, are available in straight shanks with square ends for hand reaming using a tap wrench, and with MT shanks for machine reaming. Modern reamers are HSS. For hand reaming, here are the steps:

1. Clean out the socket to be repaired by applying compressed air at the inside end of the socket, and then flush the socket out with carburetor cleaner or acetone. Visually inspect the socket to insure it is clean. Use a mirror and a flashlight to see inside the inverted spindle taper.

2. Insert the repair reamer into a tap wrench and add cutting oil.

3. If the socket is in a tailstock, turn the tap wrench while pressing it into the socket. If in a drill press, rotate the spindle by turning the pulley on top of the spindle and holding the tap wrench fixed. Turn the spindle about six times, then remove and inspect the reamer. Do not do this under motor power.

4. Look for metal scrapings on the reamer flutes because these indicate the type of imperfections.

   - If the socket has rings worn into it, there will be metal bits concentrated at points on the reamer.

   - If the socket was poorly manufactured—a fairly common situation—metal shavings will first appear in the middle of the reamer and then spread along its entire length when the reaming is completed. If the socket bulges out in its middle, the shavings will appear at the ends of the reamer and work their way toward the middle. When reaming is completed, the socket will be a cone with smooth sides.

5. Repeat Steps 2 and 3 until the socket locks up properly.

Figure 3-7. Morse taper repair hand reamer with a square shank for use in a tap wrench.

For machine reaming in a lathe, here are the steps:

1. Install the repair reamer in the lathe opposite the socket under repair. This socket could be either in the spindle or in the tailstock.

2. Put cutting oil on the repair reamer, position and lock the tailstock so that the reamer can enter the damaged socket.

3. Set the lathe to backgear, or its slowest speed, and turn it on.

4. Using the tailstock spindle crank, slowly engage the reamer into the socket using light pressure, then remove and inspect the reamer for the location of the metal shavings.

5. Repeat Steps 2–4 as needed.

Making Male MTs

Male MTs are easy to make in a lathe, but to cut the proper taper, you will need another MT with which to set the lathe compound. Although a lathe taper attachment can be used to obtain an approximate compound setting, because MTs male and female parts fit together so precisely, you must use a dial indicator to copy the correct angle from an existing MT. Figure 7-91 in *Chapter 7 – Lathes* shows this set-up.

Note: Female MTs must be ground on an ID/OD grinder and cannot be cut in a lathe unless a tool post grinder is used.

Section II – Threaded Fasteners

Fastener Facts to Remember

- For critical applications, fasteners require:

  - *Strength* – Match the application as determined by Grade (inch-based fasteners) or Class (Metric fasteners).

  - *Manufacturer* – Use only established brands like Unbrako and Holochrome. Avoid the low-quality fasteners from home improvement stores.

  - *Supplier* – Purchase from a trusted supplier with a certificate of origin stating who made the fasteners, what specs they meet, and their lot number. This additional step will increase the likelihood of getting the fastener you ordered.

- *Anti-loosening steps* – Among the many anti-loosening methods, lock washers are the least effective, skip them. Stainless steel safety wires, castellated nuts with cotter pins, split-beam nuts, which have distorted threads to increase friction (for high temperatures), nylon-inserted nuts (for lower temperatures) and anaerobic thread-locking adhesives such as Locktite are excellent choices. Military grade split-beam nuts are re-usable up to a dozen times. See Figure 3-8.

- *Fine vs. coarse threads* – Fine threads are used on steel nuts and thin tubing where coarse threads would be too deep. Coarse threads are used in castings and aluminum where they provide a better, deeper grip into the soft metal. Both have the same fatigue life.

- *Screw size numbers* – Inch-based fasteners under ¼-inch diameter run from size #0 to size #12. Each increasing screw size number doubles the fastener's tensile strength. Odd-sized number diameters are uncommon today.

- *Stress in each thread* – Stress drops off rapidly after the first few threads under load, as shown in Figure 3-9. Since the first six threads carry all the load, threads farther back from the nut or thread engagement point carry no load, so adding more engaged threads to a fastener will not make it a stronger design.

- *Nuts* – Are designed with enough thread strength to carry the same proof load as their respective screw or bolt. Nuts usually have only 6 or 7 threads; adding more threads is pointless. Always have 1½ and preferably 3 complete screw threads protruding *beyond* each nut because initial threads are likely to be weaker than those further up the fastener. See the assortment of fasteners in Figure 3-8.

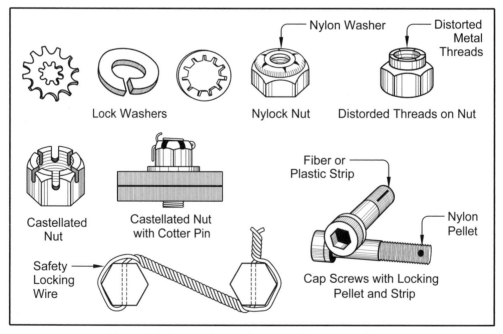

Figure 3-8. Steps to insure fasteners do not come loose.

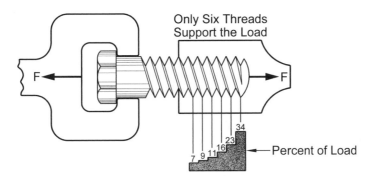

Figure 3-9. The first six threads carry all the load.

- *Washers* – Using the same grade of washers as that of the fasteners which bear on them is important to a sound design. Too soft a washer under a highly stressed bolt will cause the washer metal to *coin*, or indent, reducing the tension in the bolt and increasing the chance of the fastener loosening and decreasing fatigue life.

- *Thread height,* also called *thread engagement* – In most applications the tap drill size is unimportant as long as the thread height is greater than 60% engagement. Smaller tap drills and tap holes beyond 60% lead to more broken taps and scrapped parts without adding much strength.

- *Shear vs. tensile considerations* – In most applications, including construction, bolted joints are designed to avoid shear forces on the bolts. This is because there must be movement between the joint faces for the bolts to take up a shear load and the shear strength of most metals is only about 60% of their tensile strength. Keep in mind that bolts are much stronger in tension than in shear. Dowel pins installed in properly sized and reamed holes prevent all joint movement and take up shear load, not the bolts. In general, bolts should not be used as locators, axles, shafts or hinges unless designed specifically for this purpose.

- *Shear loading failures* – A dangerous situation occurs when bolt holes are clearance holes. That is, the bolt hole is larger than the bolt and the bolt is able to shift in the hole when loads are applied. One bolt will then fail, leading to a *cascade* of failures of the remaining bolts. Typically, for ease of assembly, bolt holes in most mechanical engineering applications are oversized. But, since many high-strength bolts have reduced shank diameters, a clearance hole for the threads leaves considerable room for bolt movement. Not a good situation. The result is that joints in shear depend on the bolts to withstand the shear load. Since the bolts are not really rigid, significant relative sideways movement must take place before the bolt shank can take any shear load as it moves from side to side in its hole. Because one bolt is likely to be loaded first, there is a good chance that it will yield before the others, making shear load failure a very real possibility.

- *Aerospace Applications* – Many joints in aerospace *do* put bolts in shear. This is possible for three reasons:

  - Aerospace bolt hole tolerances are snug, just permitting bolt insertion. This prevents bolt movement within the hole. Sometimes bolt holes are reamed to insure proper sizing. This step insures more even distribution of load forces on all of the bolts in the joint during shear load application.

  - Aerospace bolts are generally of higher strength and quality than needed for most other engineering applications.

  - Because lives depend upon it, the effect of combined loads—shear loads in addition to tensile loads—are carefully analyzed by engineers.

- *Tightening to specification* or *pre-loading the fastener* – Fasteners must be torqued to specification to put the joint under tensile load. This insures that the fastener will not loosen. Bolts under tension do not "see" fluctuating loads when the loads are below the bolt *pre-loading*, also called *pre-tension,* level. Maintaining this pre-tension level avoids fatigue failures. Generally, bolts are tightened to 75–80% of their yield stress.

- *Checking threads* – In addition to fixed thread standards and thread measuring systems, there are several other ways to check threads:

  - Comparing unknown threads with threads from a fastener of known size is a quick way to check thread count as shown in Figure 3-10.

  - Screw pitch and TPI (threads per inch) can be determined with a screw pitch gage which consists of a set of thin steel leaves. The individual leaf edges have "teeth" corresponding to a fixed thread pitch and the corresponding pitch is stamped on each leaf.

  - A thread micrometer is the fastest way to measure the minor thread diameter accurately, and is much faster than using thread wires which require the use of a formula, and so do not yield a direct answer.

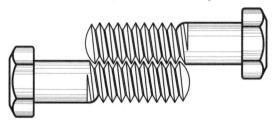

Figure 3-10. A quick way to determine a thread size is to mate
a fastener side by side with a fastener of a known size.

Section III – Dowel Pins vs. Taper Pins

Dowel Pins

- Large dowel pins are chamfered on their ends to easily go into the dowel pin hole and are domed on the other end. This dome is so the end of the dowel pin does not mushroom out when struck with a hammer. Small dowels have chamfers on both ends.

- *Hardened steel dowel pins* are the most common, but dowel pins are also available in unhardened steel, Type 316 and 416 stainless steel alloys, and in brass.

- The *pull-out dowel pin* is similar to the standard dowel pin except that the pull-out design has a threaded hole to make removal easy. The *spiral grooved-* and *flat-vent dowel pin* designs provide an escape path for air or oil when the dowel pin is installed.

- Available in both inch and metric sizes, dowel pins are typically 0.002 of an inch *larger* than their nominal size so that they stay in place. The most common dowel pins range from $^1/_{16}$- to 1-inch diameter.

- Large steel dowel pins are case hardened, but the casing process hardens pins smaller than $^3/_{16}$ inch through and through. Because of this case hardening, carbide tools are needed when shortening dowel pins in the lathe. Dowel pins may also be shortened with an abrasive cutoff wheel.

- Dowel pins are useful as pivots, axles and stops. Because they are ground to size within 2–3 thousandths of an inch, they can be used as "toolbox standards" against which to check your own calipers and micrometers, and, in an emergency, hole diameters can be checked using them. In addition, dowel pins can be used as transfer punches, and they can also remove roll pins of the same diameter without damaging the roll pins or scoring the holes.

- Oversized dowel pins are available when the original dowel holes have been waddled out. These pins are either 1 or 2 thousandths larger than the standard size pins.

Dowel pins, as shown in Figure 3-11, are usually chosen to handle shear loads and to prevent threaded fasteners from "seeing" these loads. They can also be used to *register*—also called *indexing*—or locate one part with respect to another. Dowel pins in through-holes can be driven out. Standard dowel pins in blind holes are more difficult to remove and usually require TIG welding to the dowel pin and pulling it out with a slide hammer, but, if the dowel pin has a threaded hole in one end, it is easy to remove with a slide hammer alone. If this method fails, the last resort is to use electro discharge machining (EDM) to disintegrate the dowel pin. Installing a dowel pin requires drilling a hole and performing two reaming operations. Figure 3-12 shows an example of dowel pins in use where the faceplate of a lathe is attached to the backplate by SHCSs, but the shear loads and registration between the backplate and faceplate are handled by the dowel pins. For more details about reaming holes for dowel pins, refer to Chapter 5, Figure 5-45.

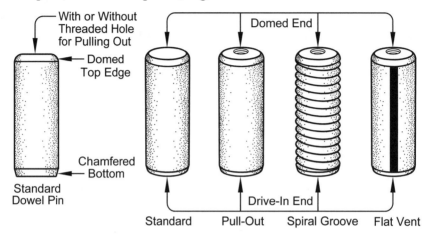

Figure 3-11. Dowel pins are available in several designs.

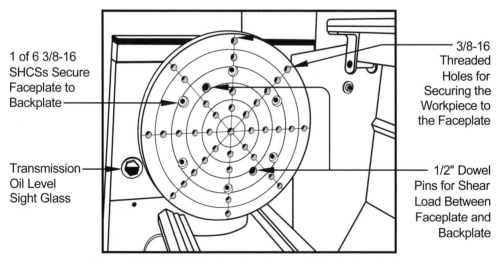

Figure 3-12. This lathe faceplate has two ½-inch dowel pins
which prevent the SHCSs from seeing shear loads.

Taper Pins

Taper pins are used for holding parts in precise alignment and for transferring low torques. *Standard taper pins* are usually installed in through-holes so that they can be removed by tapping on their small end using a punch and a hammer. *Threaded taper pins* have threaded studs, washers and nuts on their outside ends for *jacking-out*. Tightening the nut breaks the pin loose from its lock-up and permits easy removal. Installing a taper pin requires drilling several stepped holes followed by a reaming operation. Taper pins offer the advantage that when re-installed they will pull the parts back into alignment. Taper pin characteristics:

- Taper pins are supplied in sizes $\frac{7}{0}$ though 0 and 1–10 based on the large end diameter, and a variety of lengths are available. All taper pins have the same taper of 1:48 or ¼ inch per foot.

- Steel taper pins are not usually hardened. They are also available in stainless steel.

- Frequently, a large diameter taper pin is required to sustain a shear load, but the installation does not allow room for a pin of that length. The solution is simple: shorten the pin and the reamer with an abrasive disc, and then install the pin.

Here's an example of a taper pin application where a lathe tailstock must be repeatedly moved off-center for cutting tapers, then moved back into axial alignment. A perfect time-saving solution is to install a taper pin with a jacking-out screw as in Figure 3-13. To bring the tailstock back into axial alignment after cutting a taper, move the tailstock roughly into alignment, and then tap the pin into place. The taper pin will pull the tailstock back into perfect alignment and hold it there until removed.

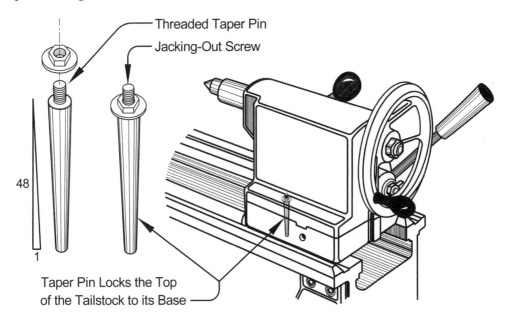

Figure 3-13. A taper pin in the tailstock simplifies re-setting the tailstock after off-setting it.

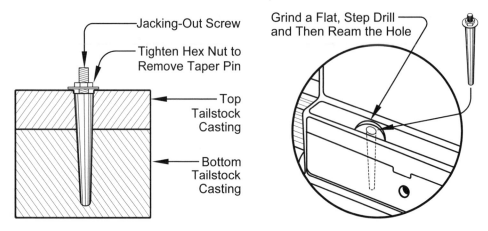

Figure 3-13. (continued) Detail of the taper pin in the lathe tailstock casting.

Section IV – Important Machining Concepts & Warnings

Removing Excess Material

When planning to make a part, see if removing large sections of unwanted material with a bandsaw *before* the start of machining will save time. It takes less time and energy to *cut out* a volume of metal than to turn it into chips.

Sacrificial Material

Many parts are best machined by using part of its raw metal stock to hold or position the part in a machine tool, then removing the sacrificial material when machining is done. In short production runs, it is not unusual to scrap a good section of the raw stock to get a good part. See Figure 9-6 for more details.

Cumulative Errors

Whenever there is a choice between using one tool holder or a series of tool holders, opt for the single tool holder. Each time one tool holder (such as a Morse taper adapter or extension) is added to another tool holder, additional inaccuracies are introduced. Here are some other situations where cumulative errors can be introduced:

- When a milling vise is mounted on a swivel base the workpiece is now two times removed from the table, first, by the swivel base, and then by the milling vise. Each of these devices introduces its own inaccuracies and uncertainties. There is no guarantee that the out-of-square errors of these two devices will cancel each other out. If a swivel base is not needed, do not leave the milling vise mounted on it.

- When a drill chuck holds a twist drill on an arbor in the tailstock of a lathe, and an MT reducing sleeve holds the drill chuck arbor, you are twice removed from the axial alignment accuracy of the tailstock. Avoid using MT reducer sleeves on tools for work that demands accuracy.

Clearcutting

Clearcutting is when a cutting tool makes a cut, but is constrained to limit the depth of cut. Clearcutting can be performed in most machine tools, but often for different reasons.

- *In the lathe* – When a lathe tool has completed its first cut at a particular depth and the tool is drawn across the workpiece a second time without increasing the depth of cut, a small amount of additional material is removed. This occurs because the large forces from the initial cut are removed from the tool after its first pass, and the tool moves inward toward the work and removes more material on a second pass. After this second pass, the forces on the tool are now much lower than on the two previous cuts, and if the cutting depth remains unchanged, little additional material will be removed on subsequent passes. This is particularly evident with boring bars because they tend to be long and springy.

- *In the drill press* – Drill presses with a threaded rod-type depth stop are often used for clearcutting. The depth stop is set for a 2–5 thousandths of an inch advance into the work, and the drill is moved into the work to the limits of the stop. Then the depth stop is advanced and the drilling repeated. Clearcutting must be performed if there is a possibility that the drill can self-feed or can take an excessive cut, which can fracture the drill or stall the drill press. Clearcutting permits completion of jobs not possible with conventional, one-step drilling.

- *In a milling machine* – Clearcutting is often necessary when using a large form cutter which would take too large a cut, such as the form tool in Figure 8-97. Clearcutting may also be used to reduce the forces on a carbide drill by limiting it to only small pecks. After each peck is cleared, the stop-nut on the micrometer depth stop is advanced for the next peck.

- *In a surface grinder* – After the grinding wheel has made repeated passes over the work, the wheel *sparks out* and ceases cutting because it has cut to its full depth.

Threads Show Distance

When making an adjustment with a screw, the question often arises, How much movement does turning this screw one turn make? For a $1/20$-20 machine screw, 20 threads/inch means that each turn represents $1/20$ of an inch or 0.050 inches. One-half turn would be 0.025 inches movement and one-quarter turn, 0.0125 inches. Other screw threads are similarly determined.

Materials Not for Welding

Welding is often performed in the machine shop, but should not be attempted on these materials:

- *Tool steels* – Pre-heat, post-heat and special welding rod are needed. Welding will also modify tool steel properties gained by heat treatment.

- *12L14 leaded steel* – This, and all other *free-machining steels,* cannot be welded because their alloying elements vaporize under welding heat before the iron in the steel melts.

- *7075 Series aluminum plate* – All members of this continuously cast aluminum tooling plate series cannot be welded, but they machine very well.

- *Cadmium-plated components* – The cadmium must be ground off before welding or brazing. Cadmium is a heavy metal and its fumes are poisionous.

Chemical Ingredients

Machinists work with many chemical products. By Federal law, industrial products must have *Material Safety Data Sheets (MSDSs)*. These are readily available on the internet, from the seller, or attached to the product itself.

Unfortunately, there are no such requirements for consumer products. Their active ingredients are often not stated on the product's container or not easily found on the internet. Only calling the poison control center will reveal their contents. Even though they are consumer products, some of them are dangerous.

Always remember that the better a product works, the more hazardous it is. Put another way, products that are intrinsically safe are usually ineffective. The converse is also true, the better they work, the faster they work, the more dangerous they are. The reason many products work is because they are able to combine with other compounds—including human flesh.

Chapter 4

Filing & Grinding

The purpose of education is to replace
an empty mind with an open one.

—Malcolm Forbes

Section I – Filing Basics

Introduction

Hammers, cold chisels and punches are blacksmith tools adopted by machinists, but files are the machinists' first and most basic tool. Since 1100 years BC, crude files in the form of stones with ridges running at right angles across them were used for the same purpose as modern files—to sharpen tool edges. The first attempt to make files by machine began in 1490, but the first successful production began in France in 1750. Before the development of machine tools, files were the only way to precisely cut and shape metal. With skill and patience, early machinists made clocks and locks using just files.

Files are inexpensive, portable and able to fit into tight spots, but because today there are faster methods to remove metal, files are mainly used to sharpen, smooth edges, remove burrs, or to make fine adjustments. Still, they remain an important and handy tool, indispensable to mold makers, tool and die makers, prototype makers and to gunsmiths.

File Terms

Figure 4-1 shows the parts of a file.

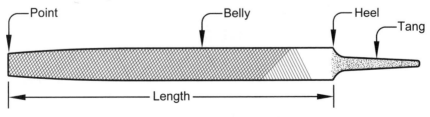

Figure 4-1. The parts of a file.

- A file's *safe edges* are smooth and have no teeth, allowing the file to cut on one surface but not on an adjoining one. See Figure 4-2. Although most files are not manufactured with safe edges, they can be applied by grinding off the teeth on an edge or face of a file using a belt, disc, pedestal or surface grinder.

Figure 4-2. A file with a safe edge (left) and one with teeth on its edge (right).

- *Single-cut files* have diagonal rows of teeth running across the width of the file. They are used with light pressure for a smooth finish with limited metal removal. See Figure 4-3 (top).
- *Double-cut files* have *two* diagonal rows of teeth running in opposite directions across the width of the file. They remove metal faster than single-cut files, but leave a rougher surface. See Figure 4-3 (bottom).

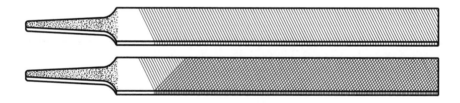

Figure 4-3. Single-cut file (top) and double-cut file (bottom).

File Cut Shapes

Figure 4-4 shows the many shapes files can create.

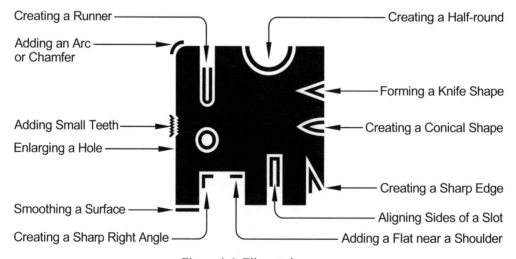

Figure 4-4. File cut shapes.

Swiss- and American-Pattern Files

- *American-pattern files,* sometimes called *engineers' files,* are the most common full-size files seen in machine shops. They remove metal rapidly and are available with both single and double cuts.

- Most American-pattern files are only available in three grades of cut—bastard, second and smooth—while *Swiss-pattern files,* also known as *needle files,* are available in eight grades. American-pattern file cut grades roughly correspond to the following Swiss-pattern grades:

  - *Bastard cut* is equivalent to Swiss-pattern cut 00.

  - *Second cut* is equivalent to Swiss-pattern cut 2.

  - *Smooth cut* is equivalent to Swiss-pattern cut 6.

  There are no American-pattern equivalents to the other five Swiss-pattern cuts, but this is not a problem because American-pattern files are used mainly for faster metal removal on rougher, larger workpieces.

- The smaller Swiss-pattern files are for more precise work and for minute adjustments, so they are available only in single-cut. Note that the terms *single-cut* and *double-cut* refer only to the number of rows of teeth, not to the number of teeth per inch. However, very fine files with high teeth per inch are not supplied in double-cut designs because that would defeat the purpose of making a file with a high tooth count—to slowly remove small, precise amounts of metal.

- The number of teeth per inch increases with decreasing file length since, proportionately, less metal is removed with a small file than with a large one. Table 4-1 shows the scale of file cut grades for Swiss-pattern files.

Swiss-Pattern Files — Scale of File Cut Grades									
00 Coarsest 0 1 2 Medium 3 4 5 6 Finest									
Teeth Per Inch	30	41	51	64	79	97	117	142	173
Files 10" and Over In Length	00	0	1	2	3	4	—	6	—
Files 4" to 9" In Length		00	0	1	2	3	4	—	6
Files 3" In Length			00	0	1	2	3	4	—
Escapement Files			00	0	1	2	3	4	—
Needle Files 4" to 7-3/4"			0	0	2	3	4	—	6
Regular Rifflers				0	—	2	3	4	6

Table 4-1. Swiss-pattern file cut grades.

Section II – File Designs

File Categories

- *American-pattern* or *engineers' files* are available in 4, 6, 8, 10, 12, 14 and sometimes 16-inch lengths. They are the most common of all files, and come in a variety of shapes. See Figure 4-5. A properly-stored, readily accessible, good selection of these files is essential for every shop.

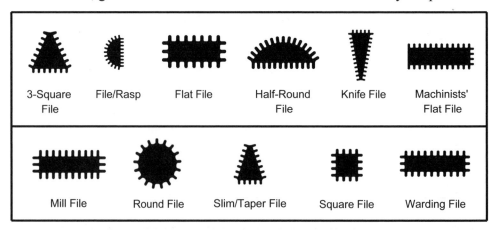

Figure 4-5. Common American-pattern file shapes.

- *Precision files* are ideal for "in-between" jobs that are too large for Swiss-pattern files and too big for American-pattern files. Precision files are typically 4-inches in length and have up to 400 teeth per inch that cut all the way to their tips. These files are manufactured with more uniformity than their larger American-pattern cousins, so the user will get consistent results year after year. Most precision files are single cut in keeping with their purpose, the precise, slow removal of metal, but a few precision file shapes are available in double-cut. See Figure 4-6 for a sampling of the many precision file shapes.

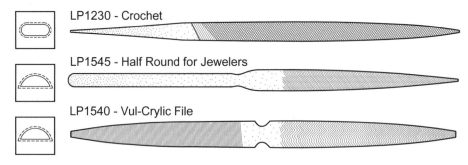

Courtesy of Usines Métallurgiques de Vallorbe SA

Figure 4-6. Precision files.

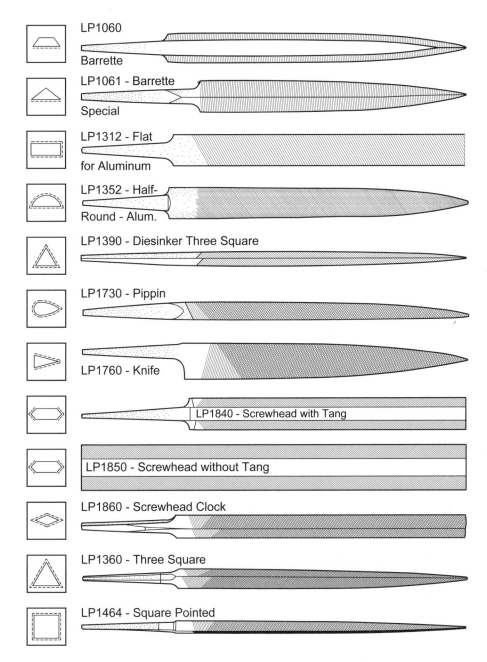

LP1060
Barrette

LP1061 - Barrette
Special

LP1312 - Flat
for Aluminum

LP1352 - Half-
Round - Alum.

LP1390 - Diesinker Three Square

LP1730 - Pippin

LP1760 - Knife

LP1840 - Screwhead with Tang

LP1850 - Screwhead without Tang

LP1860 - Screwhead Clock

LP1360 - Three Square

LP1464 - Square Pointed

Courtesy of Usines Métallurgiques de Vallorbe SA

Figure 4-6. (continued) Precision files.

- *Needle files*, also known as *Swiss-pattern files*, are used by watchmakers, instrument makers, mold makers and gunsmiths for finishing small, delicate, intricate parts, not for removing metal rapidly. See Figure 4-7. Swiss-pattern files are single-cut. They come in many lengths, but the 3-

and 4-inch sizes are the most popular. Some needle files have dipped vinyl handles and others have handles that are simply round rods with knurling. Many users insert needle files in a pin vise or other holder to increase control and reduce operator fatigue. Needle files are also available with diamond-coated surfaces instead of teeth. These files can make fine adjustments on hard materials, including carbides, tool steels and glass.

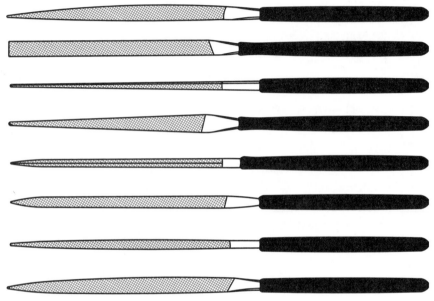

Figure 4-7. Needle files, or Swiss-pattern files, with dipped vinyl handles.

- *Escapement files* have safe edges and are specifically designed for intricate clock making and repair. They are available in many different shapes. For a sampling, see Figure 4-8.

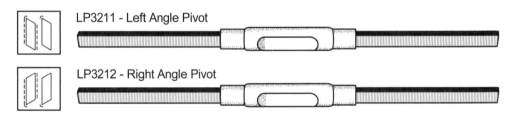

Courtesy of Usines Métallurgiques de Vallorbe SA

Figure 4-8. Escapement files.

- *Rifflers*, also known as *die sinkers,* are double-ended files with a 6-inch overall length. Both of their ends have teeth with a handle between them. Their long, thin shape allows rifflers access to very tight spaces such as the inside or bottom of cavities, making rifflers a favorite of mold makers. See Figure 4-9 for some of the many riffler shapes.

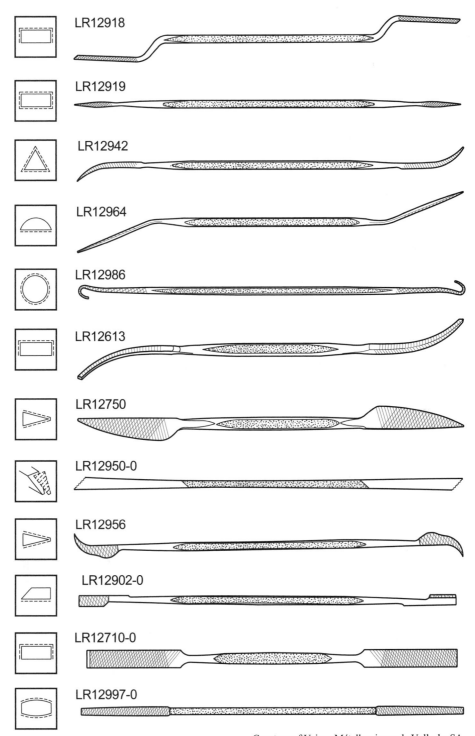

LR12918

LR12919

LR12942

LR12964

LR12986

LR12613

LR12750

LR12950-0

LR12956

LR12902-0

LR12710-0

LR12997-0

Courtesy of Usines Métallurgiques de Vallorbe SA

Figure 4-9. Rifflers and their cutting profiles.

- *Warding,* or *locksmiths' files,* are scaled down versions of engineers' files. They are used for smaller work than the typical engineers' files, but larger work than that requiring the smaller, more precise and expensive needle files or rifflers. See Figure 4-10.

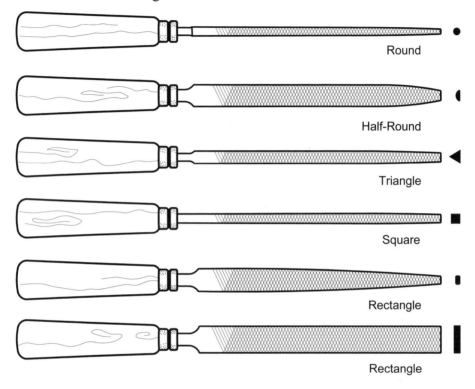

Figure 4-10. Warding, or locksmiths' files, and their cutting profiles.

Specialty Files

- *Long-angled,* or *lathe files,* have teeth set at 45° to the file's length instead of the usual 65°. They are designed for lathe filing most metals and for bench filing aluminum and copper alloys. The single-cut bastard teeth are self-clearing when used at right angles to the work. They cut cleanly without chatter and do not drag or tear. Lathe files have a rectangular cross section, taper slightly in width toward the point, and both edges are safe to protect the shoulders of work not to be filed. In the lathe, the file should not be held rigidly or stationary, but constantly stroked. A slight gliding or lateral motion assists the file to clear itself and to eliminate ridges and grooves. Use a long steady stroke across the work and move laterally about half the width of the file. Lathe filing is most often used to remove sharp edges from shoulders and for sizing shafts when only a little material needs to be removed. When lathe filing must be performed with a conventional file (65° teeth), hold the file at a 20° angle clockwise to the lathe axis as in Figure 4-11. This will place the conventional file teeth at 45° to the work as a lathe file does. When lathe filing, fill the file grooves with blackboard chalk to improve the surface finish of the work. Run the lathe at the same speed as for turning the same metal. Uneven pressure on the file and excessive use of lathe filing leads to an out-of-round condition on the work.

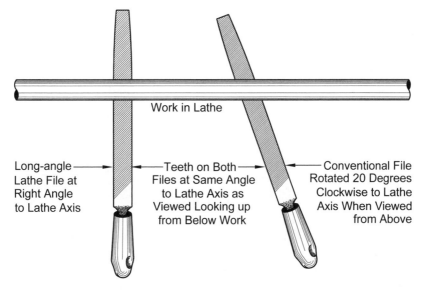

Figure 4-11. Long-angled or lathe files have teeth at 45° instead of the usual 65° angle.

• A *Three-square file* is an engineers' file used to file acute angles, grooves, corners and notches. Its triangular cross section, while similar to a taper saw blade sharpening file, has three sharp edges used for bringing rounded inside corners to square. See Figure 4-12.

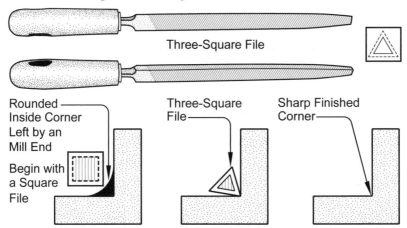

Figure 4-12. A square file begins removal of the corner web left by an end mill, and a three-square file removes the remaining metal to leave a square inside corner.

- *Tungsten carbide files* are excellent for rough work on hard phenolic plastics like electrical switch plates, and for filing work with both hardened and unhardened surfaces such as welds that must be blended with the rest of a workpiece surface. See Figure 4-13.

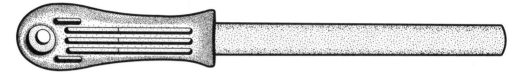

Figure 4-13. A coating of tungsten carbide particles produces a file for hard materials.

- *Rasps* and *curved-tooth files* work well on lead, leather, plastics and some softer zinc castings. When used on soft materials, they resist loading. See Figure 4-14.

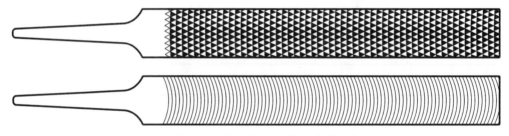

Figure 4-14. Rasp (top) and curved-tooth file (bottom).

Section III – Filing Practice

Important File Practices

- Never use a tanged file without a handle, especially when doing lathe work. The tang can push through your palm.
- Always lighten up pressure on the file when pulling *with* the direction of its teeth. The file will last longer and cut better.
- Never hammer a file on its point to seat it into its handle. Invert the file in its handle, then rap the file handle top on a hard surface.
- Avoid cross contamination of workpieces of different metals by removing particles caught in file teeth. With American-pattern files, use a file card that has steel wire bristles on a wooden handle, and with precision and Swiss-pattern files, use a new stainless steel wire brush. A file card will not work with precision or Swiss-pattern files because the card's wires are too large to fit into the small teeth of these files. See Figure 4-15. Stubborn metal particles can also be removed from file teeth using the edge of the mouth of a soft brass cartridge case, a piece of hardwood, or a soft iron point.

- Apply white blackboard chalk to lathe files to prevent metal filings from adhering to the file teeth and leaving marks from them on the work.

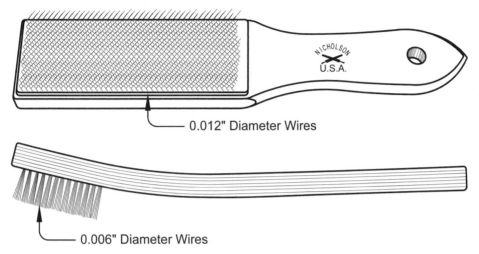

0.012" Diameter Wires

0.006" Diameter Wires

Figure 4-15. Use a file card (top) on American-pattern files, also called engineers' files, and a stainless steel wire brush (bottom) on precision and Swiss-pattern files, also called needle files, to match the wire size to the file teeth spacing.

Bent Files

Files can be easily bent to fit into tight spots or to permit flat filing as in Figure 4-16. Heat the bend point red hot with an oxyacetylene torch, bend the file to shape while holding the hot end in pliers, then quench in water to re-harden the file. Place the pliers at the desired point of the bend or the bend will not be sharp, but rounded.

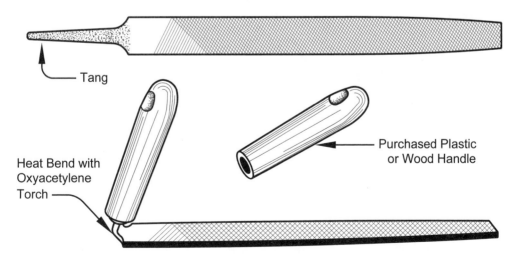

Tang

Heat Bend with
Oxyacetylene
Torch

Purchased Plastic
or Wood Handle

Figure 4-16. Bending the file handle permits the filing of flat surfaces.

Shop-Made File Holders

Tool and die makers often make their own custom file holders, usually from aluminum. See several different designs in Figures 4-17 and 4-18.

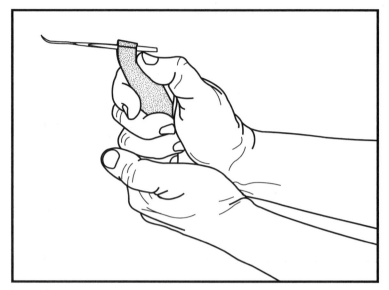

Figure 4-17. Proper way to hold a riffler or needle file in a shop-made file holder.

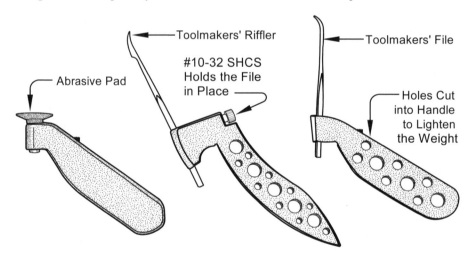

Figure 4-18. Shop-made aluminum file holders for needle files, rifflers and abrasive pads.

Flat Filing Fixture

An angle iron guide clamped to a file will improve the flatness of filing. Use a piece of Masonite or cardboard between the file and the clamp to prevent damage to the file teeth. See Figure 4-19. Since angle iron is not perfectly flat or square, milling the outside surfaces of the angle to make them square is required for fine work. A piece of CRS would also work without flattening.

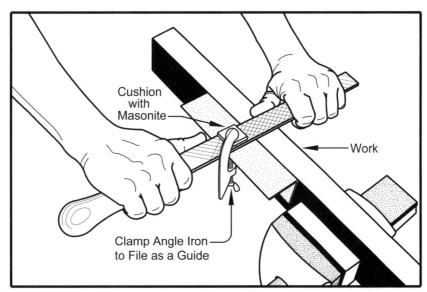

Figure 4-19. Using a clamp and an angle iron guide for filing flat, smooth surfaces.
The Masonite square is to protect the file teeth from clamping damage.

Air Files

Air files are frequently used with needle and diamond-coated needle files to dress hardened steel parts such as repaired gear teeth. Imported air files are inexpensive and work well for most shop work. See Figure 4-20.

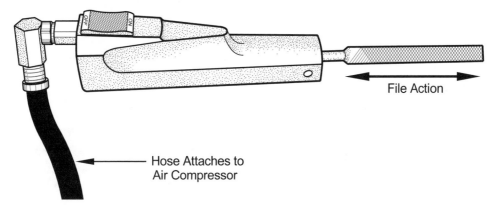

Figure 4-20. Air file has a reciprocating action.

Center-Punch Marks Gage the Filing Depth

Hacksaw cuts or a series of center-punch marks of the same depth applied over the surface of a workpiece can be used to insure that an even layer of work is filed off. See Figure 4-21. The workpiece is filed until the punch or the hacksaw marks are removed, but no farther.

An automatic center punch, or the shop-made drop center punch shown in

Figure 4-22, can be adjusted to apply a series of uniform punch marks at the desired depth. Try it first on a scrap of the same material as the workpiece to set the punch-mark depth. On softer materials, a ball bearing can be used instead of a point where a pointed punch would make too deep an impression. Hacksaw cuts across the work surface are used to mark the depth when deeper metal removal is necessary.

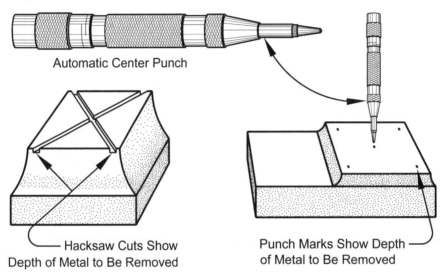

Automatic Center Punch

Hacksaw Cuts Show
Depth of Metal to Be Removed

Punch Marks Show Depth
of Metal to Be Removed

Figure 4-21. When the hacksaw cuts or center-punch
marks are filed off, final depth has been reached.

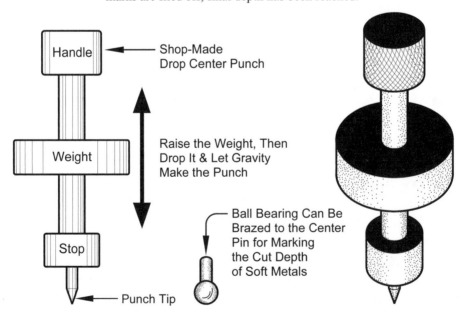

Handle — Shop-Made
Drop Center Punch

Raise the Weight, Then
Drop It & Let Gravity
Make the Punch

Weight

Ball Bearing Can Be
Brazed to the Center
Pin for Marking
the Cut Depth
of Soft Metals

Stop

Punch Tip

Figure 4-22. This shop-made drop center punch makes indents to indicate
the depth of the workpiece material to be removed by filing.

Section IV – Overview of Grinders

Different grinders are needed for different jobs. The following grinders meet the needs of a well-equipped machine shop:

- A *¾-hp 8-inch pedestal* or *bench grinder* with 60 and 80 grit aluminum oxide wheels is needed for general purpose grinding of ferrous metals. A 10-inch grinder with a 1- or 1½-hp motor would be even better, but if your workpiece is small, a 6-inch ½-hp grinder may be sufficient. All of these grinders are suitable for making and dressing HSS tool bits, sharpening center punches, and removing the burrs from parts.

- A *½-hp 6-inch pedestal* or *bench grinder* with two green wheels, a coarse (60 grit) and a fine (100 grit), for roughing carbide lathe tools, plus a *diamond wheel* for finishing them.

- A *12-inch 1½-hp disc grinder* is needed to handle non-ferrous metals, wood, fiber and plastics. It can also bevel edges and round corners.

- A *6 × 48-inch belt grinder* is needed to apply soft edges and to blend curves.

- A *½-hp 6-inch pedestal* or *bench grinder* with a 6-inch diameter by 0.032-inch wide abrasive cutoff wheel can quickly shorten hardened fasteners such as SHCSs, cut drills and drill rod, and cut away the unneeded sections of HSS tool bits. If straight-line cuts are acceptable, abrasive wheels are great for quickly removing sections of sheet metal parts.

- *Deburring* and *finishing wheels*, also called *surface conditioning wheels*, remove burrs, tool marks and sharp edges.

- *Flap wheels* are an alternative to deburring and finishing wheels. Flap wheels remove metal and can affect part dimensions.

- *Wire wheels* are excellent for removing paint and rust. Since they *do not* remove metal, wire wheels do not change the size of the part.

Section V – Bench & Pedestal Grinders

Grinder Designs

- *Grinder sizes* are specified by the diameter of their abrasive wheels. Table 4-2 shows the typical motor horsepower of each grinder size. The larger the grinder, the higher the horsepower, the faster it removes metal. In general, larger work calls for a larger grinder. Because the 7- and 10-inch grinders are less common than the 6-, 8- and 12-inch models, wheels for those machines may be harder to find and priced higher than the more popular grinder sizes. Most shops will find that 6- and 8-inch grinders are a good choice. However, surface grinders—a completely different type of machine tool—*do* use 7-inch abrasive wheels.

Wheel Diameter (inches)	Horsepower
6	⅓ or ¼
7*	½
8	¾
10*	1 or 1½
12	2 or 3
14	5 or 7½

*Less common size.

Table 4-2. Grinder wheel diameter vs. horsepower.

- *Wheel speeds* for 60 Hz grinders are either 1800 or 3600 RPM. Slower grinders are less likely to burn the work, but remove metal more slowly.

- *Arbor nuts* located on the right-side grinder wheels have right-hand threads, and arbor nuts on the left-side grinder wheels have left-hand threads.

- *Spark shields* are thin adjustable sheet metal barriers that prevent sparks from being carried completely around the grinding wheel and exiting from above the wheel and onto the user. Spark shields should be adjusted to be within $^1/_{32}$-inch of the top of the wheel. See Figure 4-23.

- *Industrial grade grinders* are likely to have built-in work lights for each wheel, a water pot on one side of the machine, and a cooling tray on the other. When grinding multiple parts, a cooling tray offers a convenient place for parts to cool as each new piece is ground in turn. Industrial grade grinders have superior motor winding insulation which allows for continuous use even though the grinder housing will get quite warm. These industrial grinders usually have cast iron shrouds around the grinding wheels which, should a wheel disintegrate, provide the user much more protection than the thin sheet metal shields found on economy grinders. Cast iron shrouds are a definite safety advantage because a spinning grinding wheel stores considerable energy that will convert to kinetic energy should the wheel come apart.

Securing the Grinder

Grinders can produce heavy vibrations, so for safety, they must be securely fastened to their pedestals or bench tops with vibration-resistant fasteners. Castle nuts or Nylocks are excellent choices. Using Locktite on the hold-down bolts is a good additional step for the "belt-and-suspenders" guys. Skip lock washers, they are more about intent than results.

Instead of securing a grinder to a pedestal or a workbench, it may be bolted to a ½- or ¾-inch steel plate which has a rubber pad glued onto its bottom. The plate should be larger than the outside dimensions of the grinder. This arrangement allows the grinder to be moved outside for messy jobs or turned to accommodate a particular job.

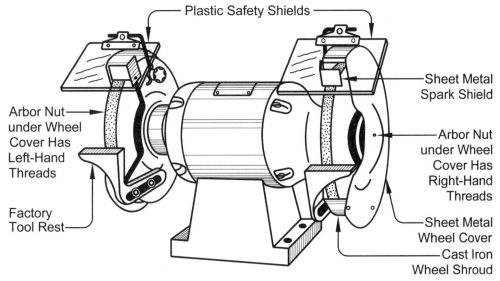

Figure 4-23. Bench grinder.

Tool Rests

Tool rests are both a critical part of a grinder and the one part most often compromised on imported economy grinders. Many of these grinders have durable motors, good bearings, and excellent dynamic balance on the motors themselves, but their flimsy sheet-metal tool rests prevent any serious grinding. And, because they are too small, these rests deflect under load, making them difficult or impossible to adjust. Cheap, cheesy tool rests also prevent the use of diamond wheel dressers.

Shop-Made Tool Rests

Figure 4-24 shows a first-class shop-made tool rest to replace the flimsy sheet metal rests on imported grinders. This tool rest has several advantages:

- Made from ⅜-inch CRS, the tool rest top surface is extremely rigid and will not deflect under load.

- The edge of the tool rest top surface is *parallel* to the grinder spindle axis, so it provides a guide for a diamond wheel dresser.

- The large area of the tool rest top surface makes it easier to support and rotate work into the grinder wheel. To prevent cut fingers, all edges of the tool rest are rounded.

- Screw slots in the base of the tool rest allow it to be adjusted toward the grinder axle to compensate for the reduction in wheel diameter with wear.

- Three different versions of this tool rest can be made from the same basic design. The tool rest in Figure 4-24, made for gray and green wheels, is notched to better support the work, not so work can be ground on the side of the wheel, which is a very dangerous practice. The surface of the tool rest is *at* or *slightly above* the wheel center height.

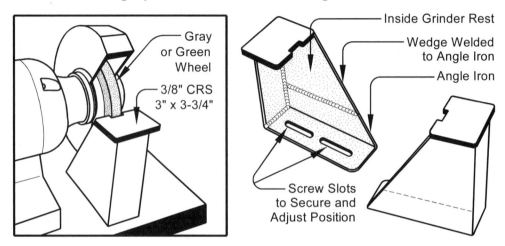

Figure 4-24. A shop-made grinder tool rest for gray or green wheels.

Figure 4-25 shows all three versions of the shop-made tool rests. The first, for gray and green abrasive wheels, the second, for diamond wheels, and the third, for abrasive cutoff wheels. Diamond wheels, like the one pictured in Figure 4-25 (bottom right), grind on their sides, not on their peripheries, so tool rests for these wheels must support work going against the side of the diamond wheel. Tool rests for abrasive cutoff wheels, Figure 4-25 (top right), have a long slot in the tool rest to support work as it moves into the cutoff wheel. Tool rest height will vary with the height of the grinder and will need to be adjusted. Figure 4-26 shows the parts needed to make the tool rests and their welding sequence. Following this welding sequence and using proper clamping methods will minimize weld distortion. Each grinder rest requires:

- Two pieces of $2 \times 2 \times \frac{1}{4}$-inch angle iron, one piece has screw slots added for adjusting the tool rest in and out with respect to the grinding wheel.

- One $4 \times 4 \times \frac{1}{4}$-inch steel gusset plate.

- One $\frac{3}{8}$-inch CRS rectangle for the tool rest top surface. For this part, cut a square notch to surround the end of the grinding wheel and remember to round the edges. Make sure that the front edge of the tool rest is parallel to the motor axle axis because this edge will guide the diamond dresser.

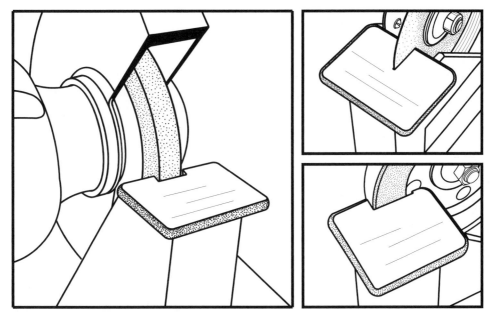

Figure 4-25. Shop-made grinder tool rest surfaces for gray or green wheels (left), for abrasive cutoff wheels (top right), and for diamond wheels (bottom right).

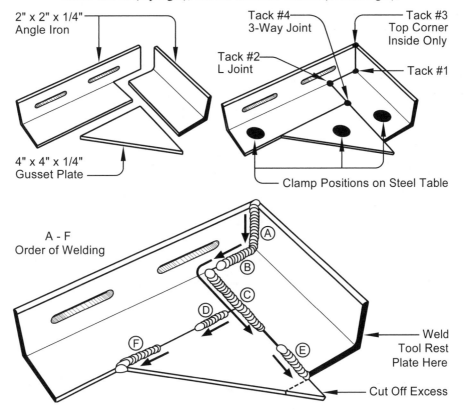

Figure 4-26. Cutting, layout, tacking and welding sequence for the tool rest base.

Improving Cast Iron Tool Rests

Some industrial-grade grinders have rigid cast iron tool rests that are too small, or, because the tool rest castings are hand-finished, are not square to the grinder spindle axis. See Figure 4-27. These tool rest deficiencies can be corrected with a little effort. First, using a disc or belt grinder, square up the top surface of the tool rest with the side of the tool rest. This will make the tool rest square with the wheel and parallel with the spindle axis. Second, make ⅜-inch thick CRS covers for the existing tool rests and fasten each cover to the original tool rests with two SHCSs. These screws are upside down going into threads tapped into the covers and do not extend above the surface of the covers. This new cover provides a larger tool rest surface *and* an edge for the diamond dresser to ride on. See Figure 4-28. This tool rest has a sturdy and rigid design, but it must never be adjusted while the grinding wheel is turning because the tool rest can jam into the wheel, causing the wheel to disintegrate.

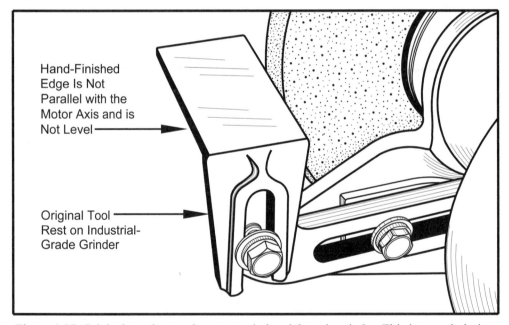

Hand-Finished Edge Is Not Parallel with the Motor Axis and is Not Level

Original Tool Rest on Industrial-Grade Grinder

Figure 4-27. Original cast iron tool rest on an industrial-grade grinder. This is a weak design which should be replaced or upgraded.

Tool Rest Height

As stated before, the tool rest should be adjusted so its top surface is *at* or *slightly above* the grinding wheel center height. When the tool rest is too far above center height, the wheel tends to push the work away, and when the tool rest is below center height, the work tends to be pulled into the wheel.

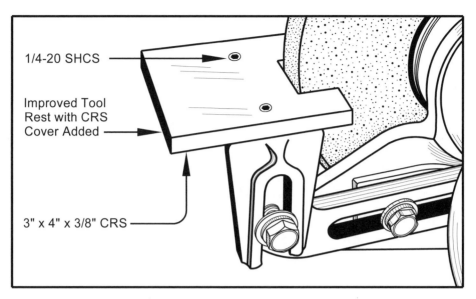

1/4-20 SHCS

Improved Tool
Rest with CRS
Cover Added

3" x 4" x 3/8" CRS

Figure 4-28. Cast iron tool rest on an industrial-grade grinder with a CRS
cover added to provide a more accurate and larger work-holding surface.

Grinding Wheels – Materials & Grits

Three materials are commonly used for bench and pedestal grinding wheels:

- *Gray aluminum oxide* is the most common wheel material and it is suitable for all ferrous materials: cast iron, steel and HSS. Most grinders are sold with a 36-grit wheel for roughing and a 60-grit wheel for finer grinding. Usually, the rougher wheel is mounted on the grinder's left side, and the finer wheel on the grinder's right side.

- *Green silicon carbide* is for the rough dressing and shaping of tungsten carbide cutting tools. These wheels are available in medium, fine and extra fine grits, but usually the medium and fine wheels are the most used.

- *Synthetic diamond* is used to sharpen carbide cutters. However, real diamond cutoff wheels are common too. These wheels have fine diamond particles which are held in place by nickel plating on a steel wheel. Diamond wheels work well on most high-tensile strength materials.

In general, the harder the work material, the softer the grinding wheel needed. When grinding very hard materials such as carbide, the green grinding wheel wears down much more rapidly than a typical gray wheel. This wearing down process constantly exposes the work to a fresh grinding surface.

Wheel grit determines how fast material is removed from the work and the quality of the finish left by grinding. See Table 4-3. Grit size also determines the sharpness of the grinding wheel's corner. The finer the grit, the more closely the edge of the wheel approaches 90° and departs from being rounded.

Work Finish & Grit Size	Grit on Aluminum Oxide Wheels (Ferrous Metals)	Grit on Silicon Carbide Wheels (Non-ferrous Metals)	Stock Removal Rate
Very Coarse	24	–	Heavy ↓ Medium ↓ Light
Coarse	36–46	–	
Medium	60–80	60	
Fine	100–120	80	
Extra Fine	–	120	

Table 4-3. Abrasive wheel grits for bench and pedestal grinders.

Mounting Grinding Wheels

Here are the steps for mounting a grinding wheel:

1. Before installing a new grinding wheel, it should be *ring tested* to insure it is free from cracks. To do this, suspend the wheel from a finger or a pin through its center hole and, using a wooden mallet or plastic hammer, strike the wheel at the 2, 4, 8 and 10 o'clock positions. A crack-free wheel will produce a clear, resonant tone when struck; a damaged wheel will produce a dull thud. The ring test is important because the bond inside these wheels is ceramic and, if damaged, they can suffer cracks like a dish.

2. For safety, it is critical that the *paper washers*, also called *wheel blotters*, are in place on each side of the spindle hole on the grinding wheel before installing the wheel. These paper washers insure that the force of the nut and abrasive wheel mounting flange is evenly distributed over the wheel's surface. The paper washers also allow the surfaces of the wheel flange and the paper washer to act as a clutch, preventing the wheel from slipping.

3. When mounting a new wheel, insure that the wheel-mounting flanges are clean, that the wheel fits over the spindle easily, and that the nut holding the wheel on the spindle is snug, but not tight. The left-hand wheel is held on the spindle by a *left-handed nut,* so it will self-tighten.

4. Allow a newly mounted wheel to run for a minute or two before using it in case of an initial failure.

5. Always stand to one side of a grinding wheel when starting it, especially during the initial start-up.

Grinding Wheel Vibration

The three most common conditions that cause grinding wheel vibration are:

- *Lack of concentricity* – This annoying condition makes the work bounce against the wheel and is caused by the mounting hole not being concentric with the edge of the wheel. This manufacturing defect, which is very common even in wheels from better manufacturers, will vary from wheel to wheel and is fully correctable by using a diamond dressing tool. Manufacturers address this hole concentricity problem differently. Many imported grinding wheels have oversized center holes shimmed out with epoxy to form the final center hole. Quality wheels have diamond-drilled holes shimmed out with a snug-fitting plastic bushing. Still, both center-hole designs may lack concentricity.

- *Lack of a flat wheel face or grinding edge* – Grinding wear changes the shape of the periphery of the wheel from a smooth cylinder to a grooved or tapered one. This condition is easily corrected with a diamond dresser.

- *Side-to-side wheel wobble* – Grinding wheels must be held perpendicular to the motor shaft axis. Wheel wobble is caused when the faces of the mounting flanges are not parallel with each other. See Figure 4-29. This problem is particularly common in economy grinders which use stamped steel wheel-mounting flanges. This may also occur in industrial grade machines with cast aluminum flanges if the flanges are used straight out of the casting mold without first being machined. This wobble condition is corrected by making the faces of the mounting flanges parallel by first lapping the flange surfaces that touch the paper washers, then taking a light milling cut on the smaller flange faces. Figure 4-30 shows how this is done. After this correction, it is common to see wheel wobble of over 0.100 inches of an inch reduced to under 0.010 inches.

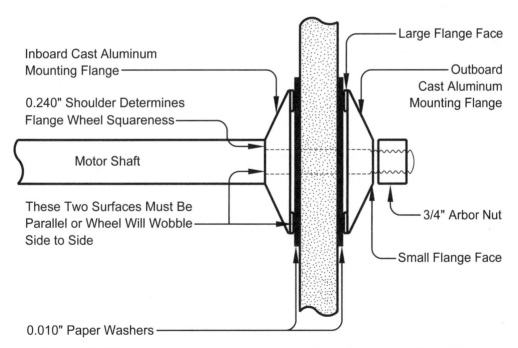

Figure 4-29. Wheel-mounting flanges determine grinding wheel side-to-side wobble.

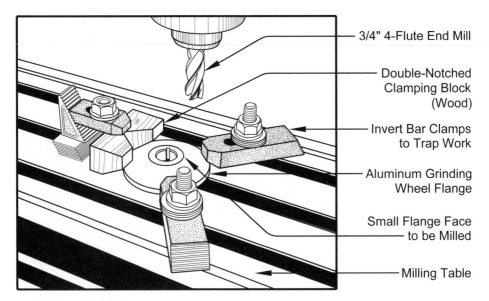

3/4" 4-Flute End Mill

Double-Notched
Clamping Block
(Wood)

Invert Bar Clamps
to Trap Work

Aluminum Grinding
Wheel Flange

Small Flange Face
to be Milled

Milling Table

Figure 4-30. Milling the small side of a grinding wheel mounting flange to make both faces parallel. Note that the tips of the bar clamps are inverted to trap the flange securely.

Another cause of grinding wheel wobble occurs when the grinder shaft has been bent—usually because the grinder was dropped during shipment. This condition cannot be fixed and the grinder is scrap.

Wheel Truing vs. Dressing

Truing and dressing are two different operations with different objectives that use different tools:

- *Truing* removes enough material from the wheel periphery to bring the wheel into roundness. That is, the wheel edge is a perfect circle which is concentric with the grinder's spindle axis. Truing also insures that the face of the wheel is flat. To make matters more confusing, truing is done with a *diamond wheel dresser*.

- *Dressing* exposes fresh abrasive material so that the wheel cuts faster, but does not bring it back into concentricity. Dressing may be necessary because the wheel has not simply been worn smooth, but has had its pores clogged with metal, usually copper, brass, or aluminum—three metals which should not be ground on an abrasive wheel. Dressing is done with a *star wheel dresser* or a stick of boron or silicon carbide, known as a *wheel dressing stick,* also called a *devil's stone*.

Truing

Diamond abrasive wheel dressers have been used for many years to true surface grinders but, until recently, diamonds were so expensive that using them on bench and pedestal grinders was cost prohibitive. For truing, machinists used star wheel dressers and dressing sticks and lived with the poor results. Neither of these tools will correct an out-of-round grinding wheel; they will mainly expose fresh abrasive material. But, now that a mounted ¼-carat diamond wheel dresser costs about as much as a large pizza, diamonds are finally cost effective to dress bench and pedestal grinding wheels.

The shop-made diamond dresser in Figure 4-31 removes wheel material in very small cuts, about one-thousandth of an inch on each pass, so the dresser must be adjusted *away from* the highest point of the grinding wheel before any dressing begins. In other words, the tip of the diamond dresser must clear the highest point on the wheel because the grinding wheel could snap off the tip of the dresser when the grinder is turned on. Failure to take small cuts can also fracture the diamond or rip it from its setting. Properly used, a diamond dresser will last a long time, dozens of dressings. The shop-made dresser in Figure 4-31 has ½-20 threads on which to mount the diamond. This means that one full turn of the dresser knob moves the diamond into the work 0.050 inches and 6° of knob movement advances the diamond about 0.001 inch into the work. Note that the diamond is held at an angle to the grinding wheel so the diamond wears evenly as it is turned inward toward the grinding wheel.

Here is how to true an abrasive wheel using a diamond dresser:

1. Wear a face mask and eye protection. Besides abrasive particles, this operation produces wheel dust, a significant long-term health hazard.
2. Place the diamond dresser with its guide rail snug against the edge of the grinder tool rest.
3. While the grinder is turned off, back off the diamond dresser screw so that the diamond does not contact any part of the grinding wheel when the wheel is slowly turned by hand and the dresser is slid back and forth across the grinding wheel's surface. At this point, the diamond should just clear the highest part of the wheel. Then, move the dresser to one side so it does not touch the wheel, and turn the diamond dresser screw knob about 18° to prepare for the first cut.
4. Start the grinder and allow it to come up to full speed.
6. Slide the diamond wheel dresser back-and-forth across the face of the wheel for several passes until the diamond sparks-out. Maintain pressure against the base of the diamond dresser to keep its guide rail against the grinder tool rest. This makes the dresser's path parallel to the grinder's spindle and puts a flat, concentric face on the grinding wheel.
7. Then take additional one-thousandth of an inch cuts, as in Step 6, until the wheel is flat and square.

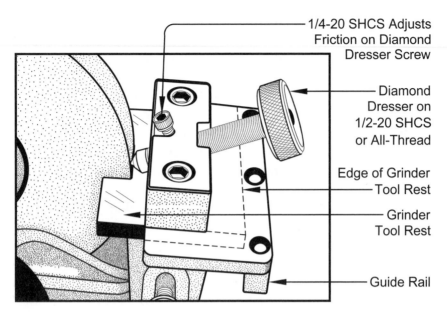

Figure 4-31. Design for the shop-made diamond wheel dresser. For plans, see Figure 9-60.

Abrasive Stick Dressing

Dressing an abrasive wheel with an *abrasive stick,* also called a *wheel dressing stick* or a *devil's stone,* exposes fresh cutting surface and flattens the wheel face. See Figure 4-32. The sticks are either boron carbide or silicon carbide. Although dressing removes much less material than truing, an abrasive dressing stick can rejuvenate a cutoff wheel that has been loaded with metal by removing its outer edge.

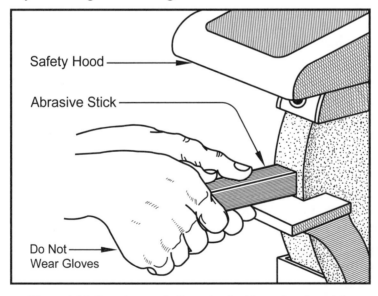

Figure 4-32. Dressing a grinding wheel with an abrasive stick.

Star Wheel Dressing

The only virtue of a star wheel dresser is that it opens up the grinding wheel surface and removes loose grains providing a fresh, rough grinding surface, but this is more of a blacksmith's tool than a machinist's tool. Star wheels will not make a wobbling wheel concentric no matter how much dressing is done, and they spew abrasive particles all over the shop and the operator. But, if you need to open up your grinding wheel's surface, here is how to use the star wheel dresser:

1. Start the grinder and allow it to come up to full speed.

2. *Wearing a face mask and eye protection,* position the handle of the star wheel dresser on the tool rest, parallel with the grinding wheel and bring the steel wheels of the dresser into contact with the edge of the rotating grinding wheel. See Figure 4-33.

3. Move the star wheel dresser side to side along the face of the grinding wheel until the grinding wheel surface is clean and approximately square with the sides. On larger diameter wheels, considerable pressure may be required. Never apply the star wheel dresser to the sides of the grinding wheel.

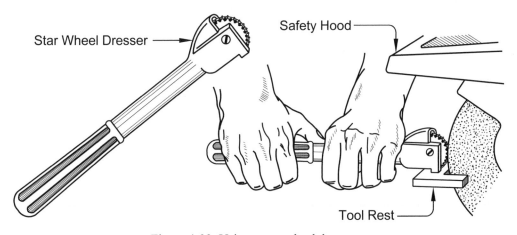

Figure 4-33. Using a star wheel dresser.

Abrasive Cutoff Wheels

These wheels are available in widths of 0.040, 0.062 and 0.128 inches and diameters from 3–14 inches. Most abrasive cutoff wheels are for ferrous metals, but green cutoff wheels are available for stainless steel and fiberglass. These wheels can:

• Shorten hardened SHCSs, machine screws and Grade 8 bolts.

• Cut drill rod to length.

- Rough shape HSS cutting tools. This saves a lot of grinding time when a large section of a HSS tool bit must be removed, such as when making a narrow cutoff tool bit from a full-width HSS tool blank.

- Shorten twist drills and end mills.

- Trim both hex and spline wrenches to remove a damaged end or to shorten the wrench to allow access to a tight spot.

- Cut away sheet metal sections. For example, an abrasive cutoff wheel can be used when a sheet metal grinding wheel cover or shroud must be opened up or widened when converting the cover from a grinding wheel to a finishing or wire wheel.

Shortening Fasteners with an Abrasive Cutoff Wheel

Figure 4-34 shows how to hold a SHCS with a wooden push block to shorten a screw using an abrasive cutoff wheel. The steps follow the figure.

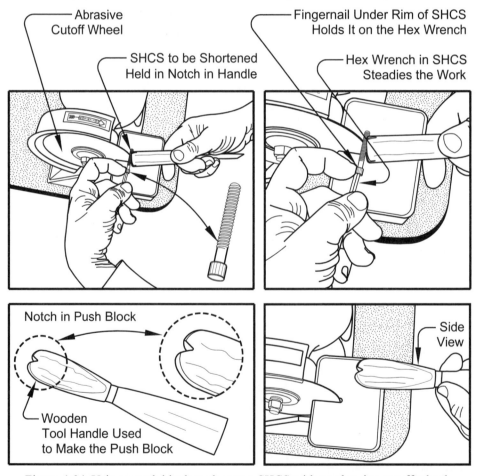

Figure 4-34. Using a push block to shorten a SHCS with an abrasive cutoff wheel.

1. To begin, make a push block. Using a hacksaw or bandsaw, cut a V-shaped notch in the end of a ¼–½-inch thick piece of wood as shown in Figure 4-34 (lower left). The handle of a small paint brush or scraper works well. Use this notched piece of wood to press the screw against the wheel to stabilize it. Fingers alone will not work for this job because the fastener is awkward to hold and gets very hot.

2. Insert a hex wrench into the head of the SHCS and catch the edge of the head with your fingernail to hold the screw on the wrench. Do not use a ball-end hex wrench; it will not provide enough stability and the SHCS will wobble.

3. Turn on the abrasive wheel, place the threaded section of the screw to be cut off in the V-notch of the push block, and press the screw into the abrasive disc to make the cut. See Figure 4-34 (upper row).

4. The abrasive wheel cuts into the notched push block, stabilizing both the block and the work it holds during the cut.

Deburring & Finishing Wheels

Deburring wheels, also called *finishing wheels,* are unlike wire wheels because they gently remove work metal. They are excellent for:

- Removing burrs around holes and keyways.

- Eliminating sharp edges and tool marks.

- Breaking edges of aluminum extrusions and removing flash from castings.

- Adding a radius to stamped sheet metal parts.

- Blending and smoothing transitions between one surface and another.

- Removing old gaskets, coatings, paint and scale.

- Applying a satin or antique finish and preparing surfaces prior to buffing.

- Polishing molds and parts before plating.

Deburring wheels work well on steel, stainless steel, chrome plate, aluminum, copper, brass, zinc, nickel, titanium, ceramics, glass, fiberglass, plastics and wood. They use aluminum oxide or silicon carbide in a nylon carrier. Aluminum oxide wheels are more durable than silicon carbide wheels, but silicon carbide cuts faster than aluminum oxide and leaves a finer finish on most materials. Compared with other grinding wheel designs, deburring wheels do not last very long and are relatively expensive, but they should still be in your shop. There are alternatives, but no exact substitute.

There are three deburring wheel designs:

- The most basic design consists of several flat layers of Scotch-Brite-like material sandwiched between two steel washers. The wider the washers, the more rigid the wheel, but the less the wheel will get down into grooves and crevices.

- Some wheel designs use round or rectangular filaments secured in a metal hub. These wheels can be quite aggressive.

- Another design uses a mesh tape wrapped around the hub in a spiral as in Figure 4-35. These wheels have directional arrows to prevent their unwinding when driven backwards.

For safety, remove the tool rest while deburring since the work is held freehand. Usually, the sheet metal or cast iron wheel guard is partially cut away to open it up for this work. This not only provides better access to the wheel, it prevents the work from becoming trapped against the wheel guard.

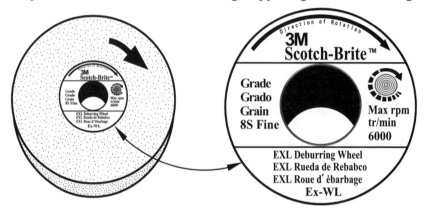

Figure 4-35. A deburring or finishing wheel which is made from a non-woven tape.

Flap Wheels

Flap wheels consist of a center metal hub which holds a series of cloth or fiber flaps. The aluminum oxide coating on the surface of each flap does the work. As the wheel wears away, fresh abrasive material is exposed which provides a uniform rate of cut and a consistent finish. See Figure 4-36.

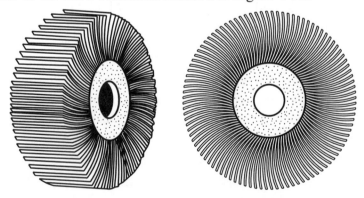

Figure 4-36. Flap wheels.

Flap wheels are used for the polishing, grinding and cleaning of metals and wood. Because their aluminum oxide coating is aggressive—unlike wire brushes—flap wheels *will* remove metal and change the dimensions of the work. Flap wheels are offered as an alternative to wire brushes and abrasive impregnated nylon finishing wheels, but each of these products produces slightly different results and are not exact substitutes for flap wheels.

Flap wheels can be shaped to better fit into and around the work. While flap wheels must be mounted to rotate so that the abrasive side of their flaps is exposed, to shape one, mount the flap wheel to run backwards and cut it to shape using a carbide insert cutter or a brazed lathe tool bit. Then, reverse the flap wheel on the arbor to use it.

Wire Wheels

The principal use for wire wheels is for rust and paint removal. The least expensive wire wheels are steel, and the more expensive ones are Type 304 stainless steel. Brass wheels are also available for more fragile work. Wire wheels with straight wires are less aggressive than wheels with the same diameter wire which has been crimped, as shown in Figure 4-37 (left). Smaller diameter wire is less aggressive than larger diameter wire.

The most aggressive wire wheels have a series of knotted or twisted steel cables extending from a metal hub. These knotted wire wheels are *extremely dangerous*. They will catch clothing or rags and wrap them around the wire brush and should only be used in a hand-held disc grinder to smooth welds. If you value your fingers, never use a knotted wire wheel in a bench or pedestal grinder because these wheels cut flesh fast and easily. See Figure 4-37 (right).

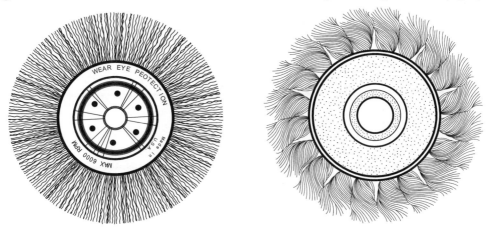

Figure 4-37. Crimped wire wheel (left) knotted wire wheel (right).

Be sure to remove the tool rest when installing and using a wire wheel. This is done because the work is held freehand and the wheel will tend to push the work downward and we do not want the work to be trapped against the tool rest. As when using finishing and abrasive wheels, the wheel shroud is usually opened up to allow more access, and, because of the flying dust, debris and loose wires, wearing eye and face protection is essential.

Section VI – Disc & Belt Grinders

Disc Grinder

Figure 4-38 shows the most basic disc grinder design where a round metal plate mounted to the end of a motor shaft holds a round abrasive sheet. An adjustable table can be used to support the work or the work may be hand held, depending on the job. To keep work at 90° to the disc, a groove in the table can hold a miter guide. Today, most abrasive discs are sold with a PSA (pressure sensitive adhesive) backing covered by a release sheet. To use, simply strip off the release sheet and adhere the abrasive disc to the round metal plate of the disc. No glue is needed.

Disc grinders have many uses, they can:

- Quickly square up sheets, bars or blocks of metal, fiberglass, plastic or wood.

- Grind parts to a precise length without sawing, milling or filing.

- Remove sharp edges, round over corners, or apply a chamfer to the ends of rods and bars.

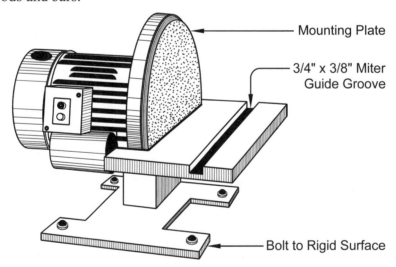

Figure 4-38. Disc grinder with a miter guide groove on its table.

- Grind both ferrous and non-ferrous metals equally well. Disc grinders are especially useful when grinding non-ferrous metals, which would quickly load the pores of a gray aluminum oxide grinding wheel, rendering it useless.

- Dress the threads on the end of a fastener that has been cut to length so the threads will fit into a nut or threaded hole.

Resting work on the grinder table and against a miter guide insures that the work is ground squarely. While not nearly as accurate as a milling machine, cuts with an accuracy of ±0.005 inches are quick and easy on a disc grinder. The only requirement is an accurately placed scribe mark to grind up to.

Most commercial miter guides are adjustable to hold the work at any angle against the abrasive disc, but because many of these guides are made of cheap die cast aluminum, they are flimsy at best. A better solution is to use the shop-made miter guide shown below in Figure 4-39.

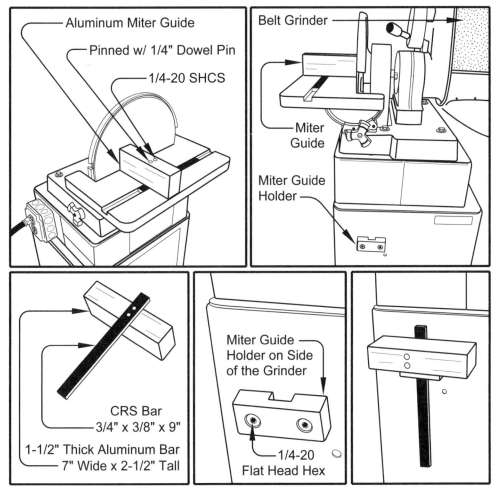

Figure 4-39. Twelve-inch pedestal disc grinder with details of
a shop-made aluminum miter guide and miter guide holder.

Fixed at 90º to the disc, this design is extremely rigid, will not fracture if dropped like the die cast guides, and will meet most shop needs. Remember that, because disc grinders vibrate, the miter guide will vibrate right onto the floor if not caught in its groove. To avoid this problem, make the simple bracket in Figure 4-39 (bottom right) to store the miter guide when not in use.

Note: The disc grinder in Figure 4-39 (top right) shares a common shaft with a belt grinder. The grinder motor is housed inside the pedestal and drives the grinders using a common shaft with a V-belt.

Corner Rounding

Here is how to round the corners on flat stock such as sheets, bars and plates:

1. Grind off the corner sections at a 45° angle, removing 80% of the final corner depth.

2. Round the corners using a disc or belt grinder by rocking the work back and forth until the desired corner is achieved. See Figure 4-40. A file can also be used to round corners, but it is a much slower process.

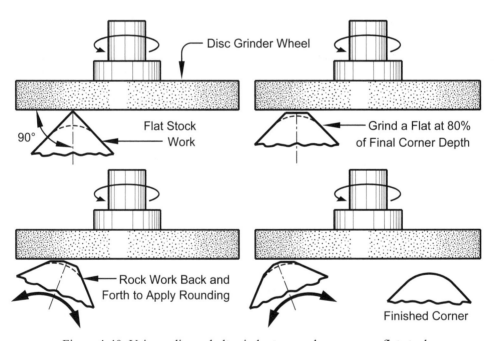

Figure 4-40. Using a disc or belt grinder to round a corner on flat stock.

Cleaning up Cut Thread Ends

The best way to dress the threads on a shortened fastener is to use a disc or belt grinder and *draw* the rough ends off the threads. This is done by turning the fastener while dragging the threads against the abrasives to produce a smooth chamfer. See Figure 4-41.

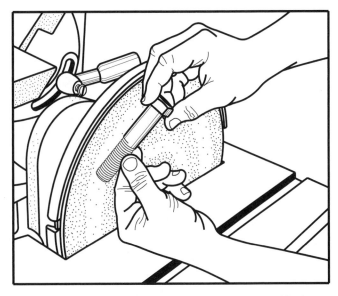

Figure 4-41. Cleaning up threads on a shortened bolt.

Because set screws and hex screws are hard to hold, place them on a hex wrench, and then drag the threads off as in Figure 4-42. Holding a set screw in a hex wrench makes it easy to turn and to maintain a constant angle against the grinder. Also, as shown before in Figure 4-34, catching the edge of the head of a SHCS with your fingernail helps keep the fastener from falling out of the hex wrench.

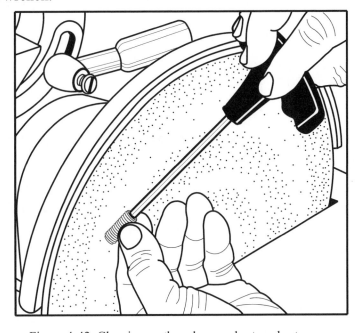

Figure 4-42. Cleaning up threads on a shortened set screw.

Belt Grinders

Although many grinding tasks on smaller workpieces can be done on either disc or belt grinders, belt grinders offer advantages over disc grinders when:

- *Large workpiece areas must be ground flat* – A 6×48-inch belt grinder, like that in Figure 4-43, can grind a 6×10-inch workpiece. A steel back-up plate supports the belt so that it grinds the entire work surface at once and the entire grinding surface is moving at the same speed. While this workpiece could also be ground on a disc grinder, because of the different geometries of the belt and disc grinders, getting a uniform flat surface with a disc grinder is much more difficult.

- *Long edges must be rounded uniformly* – Because of the longer section of the grinding belt available, belt grinders make applying a rounded surface on an edge much easier than when using a disc grinder.

- *Surfaces must be smoothly blended* – Many belt grinders have sections of belt that are not supported by a back-up plate, but this is a good thing. This unsupported area of the belt bows and flexes when work is pressed against it and this produces gradual transitions between one surface and another. Handgun finishers and knife makers use this grinding method extensively for smoothing workpieces. The small 1- and 2-inch wide belt grinders are especially popular for this smoothing work.

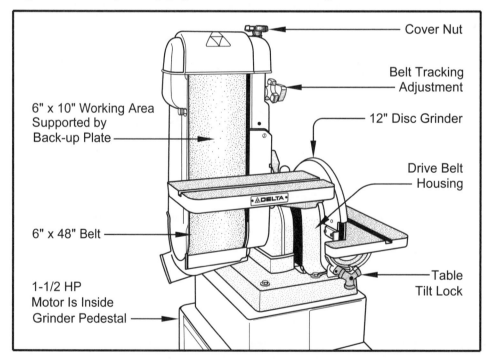

Figure 4-43. Belt grinder detail on a combination 6×48-inch belt and disc pedestal grinder.

- *Forming smooth concave curves* – On a belt grinder, the round surface of the top roller makes quick work of grinding an inside radius. Start by removing the protective cover over the roller, and then use the top surface of the belt grinder to apply a smooth concave curve. The only catch is that the radius of the work must be larger than the radius of the belt grinder's roller. See Figure 4-44.

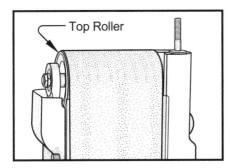
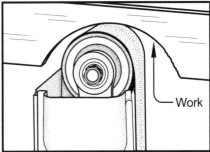

Figure 4-44. Belt grinder with the top cover removed for shaping concave curves.

Section VII – Die & Pencil Grinders

Grinder Overview

These grinders, called *die grinders* or *pencil grinders* depending on their size, are for free-hand grinding where the work is fixed or clamped and the grinder is held by hand. This is just the opposite of free-hand grinding with a bench or pedestal grinder. Available in both electric- and air-driven versions, die and pencil grinders come in many sizes and designs, and usually turn between 10,000 and 65,000 RPM. The largest of these grinders are used to smooth the edges of castings or grind out welds, the medium-sized ones are used to remove metal or smooth parts in gunsmithing and mold making operations, and the smallest hand-held grinders are used to make adjustments in dental work, to manufacture and repair jewelry, and to make molds and precision instruments. There are also very inexpensive hobby-type grinders that work well for small jobs, but they do not hold up in continuous service. See Figures 4-45 and 4-46.

Grinder Designs

There are more than a dozen designs for hand-held grinders. Here are some of their key characteristics:

- *Air or electric power* – Typical economy *air-powered grinders* require 4–5 cfm of compressed air at 90 psi. All grinders that use compressed air require continuous lubrication supplied through their air hoses to insure long life, although lightly used grinders can survive with just a few drops of oil added manually before each use. While *electric die grinders* do not require a compressed air supply or continuous lubrication, they tend to heat up quickly and, if used for more than a few minutes, their motors will burn up. Air-powered grinders do not heat up and are a better choice for continuous service. They are also more pleasant to hold and can take much more abuse without complaint, especially when their cutting tools are repeatedly stalled.

- *Tool shank diameter* – Most hand-held grinders use either $^1/_8$- or $^1/_4$-inch diameter tools and mandrels, but some tools will also accept $^3/_{32}$-inch tools. Tool bits for most small grinders are held in collets for better concentricity and balance, and for minimum weight and cost, but a few hand-held grinders use Jacobs chucks.

- *Front vs. rear exhaust (air-powered grinders only)* – In a confined space, such as a corner or a hole, the air stream of a front-exhaust grinder blows the cuttings back into the operator's face. These front-exhaust grinders are desirable out in the open where its exhaust stream blows cuttings away from the operator and the work. In confined spaces, though, use rear-exhaust grinders.

- *Quality and cost* – A quality hand-held grinder often costs ten times as much as an inexpensive import of the same size. These imports, along with hobby grinders, work well for occasional, light-duty work, but they are so inexpensive that they should be considered disposable.

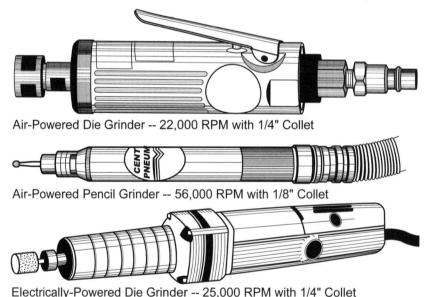

Air-Powered Die Grinder -- 22,000 RPM with 1/4" Collet

Air-Powered Pencil Grinder -- 56,000 RPM with 1/8" Collet

Electrically-Powered Die Grinder -- 25,000 RPM with 1/4" Collet

Figure 4-45. Three hand-held grinders with collets which are suitable for mounted abrasive stones and for HSS, carbide or diamond burrs.

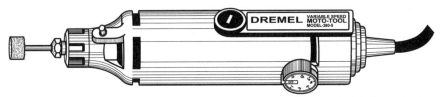

Figure 4-46. Hand-held 35,000 RPM electric hobby grinder suitable for ⅛-inch collet-mounted abrasive stones and cutoff wheels, or for HSS, carbide or diamond burrs.

Grinder Tool Bits & Their Uses

Although there are more than a dozen different tool bits available for small hand-held grinders, these are the most common:

- *HSS burrs* – These burrs are good for aluminum, wood and plastic, but quickly burn up when cutting steel. As shown in Figure 4-47, they are available in many shapes in both single- and double-cut.

- *Carbide burrs* – Although they cost more than HSS burrs, carbide burrs will stand up well when cutting carbon and hardened steel. Single-cut carbide burrs are machine made and are less expensive than double-cut burrs, which require hand cutting to get the second set of burrs in the proper location.

  Carbide burrs may be one-piece of solid carbide, but many burrs with a cutting tip larger in diameter than the shank diameter have carbide cutters brazed onto HSS shanks. This reduces the grinding of carbide and saves money.

- *Diamond burrs* – These will cut all hardened steels, glass and ceramics. They are especially effective for shaping carbide form tools when there are no other cutting alternatives except wire EDM.

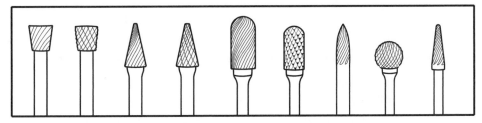

Figure 4-47. HSS and carbide burrs are available in both single- and double-cut. The most popular tool shank diameters are ⅛- and ¼-inch.

- *Cut off wheels* – These are excellent for severing and slotting plastics, fiberglass and metals. See Figure 4-48. There are three different wheel materials:

  - *Aluminum oxide abrasive in an unreinforced rubber matrix* – Both the edge and the face of these wheels can be used to cut or slot, steel, glass or ceramic. A common example is the Dremel 409 wheel which is $^{15}/_{16}$-inches in diameter and 0.024-inches thick. Other suppliers offer silicon carbide abrasive, but these wheels wear very fast and fracture easily in use. Be sure to start all jobs with a dozen or more wheels on hand.

- *Aluminum oxide abrasive in a reinforced fiberglass base* – Dremel's 426 cutoff wheels are the most widely available version of this tool, but there are many other similar versions with silicon carbide, ceramic or zirconia alumina abrasives. These wheels are $1^{1}/_{4}$-inches diameter by 0.044-inches thick and last much longer than the unreinforced wheels.

- *Diamond particles nickel-electroplated on a steel wheel* – These wheels work best on glass, ceramics and carbide.

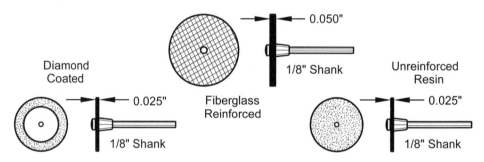

Figure 4-48. Cutoff wheels.

- *Mounted stones* – There are four reasons to use mounted stones: one, the workpiece material is too hard to shape otherwise, two, only minute and precise dimensional adjustments are needed, three, a fine surface finish is required, and four, mounted stones can be dressed to a particular diameter with a diamond dresser. Figure 4-49 shows some of the many shapes. There are three types of mounted stones:

  - *Red mounted stones* – Red-brown in color, these stones are aluminum oxide bonded by porcelain clays. They are supplied in 60, 80 and 100 grits and produce a relatively rough finish.

  - *Blue mounted stones* – Medium-dark blue in color, these stones are aluminum oxide with a porcelain clay bond. Cobalt has been added to provide lubrication and reduce heat build-up. All are 120 grit.

  - *White mounted stones* – Off-white in color, these stones contain finely divided aluminum oxide. They are used to cut glass, porcelain, metal or stone. White mounted stones are 400 grit and produce a smooth finish.

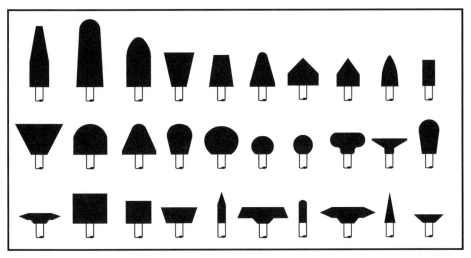

Figure 4-49. Mounted stones are available with $^1/_8$-, $^3/_{32}$- and $^1/_4$-inch shanks.

Section VIII – Other Abrasive Grinders

Hand-Held 4¼-inch Electric Angle Grinders

These powerful and versatile tools, shown in Figure 4-50, are typically 11,000 RPM and $^3/_4$ hp. They are mainly used on welding and fabrication work for dressing and removing welds, but they can also be used to clean metals of paint, rust and grime. The grinding wheels are particularly effective in removing surface oxide, sometimes called *scale* or *bark*, on hot-rolled steel before welding or brazing. Here are the tools that can be mounted on these grinders and their uses:

- *Grinding wheels* are used for improving part fit-up before welding, and for smoothing or removing welds. These wheels have a *depressed center* to space the wheel away from its mounting nut.

- *Fiber-backed abrasive sheets* are supported by a flexible rubber or plastic disc. Unlike abrasive grinding wheels, which grind on their edges, the fiber-backed sheets grind on the face of the sheet. Fiber-backed abrasive sheets are available in a variety of grits. They are suitable for smoothing, blending and paint removal on metals.

- *Wire wheels*, which are usually of carbon steel, are used for paint, rust and dirt removal, and also to remove spatter after welding.

- *Flap wheels* are similar to wheels for pedestal and table grinders, except that their flaps on the face of the wheel, not on the edge. They are used for removing paint and rust, and also for smoothing welds.

- *Abrasive cutoff wheels* are used for cutting ferrous and non-ferrous metals.

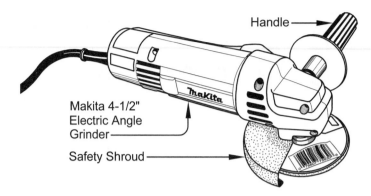

Handle

Makita 4-1/2"
Electric Angle
Grinder

Safety Shroud

Figure 4-50. This Makita grinder holds grinding wheels for weld preparation, weld removal, and dressing. It is good for removing rust, scale and surface oxides on HRS.

Abrasive Chop Saws

Although chop saws are available in a wide range of sizes, the most common and inexpensive size uses a 14-inch diameter wheel as in Figure 4-51. They are able to rapidly cut hardened alloys, rods, shapes, angles, pipe and tubing. Because their wheels are thin—usually ⅛-inch or less—little material is lost in their kerfs. Chops saws, also called *abrasive cutoff saws*, are particularly suited to cutting round and square steel tubing that has internal seam welds. These internal welded seams are very hard and rapidly wear out bandsaw blades.

With use, the abrasives on the edges of these wheels tend to become loaded with metal and can no longer cut rapidly. The solution is to apply a silicon or boron carbide dressing stone to the wheel edge to expose fresh abrasive material.

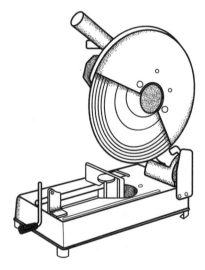

Figure 4-51 Abrasive cutoff, or chop saw, with a 14-inch wheel is excellent for rough cutting steel shapes, pipe, rebar and tubing. It also cuts steel building studs.

Section IX – Surface & Blanchard Grinders

To get precision work out of these seemingly simple machines requires patience, skill, practice and good technique, so their use cannot be covered in just a few pages. While anyone can perform simple tasks on these grinders, achieving accurate, consistent results takes years to learn. This section provides an overview of these two important machine tools.

Surface Grinders

Surface grinders are most often found in tool rooms and in die and mold shops where hardened materials need to be machined. See Figure 4-52.

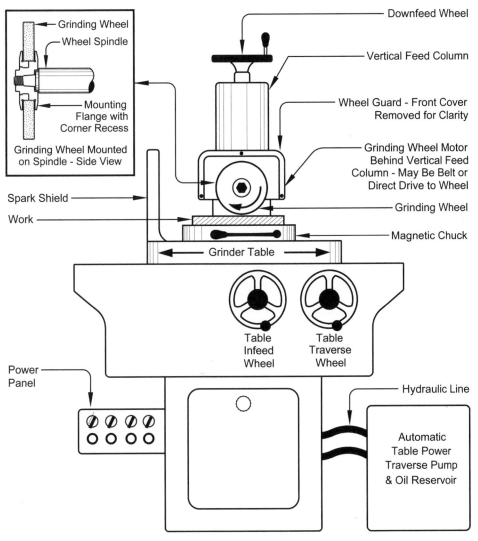

Figure 4-52. Surface grinder.

Surface grinders:

- Machine work to tolerances of fractions of a thousandth of an inch by moving the work back and forth in a reciprocating motion under a stationary grinding wheel. Many surface grinders have a hydraulic drive to move the table—and workpiece—back and forth under power, saving the machinist the effort.

- Have three main control handwheels:

   - A *table traverse wheel* that moves the table back and forth—left and right—so the grinding wheel moves over the work.

   - A *table infeed wheel* that moves the table in and out or from side to side over the work.

   - A *downfeed wheel* that controls the wheel height over the work.

- Can either grind with the work dry—that is, without any coolant—with soluble oil and water, or with a grinding fluid. The principal function of the fluid is to keep the work cool to prevent heat-caused expansion and the resulting dimensional changes. The coolant may be applied as a spray mist, a flood, or through the wheel pores with a special flange that uses centrifugal force.

- Surface grinders must hold extremely tight tolerances. To do this, their grinding wheels are dressed with a diamond dresser each time the wheel is installed to insure concentricity with the spindle axis and flatness across the face of the wheel. Some grinding tasks require the wheel to be shaped to produce a specific profile on the work. This shaping is done using a diamond dresser and an optical comparator.

- Must have work securely held in place. Ferrous metals are usually held in a magnetic chuck as shown in Figure 4-53, but work may also be clamped. Many non-magnetic materials are held in vacuum chucks or glued in place with anerobic or epoxy adhesives. After grinding, a heat gun is used to release the work from the adhesive.

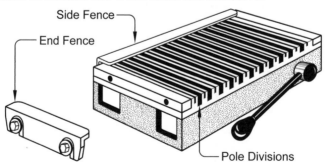

Figure 4-53. Magnetic chuck.

- Unlike table and pedestal grinders, surface grinders have mounting flanges with a tapered hole that fits on a tapered spindle. This arrangement helps to maintain wheel concentricity while on the grinder and allows the wheel to be removed from the grinder and still hold its concentricity when re-installed. In general, shops have many flanges, ideally one for each grinding wheel. This minimizes the amount of abrasive material removed during dressing with each wheel change.

- Make roughing cuts on steel that are typically 1–3 thousandths of an inch; while finishing cuts are ½–1 thousandths.

Capabilities

Work in surface grinders can be:

- Ground flat, or one or more surfaces and can be ground perfectly square or parallel with another.

- Machined to a precise thickness, everything from hardened metals to very thin stock.

- Given an extremely fine finish, which can be applied even to very hard metals.

- Cut to length, including hardened stock.

- Shaped by shaping the grinding wheel, even hardened steel alloys can be ground to specific profiles needed for punch and dies.

Typical Operations

Here are some of the most common jobs performed on a surface grinder:

- Flat steel plates for a punch, die, mold, or fixture can be ground to exact size.

- Slots or grooves with precise dimensions can be cut into all metals.

- Several hardened 1-2-3 blocks or V-blocks can be ground at the same time to bring them to the exact same height. These matching blocks are useful in the shop for supporting workpieces when grinding, milling, drilling or performing layout work on a granite plate. In this instance, uniformity of dimensions is more important that their exact height.

- A vanadium steel open-end wrench, which is hardened, can be thinned—reduced in height—to fit into tight quarters.

- Additional Weldon locking flats for set screws to bear against can be added to the shanks of end mills.

- Hardened steel parts, which have had weld metal added to them to replace worn sections, many times end up with oversize welds that must be ground down. A surface grinder can grind the welds flat to bring the parts back to their original dimensions.

- Hardened dowel pins and punches can be brought to a precise diameter.

- When using fixtures, flats and angles can be applied to work such as vises, angle vises, sine chucks and spin fixtures.

- Surface grinders can also perform cutoff operations on hardened work. For example, an end mill may be shortened to remove a damaged end, or hardened ground stock may be cut to length.

Blanchard Grinding

Blanchard grinding, also called *rotary surface grinding*, turns work on a rotary table and repeatedly brings the work under a grinding wheel that has multiple pie-shaped grinding stones. See Figure 4-54. Grinding is done under coolant flooding so there is little heat buildup. As with surface grinders, ferrous workpieces are held in magnetic chucks and non-magnetic work in vacuum chucks. This makes for fast set-ups. Blanchard grinding may be the preliminary machining for a part, but often it is adequate for final machining when only parallel, smooth surfaces are needed.

Blanchard grinding has many advantages:

- By using higher horsepower machines, Blanchard grinding removes material more accurately than many other metal removal methods. Large Blanchard grinders have 300–450 hp motors.

- Leaves a smooth surface with a distinctive swirl.

- Can be used on most materials: ferrous, non-ferrous and plastics.

- Leaves surfaces parallel and flat to 0.001 inch.

- Blanchard grinding takes a relatively rough surface and makes it flat and smooth. If a part has multiple surfaces, as in a gate valve casting with two flanges, the flanges can be made parallel with each other.

If the workpiece is ground with the Blanchard stones turning in opposite directions on each side of the work, the work is more likely to lie flat because the stresses induced by the grinding process balance out. If the internal stresses are not balanced, the work is liable to have a residual twist in it, like a flimsy cookie sheet in a hot oven.

Blanchard grinders range in size from small table top models to huge industrial models that can handle 500-pound castings.

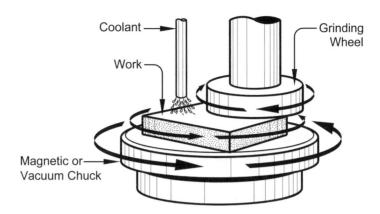

Figure 4-54. Blanchard grinding.

Blanchard Grinding in Production

In production, it is used three ways:

- Large fabricated parts and castings, which need one or more flat surfaces before other machining can begin, go into the Blanchard grinder one at a time.

- When there are many small parts, they can be placed in fixtures and many pieces can be ground at once. Using this process, all of the parts will be finished to the same height.

- Sometimes a large piece of stock is ground, then cut up into individual pieces to make other parts. This produces any number of parts of all the same thickness.

Section X – Grinding Projects

Add a Work Light to a Disc/Belt Grinder

Install a duplex receptacle on the side of the grinder base using pop rivets or sheet metal screws, then rewire the on/off switch to apply power to the receptacle when the motor is turned on. Plug magnetic-based work lights into the receptacles to illuminate the grinder's tables.

Make a Mobile Base for a Disc/Belt Grinder

There are four reasons for adding a mobile base to a grinder:

- To allow a 250-pound grinder to be easily moved *outside* the shop to reduce grinding dust *inside* the shop. This provides cleaner breathing air for the machinist and easier clean-up. The caster-base design in Figure 4-55 has a lower center of gravity than if the casters were attached directly underneath the grinder, making this design less tippy, but just as mobile. Besides, the sheet metal base of a typical grinder pedestal is too thin to support casters, or even leveling feet, because the spring in the grinder's flimsy sheet metal base would cause the grinder to rock.

- This base design permits easy leveling with the adjustment of one caster to prevent the grinder from rocking on an uneven floor surface.

- Since the base of the pedestal is open, adding a ⅛-inch steel plate to the bottom of the caster base traps dust from the grinding disc *inside* the base instead of allowing it to fall onto the shop floor.

- In a small shop, the grinder can be easily moved out of the way.

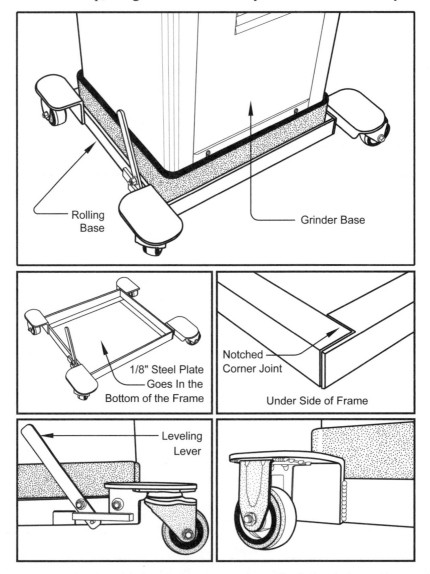

Figure 4-55. A simple welded angle-iron base makes a disc/belt grinder easily movable.

Abrasive Paper Holder

Often parts must be flattened using silicon carbide abrasive paper. Since the paper must be on a flat surface, many machinists put a few drops of oil on their granite plates as glue to hold the paper in place and flatten the part by moving it in a figure-eight pattern. Figure 4-56 shows a shop-made device that stretches and holds the abrasive paper at the same time. Some shops make several of these holders for different grits of paper. Using this paper holder avoids getting grit on your granite plate.

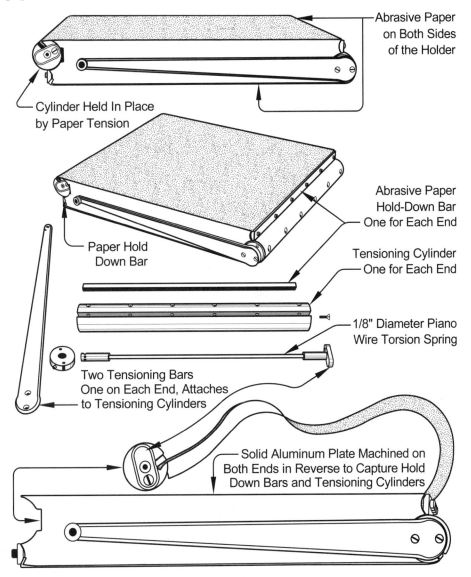

Figure 4-56. Shop-made abrasive paper holder.

Section XI – Grinding Safety

Grinding wheels present many hazards. Here are some of them, and ways to protect yourself:

- Flying metal and grit particles are an ever-present eye hazard. Wear your safety glasses and position the safety shields on the grinder between your eyes and the work.

- Grinding wheels and wire wheels can grab rags, clothing and gloves. Keep them away from grinders and *never wear gloves when grinding*.

- Plastic or wood grindings left in a grinder, disc grinder or belt grinder can ignite from the sparks created by grinding steel later. This can causes a sudden tongue of flame to shoot from the grinder's exhaust, which can start a fire in the vacuum exhaust system. Not surprisingly, this can also startle nearby workers and cause an accident.

- *Never* adjust the tool rest while the grinder is running. Doing this is extremely dangerous because many tool rests self feed and will suddenly jam themselves against the grinding wheel, causing the wheel to disintegrate. With the grinder turned off, position the tool rest to within $^1/_{16}$ of an inch of the face of the wheel.

- Do not shock the wheel by forcing the work abruptly against it. Wheels are fragile ceramic and could shatter. Bring the work up against the wheel gently and increase the cutting pressure gradually.

- *Never* exceed a wheel's maximum operating speed or it could cause the wheel to explode. This never-exceed speed is marked on the wheel or, if the wheel is small, on its packaging.

- *Never* grind on the sides of a wheel unless the wheel is specifically designed for this purpose. Grinding on the face of the wheel applies forces opposing the centrifugal forces trying to pull the wheel apart, but side grinding applies forces which *add* to the forces trying to pull the wheel apart. This can cause wheel failure.

- Always use a wheel blotter—a paper washer—between the grinding wheel and the wheel flange. If the wheel blotter becomes damaged, replace it with a new one.

- Store wheels vertically on their edges in a dry, clean place.

- Keep a fire extinguisher nearby.

- Do not wear gloves when using wire wheels.

Chapter 5

Drilling, Reaming & Tapping

Every discovery contains an irrational element of creative intuition.
—Karl Popper

Section I – Drills

Introduction

Drilling holes is the most common of all machining processes—nearly 75% of the metal removed by machining is drilled out, usually using twist drills. Drills remove metal by reducing it to chips in a fast, simple and economical process. Used in drill presses, lathes and milling machines, twist drills are among the least expensive and most versatile cutting tools. The fact that most industrial tool distributors place twist drills at the very front of their catalogs is testimony to the drill's importance and popularity. This chapter concentrates on twist drills, but also examines several other drill designs.

Twist Drill Development

Until the US Civil War, most holes in cast iron and steel were drilled using a forged spade-shaped drill on the end of a square or round steel shaft. See the spade drill in Figure 5-1. Because these spade drills had no way to remove chips from the drilled hole, peck drilling was required—making drilling a slow, laborious process. These early drills were carbon steel and annealed easily, so drill spindle speeds had to be kept low to prevent the drills from overheating and becoming annealed. Then in 1861, Stephen A. Morse of Massachusetts invented the *twist drill*.

Twist drills got their name because they were originally made by milling straight flutes into steel rounds, which were then heated red-hot and twisted to form helical flutes. Although a few twist drills are still made this way, today most twist drills are made by grinding helical flutes into solid rounds.

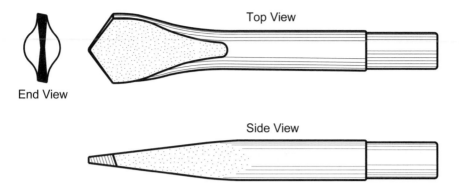

Figure 5-1. Typical spade drill design from about 1855.

The twist drill was a big improvement over the spade drills of the 1850s and 1860s because their helical drill flutes pulled chips out of the drill hole and reduced the need for peck drilling. But it wasn't until about 1900, when HSS—with its superior high temperature strength and wear resistance—became available, did the twist drill design demonstrate its superiority and become widely adopted. The term *high-speed steel* indicates that, unlike carbon steel cutting tools, HSS cutting tools can be run at high speeds without becoming annealed.

A number of doctoral candidates have done dissertations on twist drills, studying them in depth. Their conclusions are that, despite the drill's apparent simplicity, it is a complex device and very difficult to model mathematically. Over the last 160 years, however, many excellent twist drill designs have been developed by systematically experimenting with different shapes and materials, observing their performance, and choosing the most effective designs. Because of their economic impact on today's manufacturing, research continues on twist drills aimed at minimizing axial force and torque, and maximizing drill life. Even small improvements in drilling can have a huge financial impact because so much machining activity involves drilling. The most recent important developments, which have greatly increased drill life—especially in a production setting—are the addition of thin, hard, wear-resistant coatings including titanium nitride, zirconium nitride, titanium carbo-nitride, titanium aluminum nitride, chrome nitride, amorphous diamond and polycrystalline diamond.

Throughout history, most successful inventions show major design changes as they are improved over time, but not so with the twist drill. The illustration of Stephen A. Morse's original 1863 US twist drill patent, as seen in Figure 5-2, shows how closely today's twist drills follow the inventor's original design.

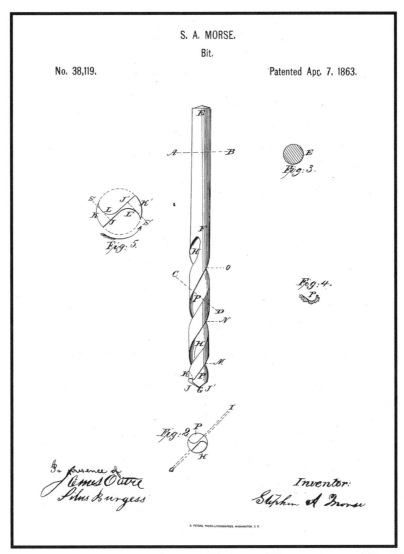

Figure 5-2. Stephen A. Morse's original twist drill patent from 1863.

Section II – Anatomy of the Twist Drill

The most common and basic twist drill is called the *conventional 118° twist drill,* or *general-purpose drill.* Because of its importance in the machine shop, Section II will concentrate on this drill.

The Shank

The twist drill *shank,* which fits into the drilling machine spindle, holds the drill in position and transmits the driving torque to the drill. Many shanks are straight and the same diameter as the nominal drill size. These shanks fit into drill chucks or collets. Other drills, usually ½-inch diameter and larger, have a Morse taper shank. Some HSS Cobalt drills have a small step on the end of the shank to differentiate them from the less expensive HSS drills. Because drills are held by the upper end of their shanks during manufacturing heat treatment, shanks tend to be much softer than the flute and point areas. See the hardness zones in Figure 5-3 (bottom). This softer area makes it easier to turn down a drill shank in the lathe, if needed, to fit into a smaller chuck.

The Body

The *drill body*, the section from the *heel* to the point, contains the *flutes*—helical grooves ground into the side of the drill to evacuate the drilling chips. The portions of the drill body *not* ground away to form the flutes are called the *lands*.

At the bottom of the flutes lies an invisible solid cone of drill steel called the drill *web,* or *web core,* which gives the drill its stiffness. The web core is usually 20–30% of the drill diameter, and is often tapered wider at the shank end to provide more stiffness and shallower at the point end to provide more room for chip clearance. See Figure 5-3 (top).

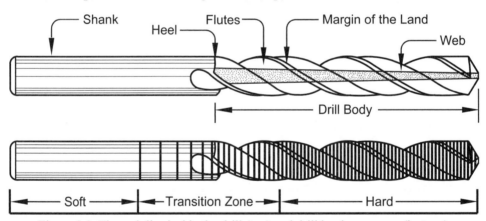

Figure 5-3. The web lies inside the drill (top) and drill hardness zones (bottom).

To reduce friction between the lands of the drill and the wall of the hole being drilled, the lands are relieved so that just a small helical strip, the *margin of the land,* is the full drill diameter. On a ¾-inch drill, the lands would typically be about 0.015 inches below the margins of the lands.

To further reduce friction, the *drill body* is usually reduced several thousandths of an inch from the point to the start of the shank. This reduction in diameter—really on the outer edge of the margins of the lands—is called *back taper*, and is typically 0.0005–0.00075 inches/inch of drill length.

Most twist drills are a compromise between a large flute space for chip removal and a heavy web thickness for drill rigidity. There are some drills, though, with extra-thick webs for applications where heavy axial force will be applied.

Helix Angle

Figure 5-4 shows the *helix angle*, which measures the twist of the drill flutes. Most twist drills have about a 30° helix angle, called the *standard helix*. This standard helix angle optimizes chip ejection, drill cross-sectional strength and drill rigidity. *High helix drills,* also called *fast spiral angle drills*, have a 40° helix. They are used for high feed rates under low spindle speeds usually on softer non-ferrous metals like aluminum, magnesium, zinc die castings, brass in deep holes and some plastics. In general, the deeper the hole, the higher the helix angle should be for chip removal. *Low helix drills*, or *slow spiral angle drills*, typically have about a 12° helix. They are used with high spindle speeds on hard-to-drill materials. These low helix drills have increased cutting edge strength and work well on materials with a tendency to *gall* or clog the drill hole. In a non-production setting, though, the standard helix angle is satisfactory for nearly every drilling task.

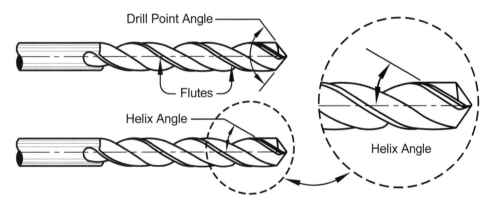

Figure 5-4. The drill helix angle and drill point angle.

The Drill Point & Point Angle

The drill *point* is geometrically complex. It is formed from the *flanks*, which are the ends of the lands at the drill point, and from the *chisel point,* which is formed by the end of the web when it reaches the point. The cutting edges of the flanks are called the *lips,* or the *cutting lips.* The sharpening of the drill during manufacturing creates the *chisel point.*

Although a twist drill can be ground to any *point angle*, the four common point angles in use today meet most drilling requirements. See Figure 5-5.

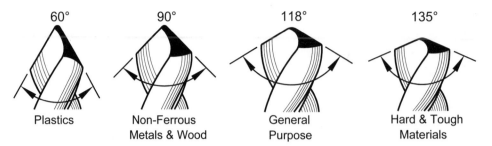

60°	90°	118°	135°
Plastics	Non-Ferrous Metals & Wood	General Purpose	Hard & Tough Materials

Figure 5-5. These are the four most common drill point angles.

Rake Angle

The *rake angle* is where the cutting lips and the flute faces meet to form the drill's cutting edges. Because the rake angle changes continuously across the lips—usually from a positive rake at the outside corner to a negative rake where the lips meet the chisel edge—the term *effective rake angle* is often used to take into account the continuous changes in the cutting edge angle across the lips. The effective rake angle is a kind of average angle that reflects the total effect of these angular changes. This angle cannot be measured as it changes continuously along the drill's cutting edge. It can only be calculated.

The *nominal rake angle* is more easily defined, visualized and measured. Figure 5-6 shows the nominal rake angle. For our purposes, this angle provides an adequate measure to see how the rake angle affects drill performance. The nominal rake angle determines:

• Sharpness of the lips and how the cutting edge gets under, or enters, the workpiece material and cuts it. Harder materials require a smaller rake angle—a sharper lip—than softer materials.

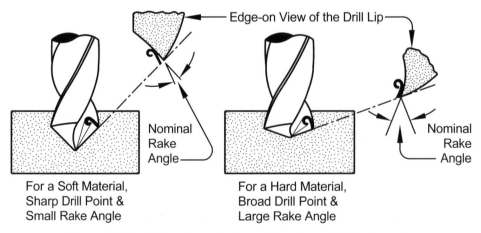

Edge-on View of the Drill Lip

Nominal Rake Angle

Nominal Rake Angle

For a Soft Material, Sharp Drill Point & Small Rake Angle

For a Hard Material, Broad Drill Point & Large Rake Angle

Figure 5-6. The drill point angle determines the nominal rake angle.
The greater the drill point angle, the smaller the rake angle.

- Cutting forces and power consumption. Generally, a smaller rake angle reduces the thrust forces while it increases the required torque.
- The strength of the tool's cutting edge. A smaller rake angle leaves less drill metal to support the cutting edge, but makes a sharper cutting edge.
- Chip shape, size and flow direction.
- The length of the lips—the cutting edges—is inversely related to the drill point angle. A 135° drill has much shorter cutting lips than a 60° drill of the same diameter and helix. Shorter lips require less torque than longer lips, a desirable situation when drilling hard materials and the available drilling torque is limited.

Flutes

Flute size and shape are important drill variables that influence chip formation, size and evacuation. Because flute design is one of the three variables that determine the lip's nominal rake angle, length and shape, flute design is a variable the drill designer can modify to improve drill performance.

Drill Design Variables

Many parameters determine a twist drill's performance. Some parameters are *independent variables*, that is, they can be chosen independently of all other variables, and other parameters are *dependent variables*. Independent variables include the point angle, helix angle and the size and shape of the flutes. Once the independent variables are set, the dependent variables are determined. The dependent variables are the nominal rake angle, lip length and lip shape. Table 5-1 shows how the three independent drill variables that the drill designer can change automatically determine the three dependent variables.

Independent Variables	Dependent Variables	Typical Design Objectives
Point Angle	Nominal Rake Angle, Lip Length & Lip Shape	Small rake angle lips for hard materials Large rake angle lips for soft materials.
Helix Angle		Length of lips.
Flute Size & Shape		Usually straight lips, not concave or convex.

Table 5-1. How three independent variables determine three dependent variables.

Figure 5-7 shows two $^{27}/_{64}$-inch diameter twist drills. By choosing the appropriate flute shape, the drill designer produced two drills with the same point angle and straight cutting lips, but different helix angles.

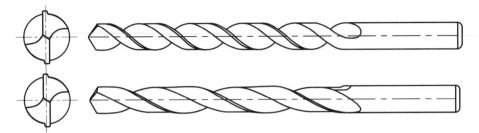

Figure 5-7. Two drills with different helix angles have the same point angle and straight cutting lip. This is possible because the flutes of the two drills are different shapes.

Point Angle & Lip Shape

Usually twist drills are designed to have straight lips because straight lips provide more support for the cutting edges than curved lips. For a 118° point angle drill with straight lips, regrinding to a sharper point makes the lips convex, while regrinding to a more blunt point makes the lips concave. See Figure 5-8. There are, though, some special-purpose drills with concave lips designed to produce tightly curled chips to flow out of the flutes more easily. Changing the drill point angle is not usually a good idea because it changes the lip shape, which in most cases is undesirable, as well as changing the nominal rake angle, which may or may not be desirable.

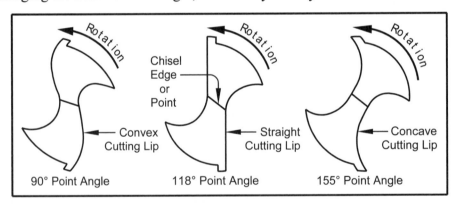

Figure 5-8. How drill point angle affects lip shape on 118° drills.

Lip Relief Angle

The *lip relief angle*, also called *lip clearance angle*, affects the strength of the cutting lips. Lower relief angles in the 8–12° range produce a stronger lip, but the lip relief angle must be large enough so that the undersides of the drill lips do not drag on the largest, thickest chip. Harder materials generally have a slower feed and produce thinner chips than softer materials, so drills for hard materials have smaller clearance angles than for soft materials. See Figure 5-9. Although important, lip relief angle is not nearly as critical to drill performance as the rake angle.

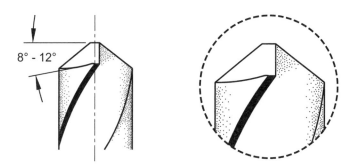

Figure 5-9. The drill lip relief angle on a 118° drill.

Drill Point Design

Drill point design refers to the overall shape of the drill point, including the rake angle, but also the relief angle, helix angle, the lip shape, the number of facets on the lips, and the shape of the chisel or starting point.

There are more than a dozen drill point designs, but only two are common: the *conventional point* and the *split point,* which is sometimes referred to as a *crankshaft drill.* Figure 5-10 shows these two point designs. Other drill point designs are used in production, usually on difficult-to-drill materials where optimum drilling speed and long tool life are critical.

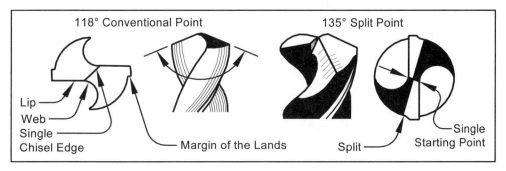

Figure 5-10. The two most common twist drill point designs.

Conventional point drills are less expensive to purchase and to resharpen than split points, but because of their straight chisel point, conventional drills tend to "walk" around on the work before they begin drilling and require center-punch starting marks for accurate hole placement. Split points are self-centering and don't walk. They start drilling where they are placed and are ideal for NC machining. Split point drills perform better on hard and "work-hardening materials" and require less torque than conventional drills. One drawback is that split points require special drill sharpening machines. Few drills of this design are made over ½-inch diameter.

Although many combinations of drill point designs, drill point angles and drill metals are available, the three most common drill combinations are:

- *118° HSS with a conventional point* – This is the least expensive drill that performs a majority of drilling tasks well.
- *135° HSS with a split point* – This self-centering drill works slightly better on hard materials than a conventional-point drill, but it is not as heat resistant as HSS cobalt, but also not as expensive.
- *135° HSS cobalt with a split point* – Other than carbide or carbide tipped drills, this is the best combination for drilling hard materials.

The 118° Drill Point Angle

There is an optimum drill point angle for every material. This optimum angle provides the maximum drill life and best hole quality. For many materials, the minimum drill thrust force occurs with a drill point angle of 118°. It also turns out that cutting lips which are straight, such as those on 118° drills, yield a longer cutting life than lips that are concave or convex. For these reasons, the standard 30° helix angle and flute contour is chosen because it produces straight lips with a 118° drill point angle. Still, there are special-purpose drills with curved cutting lips

Twist Drill Mechanics

Drilling is a complex operation because several different processes occur simultaneously and interact with each other.

- Frictional heating from rotation of the chisel point softens the workpiece metal allowing the chisel point to both extrude and cut the metal underneath it.
- The chisel point has a highly negative rake angle of $-50°$ to $-60°$ and a low tangential cutting speed because it lies close to the center of the drill point. Although the chisel point is only about 15% of the drill's diameter, it requires a disproportionate share of the axial force, as much as 70%, to maintain this extrusion, while the lip cutting action requires relatively little force.
- The lips of the drill perform cutting action similar to other machining operations. However, it is complicated by the changing rake angle along the lips, which goes from a +30° rake at the outer edges of the lips to $-30°$ where the lips meet the chisel point. The speed of the workpiece metal passing the cutting tool edge increases as the distance from the drill center increases, so the cutting speed at the outer diameter of the lip can be four to five times faster than at its inner diameter.
- The margins of the lands act as reamers, bringing the hole to final diameter. The lands also keep the drill centered and provide another path for cutting fluid to reach the tip of the drill.

- Metal removed from the hole slides along the flutes and out of the hole, while lubricant works its way down to the drill cutting face through the flutes.

Drilling Speeds & Feeds

Many factors determine the proper drilling *speed* and *feed*, but the most important one is the workpiece material. Other factors include:

- Drill design, material and coatings, if any.
- Cutting fluids, if any.
- Rigidity of the drill and drill press.
- Rigidity of the workpiece and its jig or fixture.
- Quality of the hole walls.
- Depth of the hole.

Published drilling speeds and feeds, like the extensive tables in *Machinery's Handbook,* were established by experiment just like those for lathe and milling machine cutters. These tables are not exact because there are so many variables, but they do provide a good starting point. Remember that the speeds and feeds listed in handbooks are based on the optimum trade off between maximum cutting tool life and minimum machine time in a production environment. These tables do not apply in R&D labs and prototype machine shops where only a few holes are needed and such optimization is unnecessary. But, whether in R&D labs or in production, getting a hole in the right place without excessive drill wear is the objective.

Drill speed is the rate that workpiece material and the drill bit pass by each other during drilling. The speed at the outer diameter of the drill is used in cutting speed calculations. Knowing the recommended cutting speed for a given material and the drill diameter, we can determine the drill spindle speed just as for lathe and milling machine tools, by using this formula:

$$N = \frac{4V}{D}$$

Where: N = Spindle speed of the drill press in RPM.
V = Cutting speed in feet/minute at the drill's outer diameter.
D = Diameter of the drill in inches.

Another way to determine drill spindle speed is to use the chart most drill presses have affixed to them that shows recommended speeds for common materials and a range of drill diameters. This chart makes calculations unnecessary. But, remember that these figures are for HSS drill bits. Carbide and coated bits operate at 2 to 3 times higher RPM and adding cutting fluid can increase speeds by as much as an additional 50%.

Drill feed is the rate that the drill enters the workpiece and is based on the drill diameter and the workpiece material's hardness. As with drill speeds, tables for common materials are available in machining handbooks.

Experience and observation are the twin keys to setting the proper feeds and speeds. You know you have set a satisfactory feed and speed for steel when two continuous, tightly-wound helices of chips come out of the drill flutes.

Drill Press Speeds

A common problem with many drill presses—particularly non-industrial, consumer models—is that their spindle speeds cannot be adjusted below 250 RPM. This problem becomes evident when attempting to drill some bronzes, cast irons, stainless steels or hard steels using a Silver & Deming drill of 1-inch diameter or larger. As an example, for 50 SFM, drills with a diameter larger than 1-inch require a spindle speed below 190 RPM. At 2-inches diameter, a spindle speed of 95 RPM is needed. Just because you have a large diameter S&D drill does not mean you can easily drill holes with it! You will have to step drill the hole. Fortunately, some lathes and many milling machines have variable speed drives that *do* provide spindle speeds as low as 20 RPM—low enough to use large diameter drills—offering a solution to this problem.

Dubbing Drills for Brass & Copper

On brass and other soft materials, conventional drill points tend to *hog-in* or grab the work and allow the drill flutes to act as threads, actually pulling the work up the drill flutes and off the table, particularly when breaking through to the backside of a workpiece. Sometimes the forces are enough to pull a drill chuck off its arbor. To prevent this, the edge of the drill lips is *dubbed,* or ground flat, leaving a 0° rake angle. This allows the drill to scrape the metal away and not dive into the work. See Figure 5-11. Dubbed drills must be reground if they are later used to cut other, harder metals. Many machinists keep a few dubbed drills on hand.

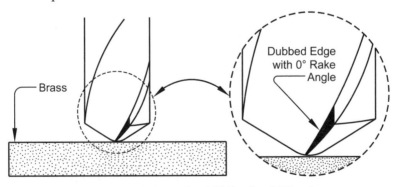

Figure 5-11. Dubbing twist drill lips for drilling brass.

Web Thinning

Drill flutes are cut deeper at the drill point end than at the shank end to increase drill rigidity and to provide a larger chip removal path where it is most often needed—at the point end of the drill. Because the *drill web*, the inner core of the drill, is smaller at the point end than at the shank end, as the drill is resharpened, the drill point moves toward the shank. This causes the web remaining at the point, the chisel point, to become larger, increasing the required thrust force on the drill. To reduce this force, the web is thinned on its lower end, or point, after sharpening to restore the web thickness to when the drill was new. This may be done after each sharpening or after several sharpenings, depending on the material being drilled. *Web thinning* is performed for both conventional and split point drills. See Figure 5-12. As a matter of practicality, thinning is usually done only on ⅝-inch diameter and larger drills using a table or pedestal grinder or hand-held die grinder.

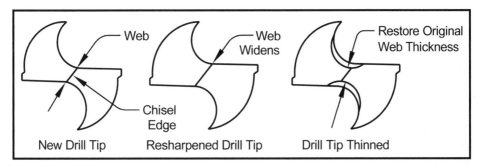

Figure 5-12. After several sharpenings, drill webs must be thinned.

Sharpening Twist Drills

Absolute symmetry in lip length and point angle are essential to drilling accurately sized and positioned, smooth-wall holes. Figure 5-13 shows the hole problems created by using a poorly sharpened drill.

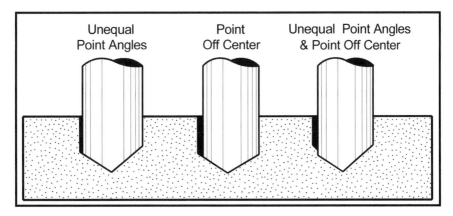

Figure 5-13. Twist drill problems caused by defective sharpening.

A few machinists can sharpen large twist drills by hand, but it takes a steady hand and a lot of practice. Small drills, under ¼-inch diameter cannot be re-ground freehand. For any machinist doing true precision work, sharpening twist drills requires professional-grade drill sharpeners which can cost between $1100 and $2500.

Since owning professional drill-grinding equipment is not cost effective for small shops, and regrinding drills without such equipment is always unsatisfactory, sending drills out for sharpening is probably the best solution. A lot of high quality drills can be bought for the cost of a good drill sharpener, and remember that, in undemanding applications—not drilling hardened materials—a drill will usually last for several hundred holes.

Basic Drill Assortment

Figure 5-14 shows many of the basic drills needed in a machine shop.

- *118° standard point HSS jobber drills* – Used for most materials, except hard and abrasive metals. Jobber drills come in standard lengths and their shanks are the same size as the drill diameter. See Figure 5-15 for a size comparison of the following four different twist drill size sets:

  - *Number drills* – Sizes #1–60 for most work and sizes #61–97 for small work.

  - *Letter drills* – Sizes A–Z.

  - *Fractional-inch drills*–Sizes $^1/_{16}$–$1^1/_2$ inch by $^1/_{64}$ increments.

  - *Metric drills* – Sizes 1–20 mm come in 1 mm steps, sizes 1–10 mm come in 0.1 mm steps, and drills larger than 10 mm come in 0.5 mm steps. These drills are needed only if your shop works with metric fasteners.

- *Silver & Deming reduced shank drills* – These drills come in $^1/_2$–$1^1/_2$ inch in $^1/_8$-inch increments. S&D drills have $^1/_2$-inch diameter shanks and usually come with 118° points. They are available in HSS and HSS cobalt. Metric sizes are also available, but these are usually special order items.

- *MT-shank drills* – These drills are used in the drill press and lathe for drilling large holes without spinning the chuck. MT shanks can also be used in milling machines, but Silver & Deming drills are preferred because MT-shank drills are about twice as long as other milling machine cutting tools. Using MT-shank drills requires the milling table to be cycled up and down each time the drill is used with other shorter cutting tools. This is a time and energy consuming process.

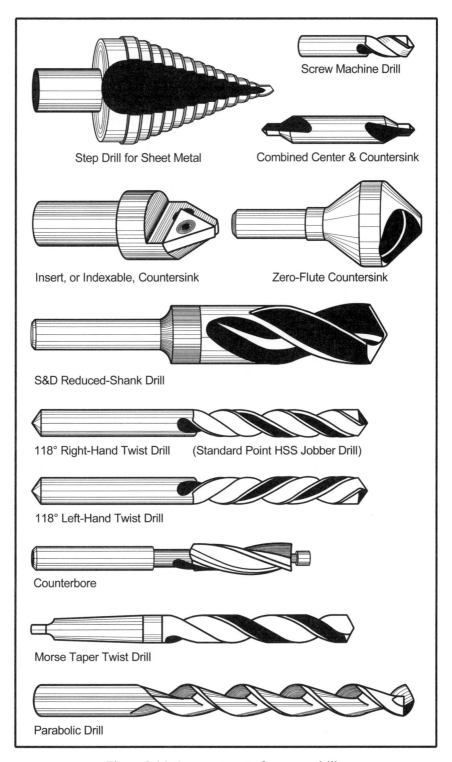

Figure 5-14. An assortment of common drills.

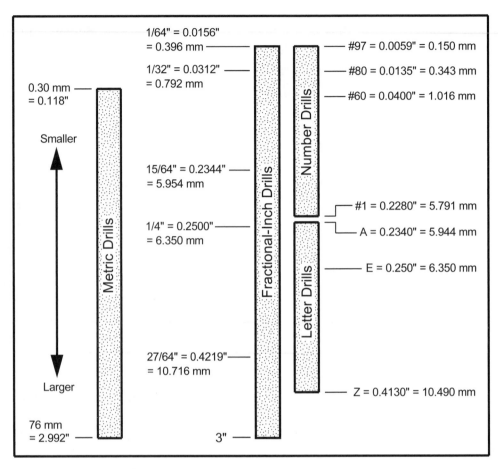

Figure 5-15. Comparison of the four twist drill size sets.

- *Countersinks* – These drills are used for countersinking screw heads, chamfering hole edges and deburring drilled holes.
- *Center drills* – These drills have two purposes:
  - They provide an accurate starting point for twist drills.
  - They produce 60° tapered holes for lathe centers.
- *Step drills for sheet metal* – These drill bits offer several advantages:
  - One bit can drill up to 13 different sized holes.
  - They deburr each hole with the cutting edge of the next larger step.

Although these bits can be started using a center drill, most have a starting point and are self-starting. They are available in both inch and metric sizes. Inch sizes from ⅛–1⅛-inch diameters are available and metric sizes are available from 4–34 mm diameter.

Other Drills

Depending on the type of work your shop performs, the following drills, shown previously in Figures 5-10 and 5-14, may be needed:

- *135° HSS* or *135° cobalt split-point drills* – For drilling hard materials, these drills are available in number, letter, inch-fractional and metric sizes.
- *Counterbores* – These are used for countersinking heads of SHCSs. Counterbores are available for screws from #4 (0.1860-inch diameter) to 1-inch diameter and 3–20 mm diameter metric fasteners.
- *Left-handed 118° HSS* – These drills, because they turn counter-clockwise, can *sometimes* remove a frozen fastener by drilling it out. Fractional drill sizes $^1/_{16}$–$^1/_2$ by $^1/_{64}$-inch increments are the most commonly available, but any other sizes can be special ordered. Both 118° and 135° split-point drills are available.
- *Large diameter Silver & Deming (S&D) reduced shank drills* – The full set of these drills covers 1–2 inches by $^1/_{64}$-inch increments with $^3/_4$-inch shanks. However, the most popular set consists of eight drills, $^9/_{16}$–1 inch by $^1/_{16}$-inch increments. Some drills come with three flats ground on their shanks to prevent them from spinning under load.
- *Screw machine drills* – Because of their shorter length, these drills are excellent for positioning holes accurately and drilling them straight. They come in the same sizes as jobber drills.
- *Parabolic drills* – The fast twist of these drills helps remove chips from deep holes. They are mainly used in production on aluminum and other non-ferrous metals. They are available ⅛–½-inch diameter in fractional and number sizes, but other sizes can be ordered.
- *Carbide-tipped* and *solid-carbide drills* – If your shop drills hardened steel, then solid carbide or carbide-tipped drills are needed. These drills require rigid set-ups to avoid drill fracture which occurs because, though these drills are very hard, they are also very brittle and can easily snap. A drill press is not rigid enough for them. Carbide drills are commonly available ⅛–½-inch diameter, but S&D drills ½–1¼-inch diameter can be special ordered. They are expensive when compared with HSS drills.

Section III – Drill Chucks

Drill Chuck Designs

As shown in Figure 5-16, there are three different drill chuck designs:

- *Keyed chucks* are the least expensive and most widely used design. Because much of the tightening torque applied by the chuck key goes to overcome friction inside the chuck, it is often not possible to tighten keyed chucks enough to keep larger drills from spinning under heavy loads. Keyed chucks, though, work well with smaller drills and are available in threaded and in arbor versions. The arbor versions cost more, but offer better concentricity. For a handy way to store a chuck key, refer to Figure 5-43.

- *Ball-bearing chucks* are two to three times more expensive than keyed chucks, but their internal ball bearings reduce frictional losses and make more key torque available for tightening. They are much less likely to allow drills to spin. Ball-bearing chucks require a separate arbor. For preventing twist drills and reamers from spinning under load, the Jacobs ball-bearing chuck is the one to buy. The Asian copies of this chuck, though less expensive, do not grip nearly as well as the authentic Jacobs chucks, and you are sure to be disappointed by them.

- *Keyless chucks* are roughly four times the cost of keyed chucks, but save time when changing drills because a chuck key is not needed. Because keyless chucks are tightened by hand, without the aid of a chuck key, many models have narrower chuck jaws which allow a better bite onto the drill. But naturally, softer drill shanks allow the jaws a more secure grip than harder ones. Keyless chucks work best on smaller drill sizes—¼-inch or less. Larger drills used in keyless chucks are likely to spin under load.

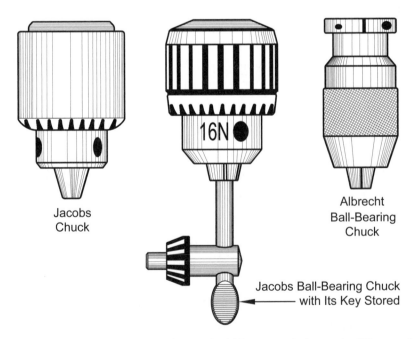

Jacobs
Chuck

16N

Albrecht
Ball-Bearing
Chuck

Jacobs Ball-Bearing Chuck
with Its Key Stored

Figure 5-16. Common chuck designs for use in drill presses, lathes and milling machines.

Removing Drill Chuck Arbors

Drill arbors, the shaft on which the drill chucks mount, must be removed before chucks can go into the arbor press for disassembly. Arbors though, can get stuck and chucks are often impossible to remove, even when using a pair of chuck removal wedges.

The solution to this problem is simple: drill a hole through the base of the chuck to admit a CRS drive pin which will apply axial force to push off the arbor as shown in Figure 5-17. Sometimes tapping the removal pin with a hammer will remove the arbor, but many times the needed removal forces are so high that an arbor press will fail to work and a hydraulic arbor press is required. Here is the arbor removal sequence:

1. Open the drill chuck jaws completely.
2. Center the drill chuck in a lathe using a three- or four-jaw chuck with the arbor of the drill chuck towards the lathe spindle.
3. Using a ⅜-inch drill in the tailstock, drill through the axis of the drill chuck to make a hole through its base. The base of the drill chuck is not hardened and you will feel the resistance on the tailstock handwheel slacken when the drill passes through the drill chuck base and before the drill hits the end of the arbor. The hole in the base of the chuck does not damage or compromise the chuck. Also, the chuck arbor will not be affected if you should drill into it.
4. With a hydraulic press, use a 3–4-inch long piece of $^5/_{16}$-inch CRS as a drive pin to press out the arbor through this hole.

Warning: When a stuck arbor releases, it will pop out of the drill chuck base with considerable force, so provide a means to capture the arbor so it does not fly off causing damage and injury.

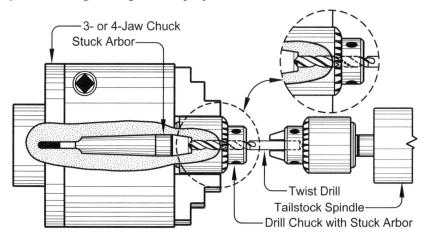

Figure 5-17. Drilling a drill chuck to admit a drive pin to remove its arbor.

Drill Chuck Repairs

Most damaged chucks are repairable if the drill chuck's manufacturer supplies replacement parts. Both Jacobs and Albrecht supply service kits. During repairs, chucks are disassembled and reassembled using an arbor press. Two cylindrical pressing-out fixtures, which are easily made in a lathe from steel or aluminum, are needed to hold the drill chuck in the arbor press. See Figure 5-18.

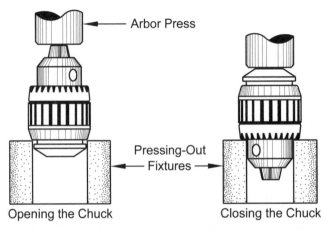

Figure 5-18. Cylindrical fixtures used to hold drill chucks in the arbor press. Note that the two fixtures have different sized openings.

Chucks become unusable most often because either their jaws get worn, the grease inside the chuck hardens, or metal chips jam the jaw threads. The actual repairs consist of arbor pressing the chuck apart, cleaning the chuck of dried grease and chips, inserting new jaws, relubricating the chuck, and pressing it back together. Ball-bearing chucks also receive new ball bearings and ball races.

Because each drill chuck jaw is ⅓ of a revolution away from it neighbors, the jaws must be replaced in the proper sequence, sometimes called *timing,* for the jaws to match up evenly. See Figure 5-19.

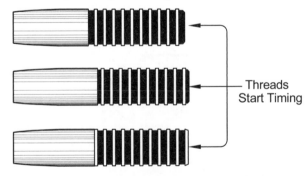

Figure 5-19. Replacement drill chuck jaws laid out in the proper order.

Manufacturers used to mark jaws with the numbers 1-2-3 to designate their replacement order, then they changed to using one, two and three tiny punch marks. Now, manufacturers use a system of stepped grooves as in Figure 5-20. As soon as a chuck is pressed apart, make a note of the jaw order and lay the jaws on the bench in this order. You will need to compare the thread pattern on the replacement jaws with those removed to install the new jaws in the correct order.

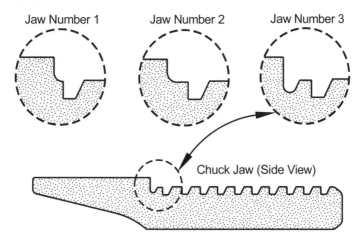

Figure 5-20. New Jacobs chuck replacement jaws showing the proper installation sequence.

Section IV – Drilling Operations

Step Drilling

Step drilling is the making of two or more progressively larger holes to reach a final hole diameter, rather than drilling the hole in a single step. The initial small hole is called the *pilot hole*. For example, making a $^5/_8$-inch diameter hole in a ½-inch thick CRS plate could be step drilled by following this procedure:

1. Center punch and center drill the part to locate where the hole is needed.

2. Start drilling with a $^1/_4$-inch twist drill for the pilot hole.

3. Drill a $^{19}/_{32}$-inch hole with a S&D reduced-shank drill, which is just $^1/_{32}$ of an inch smaller than the final hole size.

4. Also with a Silver & Deming drill, make the final $^5/_8$-inch hole.

Figure 5-21 shows how the initial, or pilot hole, relieves the next size larger drill from having to remove workpiece material to clear its web or chisel point. This considerably reduces the needed drill axial force because the material in front of the chisel point, which normally must be extruded rather than cut by the drill, has already been removed by the pilot drill.

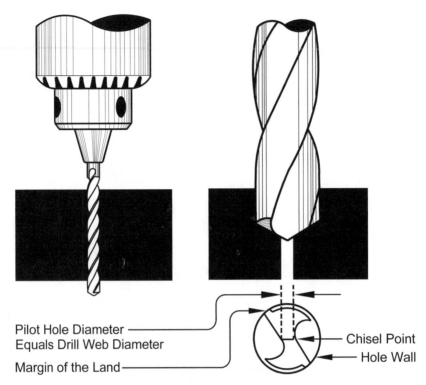

Pilot Hole Diameter
Equals Drill Web Diameter

Margin of the Land

Chisel Point

Hole Wall

Figure 5-21. Step drilling reduces the required axial force
and torque, and increases hole diameter accuracy.

Step-Drilling Advantages

There are three main advantages to step drilling:

- First, it allows you to do some drilling jobs that would otherwise be impossible. For example, it allows drilling even if your machine tool does not have enough torque to drill large holes in a single step, or if you have the torque, but your work set-up is not rigid enough to withstand such forces. Step drilling works especially well when using hand-held electric drills.

- Second, hole quality is improved:

  - Overall positional accuracy is much better than with a hole drilled in a single step.

  - Interior hole walls are smoother.

  - Final diameter tolerance is better when the final drill removes only a small amount of metal.

- Third, it is easier on the machine tool and the drill because forces are reduced. Step-drilling also reduces the chances of the drill being pulled out of its chuck or the chuck being pulled off its arbor when the drill makes its breakthrough on the back side of the work. When breaking through with single-pass drilling, the small amount of remaining metal often lets the drill flutes through at some point, allowing that metal to form a collar. This collar acts like a nut on the drill flutes, drawing the drill downward. A dangerous situation. The drill, the work, the chuck and you may be at risk when attempting to drill holes larger than ⅜-inch in a single pass. This is true whether using a drill press, a milling machine or a lathe. Just because you have the torque to drive a 1-inch drill through steel does not mean it is the best approach.

Note that in a Bridgeport-style milling machine, although the R8 collet taper transfers some of the drilling torque to the spindle, the small key inside the spindle also transfers torque and can be snapped off under high torque. Preventing damage to the spindle key is another reason to step drill holes. Replacing a Bridgeport spindle key requires removing the spindle from the quill, a time-consuming process.

Step drilling does have one disadvantage: Step drilling holes in hard materials can be very tough on drills, often damaging the drill lips because the load forces act only on the outer edges of the drill lips.

How to Drill Holes in Precise Locations

1. Before scribing the hole location, apply layout fluid to make the layout scribe lines stand out.

2. By feel, use the tip of a prick punch to locate the intersection of the scribed lines, and then, using a light ball-peen hammer, prick punch the hole location.

3. Check for proper prick-punch mark location after the *first* hammer strike. There is no point in making a deeper prick-punch mark in the wrong location. However, a prick-punch mark can be moved slightly by angling the punch in the direction you want to relocate the mark.

4. Center punch the hole location with a medium ball-peen hammer.

5. Center drill the hole location.

6. Drill the starter hole, and then step drill to the final hole diameter.

Deep-Hole Drilling

Here is how a plastic injection mold maker drilled a 26-inch long hole in hardened steel. Note that drilling is done in a milling machine from *both* sides of the mold, meeting at the mold's center. This reduces the depth of the drilling by half.

1. Center punch and center drill the hole location.

2. Using a screw machine drill for the initial hole, add cutting fluid and drill 4–6 diameters deep. Because they are shorter and more rigid than a standard jobber drill, a screw machine drill will insure a straight hole.

3. Use *peck* drilling to clear the hole of chips, followed by compressed air with a needle nozzle to get the remaining chips out from the back of the hole. Add more cutting fluid and drill 2–4 diameters. Repeat this process until the full depth of the screw machine drill is reached.

4. Change to a jobber drill, clearing chips from it frequently. With each peck cycle, add cutting fluid.

5. When the length of the jobber drill is drilled and cleared, begin using a short extension drill. Continue the peck drilling, chip clearing and cutting fluid addition cycle.

6. Use progressively longer extension drills, as in Step 5, until the hole reaches the center of the work.

7. Flip the part over and drill from the other side of the workpiece, repeating steps 1–6 until the two drilled holes meet inside the part.

Drilling Long Stock in a Drill Press

When work is too long to put on the drill press table, it can be placed *through* the table center hole as in Figure 5-22. Alternatively, the table can be swung to one side and the work drilled off the edge of the table.

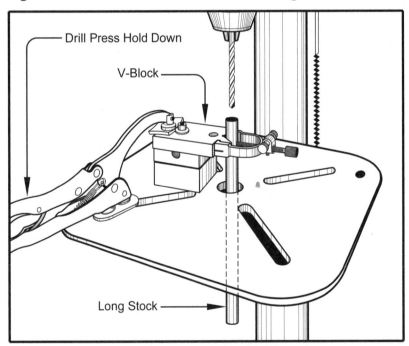

Figure 5-22. Center drilling long stock through the center hole of the drill press table.

Oversized Transfer Punches

When a transfer punch larger than those on hand is needed, make a drill bushing to hold a smaller punch as in Figure 5-23.

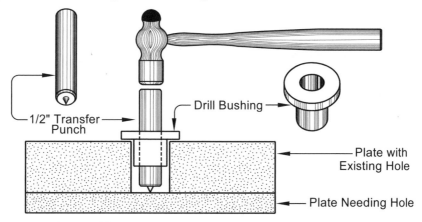

1/2" Transfer Punch

Drill Bushing

Plate with Existing Hole

Plate Needing Hole

Figure 5-23. Using a drill bushing to adapt a transfer punch for a larger-sized hole.

Drilling 90° Holes in Machinery Castings

When a casting cannot be brought to a drill press or milling machine, use a hand-held drill and a predrilled wood or aluminum block to insure that the drill is perpendicular to the work. Sometimes the drilling guide can be clamped to the work or adhered with double-sided tape. See Figure 5-24.

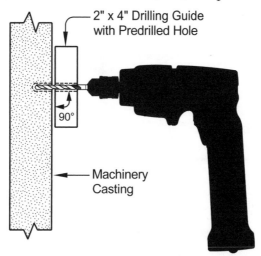

2" x 4" Drilling Guide with Predrilled Hole

90°

Machinery Casting

Figure 5-24. Using a drilling guide to drill holes perpendicular to a casting.

Accurately Drilling & Tapping a Machinery Shaft in Place

When a machinery shaft must be drilled and tapped in place, follow the 9-Step procedure in Figure 5-25 which uses shop-made drilling and tapping guides to insure that holes and threads are centered in the shaft.

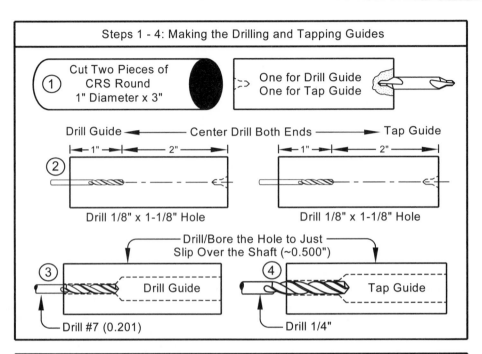

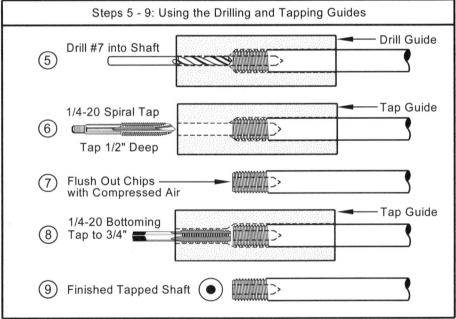

Figure 5-25. The 9-Step procedure for drilling and tapping a machinery shaft in place.

Drilling Pilot Holes in Tight Locations

Sometimes holes must be drilled after other parts are in position. Such was the case with a steel tool holder shelf that needed to be attached to the electrical box of a large lathe. With no way to determine the exact hole positions in advance, the shelf was leveled and braced in the final position, and the pilot holes were then drilled as in Figure 5-26. A long flexible twist drill and a custom-made drill bushing were used for this job because the drill chuck was too large to fit into the clearance space to drill the pilot holes. To see the finished shelf, see Figure 7-117.

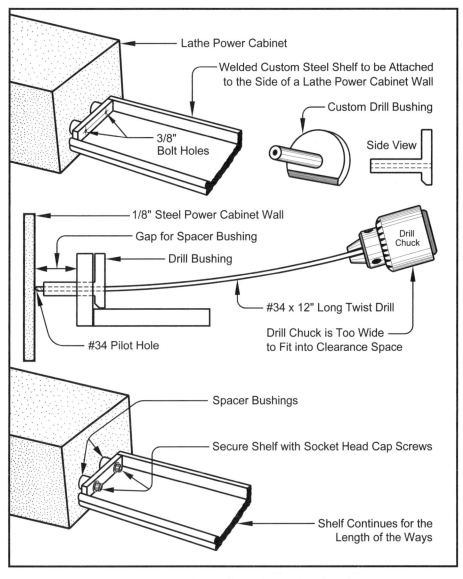

Figure 5-26. Drilling a pilot hole in a tight location.

Accurate Depth Control with Shims

When drill depth must be precise, use the depth stop nut and a feeler gage as pictured in Figure 5-27. This is a good way to perform clearcutting when the cutter will take too large a bite if not constrained.

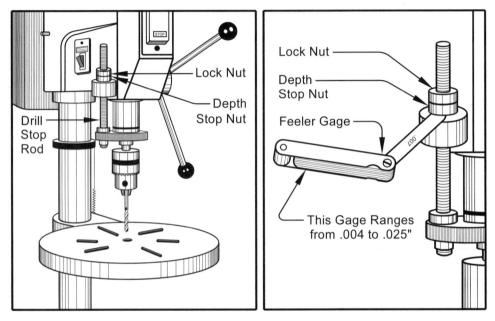

Figure 5-27. Using a depth stop nut and a feeler gage to control drill depth.

Cutting Fluids for Aluminum

Cutting fluids are very effective in cooling drills, extending tool life, reducing the problem of the welding of work material to the drill lips and for easing chip removal along the flutes. There are several cutting fluids which are commonly used for aluminum:

- Commercial Cutting Fluids: A-9 (Relton Corporation) or Tap Magic Aluminum (Steco Corporation).
- Unflavored (and unscented) PAM Non-Stick Cooking Spray (ConAgra Foods).
- Shop-made mix: 7 parts kerosene with 3 parts mineral oil.

Drilling Large Holes in Stainless Steel Plates

Drilling stainless steel can be a problem. Typically, the drill does not start where wanted and wanders about making an oversized tri-lobal hole, scratching the work surface in the process. Figure 5-28 shows how to drill a large diameter hole in a stainless steel receptacle cover plate. This same technique can be used on any thickness stainless steel plate.

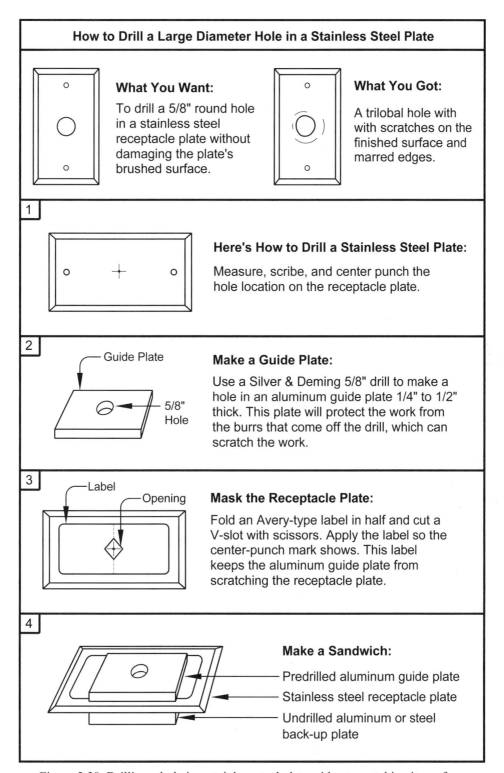

How to Drill a Large Diameter Hole in a Stainless Steel Plate

What You Want:

To drill a 5/8" round hole in a stainless steel receptacle plate without damaging the plate's brushed surface.

What You Got:

A trilobal hole with with scratches on the finished surface and marred edges.

1

Here's How to Drill a Stainless Steel Plate:

Measure, scribe, and center punch the hole location on the receptacle plate.

2

Guide Plate

5/8" Hole

Make a Guide Plate:

Use a Silver & Deming 5/8" drill to make a hole in an aluminum guide plate 1/4" to 1/2" thick. This plate will protect the work from the burrs that come off the drill, which can scratch the work.

3

Label

Opening

Mask the Receptacle Plate:

Fold an Avery-type label in half and cut a V-slot with scissors. Apply the label so the center-punch mark shows. This label keeps the aluminum guide plate from scratching the receptacle plate.

4

Make a Sandwich:

Predrilled aluminum guide plate

Stainless steel receptacle plate

Undrilled aluminum or steel back-up plate

Figure 5-28. Drilling a hole in a stainless steel plate without scratching its surface.

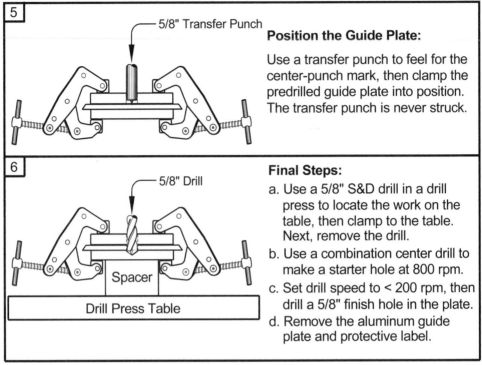

Figure 5-28. (continued) Drilling a hole in a stainless
steel plate without scratching its surface.

Magnetic Drill Presses

Magnetic drill presses are used for drilling machinery and structures that are too big or too immovable to fit into a drill press or a milling machine. Magnetic drill presses have several advantages over hand-held drills:

- The electromagnet in the base holds the drill press in place with as much as 3000 pounds of force, so the user does not have to hold the electric drill in place while drilling.

- The magnetic drill press can be positioned exactly over a center-punch mark, and then the magnet energized.

- The spindle is advanced using a three-spoke handle, a design with a big mechanical advantage. Because the handle is turned from the side of the drill press, the user need not stand behind the drill press when drilling and the spindle can exert up to 1600 pounds of axial force on the drill.

- There are three different magnetic drill press spindle designs:

    - The Jacobs drill chuck design holds twist drills and can drill ½-inch holes in steel with ease. See Figure 5-29 (right).

    - Many other drill presses have № 3 Morse tapers for holding twist drills up to 1¼-inches diameter.

- Threaded or proprietary spindle designs are used with trepanning tools or hole saws to cut holes up to 2-inches in diameter in steel. These larger holes can be drilled with hole saws in a single step because the hole saw need only remove a thin donut-shaped metal section, it does not need to turn the entire volume of the hole metal into chips. See Figure 5-29 (left).

• The magnetic drill press can not only hold the drill perpendicular to the work, it can get into tight spots where it would be impossible to use a hand drill, for example, between the platens of a hydraulic press.

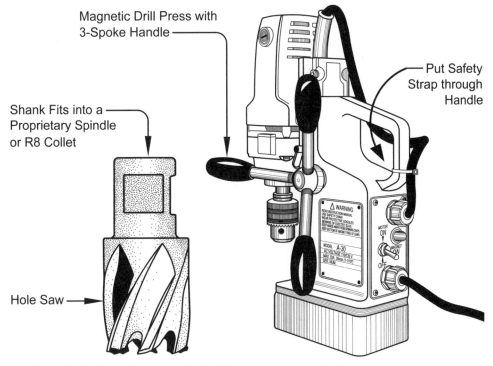

Figure 5-29. The hole saw on the left fits on a magnetic drill press with a proprietary spindle design. The magnetic drill press on the right has a Jacobs chuck for twist drills. Note the location of the safety strap.

Drilling Holes Deeper Than the Drill Press Stroke

By drilling a hole, or pocket, through the back of the drill chuck and into its Morse taper arbor, holes deeper than the travel of the drill press chuck can be drilled without using individual drills of increasing lengths. As shown in Figure 5-30, one long drill can be progressively lowered until the desired drill depth is achieved. Drilling this pocket hole does not ruin the Morse taper arbor or the drill chuck.

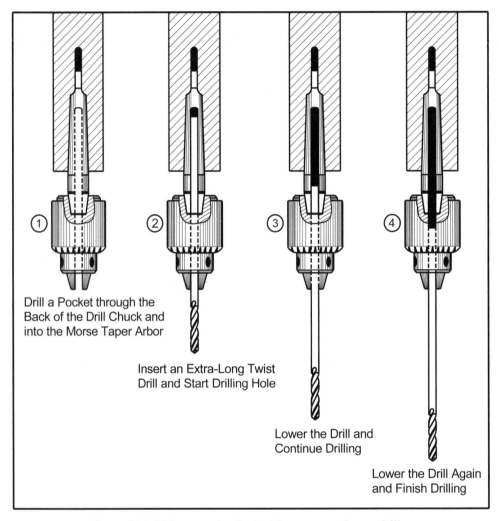

① Drill a Pocket through the Back of the Drill Chuck and into the Morse Taper Arbor

② Insert an Extra-Long Twist Drill and Start Drilling Hole

③ Lower the Drill and Continue Drilling

④ Lower the Drill Again and Finish Drilling

Figure 5-30. Using a pocket in the Morse taper arbor to drill a
hole deeper than the travel of the drill press.

Drill Press Safety

- Wear safety glasses, and to further reduce eye hazards, always keep your eyes out of the plane of the drill press table.
- Drill presses are top heavy, particularly the floor-mounted models. They tip over easily so must be secured to the floor.
- Use a drill press vise to hold smaller parts. Sometimes clamping the drill press vise to the table is helpful when a hole must be drilled very accurately.
- When drilling many materials, long continuous chip strands come out off the drill flutes. These chips may be easily interrupted by momentarily letting up on the drilling pressure to let the strand break.

- Use quick-release drill press clamps on plates and sheet metal to prevent them from spinning on the drill as the drill breaks through the back side of the hole. See Figure 5-31.

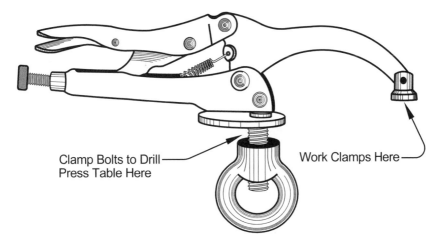

Clamp Bolts to Drill Press Table Here

Work Clamps Here

Figure 5-31. A quick-release drill press clamp.

- Hold small parts in an inexpensive drill press vise. The model in Figure 5-32 can also hold parts on an angle as well as be clamped to the drill press table.

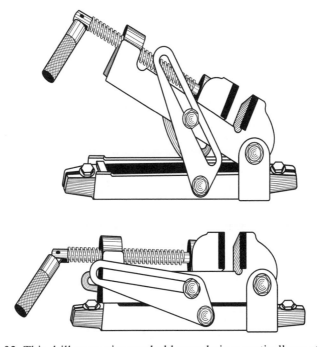

Figure 5-32. This drill press vise can hold a workpiece vertically or at an angle.

Good Drill Press Practices

- On a shelf near the drill press, keep the most frequently used drills, drilling and tapping fluids, drill chucks, chuck keys and Morse taper drifts. This will save many steps.

- Keeping a tap, its tap drill and its clearance drill in the most common size fastener used in the shop close to the drill press saves time hunting for them. Many machinists choose a ¼-20 tap, a #7 drill (its tap drill) and a ¼-inch drill (its clearance drill).

- Avoid using keyless drill chucks on drills larger than ¼-inch. Larger drills will spin in keyless chucks and have their shanks gouged, permanently reducing their concentricity and damaging the chuck jaws.

- Using an abrasive stone or file, remove the burrs from drill shanks that have been spun to minimize further damage to the drill chuck jaws.

- Using a Jacobs ball-bearing chuck for drills larger than ¼-inch will stop twist drills from spinning in their chucks. The ball bearings insure that the force applied to the chuck to tighten it is not consumed by friction in the chuck mechanism itself and really does go to tighten the jaws on the drill. Budget imported ball-bearing chucks do not grip as well as Jacobs chucks, so pay the premium and avoid the problems that go with cheap chucks.

- Step-drill all holes larger than ⅜-inch diameter. Most drill presses lack the torque, rigidity and slow spindle speed needed to drill large holes in a single pass.

- Placing the work on top of an aluminum block instead of on the drill press table accomplishes four functions:

  - Removing heat from the work.

  - Preventing softer work material from *breaking out* where the drill emerges on the backside of the work.

  - Avoiding drilling holes in the drill press table.

  - Using an aluminum block also permits the drilling of very hard materials such as hacksaw blades. When cutting hard materials, be sure to use cutting lubricant, the slowest spindle speed available and a 135° split-point drill. And, be aware that considerable axial force is needed to get the hole started.

- Use peck drilling when the drill and the work material do not permit the chips to exit along the flutes. After the initial peck, withdraw the drill from the work, brush away the chips, add cutting fluid and drill further.

- Most floor-mounted drill presses have spindles positioned so a person of average height sees his work from a steep angle. This provides little side view of the work. Depending on your own height and the size of your work, you may want to raise the base of the drill press to get a better side-on view of your drilling. For bench-mounted drill presses, the drill press column can be shortened 5–6 inches to provide a better view of the work.

• Using cutting fluid reduces drill wear and increases drilling speed for almost all materials.

A Typical Drill Press Mishap

You are drilling a hole in the far end of an aluminum bar $1 \times 1 \times 15$ inches with a ¼-inch twist drill in a drill press. Since the aluminum bar is large and easy to hang on to, you fail to clamp the work to the drill press table. After all, the hole being drilled is small and relatively little torque is involved; so you think you can hold it with just your hands.

Here's how things can quickly go awry:

1. The drill enters the work easily, and the chips slide up and out the drill flutes. So far, so good, but the smoothness of this initial step is deceptive.

2. When the drill gets about ¾ of the way through the aluminum bar, the chips jam up inside the drill flutes, stop coming out of the hole, and you now realize that you must withdraw the drill from the hole to clear the chips so you can finish drilling the hole. But this is not as easy as it sounds.

3. While hanging on to your end of the bar, you begin to withdraw the drill from the hole. But, since the drill has been turning with the chips stuck in the flutes, the chips get hot and expand, *locking* the drill in the hole.

4. The result is, the hole end of the aluminum bar lifts up off the table while at the same time you are trying to hold your end down against the drill press table.

5. The drill fails to bend and snaps off in the hole. If the drill is large, the drill press may tear the work out of your hand and begin to whirl the work around. Oops.

Important tip: *Always clamp your work against the drill press table.* Even a light clamping that allows you to slide the work around under the clamp and drill will prevent the work from lifting off the table and snapping the drill.

Recovery from a Broken Center Drill

When the tip of a center drill snaps off inside a part, it cannot be drilled out because it is hardened HSS. But, there's more you can do than just curse. The solution lies in the ruined end of the center drill itself. Remove the broken center drill from the drill press or lathe, and, as shown in Figure 5-33, use a small abrasive wheel in a hand-held air or electric grinder to form a slot. The slot should be just wide enough to fit around the broken tip. Then, use this modified center drill to redrill the center hole. When the slot in the tip of the center drill fits *around* the snapped tip, the modified center drill removes the metal *surrounding* the broken-off tip, releasing it.

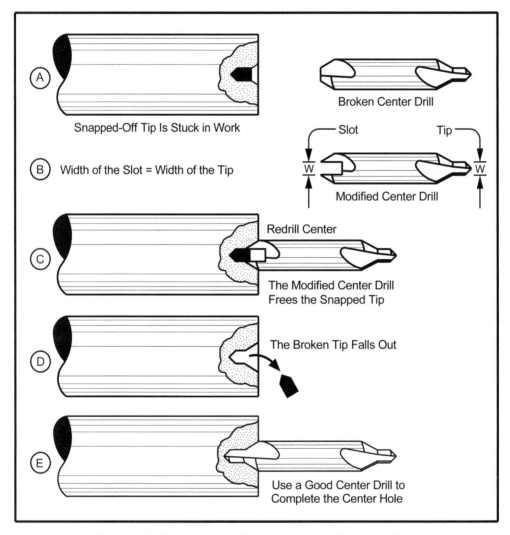

Figure 5-33. How to recover from a snapped-off center-drill tip.

Drill & Tap Extensions

Although 6-, 12- and 18-inch long twist drills are commercially available from industrial tool houses, sometimes twist drills with even longer-shanks are required. Here are two shop-made solutions:

• Figure 5-34 shows the steps for making a drill extension from CRS rod stock. Center drilling the rod and filing away a cut-out are the only processes required. This method can also be used to extend taps for tapping pulley hubs.

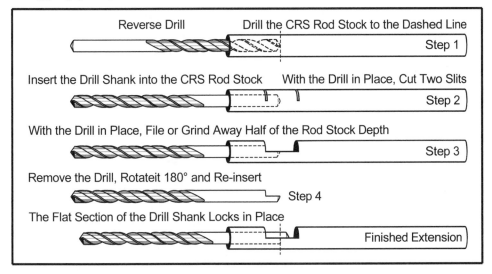

Figure 5-34. Making a twist drill extension using CRS rod stock.

• Figures 5-35 and 5-36 show two shop-made fixtures that hold a drill and a section of CRS rod stock in axial alignment for brazing. Both of these fixtures maintain the drill shank at the same diameter along its entire length. Although drill rod could be used for making the extension, brazing heat could harden and embrittle it, causing a fracture. CRS is a better choice because it is less expensive and tougher.

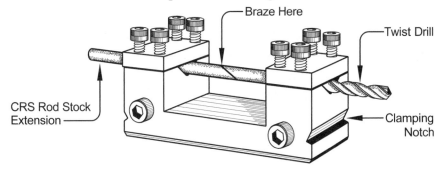

Figure 5-35. Shop-made fixture for brazing a twist drill extension.

To make the drill extension stronger, be sure to cut both the drill shank and the CRS rod stock at an angle. This distributes forces around a larger braze area and reduces the nature of the forces acting on the joint from all shear to a mixture of shear, compression and tension.

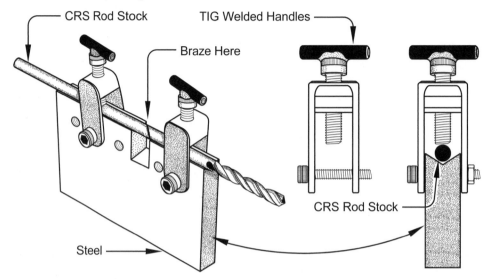

Figure 5-36. Shop-made fixture for brazing a twist drill extension.

Countersinks

Countersinks are cone-shaped cutting tools which chamfer or bevel the edges of an existing hole. This is done to seat flat head screws below a workpiece surface, to deburr holes, and sometimes it is done so a thread tap starts more easily. Countersinks are available in HSS, solid carbide, or with carbide inserts in a variety of point angles. Countersinking can be done in a drill press, lathe, milling machine, or in a hand-held electric drill. Carbide countersinks, because of their brittleness, should be used in a lathe or drill press, not a hand-held drill.

Countersinks are available in 30º, 60º, 82º, 90º, 100º, 110º, 120º and 130º angles. The three most popular angles are:

- 60° for flat head screws and rivets, and also for chamfering the edges of holes tapped with 60° threads.
- 82° for countersinking inch-based flat head screws.
- 90° for countersinking rivets, metric screws, and for chamfering and deburring.

The choice of countersink design involves trade-offs between self-centering properties, tool life, work hardness, speed and surface finish.

Here are the different types of countersinks:

- *Single-flute countersinks* self-center the best, but cut slower than other designs. In HSS they can be used in hand-held electric drills and other non-rigid set-ups. Single-flute countersinks are often used where the holes are too small for multi-flute countersinks.
- *Three-* and *four-flute countersinks* have the most chip clearance of all the designs and should be used on stringy materials like plastics and non-ferrous metals.
- *Six-flute countersinks* can be fed 250% faster than other countersink designs. They offer long life because of their multiple cutting edges and are used for both ferrous and non-ferrous materials.
- *Carbide indexable countersinks* are not self-centering and must be used in lathes or milling machines. Most solid carbide countersinks can last up to ten times as long as their HSS versions, but carbide countersinks must be used in a rigid set-up or they will chip, fracture or crack under load. See both the carbide and carbide insert countersinks in Figure 5-37.

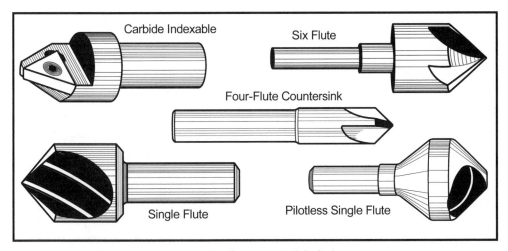

Figure 5-37. Five countersink designs.

Section V – Drill Press Projects

Drill Press Tray

Figure 5-38 shows a shop-made industrial-grade steel drill press tray that keeps cutting fluid and often-used drills and taps within easy reach. Hose clamps secure the tray to the drill press column making it unnecessary to drill mounting holes in the drill press column.

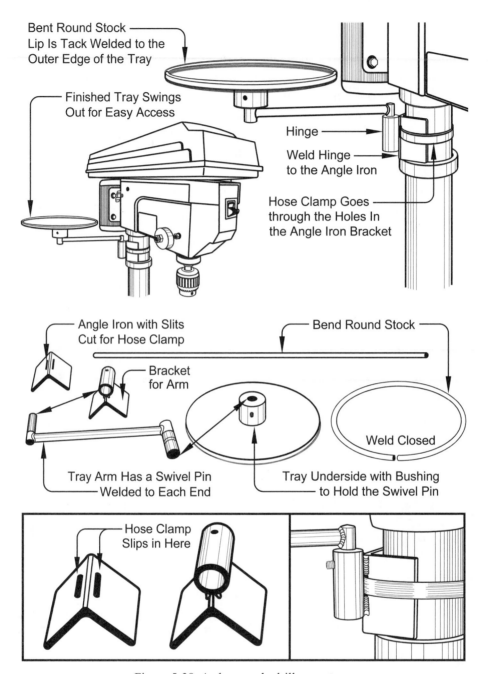

Figure 5-38. A shop-made drill press tray.

Silver & Deming Drill Stand

In addition to some basic milling and drilling of the aluminum block which forms the stand top rack, the project shown in Figure 5-39 provides an opportunity to practice accurately positioning drilled holes for the four flat head hex screws that hold the base plate to the top of the stand.

The challenge in making this aluminum drill stand is in placing the four clearance holes and their matching tapped holes in exactly the right position on the base plate and the drill stand top rack. These holes must be in precise symmetrical locations and their clearance holes must align with their tapped holes. Although this could be done using X-Y coordinates on a milling machine, the following is a method that requires only a height gage, a granite plate, an angle plate, and some simple addition.

To make the drill stand, follow the plan in Figure 5-40 and the step-by-step instructions which begin below.

1. After machining the aluminum drill stand top rack, turn it bottom-side-up and choose the location of the first corner hole. Mark this location with a prick punch.

2. Hold the aluminum top rack against a right angle plate and scribe a line through the punch mark. As shown in Figure 5-41, the work must always be scribed against the right angle plate to get an accurate scribe.

3. Turn the block one-half turn and scribe the same line height across the other end of the block.

4. Leaving the height gage setting unchanged, hold the base plate to the angle plate and scribe a hole line across one end of the base plate.

5. Turn the base plate one-half turn and scribe the same line height across the other end of the plate.

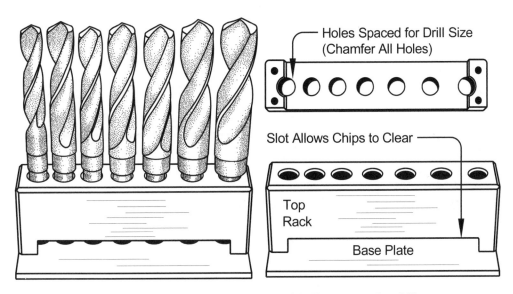

Figure 5-39. An aluminum stand to hold Silver & Deming drills.

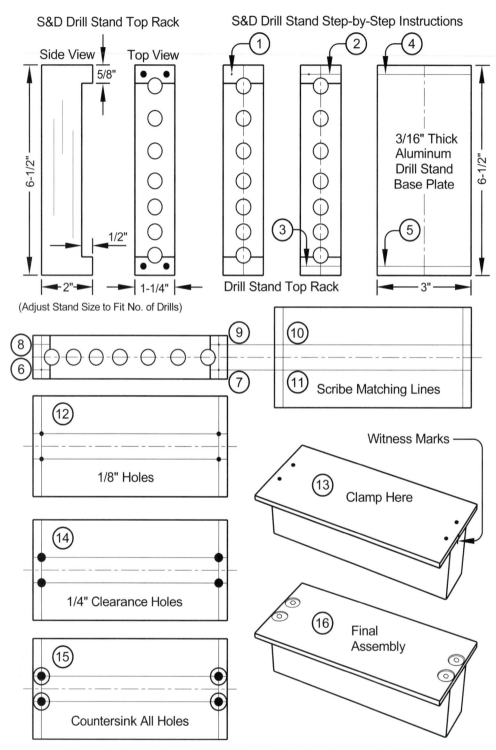

Figure 5-40. Plan for an S&D drill stand showing the steps for drilling accurately placed holes in the base plate and in the top rack of the drill stand.

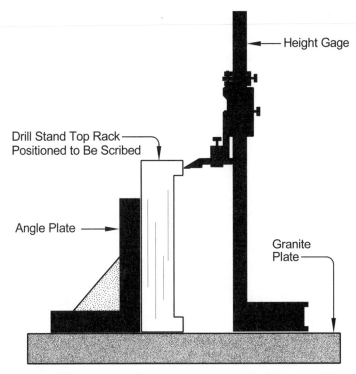

Figure 5-41. Holding work vertically against a right angle plate for scribing with height gage.

6. Lay the aluminum top rack on its side, set the height gage on the prick-punch mark and scribe the hole height. Record the height of this hole for use in Step 10.

7. Leave the height gage setting unchanged and scribe the hole height at the other end of the top rack.

8. Turn the aluminum top rack one-half turn and scribe the line height across the other end of the rack.

9. Scribe a line for the height of the remaining hole.

10. Measure the width of the base plate with the height gage, set the height gage to *half* the width of the base plate and scribe a centerline. Zero the height gage, then raise it to the hole height recorded in Step 6. Scribe a line across the length of the plate to mark two of the base holes.

11. Turn the base plate one-half turn and scribe the line height across the other side of the plate. The location of all four holes on the aluminum top rack and on the base plate are now marked.

12. Prick punch and center punch the four hole marks on the base plate, center drill and drill four ⅛-holes in the base plate.

13. Align the base plate over the aluminum top rack's scribe lines by looking through the ⅛-inch holes. The scribe lines on the top rack will align with

those on the base plate. Clamp the base plate to the top rack. A single Kant-Twist 4½-inch clamp works well here. Also, using a prick punch, put two witness marks on the edge of the base plate and the aluminum top rack so these two parts can be assembled this way later.

14. Using the four existing ⅛-inch holes in the base plate as starter holes, use a #7 drill to drill tap holes though the base plate and into the top rack.

15. Separate the clamped parts and enlarge the #7 tap holes in the base plate to ¼-inch clearance holes, then countersink these holes for ¼-20 flat head hex screws.

16. Tap the four holes in the aluminum top rack, drill the holes for your S&D drills, then fasten on the base plate with four flat head screws.

Hex Wrench Stand

Many hex wrenches are supplied with flimsy z-shaped sheet metal stands which require you to wiggle the wrench around blindly to find the bottom hole. Figure 5-42 shows an aluminum stand that allows the wrench to drop in easily, without fishing for the bottom hole. Also, for easy hex wrench insertion, holes for the wrenches have 60° countersunk entrances.

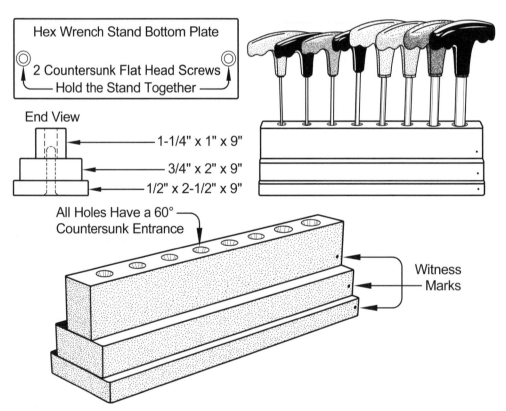

Figure 5-42. Shop-made hex wrench stand of aluminum bar stock.

Chuck Key Storage

Drilling a hole near the back right-hand edge of the drill press table to hold the chuck key keeps the key handy, yet out of the way. For lefties, drill the hole on the left-hand edge. See Figure 5-43.

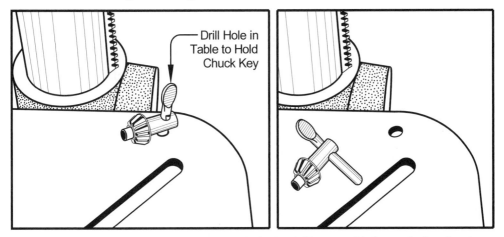

Figure 5-43. Storing the chuck key in a hole in the drill press table keeps the key handy.

Section VI – Reaming

Basic Reamer Assortment

Most shops require a set of *dowel pin reamers*, also called *over/under chucking reamers,* for installing dowel pins. The typical set consists of seven reamer pairs. One member of each pair is one-thousandth of an inch undersized and the other one-thousandth of an inch oversized. For example, with the $^1/_4$-inch diameter pair, one reamer is 0.249-inches diameter and the other is 0.251-inches diameter. The smaller reamer hole is used to lock the dowel pin in place and the larger one is used to allow the dowel pin to be easily removed. A typical inch-based reamer set covers $^1/_8$-, $^3/_{16}$-, $^1/_4$-, $^5/_{16}$-, $^3/_8$-, $^7/_{16}$- and $^1/_2$-inch diameter dowels. Smaller diameter reamers are usually straight shank and larger diameter reamers have an MT shank to transmit the needed torque. See Figure 5-44.

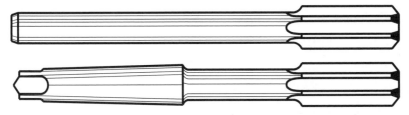

Figure 5-44. Chucking reamers: straight shank (top) and Morse taper (bottom). Straight shanks are found on smaller chucking reamers and Morse tapers on larger chucking reamers. Note: These two reamers are not drawn to scale.

Other chucking reamer sets are also available in:

- *Fractional inch* – Sized $\frac{1}{32}$–$1\frac{1}{2}$-inch diameter, *exactly* the fractional diameter to four decimal places.
- *Letter size*, also called *wire gage size* – Sized from A–Z.
- *Number size* – Sized 1–60.
- *Metric* – Sized 1–25 mm in 0.5 mm increments.
- *Decimal inch* – Any decimal size from 0.047–1.50-inches may be ordered and some industrial tool distributors stock several thousand decimal sizes from 0.050–0.997-inches.

The five sets of reamers above may be needed depending on the type of work your shop performs, but usually these reamers are less frequently used than the over/under dowel pin reamers. Note that both the over/under and the exact-size reamers are called chucking reamers.

Although straight-flute reamers are the most common because of their lower cost and usually adequate performance, reamers with a right-hand cut and a left-hand spiral must be used when the best surface finish is needed. But keep in mind that these reamers are more expensive and less common than the straight-flute reamers.

Reaming Speeds & Feeds

Reaming speeds are usually about $\frac{2}{3}$ of the speed used for drilling the same size hole. *Reaming feeds* are usually 200–300% of drill feeds. Too low a feed can cause excessive reamer wear and sometimes allow the reamer to merely burnish or rub, rather than cut. Very high feeds can cause poor hole finish and reduced diameter accuracy.

Chatter

Chatter, which affects hole finish and reamer life, has several possible causes:

- Too high a spindle speed.
- Poor rigidity in the set-up.
- Too slow, or too fast a feed.
- Work not held securely.

Here are three steps that may stop chatter:

- Chamfering the hole before reaming.
- Using a piloted reamer.
- Packing the reamer flutes with grease or Crisco.

Reaming Procedure for Chucking Reamers

1. To begin, measure, scribe mark, prick punch, center punch and center drill for an undersized hole.

2. Drill the undersized hole. The objective is to leave enough material for the reamer to remove rather than too little and have the reamer merely burnish the existing hole and fail to cut the hole to size. See Graph 5-1 for undersized hole allowances.

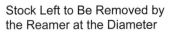
Stock Left to Be Removed by
the Reamer at the Diameter

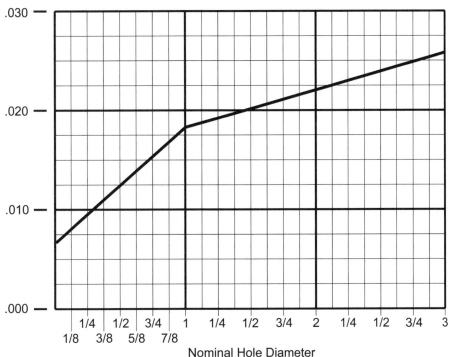

Graph 5-1. Recommended hole undersizing for reaming vs. hole diameter.

3. Secure about ⅜ inch of the chucking reamer shaft inside the drill chuck or collet. The less shaft in the chuck is better. Too much reamer shaft in the chuck (or collet) stiffens the reamer and prevents it from following the existing, undersized hole.

4. For maximum symmetry, chamfer the hole entrance with a countersink under machine power, not by hand.

5. Set the spindle speed to about 200 RPM. This slow speed will make reaming take longer, but prevents tool chatter. Reaming speeds can be increased with experience.

6. Apply cutting fluid to the hole entrance and to the reamer flutes. Generally, the same cutting fluid used for drilling will be acceptable.

7. Use light, steady pressure to get the reamer tip to exit the far end of the hole.

8. Do not allow the reamer flutes to pass completely through the reamed hole. This forces the flutes to back into the already reamed hole and can damage both the flutes and the hole.

9. Withdraw the reamer and clean out the chips and cutting fluid.

Reaming Procedure for Dowel Pins

Dowel pins for indexing two parts have an *interference fit,* also called a *press fit* or *drive fit,* which retains the dowel pin permanently in one part and has a snug, but *sliding fit* on the other part. This arrangement allows the two parts to be separated while the dowel pin with the interference fit is retained in the part. See Figure 5-45. In this procedure the dowel pin hole is reamed to two different diameters. Here are the steps:

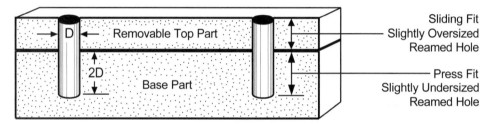

Figure 5-45. Cut view of installing a dowel pin for indexing two parts.

1. To begin, measure, scribe mark, prick punch and center punch for the dowel pin holes.

2. Match up the two parts to be aligned by the dowels and clamp them together so they do not move when drilling or reaming.

3. Center drill for the undersized hole.

4. Drill the undersized hole through *both* of the parts. Again, be sure to leave enough metal inside the hole so that the reamer has sufficient metal to engage and cut to full size.

5. Without disturbing the alignment of the two parts, ream the *undersized hole* through both parts. Put just ⅜-inch of the reamer shank into the drill chuck and do not choke up on the shank. This allows the reamer to *float,* giving it more freedom to find its own center.

6. Withdraw the undersized reamer and replace it with the clearance, or oversized reamer. The clearance reamer will allow the dowel pin to be withdrawn through the upper removable part.

7. Be sure that the clearance reamer passes completely through the upper removable part and just into the lower part.

8. Remove all the chips, apply lubricants, and press or drive the dowel pin through both parts.

Tip: If the dowel pin goes into a blind hole, use a piece of tape on the reamer to indicate that the reamer has reached full depth. Failure to reach full depth can leave a dowel pin stuck in the blind hole. Often the only way to correct such a mishap is with EDM. This process erodes the center of the dowel pin and the weakened outer shell of the pin is then cracked out.

Shortening Dowel Pins

Dowel pins are easy to shorten in a lathe even though they may be case hardened. Here is the procedure:

1. Place the dowel pin in a lathe collet. Smaller dowel pins have chamfers on both ends, but larger diameter dowel pins have a dome or crown on their the hammer ends. The other end of the pin will have a chamfer, making it the end that goes into the reamed hole. If your dowel pin is large enough to have a dome, put the domed end into the collet.

2. Use a carbide lathe tool with a nick-off as described in Chapter 7, Lathes, Figure 7-29.

3. Set the lathe for about half the speed used for drilling the same diameter part, and, using cutting fluid, make the cut. Put a chamfer on the dowel pin, cutting it similarly to the original chamfer.

4. Touch up the chamfer with emery cloth to insure it has no burrs.

Common Dowel Pin Problems

Here are some of the problems that arise when installing dowel pins:

*   After an undersized blind hole is drilled and reamed, the two workpieces move and the upper and lower holes shift slightly out of axial alignment. When the dowel pin is installed, it gets stuck. The pin will not go all the way into the blind hole, and it will not come out either. Don't panic. Though nearly impossible to drill out, if there is access to the dowel pin hole at both ends, drill an access hole and the stuck dowel pin can be driven out with a punch. But, if there is not access at both ends, EDM is the usual solution to remove a stuck dowel pin.

*   A blind undersized dowel pin hole for some reason was not drilled—or reamed—to full depth, and the machinist is not aware of this and inserts the dowel, which will not seat. Once more EDM is called for to remove the pin, but the best plan is to avoid this problem entirely by putting a small piece of tape on the drill or reamer to signal that the hole has reached full depth.

*   The dowel pin has been shortened, but a burr has been left on the chamfered end and the dowel pin will not seat because the burr has caused it to jam. To avoid this situation, be sure to polish the end of the dowel pin after shortening it.

Reaming Tips & Techniques

- To *decrease* the size of a reamed hole by several fractions of one-thousandths of an inch, raise the temperature of the part with a heat gun before reaming. This will increase the dowel hole size from thermal expansion, leaving less metal in place for the reamer to remove.

- To *increase* the hole size made by a reamer, place a small shred of fabric down a flute of the reamer. A strip of the overlocked edge of a shop towel works well. Ream a test hole first. See Figure 5-46.

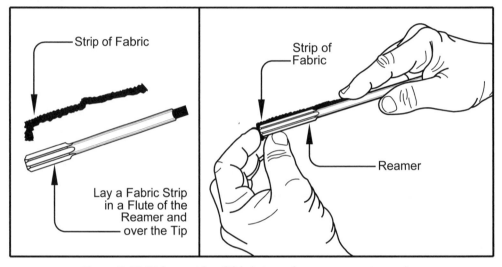

Figure 5-46. Using a strip of fabric to make a reamer cut oversize.

- Allowing a reamed hole to intersect with a drilled hole will reduce the accuracy and symmetry of the reamed hole.

- When reaming a blind hole, do not ream all the way to the bottom; leave a space, or pocket, to hold the reamer chips.

- Because only a 45° chamfer is applied to the front flutes, sharpening a chucking reamer in a tool or cutter grinder is relatively quick and simple. Sharpening, though, cannot be done by hand because symmetry is required—each flute must be ground alike or the reamer will cut oversize.

Section VII – Tapping

Spiral Point Taps

Spiral point taps, also called *gun taps,* are similar to standard taper taps except they have a spiral slash ground in their point. See Figure 5-47.

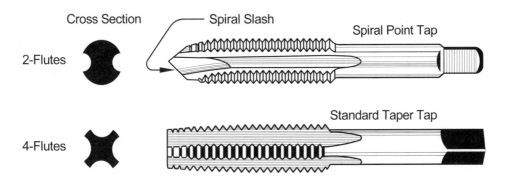

Figure 5-47. A spiral point tap and a standard taper tap.

This slash ejects thread cuttings *ahead* of the tap and avoids clogging in the flutes. See Figure 5-48. Spiral point taps work well in through-holes where their two-flute design makes them stronger than standard taps. And, because of their increased cross section, as shown in Figure 5-47 (top), spiral taps are less likely to snap off. These taps do not need to be reversed to break the chips as conventional taps require. In fact, spiral taps should not be reversed because their chips may jam the threads.

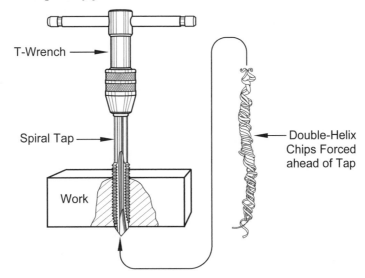

Figure 5-48. Spiral point taps produce a single string of double-helix chips.

Although spiral point taps are not recommended for use in blind holes because their helical chips have no place to go and tend to jam the tap, if the hole is made three times the depth of the required threads, blind holes can be tapped. But this is not considered a good practice. When tapping, always remember to remove the chip string so it will not cause jams later.

With caution, spiral taps can be used under lathe, mill or drill press power.

Spiral taps can tap threads entirely though the tap hole and be removed from the work by passing the shank out the far end of the hole. This saves backing out the tap.

Tapping Tip

Because there is little springiness in a tap wrench assembly, it is all but impossible to adequately tighten it by using only the knurled shaft. Using the shaft alone will cause the tap to fall out and likely chip when it hits the floor. To solve this problem, tighten the tapping wrench by using a nail or a scrap steel rod. Do not use a small drill unless it is a discard because the drill will get bent. See Figure 5-49.

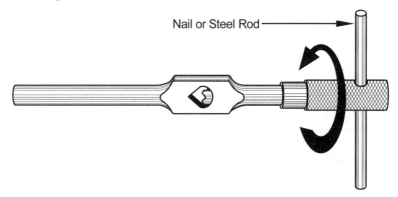

Figure 5-49. Tighten a straight-handled tap wrench with
a nail or steel rod though the handle hole.

Tapping Small Screw Threads

Because the threads in small-diameter holes are just a few thousandths of an inch high, and a drilled tapping hole may have considerable variance in diameter, reaming the tap hole to size before tapping insures that the hole is not too large to develop full-depth threads. Here are the steps to tap small screw threads:

1. Determine the hole size required from *Machinery's Handbook* or other machining tables.
2. Select a drill 3–6 thousandths of an inch *under* the final hole size needed prior to tapping.
3. Center drill the hole location.
4. Drill the "starter" hole.
5. Ream the hole to final size for tapping. This procedure eliminates the scoring that drills and their chips make on the hole walls when drilling and when withdrawing the drill. These scoring marks pose a problem when tapping fine or extra fine threads.

6. Do the first tapping pass with a starter tap.

7. Finish the threads with a finishing tap. This insures that chips from the initial threading do not damage the final threads.

Tapping Blocks

Tapping blocks are guides that greatly reduce the chances of snapping off a tap and insure that the tap enters the work on axis. As shown in Figure 5-50, they may be shop-made or commercially-made.

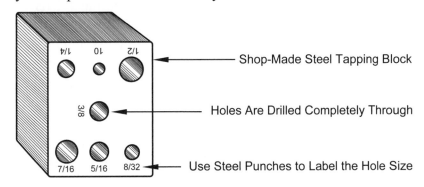

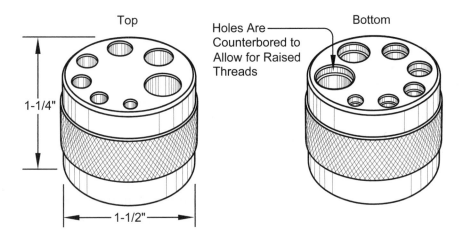

Figure 5-50. Tapping blocks: shop-made (top) and commercially-made (bottom).

Section VIII – Tapping Projects

Shop-Made Precision Tap Guide

Using the shop-made precision tap guide shown in Figure 5-51 will insure better tapping results. This is because the Morse taper in a lathe tailstock or in an R8 collet in a milling machine spindle holds the shop-made tap guide on the machine axis. This does three things:

- Forces taps to enter the work on axis, so the threads are coaxial.
- Prevents taps from being broken.
- Allows taps to be used with either hand or machine power.

To make the precision tap guide in Figure 5-51, start with a standard T-wrench. Here is how to modify the wrench to make the tap guide:

1. Remove the original T-wrench handle cross rod.

2. Drill a new through-hole in the T-wrench closer to the T-wrench chuck. This moves the handle cross rod out of the way of the new guide shaft.

3. Take the T-wrench chuck apart, then drill and tap an axial hole into the bottom of the chuck cavity for a set screw to secure the handle cross rod in its new location. This hole and set screw are only visible when looking into the chuck.

4. With the T-wrench chuck still disassembled, place the T-wrench body into a lathe chuck with access to the back end of the T-wrench body. Center drill, drill and ream the T-wrench body to fit a guide shaft which will extend from the back of the T-wrench. About ¾ inch of the guide shaft fits inside the T-wrench and 2½ inches projects beyond the T-wrench. The guide shaft may be O-1 drill rod or CRS. If using drill rod, there is no need to harden the guide shaft.

5. Place the Morse taper drill chuck arbor in the lathe tailstock and put a drill chuck in the lathe spindle. Then, center drill, drill and ream a hole in the center of the MT in the tailstock to accept the guide shaft for the modified T-wrench. Size the hole so the guide shaft slides smoothly in and out of the Morse taper.

6. Center drill, drill and tap a hole for a small set screw to hold the guide shaft in place.

7. To assemble the modified T-wrench, insert the handle cross rod and insert the set screw in the back of the chuck to hold the handle in place. Then, insert the guide shaft and tighten its set screw. Your precision tap guide is now ready for use.

If using machine power, when the tap reaches full depth, let go of the T-wrench handle and stop the machine. Letting go of the handle causes the T-wrench to stop tapping. Very low speeds should be used for power tapping.

No modification of the R8 collet is necessary to use this tapping guide in a mill. Just choose a collet that matches the size of the guide shaft. Do not pull the collet tight with the mill drawbar because the T-wrench shaft must be free to slide in and out of the collet.

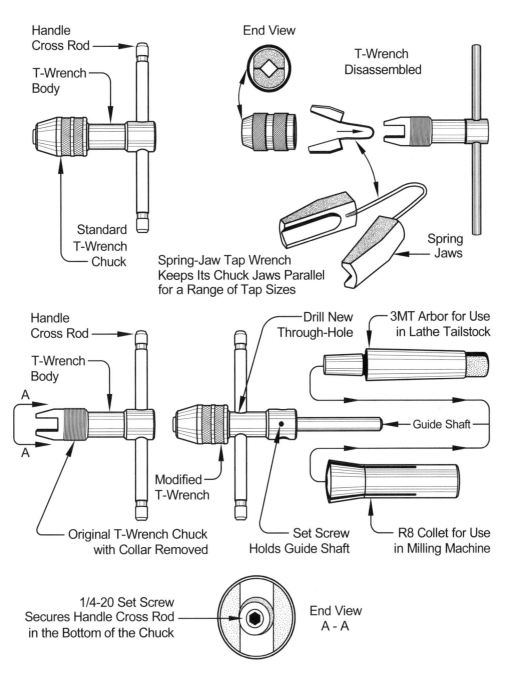

Handle
Cross Rod

T-Wrench
Body

Standard
T-Wrench
Chuck

End View

T-Wrench
Disassembled

Spring
Jaws

Spring-Jaw Tap Wrench
Keeps Its Chuck Jaws Parallel
for a Range of Tap Sizes

Handle
Cross Rod

T-Wrench
Body

A

A

Original T-Wrench Chuck
with Collar Removed

Modified
T-Wrench

Drill New
Through-Hole

3MT Arbor for Use
in Lathe Tailstock

Guide Shaft

Set Screw
Holds Guide Shaft

R8 Collet for Use
in Milling Machine

1/4-20 Set Screw
Secures Handle Cross Rod
in the Bottom of the Chuck

End View
A - A

Figure 5-51. A standard T-wrench modified into a shop-made precision tap guide.

Tap Extensions

Tap extensions are necessary when tapping gears and pulleys that have diameters that are too large for regular length taps to reach their hubs. Here are the steps to make the tap extension shown in Figure 5-52.

1. Drill one end of a CRS round. Select a drill diameter that best fits the diameter of your tap.

2. Mill a though slot in the CRS round for the square shank of the tap.

3. Slip the tap into the milled slot where the square shank locks in place.

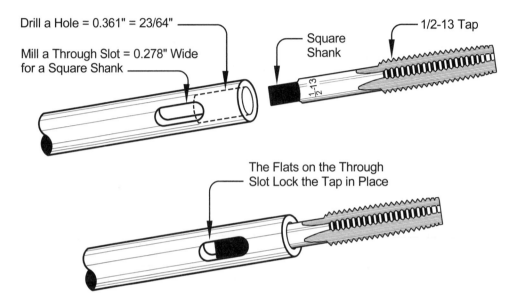

Figure 5-52. A center-drilled hole and milled slot in a CRS round make a simple but effective tap extension.

Chapter 6

Bandsaws

Nine tenths of education is encouragement.

—Anatole France

Section I – Vertical Bandsaws

Introduction

The *vertical metal-cutting bandsaw* or *contour saw*, shown in Figure 6-1, is the most common bandsaw design. Although this saw can perform cutoff operations on raw metal stock, its real value is in removing large amounts of metal quickly.

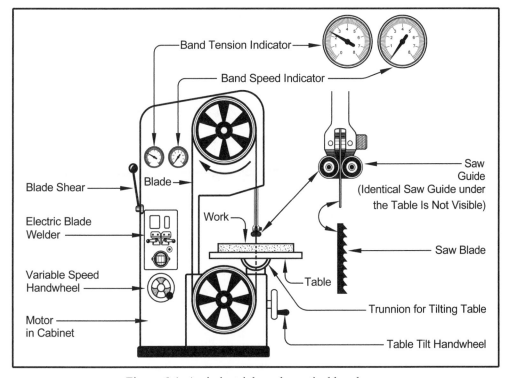

Figure 6-1. An industrial-grade vertical bandsaw.

Vertical bandsaws have a continuous, endless blade called a *band*, which is tensioned on two or three wheels. Bands are made by electrically welding or silver brazing a strip of steel-toothed blade material end-to-end. The most common blade is 0.035-inches thick and can be broken and rejoined to cut out internal sections of a workpiece as in Figure 6-2. A typical industrial-grade bandsaw has an integral electric band welder to do the rejoining. Although a new bandsaw blade has one splice, older used blades often have several splices from being broken and rejoined for multiple interior cuts.

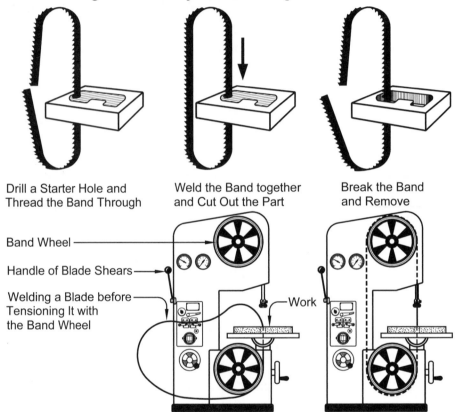

| Drill a Starter Hole and Thread the Band Through | Weld the Band together and Cut Out the Part | Break the Band and Remove |

Figure 6-2. Cutting out an internal section in a workpiece (top).
When cutting out an internal section, the band passes through the work, the saw table and around the lower band wheel during the splicing operation (bottom).

Functions

There are three different types of cutting that vertical bandsaws can perform:

- Cutting out parts from raw stock, also called *band machining*.

- Removing excess workpiece material *before* performing other, more precise machining operations. This eliminates the need to spend machining time and energy turning large sections of unwanted metal into chips. Often the excess material can be used on other jobs.

- Severing raw stock to length so it can be machined. Although a vertical bandsaw can perform this task, a *horizontal bandsaw* permits long pieces of stock—some up to 20 feet—to be held and handled more easily.

Bandsaw Operations

Figure 6-3 shows some of the different types of cuts bandsaws can make. On many parts, where dimensions are less critical, bandsaws can do nearly all the machining required. On parts with tighter dimensional tolerances, bandsaws can be used for slitting, and the rest of the machining done on mills or lathes.

Slitting is often done on the bandsaw instead of using a slitting saw because of the bandsaw's greater speed and lower cost. Also, bandsaw blades cost less to remove the same volume of metal as slitting saws, which have relatively short lives and are not easily resharpened. In addition, bandsaw blades last longer because they distribute wear over many more teeth than a slitting saw.

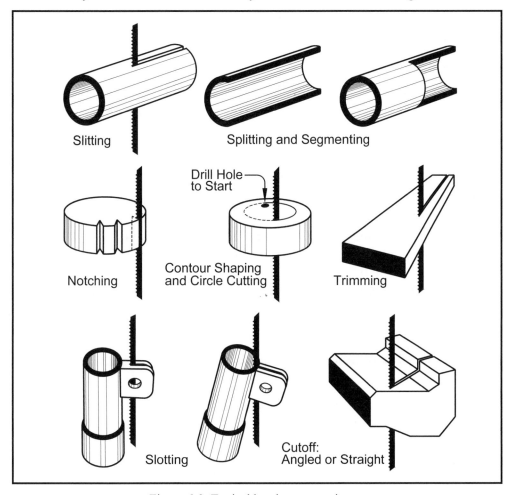

Figure 6-3. Typical bandsaw operations.

Contour Bandsawing Procedure

Here are the steps to use a vertical bandsaw:

1. Check the workpiece material to make sure it is smooth on its bottom so when the cut is made it is square with the work. Stone, grind or file away any projections.

2. Lay out the part shape using layout fluid and a scriber. Then prick punch on top of the scribe lines to insure the cutting lines remain visible.

3. If the part is complex, plan a sequence of cuts which allows the most secure part holding.

4. Select the saw blade to match the work, taking into consideration:

   - *Tooth pattern* – See page 193.

   - *Width* – See pages 192 and 193.

   - *Gage* or *blade thickness* – See pages 192 and 193.

   - *Tooth set* – See page 194.

   - *Rake angle* – See pages 194 and 195.

   - *Blade material* – See page 195.

   - *Pitch* or *teeth per inch (TPI)* – See pages 195 and 196.

5. Mount the proper saw blade and guides on the machine.

6. If an interior section of the part is to be removed, drill an access hole for the band in the part, thread the saw blade through the hole, and then splice together the blade ends.

7. Set the blade speed for the workpiece material. Many bandsaws have recommended blade speeds for common materials listed on or inside their covers. *Machinery's Handbook* also lists this data for virtually all materials you are likely to cut.

8. Place the work on the saw table and position the upper saw guide to clear the work by ¼-inch.

9. Secure the work against a piece of wood or in a *work holder*.

10. Turn on the lubrication system, mister or compressed air, if present.

11. Turn on the saw.

12. Gradually bring the work up to the saw blade and, following the layout lines, begin the cut.

Bandsawing Techniques

- If the workpiece is small, use a work holder, which is a really big clamp that will keep your fingers away from the blade while giving you better control of the work. To see a shop-made work holder, go to Section III of this chapter, pages 213 and 214.

- For easier and faster cutting, lubricate the blade with something like Castrol Stick Wax. To use this product, hold the stick lubricant against each side of the saw blade while the saw is running.

- When making a cut and then entering a hole, reduce the cutting pressure on the work or you will not only enter the hole, you will skip across the hole space and damage the opposite side of the hole with the saw blade.

- Never go back into an existing bandsaw cut with a new blade—rotate the work 180 degrees and start a new cut. This is necessary because the new blade is likely to be wider than the original blade, which has been worn narrower with use. The existing kerf will tend to squeeze the new blade teeth, damaging their sharp edges rather than letting them cut.

- Bandsaw blades dulled on steel will still cut aluminum, wood and plastics.

- Use either a toolmakers' grinding vise or a drill press vise to hold small parts while cutting. This will keep your fingers farther away from the blade and provide better control of the part. See Figure 6-4.

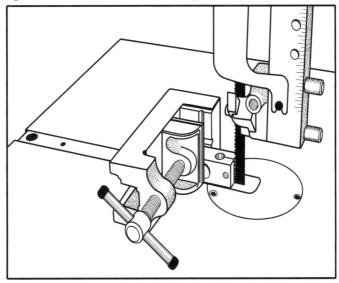

Figure 6-4. A toolmakers' grinding vise is helpful in holding small parts in the bandsaw.

- When a series of cuts is needed along cylindrical stock, use a lathe tool bit to make light rings, or stabs, to locate the cuts. The carriage dial calibrations can accurately space the stab marks.

- Drill holes through the work where there are abrupt changes of direction. Holes permit the work to be rotated and allow the blade to be positioned along the new line of cut.

- When storing blades for long periods of time, it's a good idea to spray them with a rust preventive. This usually isn't necessary for new blades because most new blades are coated at the factory before they are shipped.

- Be careful when handling your blades. The fastest way to cut short a blade's life is to drop it on a cement floor.

The Parts of a Bandsaw Blade

Bandsaw blades are more complicated than they look as evidenced by their many parts shown in Figure 6-5.

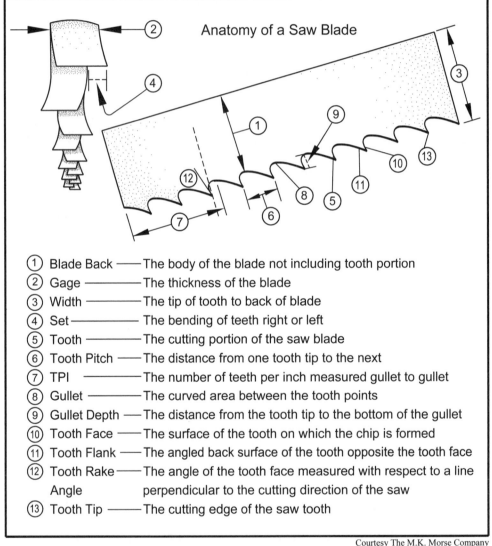

Anatomy of a Saw Blade

① Blade Back ——— The body of the blade not including tooth portion
② Gage ——————— The thickness of the blade
③ Width ——————— The tip of tooth to back of blade
④ Set —————————— The bending of teeth right or left
⑤ Tooth ——————— The cutting portion of the saw blade
⑥ Tooth Pitch ——— The distance from one tooth tip to the next
⑦ TPI ——————————— The number of teeth per inch measured gullet to gullet
⑧ Gullet ——————— The curved area between the tooth points
⑨ Gullet Depth ——— The distance from the tooth tip to the bottom of the gullet
⑩ Tooth Face ——— The surface of the tooth on which the chip is formed
⑪ Tooth Flank ——— The angled back surface of the tooth opposite the tooth face
⑫ Tooth Rake ——— The angle of the tooth face measured with respect to a line
   Angle   perpendicular to the cutting direction of the saw
⑬ Tooth Tip ——— The cutting edge of the saw tooth

Figure 6-5. Anatomy of a bandsaw blade.

Blade Gage

There are five common blade gages, or thicknesses: 0.025-, 0.035-, 0.042-, 0.050- and 0.063-inches. The 0.035-inch gage is used for most blades of 1-inch or less in width and is by far the most common gage. The thinnest gage, 0.025 inches, is chosen when small radii must be cut. In general, the smaller gages are used for the best flex life when operating with small band wheels. Larger gages are used on blades of 1¼- to 3-inches wide for straight cuts under heavy feed force, and are usually only seen in industrial settings.

Blade Tooth Patterns

Figure 6-6 shows the four common bandsaw blade tooth patterns.

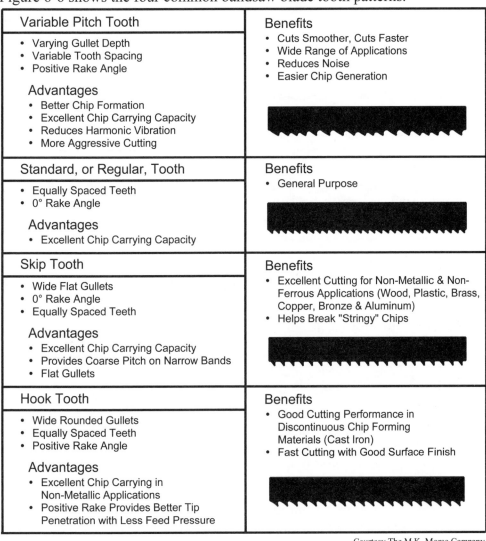

Variable Pitch Tooth	Benefits
• Varying Gullet Depth • Variable Tooth Spacing • Positive Rake Angle **Advantages** • Better Chip Formation • Excellent Chip Carrying Capacity • Reduces Harmonic Vibration • More Aggressive Cutting	• Cuts Smoother, Cuts Faster • Wide Range of Applications • Reduces Noise • Easier Chip Generation
Standard, or Regular, Tooth	Benefits
• Equally Spaced Teeth • 0° Rake Angle **Advantages** • Excellent Chip Carrying Capacity	• General Purpose
Skip Tooth	Benefits
• Wide Flat Gullets • 0° Rake Angle • Equally Spaced Teeth **Advantages** • Excellent Chip Carrying Capacity • Provides Coarse Pitch on Narrow Bands • Flat Gullets	• Excellent Cutting for Non-Metallic & Non-Ferrous Applications (Wood, Plastic, Brass, Copper, Bronze & Aluminum) • Helps Break "Stringy" Chips
Hook Tooth	Benefits
• Wide Rounded Gullets • Equally Spaced Teeth • Positive Rake Angle **Advantages** • Excellent Chip Carrying in Non-Metallic Applications • Positive Rake Provides Better Tip Penetration with Less Feed Pressure	• Good Cutting Performance in Discontinuous Chip Forming Materials (Cast Iron) • Fast Cutting with Good Surface Finish

Courtesy The M.K. Morse Company

Figure 6-6. Common bandsaw blade tooth patterns.

Blade Tooth Set

Bandsaw blade tooth set is the amount that a blade's teeth are offset from either side of the blade center. Blade tooth set widens the saw kerf to provide clearance so that the back of the blade does not rub on the work. Although there are many blade set designs, *raker set* is the most common. *Wavy set* is used when the cross section of the workpiece changes, such as with structural steel and pipe. *Alternate* or *Straight set* works well for non-ferrous castings, thin sheet metal, tubing and some plastics. See Figure 6-7.

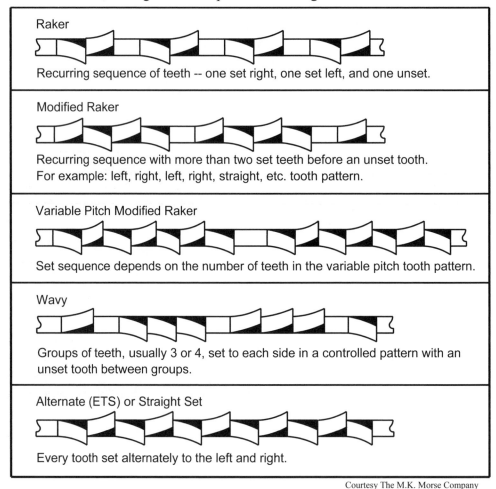

Raker

Recurring sequence of teeth -- one set right, one set left, and one unset.

Modified Raker

Recurring sequence with more than two set teeth before an unset tooth.
For example: left, right, left, right, straight, etc. tooth pattern.

Variable Pitch Modified Raker

Set sequence depends on the number of teeth in the variable pitch tooth pattern.

Wavy

Groups of teeth, usually 3 or 4, set to each side in a controlled pattern with an unset tooth between groups.

Alternate (ETS) or Straight Set

Every tooth set alternately to the left and right.

Courtesy The M.K. Morse Company

Figure 6-7. Common, or standard, blade tooth set patterns.

Rake Angle

Rake angle is a measure of the tooth face inclination to the work. Bandsaw blade rake angles are either neutral or positive. Choose a standard, or *neutral rake angle,* for most work narrower than 2 inches and a hook, or *positive rake angle*, for wider, tougher-to-penetrate work. See Figure 6-8.

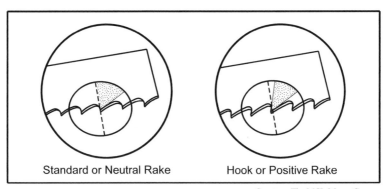

Figure 6-8. Neutral and positive bandsaw blade rake angles.

Blade Metal

- *Carbon steel* is for the easiest-to-cut materials: non-metals, including wood, plastic and rubber, and non-ferrous metals, including aluminum, copper, brass and free-machining steel. Carbon steel blades are the least expensive, but they have a shorter life than other types of blades.

- *Bi-metal* is an all-purpose blade with an M42 HSS cutting edge that is welded to a spring steel back. Bi-metal blades cut a wide range of materials and shapes. They have the highest initial cost, but they also have a longer life, up to ten times longer than carbon steel. They can be tensioned higher than carbon steel blades and so produce straighter cuts. These blades are the most cost effective for cutting steel pipe and tubing with welded seams. Weld-seam metal becomes hardened with the absorption of carbon and rapid cooling, making it exceptionally hard.

- *Carbide edge* blades are similar to bi-metal blades, but have tungsten carbide teeth welded to a spring steel back. These blades have greater wear and high-temperature resistance than carbon steel and bi-metal blades. They are normally used on cobalt, nickel and titanium alloys as well as aluminum castings and fiberglass.

- *Carbide grit* and *diamond edge* blades cut materials that other blades cannot, including reinforced plastics, some cast irons and tool steels.

Selecting Blade Tooth/Inch (TPI)

In general, a minimum of three saw teeth must be on the work: one entering, one cutting and one leaving. When the blade has too many small teeth for the size of the workpiece, the tooth gullets rapidly clog with chips. This drags the tooth tips through the work, wearing and overheating them while not allowing them to cut. Use Figure 6-9 to select the proper blade TPI by finding the material dimension in the left-hand column and then moving right to find the tooth count.

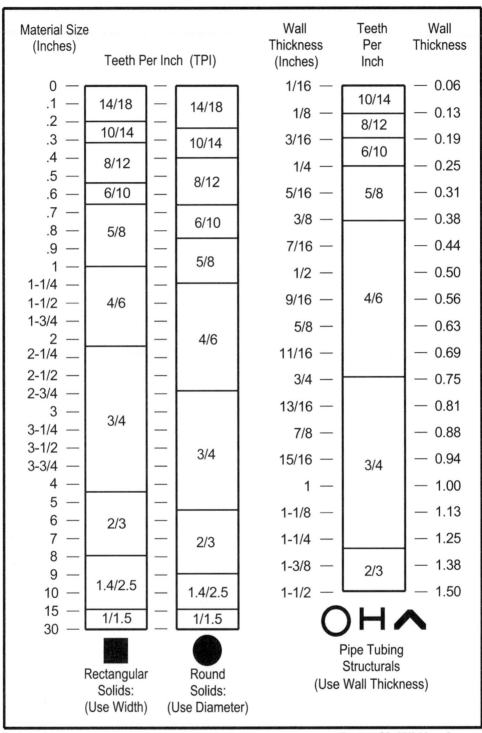

Courtesy of the M.K. Morse Company

Figure 6-9. Blade selection chart.

Bandsaw Minimum Radius

Figure 6-10 shows that the smaller the bandsaw blade width, the smaller the radius it can cut in the workpiece. A tradeoff must be made between blade stiffness to resist lateral forces and the ability to make a tight turn.

Minimum Radius per Blade Width		
Blade Width	Minimum Radius	Material Thickness 1"
1"	7-1/4"	
3/4"	5-7/16"	
5/8"	3-3/4"	
1/2"	2-1/2"	
3/8"	1-1/4"	
1/4"	5/8"	
3/16"	3/8"	
1/8"	7/32"	

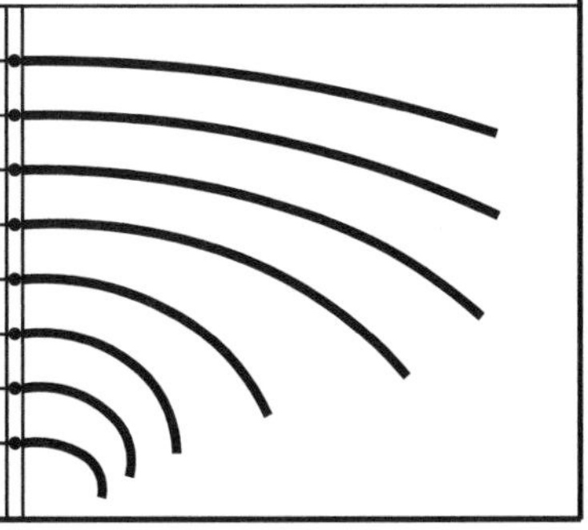

Courtesy of the M.K. Morse Company

Figure 6-10. Minimum bandsaw blade radius vs. bandsaw blade width.

Blade Tension

Bandsaw blades must be under enough tension to prevent them from deflecting under cutting forces. Many large industrial-grade bandsaws have built-in tension meters. Satisfactory tension on many bandsaw blades is in the 15,000–30,000 psi range, so a ½-inch 0.035-inch thick blade would be under 260–520 pounds of tension, respectively. Not only are bandsaw frames constructed to easily handle these forces, so are the steel bandsaw blades and the two methods of joining them: electric welding and silver brazing.

Breaking In Blades

Regardless of manufacturer, all bandsaw blades must be *broken-in*. When new, the teeth are just too sharp and cutting at full rate—or pressure—will cause fracturing of the feather edges leading to premature blade failure. Breaking in a bandsaw blade wears off these ultra sharp edges and allows the blade to retain its cutting ability longer. Each blade maker has its own procedure, but they all have these general steps:

1. Maintain the proper blade speed for the work material.

2. Reduce feed pressure or feed rate by 50% for the first 50–100 square inches of material cut.

3. After the break-in period, gradually increase the feed pressure, or feed rate, to full pressure or rate. If you are unsure what the normal feed pressure is, start light, and increase the feed pressure until good curly chips start to form.

When the Blade Stalls in Aluminum

When a bandsaw stalls while sawing aluminum there are the four possible causes:

- Tooth count is wrong, usually too high, allowing chips to clog the teeth.
- Bandsaw slot has closed up and pinched the blade. This is caused by residual stresses in the workpiece metal and may require that the kerf be kept open with a wedge.
- Saw set is inadequate and does not provide a wide enough saw kerf.
- Work moved in the vise.

Trouble Shooting Tips

Here are a couple of bandsawing guidelines you should follow:

- Listen to the machine. Squealing or grinding sounds often are indications of over feeding and blade strain.
- Inspect the chips. Typically, chips should be brightly colored, not blue or brown. Chips should have some mass to them, be moderately or tightly curled, and never be of a powdery consistency. See the chip form chart in Figure 6-11.

Figure 6-12 shows many other bandsawing problems and their solutions.

Chip Form	Chip Condition	Chip Color	Blade Speed	Blade Feed	Other
 (symbol)	Thick, Hard and Short	Blue or Brown	Decrease	Decrease	Check Cutting Fluid and Mix
 (symbol)	Thin and Curled	Silver	Suitable	Suitable	
 (symbol)	Powder	Silver	Decrease	Increase	
 (symbol)	Thin and Curl Tight	Silver	Suitable	Decrease	Check Tooth Pitch

Figure 6-11. Examining chips to check proper bandsaw blade speed and feed.

Problem	Cause	Solution
 Premature Blade Breakage Straight Break Indicates Fatigue	• Incorrect blade—teeth too coarse • Blade tension too high • Side guides too tight • Damaged or misadjusted blade guides • Excessive feed • Incorrect cutting fluid • Wheel diameter too small for blade • Blade rubbing on wheel flanges • Teeth in contact with work before starting saw • Incorrect blade speed	• Use finer tooth pitch • Reduce blade tension • Check side guide clearance • Check all guides for alignment • Reduce feed pressure • Check coolant • Use thinner blade • Adjust wheel alignment • Allow ½" clearance before starting cut • Increase/decrease blade speed
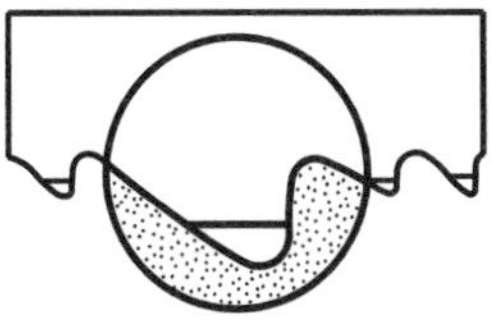 Premature Dulling of Teeth	• Teeth pointing in wrong direction • Improper or no blade break-in • Hard spots in material • Material work hardened • Improper coolant • Improper coolant concentration • Speed too high • Feed too light • Teeth too small	• Install blade correctly. • Break in the blade properly • Check for hardness or hard spots • Increase feed pressure • Check coolant type • Check coolant mixture • Check recommended blade speed • Increase feed pressure • Increase tooth size
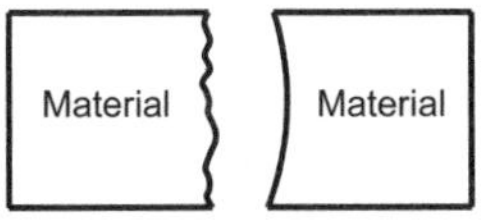 Material { } Material Inaccurate Cut	• Tooth set damage • Excessive feed pressure • Improper tooth size • Cutting fluid not applied evenly • Guides worn or loose • Insufficient blade tension	• Check for worn set on side of blade • Reduce feed pressure • Check tooth size chart • Check coolant nozzles • Tighten or replace guides • Adjust to recommended tension
Band Leading In Cut 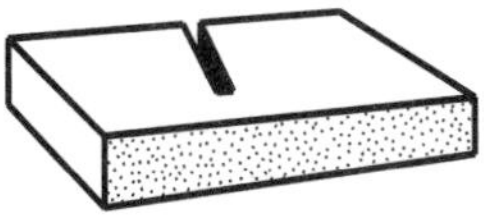	• Over feed • Insufficient blade tension • Tooth set damage • Guide arms loose/ set too far apart • Teeth too small	• Reduce feed force • Adjust recommended tension • Check material for hard inclusions • Position arms close to work as possible • Increase tooth size
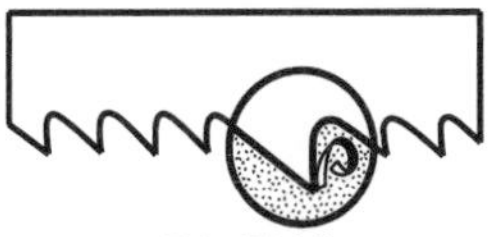 Chip Welding	• Insufficient coolant flow • Wrong coolant concentration • Excessive feed and/or pressure • Tooth size too small	• Check coolant level and flow • Check coolant ration • Reduce speed and/or pressure • Use coarser tooth pitch
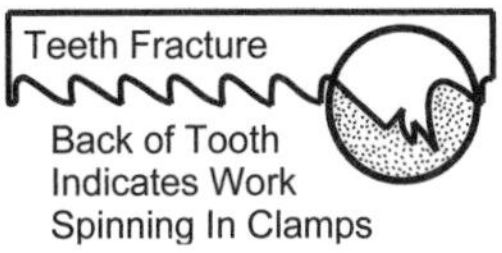 Teeth Fracture Back of Tooth Indicates Work Spinning In Clamps	• Incorrect speed and/or feed • Incorrect blade pitch • Saw guides not adjusted properly • Chip brush not working • Work spinning or moving in vise	• Check cutting chart • Check tooth size chart • Adjust and replace saw guides • Repair or replace chip brush • Check bundle configuration/adjust vise pressure
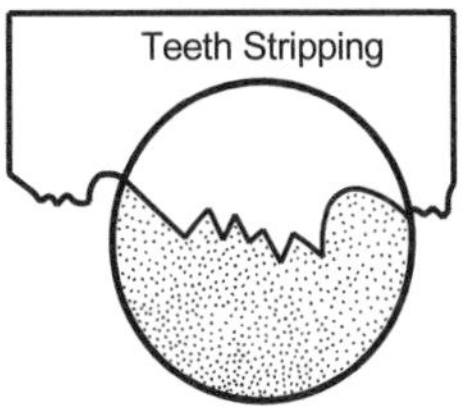 Teeth Stripping	• Feed pressure too high • Tooth stuck in cut • Improper or insufficient coolant • Incorrect tooth size • Hard spots in material • Work spinning in vise • Blade teeth running backwards	• Reduce feed pressure • Do not enter old cut with a new blade • Check coolant flow and concentration • Check tooth size chart • Check material for hard inclusions • Check clamping pressure • Reverse blade (turn inside out)

Courtesy of the M.K. Morse Company

Figure 6-12. Bandsaw blade troubleshooting.

Problem	Cause	Solution
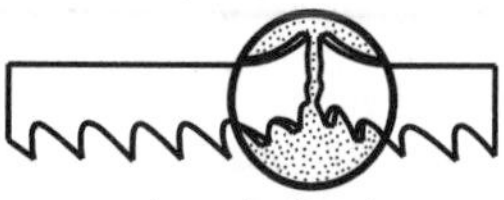 Irregular Break Indicates Material Movement	• Indexing out of sequence • Material loose in vise	• Check proper machine movement • Check vise or clamp
Wear on Back of Blades 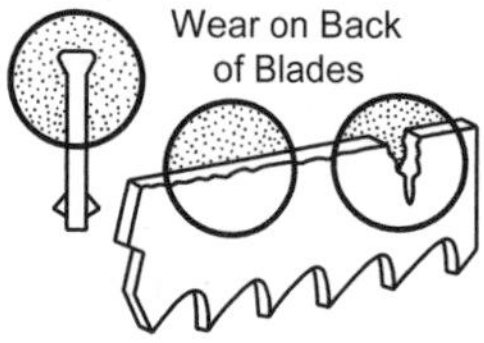	• Excessive feed pressure • Insufficient blade tension • Back-up guide roll frozen, or damaged • Blade rubbing on wheel flange	• Decrease feed pressure • Increase blade tension and readjust guides • Repair or replace back-up roll or guide • Adjust wheel cant
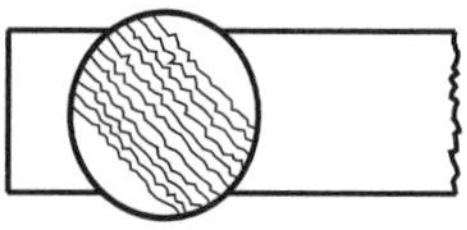 Rough Cut Washboard Surface Vibration and/or Chatter	• Dull or damaged blade • Incorrect speed or feed • Insufficient blade support • Incorrect tooth pitch • Insufficient coolant	• Replace with new blade • Increase speed or decrease feed • Move guide arms as close as possible to the work • Use finer pitch blade • Check coolant flow
Wear Lines, Loss of Set 	• Saw guide insert or wheel flange are riding on teeth • Insufficient blade tension • Hard spots in material • Back-up guide worn	• Check machine manual for correct blade width • Tension blade properly • Check material for inclusions • Replace guide
Twisted Blade Profile Sawing 	• Blade binding in cut • Side guides too tight • Radius too small for blade width • Work not firmly held • Erratic coolant flow • Excessive blade tension	• Decrease feed pressure • Adjust side guide gap • User narrower blade • Check clamping pressure • Check coolant nozzles • Decrease blade tension
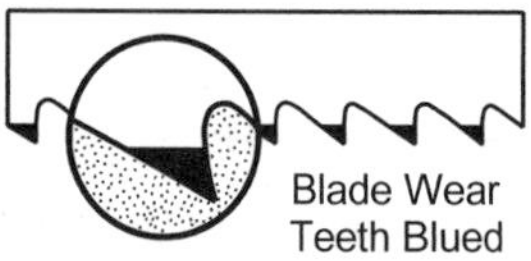 Blade Wear Teeth Blued	• Incorrect blade • Incorrect feed or speed • Improper or insufficient coolant	• Use Coarser tooth pitch • Increase feed or decrease speed • Check coolant flow

Courtesy of the M.K. Morse Company

Figure 6-12. (continued) Bandsaw blade troubleshooting.

Blade Splicing Methods

There are two methods for splicing bandsaw blades: *electric welding* and *silver brazing*. Each method has its advantages:

• Welding is much faster than silver brazing, but requires an electric welder. Once the welding/annealing cycle is determined for a particular blade metal, relatively little skill or technique is needed for good splices.

- Silver brazing requires an oxyacetylene torch, flux, silver braze filler metal and a brazing fixture. Although the process does not vary with the blade metal or manufacturer, there is a technique to getting a sound silver braze joint.

Blade Welding Procedure

Bandsaw blade welding is complicated by differences in the blade steel metallurgy and the annealing requirements. Blade annealing varies not only with manufacturer and type of blade—carbon steel, molybdenum HSS steel or bi-metal—but between blade widths. Once a satisfactory annealing cycle for a particular blade material has been found after experimentation, an experienced machinist will make note of the cycle on the blade box for the next time this blade material is welded.

Here are the steps for blade welding:

1. Wear heavy-duty leather gloves when handling bandsaw blades, particularly the wider blades. The wider and thicker the blade, the greater the need for gloves.

2. If the blade has been welded before, trim about ¼ inch from each end of the blade. Use a blade shear, usually found on bandsaws which have electric welders, or use an abrasive cutoff wheel.

3. As in Figure 6-13 (top), lay up the two bandsaw blade ends so the teeth of each blade end point in opposite directions, then adjust the blades so their ends are even, as in Figure 6-13 (middle). Be sure to align the blade edges parallel. This alignment method insures that even if the blade ends are not exactly square, they will fit snugly in the welder when butted together.

4. With the blades held as in Figure 6-13 (middle), grind the ends square using the grinding wheel on the electric welder. Unlike the typical pedestal or bench grinder, these grinding wheels grind on the *sides* of their wheels as well as their edges. Rest the blades on the metal shroud around the grinding wheel and feed the blades into the grinding wheel. Be sure that the trimmed edges are ground so that they both end at a gullet, not at a point. Remove all burrs, then using emery cloth, lightly clean the side face of each blade down to fresh metal for ¼ inch from their ends. With acetone or alcohol, remove all dirt, grease, coatings and oil.

5. For the following steps refer also to Figures 6-14 and 6-15. Turn the *pressure knob,* sometimes known as the *blade infeed,* to zero. This setting determines the spring force applied between the bandsaw blade ends during the welding cycle. This spring force is applied to one of the electrodes which is moveable—usually the right-hand electrode. This forces one blade end into the other during the welding process.

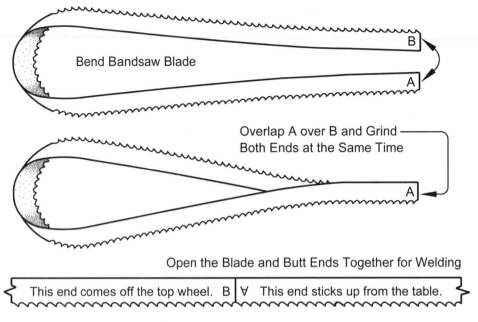

Figure 6-13. Bandsaw blade ends aligned and folded (top), ready for grinding (middle), and the blade untwisted with the ends aligned for welding (bottom).

6. Loosen the right- and left-hand *electrode clamps*.

7. Place the *A* end of the saw blade under the right-hand electrode. Make sure the blade is aligned squarely and the teeth are facing back towards you, then tighten the right-hand blade clamp to secure the blade in place. The saw blade end should protrude about ¼ inch out of the clamp, halfway into the space between the two electrodes.

8. Place the *B* end of the saw blade under the left electrode. Make sure that the blade is aligned squarely, its teeth are facing back towards you, and the ends of both blades meet each other. Tighten the left-hand blade clamp to secure the blade in place. Putting the *A* and *B* ends of the band in the right and left electrodes, respectively, is only important if the band has been left threaded through the bandsaw table—and sometimes through the workpiece starting hole, too.

9. Set the *pressure knob* for the appropriate blade width. Wider blades need more pressure between their ends during welding, while narrower blades require less pressure.

10. Perform the weld by pushing down the *weld switch lever* to turn on the welding electricity between the electrodes and apply the spring force between the blade ends. After the ends of the blade meet and fuse, and about $^3/_{16}$ of an inch on each side of the weld becomes red, release the weld lever. This entire process takes only 1–2 seconds, depending on the blade

width and the type of metal. Other blade welders have a push button that starts the welding cycle. Typical blade welders on bandsaws do not have an automatic welding cycle and require the operator to watch carefully and release the weld lever or button after the weld is completed.

11. Allow the weld to cool for 3–5 minutes.

12. Because bandsaw blades are made of O-1 air-hardening steel, welding makes the weld area steel hard and brittle so the weld must be annealed so it properly flexes in the bandsaw. To do this, open one of the electrode clamps to release the spring compression pressure on the weld and retighten this electrode clamp in preparation for the application of annealing heat.

13. Gradually heat the weld by pushing the *anneal button* until the weld turns cherry red—not orange or yellow. A typical ½-inch blade requires 4–5 button pushes to reach red heat over 2–3 seconds, then another 4–6 button pushes at ¾-second intervals to anneal the weld zone. Cool the weld slowly by lengthening the time interval between pushes to the anneal button. You may need to shield the weld from ambient light to better see its color during annealing. (Some blades require two annealing cycles.)

14. Let the saw blade cool for 3–5 minutes, then remove it from the welder.

15. Use the top edge of the small grinding wheel on the side of the bandsaw to remove the welding flash from the bottom of the weld, and use the bottom edge of the grinding wheel to remove the flash from the top side of the weld. Using both the top and bottom of this grinding wheel avoids the need to flip the blade over to grind its other side. See Figure 6-15.

16. Slide the weld section through the 0.035-inch gap gage on the bottom of the welder—see the bottom of Figure 6-14—to verify that the blade has been ground to the proper thickness.

17. Test the weld by bending the blade in an 8–10-inch radius.

   - If the blade forms a smooth, continuous arc and does not crack, the weld is good.

   - If the blade bends into a V-shape at the weld, the blade is too soft and is over-annealed. Cut off the bad weld, regrind the band ends, and repeat the welding and the annealing cycle with longer time intervals between pushes to shorten the annealing time.

   - If the blade snaps at the weld, the weld did not cool slowly enough during annealing. Cut off the bad weld, regrind the band ends and repeat the welding and annealing cycle, increasing the annealing time.

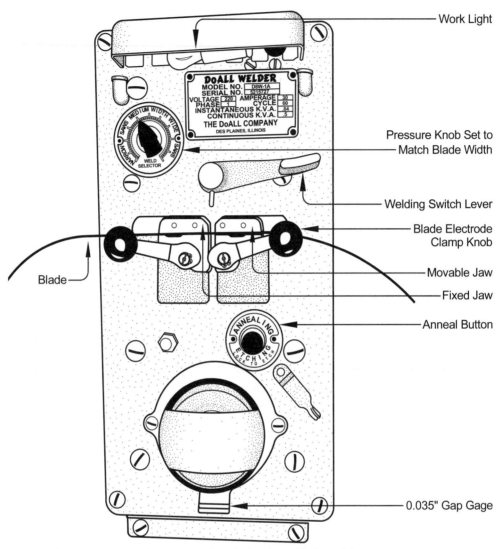

Figure 6-14. Electric bandsaw blade welder.

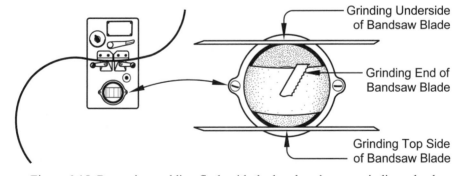

Figure 6-15. Removing welding flash with the bandsaw's own grinding wheel.

Blade Welding Troubleshooting

The proper settings of heat and blade infeed are made initially by experimentation. Here are some welding problems and their likely cures:

- Blades that overlap as they weld do not have enough heat and/or too much infeed.

- A complete blowout at the weld is the result of too much heat.

- Too little pressure causes a partial weld across the blade. This is from not enough infeed.

- More than $\frac{1}{16}$-inch of weld flash on both sides of the blade usually indicates a good weld. Less than $\frac{1}{16}$-inch of flash indicates a little too much infeed, and typically, incomplete welds.

Silver Brazing Procedure for Saw Blades

Here are the materials required to silver braze bandsaw blades:

- An oxyacetylene torch with a #0 tip, regulators, hoses, flint lighter and gas cylinders.

- 0.035 or 0.045-inch diameter silver braze wire containing 45% silver. From some suppliers this wire is available with cadmium, which has better wetting characteristics and a wider fluid temperature range than the braze alloys without cadmium. Using 0.062-inch silver braze filler metal is a poor choice because it is difficult to initiate melting.

- Paste brazing flux for silver brazing of steel.

- Wooden stir sticks for flux application—flux brushes are far too large.

- A shop-made saw blade brazing fixture. See Figures 6-16 and 6-17.

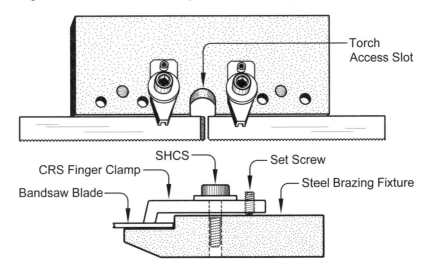

Figure 6-16. A simple shop-made fixture for brazing bandsaw blades.

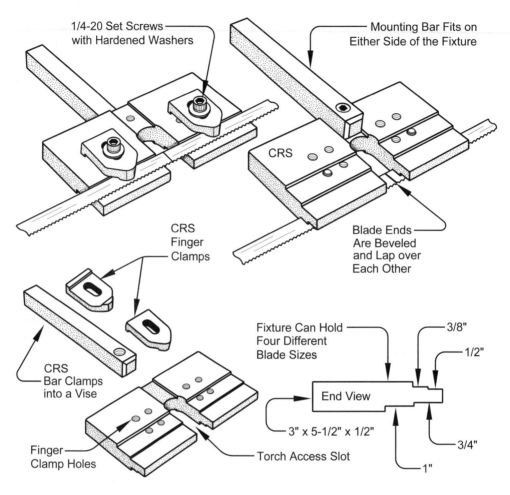

Figure 6-17. A deluxe shop-made silver brazing fixture
which will hold four different widths of bandsaw blades.

Here is the silver brazing procedure for saw blades:

1. If the saw blade has been spliced before, trim the blade ¼ inch away from each side of the previous splice. Lay up the two blade ends so they are parallel and the teeth are on the same side as in Figure 6-18 (left).

2. Using a pedestal, table, disc or belt grinder with an aluminum oxide abrasive, grind the ends of the two blades square. Make sure that the ends stop at a gullet so there are no partial teeth on the blade ends. Then, holding them together, grind a 20° bevel on the blade ends. See Figure 6-18 (middle). By grinding the two blade ends at the same time, when the blades are matched up in a continuous band, the bevels will be identical and the blades will butt up tightly as in Figure 6-18 (right).

3. Remove all burrs from the blade ends and lightly grind the flats of the blades ⅜ inch back from the ends on both sides down to fresh metal.

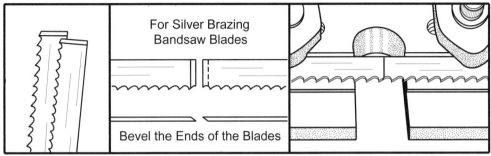

Figure 6-18. Aligning bandsaw blade ends for beveling before silver brazing (left). Ground beveled edges (middle) and blade ends in brazing fixture ready to braze (right).

4. Wipe down the blade ends with acetone or alcohol to remove all grease and oils. Do not touch the cleaned ends with your fingers.

5. Your silver brazing flux should be a paste. If it has dried out, add distilled water and remix it into a paste. Apply the flux in a *thin* layer over the beveled ends of the blade using a thin wooden stir stick. Avoid getting flux on the flats of the blade because this will only put silver braze metal where it is not needed and will have to be removed.

6. Secure the brazing fixture in a vise so the fixture will not move when pulled on by the weight of the blade ends.

7. Secure the blade ends in the brazing fixture:

    -   If you are splicing the blade *through* a workpiece, make sure you have the teeth running in the correct direction when the work sits flat on the bandsaw table. Also, make sure that the marked cut lines on the work face up when the work is on the saw table.

    -   Face the teeth outward away from the brazing fixture.

    -   Insure the back edge of the blade is snug against the back ledge of the brazing fixture.

    -   When the blades are butted, the upper beveled blade should exert a little force on the lower beveled blade. The two bevels should join evenly.

8. Cut off about 10–12 inches of silver brazing wire and straighten it.

9. Light the oxyacetylene torch and adjust it for a neutral flame, then increase the acetylene slightly for a mildly carburizing flame with a ¾-inch long inner cone. The flame should be neither wispy—likely to go out if the torch is waived back and forth—or hissing. The torch should show a 1½-inch diameter flat heat area when played against a flat plate.

10. In preparation for heating the blade, position the torch upside down inside the torch access slot so the tip of the blue inner cone is level with the bottom of the saw blade.

11. Move the torch up and down each side of the braze line several times. Remember that the torch flame is about 5600°F and the silver braze metal will flow at 1200–1400°F. The blade will come up to the brazing temperature within a few seconds. Note that the silver braze metal's data sheet specifies a melting point of 1100–1200°F, but it will not *flow* until it gets 150–200°F hotter. Melting is of no help here, flow is what is needed.

12. The brazing flux goes through three phases when heated:

    - *White powder* – From the paste it becomes a dry, white powder.

    - *Semi-transparent spheres* – From a white powder it transforms to a series of small semi-transparent spheres.

    - *Glassy coating* – From the spheres it becomes a milky, glass-like coating. When the flux reaches this phase, it has done its work of chemically cleaning the steel's surface to prepare it to accept the silver braze alloy, and the steel is hot enough to melt and flow the alloy on contact. *At this time the silver braze metal should be touched to the joint.*

13. In a second or less, the braze metal will melt and a silver line will appear in the braze joint. Do not apply additional braze metal. The joint is complete. Very little braze metal is actually needed; a ½-inch blade requires only 2–4 *pinheads* of filler metal for a solid joint.

14. Allow the joint to cool for 3–5 minutes and remove the blade. Remember, the brazing fixture will still be hot.

15. A well-made joint has almost no braze metal outside of the joint, but if there is any, remove it by grinding or filing.

Blade Splicing Tips

- Determine the maximum length blade your bandsaw will accept, and make your blade this length. By doing this you will be able to make the maximum number of splices before having to add in a second length of saw blade. Remember, each splice requires two ¼-inch sections of blade to be trimmed around the splice. This can be important if you must break a blade and resplice it through workpieces to saw out island sections.

- Measuring and marking off the length of a saw blade by painting lines on the shop floor eliminates having to repeatedly measure off saw blade stock when welding up new blades. It will also save you some cuts and scars.

Removing Island Material without Breaking Bandsaw Blades

Here is a time-saving shortcut to avoid a bandsaw blade breaking-splicing-breaking cycle to remove an interior island of material. As shown in Figure 6-19, a steel collar $6 \times 6 \times 1$ inches is needed with an interior square opening to fit around 4×4-inch steel tubing. The rounded corners of the collar must match the rounded corners on the tubing. Although this part could be made on a milling machine or by threading a bandsaw blade through an interior hole and cutting out the interior island, there is a faster method. Here's how to make this part:

1. Apply layout fluid, then scribe out the desired opening.
2. To form the corners, drill four holes that match the radius of the interior corners.
3. Starting at the edge of a corner, bandsaw through the side wall of the part and saw out the island.
4. Use TIG or MIG to weld up the saw kerf in the side of the part.
5. Grind the weld flat.

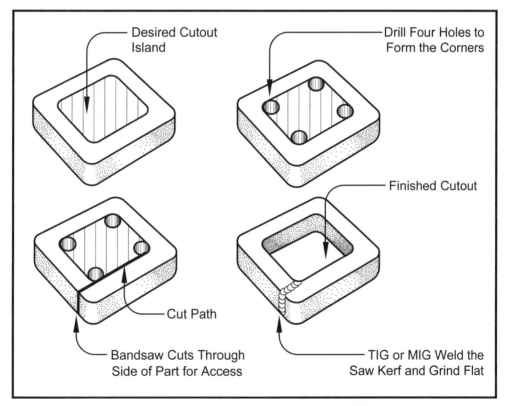

Figure 6-19. Cutting into the island material and then welding up the saw kerf avoids the cycle of breaking and welding bandsaw blades.

Section II – Upgrading a Budget Horizontal/Vertical Bandsaw

Upgrades

Bandsaws of the design shown in Figure 6-20 have been available for the last 40 years from several manufacturers. Many of these machines have been at work for years with only the replacement of bearings, motors and drive gears. These bandsaws are inexpensive and durable, and, in a non-production setting, they are capable of performing thousands of cuts in ferrous and non-ferrous metal quickly and accurately. Although mainly used as cutoff saws for preparing raw metal stock for machining, they can also be used like a vertical bandsaw.

While these budget bandsaws can be put to work straight from the carton, there are several small shop-made improvements which will not only add convenience, but years to the life of the saw.

Below are some of the more useful upgrades:

- *Adding a Tilt Lock* – If the saw is moved with the bandsaw blade positioned horizontally, the blade portion of the saw has a tendency to fly up and snap the 3-inch leg on the U-shaped upper casting. This can be avoided by adding the steel or aluminum block and pin shown in Figure 6-21. This pin arrangement locks the hinged upper casting in either the horizontal or the vertical position, preventing this damage. A satisfactory repair on a snapped leg is usually not possible.

- *Custom Transmission Cover* – The bandsaw transmission contains a speed-reduction worm gear drive. On older saws, this worm drive was lubricated with a smear of grease. But, improving upon the design, newer saws now have an oil-filled transmission. However, because the transmission cover is made of thin sheet metal, it is hard to get an oil-tight seal when the cover is replaced after changing the transmission oil. The best solution is to make a new ¼-inch thick aluminum or steel cover patterned on the original one. Then, replace the original rubber gasket with Permatex Blue RTV Silicone Gasket Maker, which is supplied in a tube. Putting a $\frac{1}{16}$-inch breather hole in the new cover reduces the chance of oil leaks through the shaft seals due to temperature changes. See the insert in Figure 6-20 (top right) for the breather-hole location.

  Caution: Be sure the breather hole is above the oil level or, as stated above, the oil will seep out with temperature changes. Remember that the oil level shifts as the upper arm of the bandsaw is repositioned.

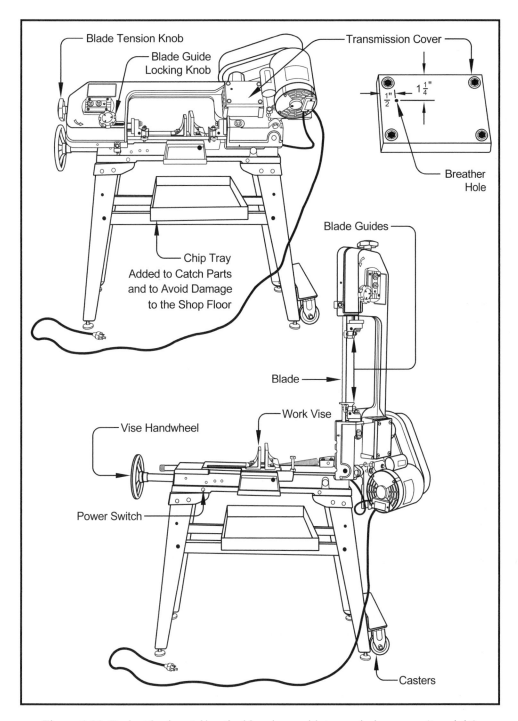

Figure 6-20. Budget horizontal/vertical bandsaw with transmission cover (top right). Note the chip tray which is added to catch chips and small parts.

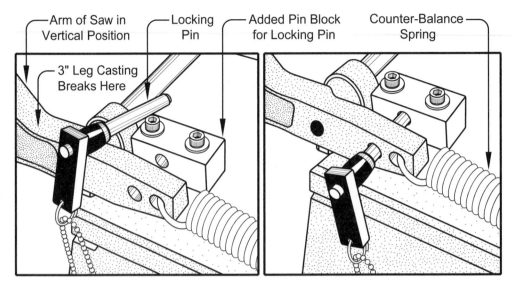

Figure 6-21. Adding a locking pin and block so the 3-inch leg on the upper saw casting does not get snapped off when the saw is moved.

- *Adding Wheels* – Some bandsaw manufacturers furnish their saws with wheels, some do not. See Figure 6-22 for a quick way to add wheels to your saw. Only one set of wheels is needed, and when pop riveted to the motor end of the saw, the unit can be wheeled about like a wheel barrow.

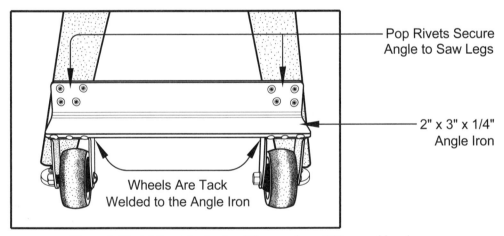

Figure 6-22. Adding wheels simplifies moving a 200-pound bandsaw.

Horizontal or Cutoff Bandsaw Safety

- Do not touch the work after cutting begins; wait until the blade stops moving, then remove the work from the vise.

- Be aware that smaller workpieces means hotter workpieces coming out after sawing. Do not get burned.

- Never re-enter an existing cut; turn the workpiece over and start a new cut on the other side of the work.

- If the blade comes off its drive wheels, stop the saw. Remove the blade and the work together and then open up the saw cut to remove the blade. You may need to wedge the cut open.

- When cutting pipe or tubing, never put your finger *into* the pipe to catch it when the cut is complete. Your finger will also be cut off.

- Do not leave length stops in place while cutting because the cut off end of the work can jam against the length stop as the work falls free.

- When bandsawing a steel part which has been previously flame cut, do not cut into the *recast metal*. This material, which appears along the flame-cut edge, is exceptionally hard and can destroy an expensive bi-metal bandsaw blade in seconds. To avoid this blade damage, grind off about ⅛-inch of the recast steel where the saw will enter the work. This allows the blade access to the work without touching recast metal.

Section III – Work Holding

Making a Bandsaw Work Holder

Most machinists require a work holder, or work guide, like the ones shown in Figures 6-23 and 6-24. Used to hold workpieces, these guides keep fingers away from the blade, yet allow the machinist to apply heavy cutting pressure and guidance to the work. The guide, which holds many different sizes and shapes of work, can be made of steel or aluminum. The welded-on handles can be shop-made or cut from discarded tools. To avoid breaking and resplicing the band, the island metal can be removed using the method in Figure 6-19.

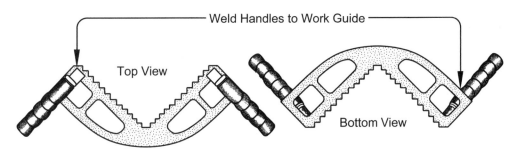

Figure 6-23. Shop-made bandsaw work holder made of aluminum or steel. Islands are cut out to reduce the weight of the holder.

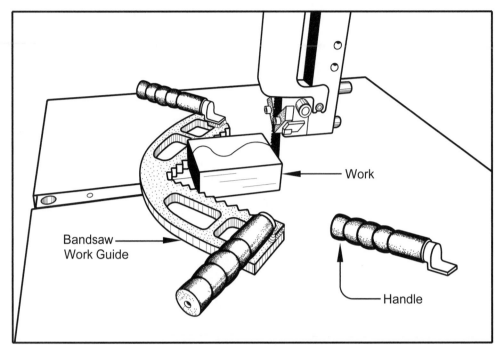

Figure 6-24. Shop-made bandsaw work holder in use. The 90º steps cut
into the V-shaped holding section can grip almost any shaped part.

Chapter 7

Lathes

All great ideas are rejected by 'experts.'

Anon.

Section I – Lathe Design

Lathe Operations

Lathes are the most versatile of all machine tools; they can face, turn, chamfer, neck, taper, drill, bore, ream, spin, file, polish, hone, buff, knurl, cut internal and external threads and cut off work. No other machine tool performs as many operations.

Lathe Construction

- *Castings* – Most lathes use iron castings as their basic structure. Besides providing a rough shape on which to begin machining, castings hold all the other lathe components in position and dampen tool vibrations. Both rigidity and damping affect accuracy, maximum cut depth and chatter tendency. In general, with two lathes of the same swing and bed length dimensions, the one with the larger castings—and greater weight—will perform better, allowing larger cuts before the tendency to chatter. When evaluating a lathe, check its net weight. Heavier is usually better.

- *Pedestals vs. Cabinets* – There are many medium-sized lathes of the same dimensions available in both bench-top and pedestal designs. In most cases, pedestal designs are superior because they weigh more and are more rigid. If the pedestals are castings rather than sheet metal cabinets, they will definitely perform better.

- *Motor Integration* – Many smaller lathes have motors which are *integral* to their castings. That is, the lathe casting actually holds the motor bearings, making it necessary to obtain an exact duplicate motor for a replacement. A much better approach is to have a lathe designed so that when its motor burns out, or the AC power requirements change, the motor can be easily replaced with a standard motor.

- *Gap-Bed Lathes* – With this type of lathe, a section of the lathe bed at the spindle end is removable, as in Figure 7-1. When this bed section is removed, short workpieces with large diameters can be machined. For example, when a 9-inch bed section of a 13 × 40-inch lathe is removed, work as large as 18-inches diameter may be turned. However, there is only about 6½ inches of additional bed freed up because the D1-4 chuck mount extends over the bed. Because of this, work is usually held on faceplates when the gap is removed to provide the maximum usable gap length.

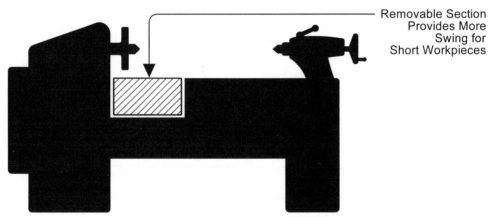

Removable Section
Provides More
Swing for
Short Workpieces

Figure 7-1. Gap-bed lathes provide additional swing, but only for short workpieces. Though handy at times, the removable gap section is easily damaged when it has been removed from the lathe and may be troublesome to re-install accurately.

This removable section is secured by several SHCSs and one or more taper or dowel pins at the factory *before* the lathe bed is machined. Then the entire lathe bed is machined as if it were one piece. While a removable gap provides more machining capability, re-installing the gap is tricky and may not always come out well. If you do not really need this extra swing, do not remove the gap. Inflicting even the slightest damage on the gap-bed section when it is removed will prevent a perfect re-installation.

Lathe Drives

There are many different ways that electric motors connect to lathe spindles. Here are some of the main designs:

- *A single-belt drive with a pair of step pulleys,* shown in Figures 7-2 and 7-3, is the most basic design. Jewelers' lathes, Sherline lathes, and small instrument lathes use a single round rubber, leather or plastic drive belt between two step pulleys. This arrangement provides a range of speeds. Some older jewelers' lathes have foot-pedal speed controls like sewing machines. The drive belt also serves as a protective link by slipping and acting as a mechanical fuse should the lathe become overloaded or stalled.

Since the diameter of work in these lathes is small, a single pair of step pulleys provides a range of speeds matching the needed work SFM. This is a valuable feature. Older jewelers' lathes use AC–DC motors running on AC, sometimes called *universal motors*, but more recently, permanent magnet DC motors with an SCR speed control are used. The Sherline lathe in Figure 7-3 has a 70–2800 RPM speed range, while Levin lathes have a range of 0–5000 RPM. Traditional jewelers' lathes run from several hundred to 4000 RPM in 4 or 5 fixed steps.

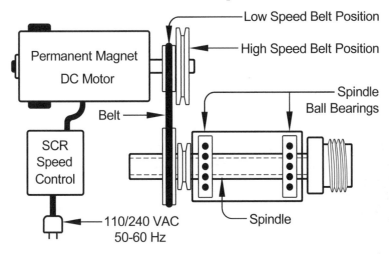

Figure 7-2. Schematic of a single-belt drive with step pulleys typical of jewelers' lathes, Sherline lathes and imported mini-lathes.

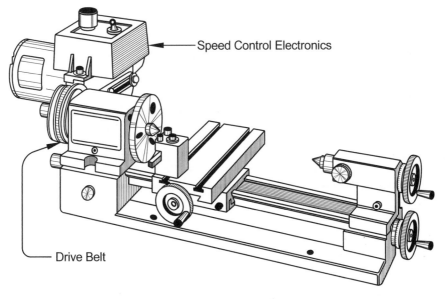

Figure 7-3. A single-belt drive—also called a direct drive—with a pair of step pulleys on the lathe is typical of small instrument and jewelers' lathes.

- *A countershaft with two pairs of step pulleys,* as in Figures 7-4, provides both greater speed reduction and more speed increments than a single-belt drive. Single-phase 60 Hz induction motors on these lathes have a fixed speed of 1750 RPM, so more speed reduction is needed than on smaller lathes. This drive design is standard on Atlas, Myford, South Bend, Logan, Clausing and many other lathes with swings of 5–15 inches. Older lathes have flat leather belts, while newer ones use one or more V-belts.

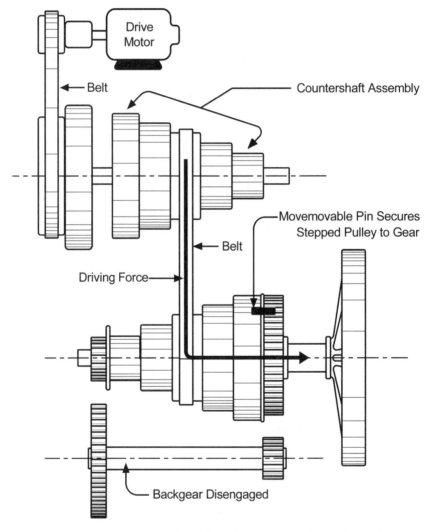

Figure 7-4. Countershaft with two step pulleys and a backgear for
small- and medium-sized lathes; backgear disengaged.

This lathe design has a *backgear*, a clever arrangement of gears which, in addition to the speed reduction provided by the countershaft, provides low spindle speeds—25–50 RPM—and high torque. This enables the lathe to turn large diameter work without stalling. Low spindle speeds are also useful when cutting threads which run up to a shoulder because a slow spindle speed gives the operator time to stop the carriage before running the tool into the shoulder. For the *higher speed range*, the backgear is disengaged and a movable steel pin on the bull gear is pushed to the left. This locks the bull gear to the spindle, making the spindle turn at the same speed as the drive pulley. Figure 7-4 shows the backgear disengaged, which makes the spindle-drive belt and the spindle turn at the same speed. This is what provides the higher speed range.

When the moveable steel pin on the bull gear is pushed to the right, the pin remains inside the bull gear, and the bull gear turns independently on the spindle shaft. When the backgears are swung into position, as in Figure 7-5, the backgear is engaged and torque feeds through them, producing a lower spindle speed, but more torque.

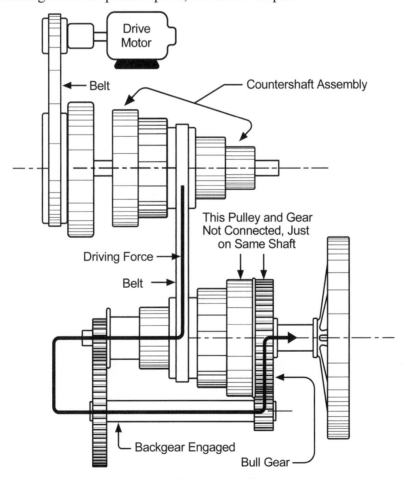

Figure 7-5. Countershaft with two step pulleys and a backgear for small- and medium-sized lathes; backgear is engaged.

To engage or disengage the backgear, the lathe operator must stop the machine, open the headstock cover, move the bull gear pin and change the backgear position. Belts may also have to be repositioned.

- *Belt and pulleys driving a geared transmission*, similar to those of a car, provide a range of spindle speeds for larger lathes. See Figure 7-6. Lathes with swings of 15 inches and over used this design until the introduction of variable-frequency drive lathes. These larger belt-and-pulley lathes have two or three V-belts from the motor to the transmission. Several levers on the face of the headstock shift the transmission gears for different speeds. There is no need to open the headstock lid to change gears. The available speeds are in fixed increments, ranging from 35 to 1500 RPM.

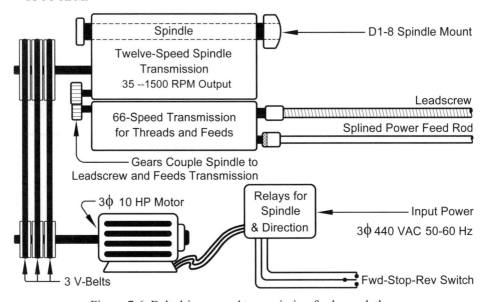

Figure 7-6. Belt-drive geared transmission for larger lathes.

- *A variable-frequency drive (VFD)* controls the speed of a three-phase induction motor which drives a geared transmission through V-belts. See Figure 7-7. This arrangement offers several advantages:

  - The two-speed transmission for these machines is much less complicated than the older style lathe transmission because it has only a LOW speed range (85–500 RPM) and a HIGH speed range (500–3000 RPM). The rest of the speed adjustment is done with a speed-control knob.

  - A VFD provides infinitely variable speeds at the turn of a knob and the optimum spindle speed can be adjusted without shifting belts or gears.

- The VFD electronics provides a gradual "soft start" and a smooth, rapid electronic braking action to the spindle when the motor is shut off. There is no need to use the mechanical brake or wait for the spindle to coast to a stop. Both starting and stopping rates are programmable.

- The VFD electronics permits these drives to operate on either single-phase or three-phase input power. This is a very big advantage to a home shop because three-phase power is generally not available to a residence, yet larger lathe motors require it.

- A pair of gears couple the two-speed transmission to the threads and feeds the transmission.

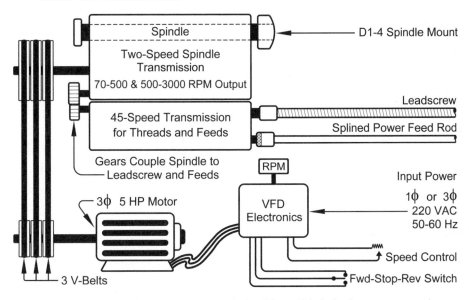

Figure 7-7. Kent TRL-13 × 40 VFD lathe drive. This lathe has a two-speed transmission and a VFD to adjust the speed of the three-phase motor.

- The VFD has a jog feature, typically 6–8 RPM. Not only can this be used to reposition the chuck to get at the key squares, this feature can be used to rotate the workpiece or to get the transmission gears to engage. It can also be used for thread tapping where very low speeds are needed.

- Most VFDs have analog outputs for motor current which makes it possible to also install a low-cost 0–10 volt meter to show motor current. Because dull tools draw more current than sharp ones, ammeters can often be used to indicate the lathe tool's condition.

Retrofitting VFDs on Older Machines

Here are the considerations for VFD retrofits:

- VFDs will control the speed of three-phase induction motors whether they are older motors designed for fixed-speed use at 60 Hz or specifically labeled as suitable for VFD service by the phrase *for inverter service* on the name plate.

- There is no sure way to know whether an older three-phase induction motor will perform *satisfactorily* when used on a VFD. The two reasons for this uncertainty are:

  - Some VFDs allow high voltage spikes to reach the motor where these spikes can damage the winding insulation. These voltage spikes are incidental to the generation of the waveform to drive the motor and may be filtered out by some VFDs or by external components between the VFD and the motor. The condition of the motor winding insulation is a key factor in the motor's tolerance of voltage spikes.

  - Three-phase motors designed for 60 Hz service may heat up excessively when subjected to the lower frequencies VFDs generate for lower motor speeds. In fact, some motors specifically designed for VFD service have additional cooling fans to counter this heating. Other motors for inverter service electrically insulate just one shaft bearing to control low-frequency current heating.

- While VFDs can control the speed of single-phase induction motors, these motors have speed-sensitive starting switches and additional windings to get the motor started, which interfere with the operation of the motor at low speeds. This prevents the use of single-phase motors on VFDs.

- On smaller lathes and drill presses, a permanent-magnet DC motor—such as those from a treadmill—powered by a Variac may be satisfactory. Despite their shortcomings, a DC motor and a Variac may still be an improvement over a fixed-speed motor with multiple belts and pulleys. Such arrangements have two potential shortcomings:

  - They may have poor no-load to full-load speed regulation.

  - Although the motor may be rated at 1.5 hp, it will only deliver this torque at full speed, delivering less torque at lower speeds.

Drive Belts

Belts are used between lathe motors and lathes because, in this application, gears would not only turn too fast, they would wear rapidly and be noisy. Today, V-belts are used, but older lathes usually used flat leather belts. These leather belts could be scarfed and glued, laced, or joined with interlocking metal grippers. The latter two methods can affect the finish on fine work as the joint passes a pulley, especially in a cold shop if the belt had been sitting. Modern V-belts can do the same until they warm up. Drive belts offer the lathe operator more flexibility when replacing a motor because the motor size and shape are more easily changed than when a motor is integrated into the lathe casting itself. The motor pulley size can also be changed to modify the spindle speeds.

Power Feed Designs

There are three ways that power is sent to the carriage to move the cross feed and the longitudinal feed:

- Smaller lathes use the leadscrew both for cutting threads and to drive the power feeds. See Figure 7-8.

- Larger lathes usually have a separate round, splined shaft to transmit this power. Having a separate shaft saves wear on the leadscrew, extending its accuracy. See Figure 7-9.

- Some high-quality lathes, like Hardinge and Kent tool room lathes, employ a small separate DC motor on the carriage to power the carriage feeds. This design also saves the leadscrew for threading and provides a wide range of feed rates.

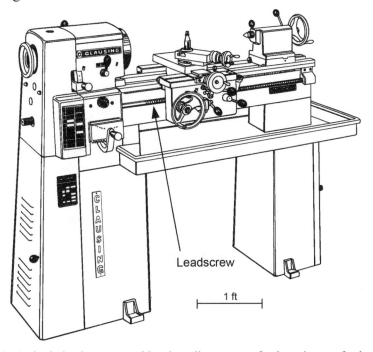

Figure 7-8. A single leadscrew provides threading, power feeds and cross-feed power.

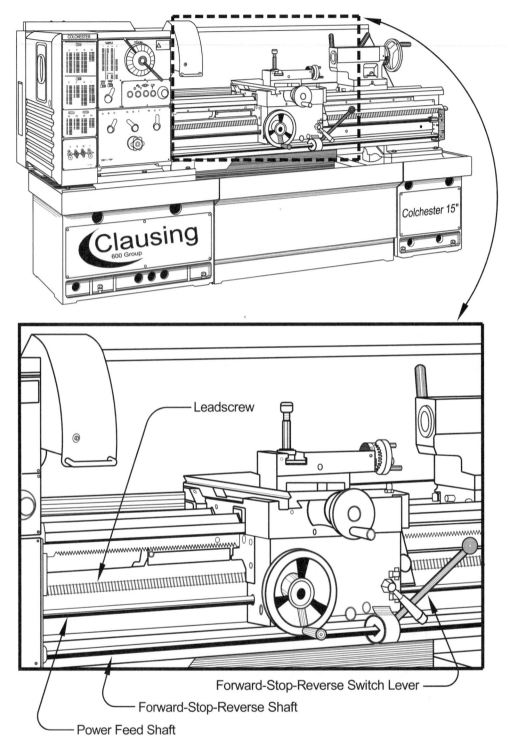

Figure 7-9. The motor FORWARD-STOP-REVERSE switch lever is mounted on the lathe apron for ready access on larger lathes as on this Clausing Colchester 15 × 50 model.

Forward-Stop-Reverse Motor Switch

Smaller lathes have a *motor control switch* above or on the face of the headstock housing, but larger lathes have a *motor control lever* on the right side of the carriage. On larger lathes there are two reasons for this. First, because larger lathes have long beds, the operator often stands far away from the headstock when the motor must be stopped, and second, by keeping the machinist's left hand away from the headstock area, chances of an accident are reduced.

Emergency-Stop Foot Bars

Many medium- and large-sized lathes made today have an *emergency-stop foot bar* along their base. Stepping on this bar turns off the spindle drive motor, and additional pressure actuates a mechanical brake band to quickly stop spindle rotation. This is not only a major safety improvement, when running multiple parts or setting up the next operation, this feature avoids the need to wait for the spindle to coast to a stop.

Lubrication

Small lathes, like jewelers' and Sherline lathes, have sealed ball bearings which require no oiling. For other lathes, there are three arrangements for lathe spindle bearing lubrication:

- *Splash lubrication* – Many lathes utilize splash lubrication which puts lube oil on the inside of the transmission top cover and channels the oil to specific bearings and gears as it drips downward off the cover.

- *Oil baths* – Medium-sized lathes, such as the Kent 13×40 series, have ball bearings with their transmissions running in oil baths. Many larger lathes, such as the Colchester lathes, also run with their apron gears in oil baths for longer life. Sometimes this oil bath is used as a reservoir for the one-shot plunger that lubricates the cross feed and leadscrew.

- *Oil pumps* – Large lathes have oil pumps to provide transmission lubrication under pressure just like automobile engines.

Tip: Many lathe transmissions and aprons have sight glasses to show the oil level. Years ago these little windows had a red level line across their middle to show the proper fill level. *Today they do not.* You need to know that, unless otherwise indicated, the oil level should cover up just half the window, not any more. If you exceed the proper oil level in the apron, oil will leak out the shaft holes and bearings and drip onto the floor. See Figure 7-10.

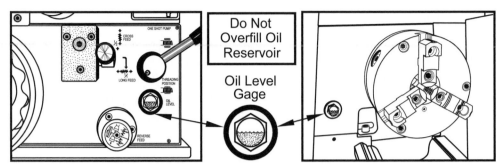

Figure 7-10. Two of the three oil level sight gages on a Kent 13 × 40 lathe. The left shows the
lathe apron and its sight glass; the right shows the transmission sight gage.

Read Outs

Depending on the size and sophistication of the lathe, four other read outs are
possible:

- *DROs* (*Digital Read Outs*) indicate the carriage position to 3 or 3½
  decimal places. As with milling machine DROs, these may be zeroed at
  any time, which simplifies making accurate parts and reduces errors.

- *RPM Meters* show spindle speed. They can be a stand-alone digital read
  out or can be part of the DRO display.

- *Ammeters* show spindle motor current, which is helpful in spotting dull
  cutting tools. Dull tools draw more current and generate more heat on the
  work than sharp tools.

- *Running Time Meters* help with scheduling maintenance.

Section II – Lathe Set-up & Tooling

Set-up Checklist

Here are the items to check or inspect when a lathe is installed or moved:

- Power must be supplied and electrical grounding checked. To do this,
  first, with the lathe wired and its motor running, use a voltmeter to verify
  that there is no voltage between the frame of the machine and ground. If
  there is no voltage, then check for a solid ground between the frame of the
  lathe and ground. The ground can be a water pipe ground, building
  structural steel or an earth-driven ground rod. To insure life safety,
  resistance should be a fraction of an ohm.

- Machinery movers use a fork lift to move large lathes and then several
  "mice" to position them inside buildings when a fork lift does not fit. Mice
  are sets of small steel wheels on a steel frame which enable the lathe to be
  pushed or pulled around. Large pry bars are also used to lever lathes into
  their exact positions. Get plenty of manpower to make a move. If mice are

not available, another approach is to place two 2 × 6-inch pieces of lumber under the lathe parallel to the ways, then use four or five 15-inch long sections of 1-inch diameter steel water pipe as rollers under the lumber. As the lathe moves off one roller, cycle it ahead of the lumber and use it again. Remember that pedestal-mounted lathes are top heavy and tip over easily. If one starts to tip, get out of the way. It is almost impossible to prevent a lathe from falling over once it begins.

- Most lathes larger than a Sherline or a Levin must be leveled with a precision level to remove the twist in the ways an uneven floor creates. Not only should the ways be level side-to-side, front-to-back leveling is critical to insure that the ways are not twisted. Twisted ways turn a cone, not a true cylinder. If a lathe is supported on a wooden floor, the level should be checked periodically because wooden floors may settle.

- Check these locations on the lathe for proper lubrication:

  - Oil level in the main transmission, feed transmission and apron gears.

  - Spindle lubrication – Some lathes, like the Sherline, have permanently lubricated and sealed ball bearings and do not need lubrication, but older lathes have oil drip cups which must be filled.

  - Ways, tailstock spindle, thread-cutting and feed drives.

- Degrease new machines fully. Remaining Cosmoline preservative will only harden and be more difficult to remove later.

- Check tailstock alignment by turning a cylinder between centers and insuring that the diameter is the same at each end. Tailstock alignment can also be checked using a test bar and a dial indicator on the carriage to verify that the test bar is parallel to the ways.

- Install basic cutters in their QCTP tool holders and set the cutters to center —or proper—height.

- Using a small ball-shaped abrasive wheel in a hand-held grinder, engrave a number on each of the chuck jaws, then place a matching number on the face of the chuck beside each jaw. This will prevent installing the jaws out of their factory sequence which can reduce concentricity.

- Before installing a new drill chuck in place on its JT-MT arbor, orient the drill chuck so one key hole is in the UP position when in the tailstock.

- For safety, covers are needed on all belts and pulleys on older machines. Although they pass OSHA requirements, some lathes with pedestal-mounted motors need covers over the partially open face of the pedestal to keep pets and small children from getting tangled in the motor drive belts.

- Install a compressed air supply or vacuum cleaner for chip removal.

Basic Lathe Tooling

A good selection of lathe tooling can easily equal the cost of the lathe itself. Here is a basic selection:

- Three-jaw and four-jaw chucks.

- Faceplate and/or driveplate with bolts or clamps.

- Lever-type collet closer and collets. A set of inch-collets—$1/_{16}$–$1^1/_{16}$—for round work, and if you will be working with metric stock and parts, a metric collet set too. A drawbar, collet spindle adapter and knock-out bar are also needed.

- Two dead centers and a live center. A quality live center will have three or more sets of ball and roller bearings to sustain the cutting forces. Centers with just one or two bearing sets will not last long.

- QCTP and cutting tool holders. A dozen would be nice, but twenty would be better because it cuts down on tool height adjustments.

- HSS and brazed carbide cutting tool selection.

- Boring bars.

- Drill chucks installed on JT-MT arbors for the lathe tailstock. Ball-bearing Jacobs chucks cost more than plain drill chucks, but they are worth it because they keep drills from spinning under load, which can damage their shanks. Ball-bearing Jacobs chucks retain their accuracy longer than conventional chucks.

- Collets for hex and square stock are sometimes needed.

- If there is no QCTP installed, keep the shims, sometimes called *packing,* with the tool itself. These shims are used to bring each cutting tool bit to center height. This will make for faster tool changes.

- Make or buy a collet rack for storing collets in size order. Do not store collets loose in a drawer. This makes it hard to find the right one, and rolling around may damage the collets.

- Steady and follower rests usually are supplied with larger lathes, but must be purchased as accessories for smaller ones. See Figure 7-11.

- Twist drills, center drills, Silver & Deming drills and MT-shank drills.

Depending on the type of work you're doing, this tooling may also be desirable:

- Taper attachment.

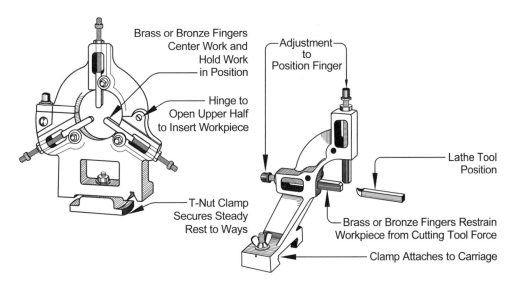

Figure 7-11. Steady rest (left) and follower rest (right).

- Mandrel assortment.
- Collet chuck.
- Three- or four-jaw 4-inch chuck mounted for use in the collet adapter on the spindle.
- Knurling tools with knurl assortment.
- DRO on carriage and cross slide.
- Sensitive drilling attachment for use in the tailstock with small twist drills.

Essential Accessories
- Knock-out bar.
- Tool box or tool board positioned on the ways.
- Chip brush and chip hook.
- Oil cans.
- Work lights.
- Chip shields.

Section III – Quick-Change Tool Post Systems (QCTPSs)

Quick-Change Tool Post Systems make it unnecessary to reset the lathe tool height with each tool change. See Figure 7-12. With the knurled wheel on the top of the tool holder, tool height is set the first time a tool is mounted in its holder. A well-equipped shop will have a dozen or more tool holders with many tools set up and ready to run.

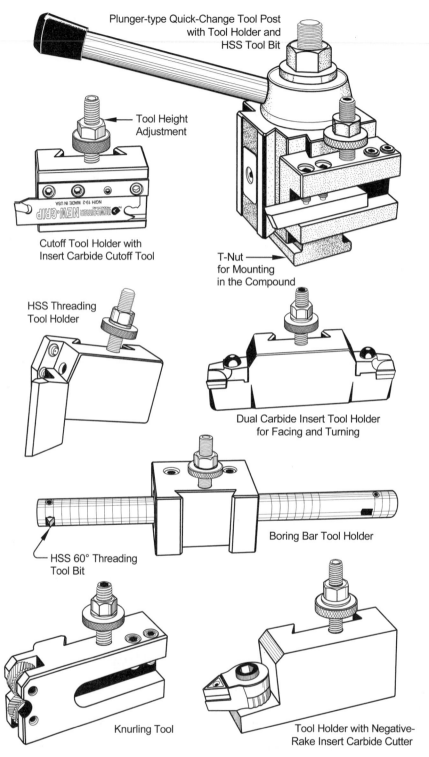

Plunger-type Quick-Change Tool Post
with Tool Holder and
HSS Tool Bit

Tool Height
Adjustment

Cutoff Tool Holder with
Insert Carbide Cutoff Tool

T-Nut
for Mounting
in the Compound

HSS Threading
Tool Holder

Dual Carbide Insert Tool Holder
for Facing and Turning

Boring Bar Tool Holder

HSS 60° Threading
Tool Bit

Knurling Tool

Tool Holder with Negative-
Rake Insert Carbide Cutter

Figure 7-12. Quick-change tool post (upper right) and tool holders.

Tool holders for MT-shank drills are also available. See Figure 7-13. These tool holders capture the MT drill shank tang and prevent the drill from spinning under load, and they also permit the use of the lathe's power feed during drilling. This is not only a great convenience when heavy drilling must be done, it is also a great time saver. See Figure 7-13.

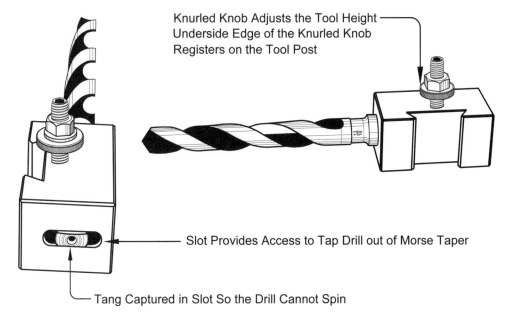

Knurled Knob Adjusts the Tool Height
Underside Edge of the Knurled Knob
Registers on the Tool Post

Slot Provides Access to Tap Drill out of Morse Taper

Tang Captured in Slot So the Drill Cannot Spin

Figure 7-13. Quick-change tool holders for Morse taper drills. The drill tang is captured in the back of the tool holder so it cannot spin under the drilling loads.

5C Collet Tool Holders

QCTP *5C collet tool holders* secure twist drills, boring bars and reamers. This quick-change system allows these tools to be used with the power feed instead of with the tailstock. This is important for larger drills and for production runs because it substitutes the lathe's carriage feed power for human feed power from the tailstock handwheel. Using the power feed also produces a smoother, more uniform surface finish. See Figure 7-14.

A similar tool holder with a drill chuck on a dovetail is available, but relatively uncommon—and expensive. A less expensive alternative would be to use a drill chuck on a Morse taper shank in the quick-change Morse taper tool holder shown in Figure 7-13.

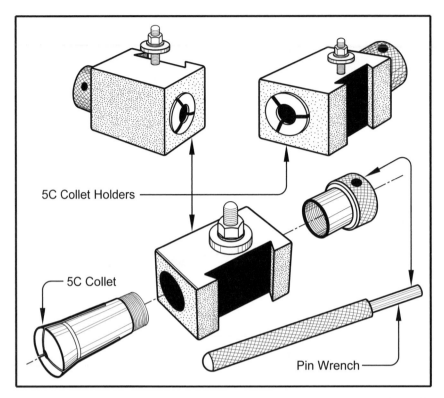

Figure 7-14. QCTP 5C collet tool holder with its pin wrench for tightening the back nut.

T-Nuts

Most new lathes are supplied with only a tool block or tool post to secure tooling, leaving the owner to purchase a QCTP separately. The T-nuts, which are supplied with the QCTP and hold the QCTP in its compound, usually arrive uncut as in Figure 7-15 (middle). Milling must be done on the T-nut to fit the dimensions of its particular compound T-slot. See Figure 7-15 (right).

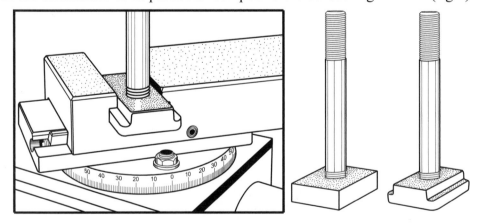

Figure 7-15. Lathe tool holder T-nut is usually left to the user to machine.

Reclocking a QCTP

Clocking, also called *indexing*, is the stopping position of the QCTP locking handle in relation to the arms of a clock.

On one style of QCTP, the locking lever arm turns a cam that pushes a plunger out to secure the tool holder. When the tool is locked in the cutting position, the lever arm should stop in the 4 o'clock position, as in Figure 7-16 (top). Sometimes this does not happen and the clocking position of the locking lever ends up in the way of the cutting tool, as in 7-16 (bottom). The solution is to adjust the length of the plungers by cutting them down in the lathe. Because there are usually two cutting tool positions and just one locking cam, the two plungers must be cut to *different* lengths. About a half-hour and a little lathe work will complete this job and make a big difference in lathe operation. This *reclocking* adjustment will keep the locking lever arm out of the way of the chuck jaws and the work it holds. See Figure 7-17.

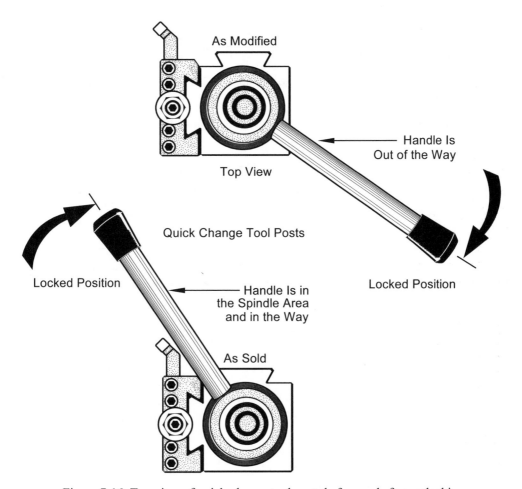

Figure 7-16. Top view of quick-change tool posts before and after reclocking.

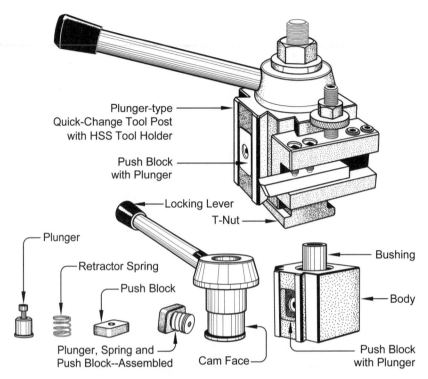

Figure 7-17. QCTP with tool holder. Shortening the length of the plunger adjusts the clocking position of the locking lever arm when in the locked position.

Industry QCTP Size Codes

There are standard industry sizes for QCTPSs as seen in Table 7-1.

Import Industry Series	American Industry Series	Lathe Swing (inches)
–	00	2–8
–	0	8–12
AXA	100	9–12
BXA	200	10–15
CXA	300	13–18
CA	400	14–20

Table 7-1. Standard industry codes and sizes for Quick-Change Tool Post Systems.

QCTP Compatibility between Brands

Tool holder compatibility is an important consideration when setting up a shop in terms of flexibility, time and cost savings. Aloris, Dorian and Phase II brand tool holders are interchangeable and some Asian budget imports fit these popular brands as well. KDK-brand, which is a different design, does *not* interchange with other brands.

Fine Tuning Imported Cutoff QCTPs

Many imported tool holders perform as well as their domestic counterparts and cost about a quarter of the price. See Figure 7-18 (top). However, a little tweaking may be needed to correct a minor shortcoming; clearance must be made so the cutoff tool can lay flat against the wall of the tool holder, not tilted at an angle away from it. This poor fit occurs when the bottom inside corner of the tool holder is rounded instead of square. See Figure 7-18 (middle). The fastest fix is to grind off the corner of the cutoff tool with a belt grinder, but the best fix is to cut a relief groove in the tool holder just as the quality domestic tool holders have. See Figure 7-18 (bottom).

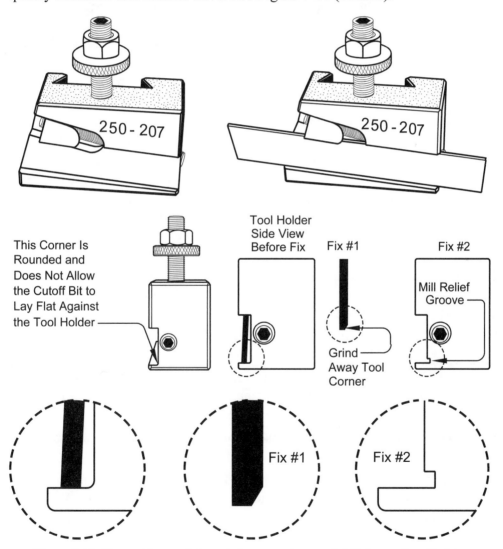

Figure 7-18. The problem and the solution on an imported QCTP cutoff tool holder.

Section IV – Cutting Tools

HSS vs. Tungsten Carbide Cutting Tool Bits

Most non-production shops use HSS, both with and without cobalt, and brazed tungsten carbide lathe tool bits depending on the work. See Figure 7-19. Usually HSS tool bits are sold unground and brazed tungsten carbide tool bits are sold ground and ready to use.

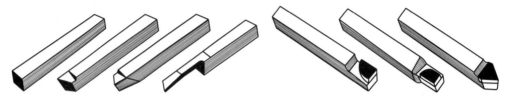

Figure 7-19. HSS tool bits (left) and brazed tungsten carbide tool bits (right). The HSS bit on the extreme left is unground, the other HSS bits are ground and ready to use.

Unless you are cutting hardened steels or exotic materials, or you require specially-shaped profiles on the cutting tools, using carbide insert cutters in a prototype or instrument shop is overkill and a needless expense.

However, production shops with NC tools must use carbide insert tool bits because these tool bits maintain a precise and uniform location of their cutting edge. This means that when changing worn-out cutters, the lathe does not need to be reset for the dimensions of the new tool bit.

For many tasks either HSS or brazed tungsten carbide will work, but usually cutting speed, workpiece material, hardness, and desired surface finish determine which of these tool materials is better for a particular job. Below are the pros and cons of each type of tool bit.

HSS tool bits:

- Are easily shaped and sharpened with aluminum oxide (gray) grinding wheels. This allows the machinist to make his own shaped or formed bits as needed. HSS also permits the machinist to modify the cutting angles of a bit to match the requirements of the work metal.

- Leave a smoother surface on many materials than carbide bits because HSS bits have sharper edges than carbide bits.

- On the con side, HSS tool bits have lower maximum temperature limits than brazed tungsten carbide bits and require lower spindle speeds.

- Will not stay sharp as long as carbide bits, so they have shorter operating lives.

Brazed tungsten carbide brazed tool bits:

- Tolerate higher maximum temperatures, permitting spindle speeds 3–4 times faster than HSS tool bits. They also have a longer operating life than HSS toolbits.

- For shaping and sharpening, brazed tungsten carbide toolbits require a silicon carbide (green) grinding wheel for roughing and a diamond wheel for finishing, not an aluminum oxide (gray) wheel.

- Readily cut hardened steel, such as SHCSs and dowel pins, which HSS bits cannot cut.

- On the con side, brazed tungsten carbide brazed tool bits are more brittle than HSS tool bits, require more rigid support, and may be damaged during interrupted cuts.

- Because the edges of tungsten carbide cutting toolbits are not as sharp as those of HSS bits, the minimum cut depth is around 0.010 inches. *This requires planning ahead to leave a minimum cut depth for the final cut.*

Cooling During Tool Bit Grinding

Because HSS tool bits are sold hardened and grinding heats them up enough to reduce their hardness, bits must be kept cool during grinding. If the tool bit shows blue oxide in the grind area, its temperature has been raised too high. This bit is now annealed and must be discarded or ground on the opposite end. You cannot grind away heat damage without removing a lot of metal.

Grinding heat will also make the cutting bit too hot to hold, so grind an HSS bit for 3–4 seconds, then dip it in room temperature water for a few seconds. This not only cools the bit, it preserves its hardness. If there are several tool bits to be ground, grind one bit, then set it aside to cool, and grind the next bit. Many grinders have cooling trays for this purpose. Most cooling trays are aluminum, which dissipates heat. And remember, if you value your fingers, never wear gloves during grinding because the grinder can pull in your hand.

Brazed tungsten carbide tool bits, on the other hand, must *not* be dipped for cooling because they are likely to crack from the thermal shock. Although grinding will not subject carbide bits to temperatures above what they will see during use, they do need time to cool between grinding cycles because you will not be able to hold them when they get hot. Tungsten carbide tool bits will become too hot to hold before they will be damaged from grinding heat.

Some large tool bit grinders, particularly those on which grinding is done on the side faces of their grinding wheels, have drip cups for kerosene. *These cups are not intended for water.* The kerosene is mainly for removing grindings from the wheels, not to cool the tool bits. But, because the tool bits are continuously bathed in kerosene, they are not subjected to thermal shock, and cracking is avoided.

Holding Tool Bits for Grinding

Grind tool bits by supporting them on a tool rest for better control, not by holding them in mid-air. Figure 7-20 (bottom) shows the correct finger positions for grinding tool bits: hooking your right middle finger (bottom left) and your left index finger (top and bottom right) under the tool rest improves your control, allows much greater pressure on the tool bit, and makes grinding your own fingers less likely. Figure 7-20 (top) also shows how the left thumb applies pressure to the tool, while the right hand holds and guides it. Use the mirror image of this figure when grinding the other side of the tool bit. This technique requires an adequate tool rest, like the ones in Figures 4-25 and 4-28, not the flimsy piece of stamped sheet metal commonly found on inexpensive grinders.

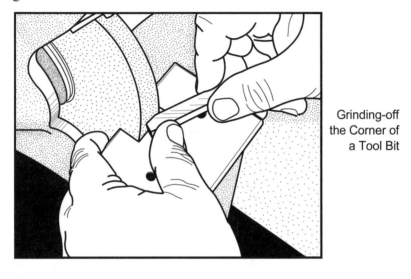

Grinding-off
the Corner of
a Tool Bit

Hook Your Right Middle Finger
against Bottom of Tool Rest

Hook Your Left Index Finger
against Bottom of Tool Rest

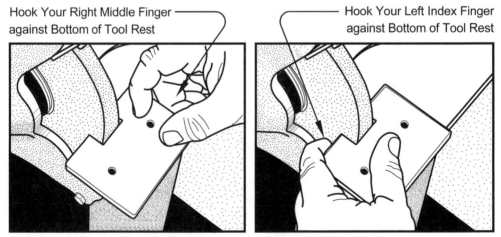

Figure 7-20. Finger positions for safe tool bit grinding.

Tool Bit Nomenclature & Angles

Figure 7-21 shows cutting tool nomenclature. The terms *clearance angle* and *relief angle* are used interchangeably. Figure 7-22 shows the steps to grind a typical cutting tool, and Table 7-2 contains typical clearance angles. With experience, you will develop and select cutting tools which work best for you and your machining tasks. For the most part, rake and clearance angles are not critical and your tool bit will cut adequately, but finding the optimum angle for the work material will result in less chatter and a better surface finish.

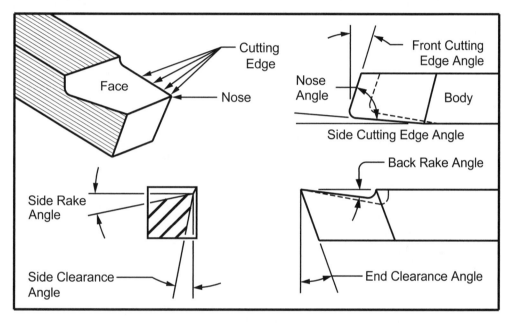

Figure 7-21. Cutting tool nomenclature.

Material	Side Clearance Angle (degrees)	Front Clearance Angle (degrees)	Side Rake Angle (degrees)	Back Rake Angle (degrees)
Aluminum	12	8	16	35
Brass	10	8	5 to −4	0
Bronze	10	8	5 to −4	0
Cast Iron	10	8	12	5
Copper	12	10	20	16
Machine Steel	10–12	8	12–18	8–15
Tool Steel (unhardened)	10	8	12	8
Stainless Steel	10	8	15–20	8

Table 7-2. Clearance and rake angles for common metals.

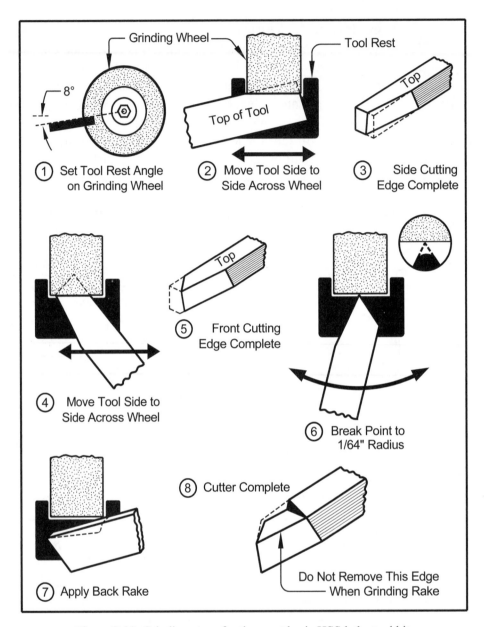

Figure 7-22. Grinding steps for the most basic HSS lathe tool bit.

Grinding a Double-Sided Cutter

Here is the progression of steps to make the double-sided HSS cutter in Figure 7-23. Grinding this cutter would take an experienced machinist 10–15 minutes. This cutter is similar to a threading tool, except that it has more front clearance. Figure 4-24 shows inside and outside faces that have been cut using this tool on a cup center for turning wood in a metal lathe. For more details on making this tool, see Chapter 8 – Milling, Figure 8-106.

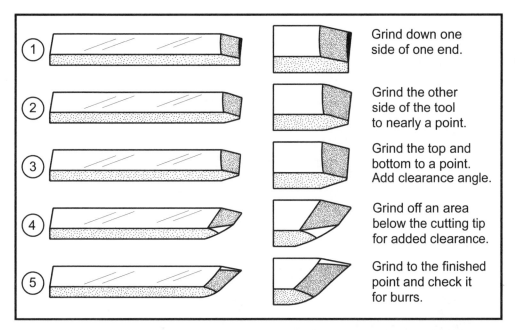

① Grind down one side of one end.

② Grind the other side of the tool to nearly a point.

③ Grind the top and bottom to a point. Add clearance angle.

④ Grind off an area below the cutting tip for added clearance.

⑤ Grind to the finished point and check it for burrs.

Figure 7-23. Steps to grind a double-sided HSS cutter for cutting both the inner and outer faces of the tool shown in Figure 7-24, a tailstock center for turning wood in a metal lathe.

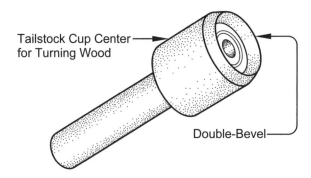

Tailstock Cup Center for Turning Wood

Double-Bevel

Figure 7-24. Ring-shaped double-bevel cup center.

Formed Tool Bits

Many jobs require specially-shaped tool bits, called *form bits*. Because HSS is easy to grind, it is usually chosen for making these bits. See Figure 7-25. However, if a workpiece metal is hardened, brazed tungsten carbide bits, as shown in Figure 7-26, may be required. Although harder to grind than HSS tool bits, brazed tungsten carbide bits can be ground by first applying *layout fluid,* scribing the outline of the finished tool bit, and then grinding out the shape. Angle gages, radii gages and templates are often used as grinding guides for formed tool bits. Figure 7-27 shows round shop-ground brazed tungsten carbide form tool bits, and Figure 7-28 shows standard stock tungsten carbide form tool bits.

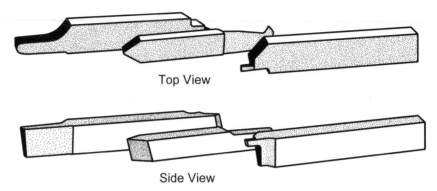

Top View

Side View

Figure 7-25. HSS shop-ground form tool bits.

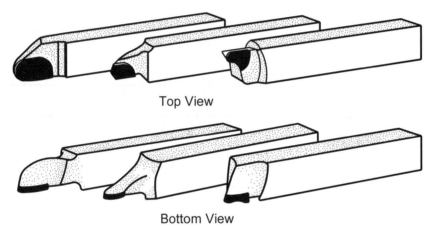

Top View

Bottom View

Figure 7-26. Shop-ground brazed tungsten carbide form tool bits.

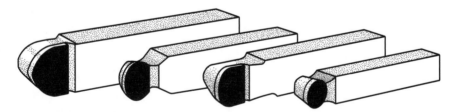

Figure 7-27. Round shop-ground brazed tungsten carbide form tool bits.

Brazed tungsten carbide form tools are commercially available, but the choice of standard stock shapes is limited and they typically cost ten times as much as a standard carbide cutter. If you have a green and a diamond wheel, in a few minutes you can make your own brazed tungsten carbide form tool for the cost of a standard carbide cutting tool.

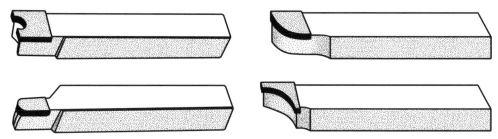

Figure 7-28. Standard stock tungsten carbide form tool bits.

Preparing Brazed Tungsten Carbide Tool Bits for Use

Although these cutters are ground to shape and sold as "ready to use," nearly all tungsten carbide cutters can be improved by honing—a very light sharpening. To hone these cutters:

1. Remove any protective dip coating, paint or plastic wrap.

2. Examine the steel of the tool bit below the cutting edge to see if additional steel should be removed to insure adequate clearance so little or no steel rubs against the diamond wheel during touch-up. Use a gray wheel for steel removal because using a diamond wheel for removing steel shortens the life of the diamond wheel.

3. Maintaining the original tool angles, lightly grind the cutting edges against the diamond wheel.

4. To finish, follow up with a few strokes with a fine-grade diamond file.

The "Nick-Off" for Improving Lathe Tool Performance

In addition to the light sharpening described above, here is an important, yet simple modification which improves the performance of many lathe tools, flycutters, boring bars and boring head cutters of either HSS or tungsten carbide. This modification works well except where a very sharp inside corner is required, where a specific tool is needed, or where threads must be cut. Figure 7-29 shows typical tungsten carbide and HSS cutters as purchased and the improved versions, which have a small nick ground from their outside corners.

By grinding this nick-off:

• The weakest, most unsupported corner of the tool is removed and is no longer subject to chipping damage and rapid wear. This helps the tool stay sharp longer.

• The remaining tool metal better transfers heat away from the cutting edge where the most heat is generated. Heat gets trapped in sharp points on cutters and removing the sharp points helps the tool to keep its shape longer.

- Stresses on the tool and tool holder are reduced. When this improved cutter is used for boring in a lathe or milling machine, the nick-off provides a more gradual entry into the bored hole and therefore less chance of chipping the cutter.

- When used in a flycutter performing interrupted cuts, the nick-off reduces the shock the cutter is subjected to as it contacts the work.

- Because the cutting tool is rounded and no longer sharply pointed, the tool produces a much smoother finish and will not cut "threads" or leave a grooved finish.

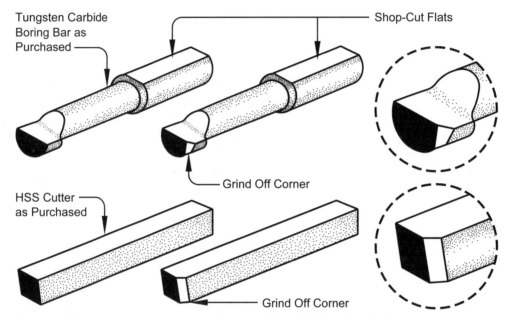

Figure 7-29. Improving cutting tools with the "nick-off." Note that the flats on the mounting stubs of the boring bars insure that they are properly indexed, or clocked, in the tool holder.

Shop-Made Boring Bars

The top of Figure 7-30 shows a 45° boring bar which could be made from CRS round stock, 4130 or 4140 steel. This design has two advantages:

- The tool holder location is made using only a twist drill, so cutting square holes to hold the boring tool is unnecessary.

- Used and damaged HSS end mills make excellent boring bar tool bits and fit into the round hole in the boring bar. These end mills are simple to grind and can be easily modified.

The bottom of Figure 7-30 shows two boring bars made with discarded brazed tungsten carbide lathe tool bits TIG welded onto a steel base. These boring bars are easy to make, cost very little and can be modified for a specific job.

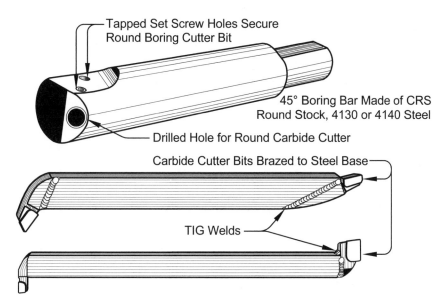

Figure 7-30. Three shop-made boring bars. Each cutter is about six inches long.

Section V – Chucks

Chuck Jaw Count

There are four common chuck designs:

- *Two-jaw scroll chucks* are self-centering and are used in production work with the jaws modified to hold a particular part. See Figure 7-31. Two-jaw chucks are not a general purpose tool because the jaws must be machined to fit a specific part, but they excel in handling irregularly-shaped work. These chucks are usually supplied with two-piece unhardened steel jaws for the customer to customize, but shop-made aluminum, brass or bronze jaws are suitable for many jobs and are easier to cut.

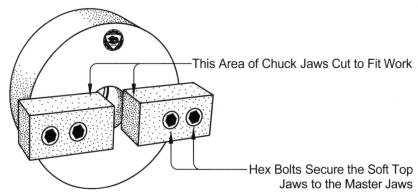

Figure 7-31. Two-jaw chucks have unhardened steel top jaws so they can be customized to hold parts for a specific job. Parts machined in these chucks may be asymmetrical.

- *Three-jaw universal scroll chucks* are the most common design and the most convenient to use because they automatically self-center the work as they close. See Figure 7-32. A quality three-jaw chuck will center round stock within 3–5 thousandths of an inch over is entire size range when new. This centering accuracy will decline with abuse and wear.

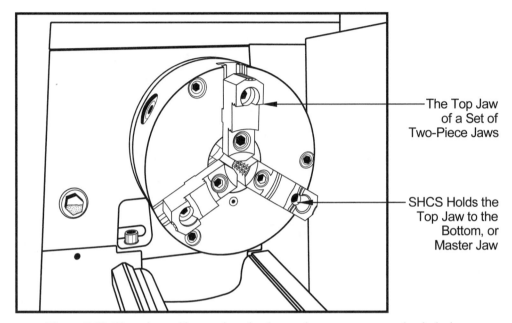

The Top Jaw
of a Set of
Two-Piece Jaws

SHCS Holds the
Top Jaw to the
Bottom, or
Master Jaw

Figure 7-32. Three-jaw self-centering chucks are the most common chuck design.
This three-jaw universal scroll chuck has reversible two-piece jaws and is
more expensive than the more common one-piece jaw model.

- *Four-jaw independent chucks* are the second most common design. See Figure 7-33. They have three advantages; they can hold:

  - The same work as a three-jaw chuck.

  - Irregular work.

  - Symmetrical work off center.

  Their disadvantage is that they do not automatically self-center work as does the three-jaw chuck. Four-jaw chucks work much better for holding square and rectangular work than three-jaw designs. If you can have only one chuck, this is the one to get. In general, a four-jaw chuck centers work much more accurately than a three-jaw chuck because with a four-jaw the machinist must center the work with a DTI. Though using a dial test indicator requires a bit more time, with a little practice centering work to within one-half a thousandth of an inch will take only 20–30 seconds.

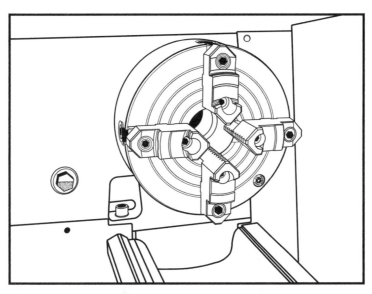

Figure 7-33. Four-jaw independent chucks are ideal for precisely centered
work and for holding square, rectangular or eccentric parts.

- *Six-jaw chucks* cost about 50% more than the same size three-jaw chuck,
  but they offer more gripping force with less part distortion. See Figure 7-
  34. Six-jaw chucks are mainly used for holding thin tubing which is too
  large to fit into collets. Remember though, the most common lathe collet,
  the 5C, has a workpiece maximum diameter of $1^1/_{16}$ inches. If the diameter
  of your thin tubing is larger, you will need to use a six-jaw chuck because
  the work will not fit into a collet.

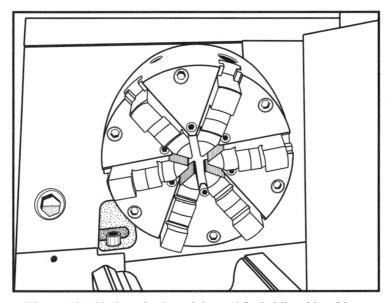

Figure 7-34. Six-jaw chuck, mainly used for holding thin tubing.

Adjustable Runout Chucks

Both three-jaw and six-jaw *adjustable runout chucks*—also called *precision chucks*—are available under several trade names: *Buck Adjust True Style, Adjust-Tru, Set-Tru, Zero-Set, Set-Rite, Hi-Tru* and *Accu-Chuck*.

With precision chucks, four opposing adjustment screws provide fine adjustment between the chuck and the chuck mounting plate resulting in a TIR (Total Indicated Runout, or concentricity) of 0.0005 inches on identical parts. See Figure 7-35. These chucks can achieve the centering accuracy of an independent chuck without the effort, but they are more expensive. Most three-jaw precision chucks are adjusted for minimum runout at a *particular diameter*—the diameter of the identical parts being run. Because of manufacturing and wear inaccuracies in the scroll—the internal spiral that moves the chuck jaws—runout is not usually the same at all work diameters.

Some clarification is required here. All chucks made by the Buck Chuck Company, now part of ITW Workholding, are Buck chucks. But those with adjustment screws between the backplate and the chuck are called Adjust-True Style Chucks, abbreviated by the Buck Chuck Company as ATSC. Many machinists call chucks of any brand that have adjusting screws "buck chucks."

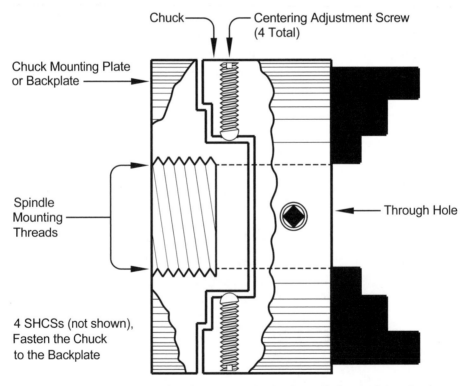

Figure 7-35. Three-jaw adjustable runout chuck, also called a precision chuck.

Jaw Design Options

There are several other important jaw options which should be considered when purchasing a scroll chuck:

- *Non-reversible one-piece jaws*, often called *solid jaws*, are used on both three-jaw and four-jaw chucks. See Figure 7-36. Chucks with this jaw design are furnished with two sets of jaws, one set for clamping work externally and one set for clamping internally. The disadvantage of this design is that when the jaws need to be reversed, one set of jaws must be wound out before the other set of jaws can be wound in. Besides being time-consuming, winding jaws in and out wears down the jaw sides and widens the chuck jaw grooves, eventually reducing chuck accuracy.

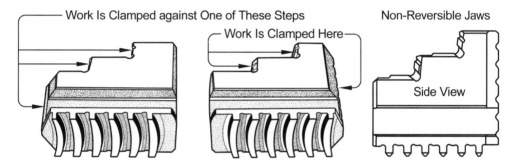

Figure 7-36. Non-reversible one-piece chuck jaws.

- *Reversible one-piece jaws* hold work with their steps either inside or outside the workpiece, so only one set of jaws is needed. Making jaws reversible though, has one drawback, it weakens the jaw teeth that fit into the chuck scroll. To see this, compare the relative mass of metal on the teeth of the reversible jaws in Figure 7-37 with that of the teeth of the non-reversible chuck jaws in Figure 7-36. The reversible teeth are much smaller and wear out much more quickly due to their small point of contact with the scroll.

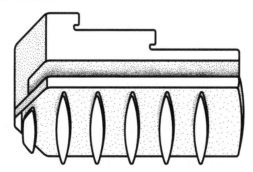

Figure 7-37. Reversible one-piece chuck jaws have teeth that fit into the scroll in either direction. This jaw is from a Sherline three-jaw chuck.

- *Reversible two-piece jaws* in Figure 7-38 increase the price of a chuck 20–30% over similar one-piece jaw chucks of the same size. Yet, despite the extra cost, reversible two-piece jaws have several advantages:

  - When a different size workpiece requires the jaws to be reversed, this is done by undoing the two SHCSs in each jaw and reversing the jaw. Not only is this a real time saver, it reduces wear on the jaw slots and avoids the hassle of scrolling each jaw out of the chuck, reversing it, and then cranking it back into position.

  - There are international standards for chuck jaws so that new jaws can be readily purchased to replace old worn ones.

  - Although most chucks are sold with hardened top jaws, many suppliers offer unhardened, or *soft* jaws, so the user can machine them to fit a particular part.

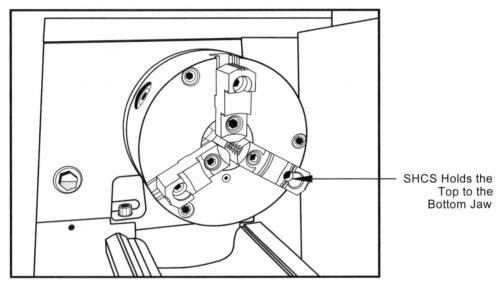

SHCS Holds the
Top to the
Bottom Jaw

Figure 7-38. Three-jaw chuck with reversible two-piece jaws. Two SHCSs hold each jaw in place and allow the jaws to be rotated 180° without scrolling the jaws out and then in again.

Reversing One-Piece Jaws

When self-centering three-jaw chuck jaws have been removed, reversed, and are ready to be rescrolled inward, the jaws must be engaged, or caught, by the starting point of the scroll in a particular sequence. Figure 7-39 shows how this process works when reversing jaws to accommodate larger work. *If this sequence is not followed, the jaws will not center the work.*

Most larger chuck jaws have numbers on their sides. If your chuck jaws do not, add numbers to the sides of the jaws with an engraving pen. Steel stamps cannot be used for marking the jaws because the jaws are hardened.

Since each jaw of a four-jaw independent chuck operates individually, jaws may be replaced in any order, but it is still good practice to replace them in the same slots they came from since the factory may have made each a slightly different size.

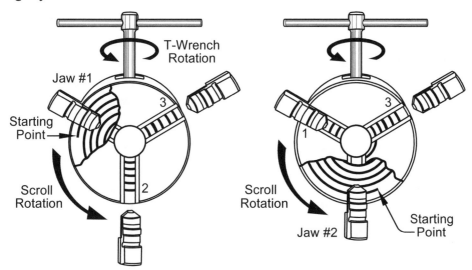

Step 1: With the Scroll in this Position, Enter Jaw #1 into Slot #1.

Step 2: Rotate the Scroll to This Position, and Enter Jaw #2 into Slot #2.

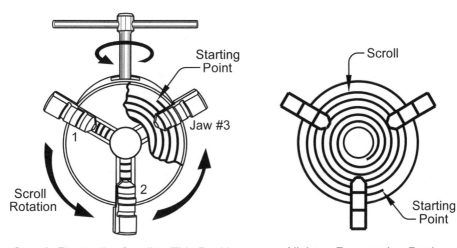

Step 3: Rotate the Scroll to This Position, and Enter Jaw #3 into Slot #3.

All Jaws Reversed or Replaced and Engaged.

Figure 7-39. Steps to reverse one-piece jaws to accommodate larger diameter work.

Sherline Jaw Reversal

Sherline three-jaw chucks are not marked for sequence. You must compare your jaws with those in Figure 7-40 to determine the starting sequence. There are three important things to note:

- The starting sequence is different for the standard-jaw and the reversed-jaw positions.

- The small punch mark on the left-side of jaw groove B identifies the position of the second-starting jaw.

- Jaws on Sherline four-jaw independent chucks should be kept in the same jaw grooves in which they left the factory. By only swapping out one jaw at a time, you can avoid any mixups.

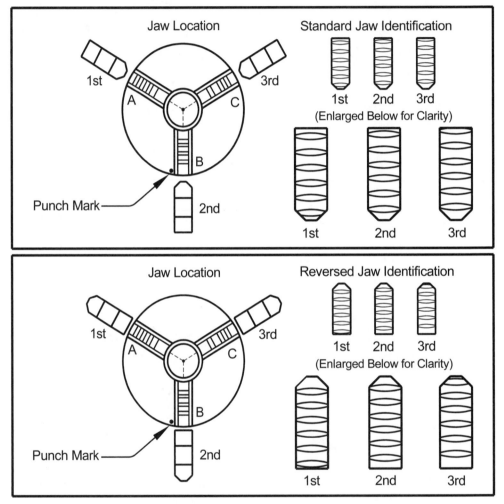

Figure 7-40. Reversing Sherline jaws. The proper sequence
is different for holding work "inside" or "outside."

Reversing Two-Piece Jaws

Two-piece jaws are removed, reversed, and re-installed when their chucks are reconfigured for different sized parts. The jaws are also removed when new replacement jaws or custom-machined jaws are installed.

Reversing two-piece jaws is a four-step process:

1. The two SHCSs which hold each top jaw must be loosened and unscrewed. These screws are usually very tight. To loosen them, you may use a breaker bar holding a hex wrench fitting. But, if you slip, this method is a sure knuckle-buster. Or, you can use a hex wrench and a dead-blow hammer as shown in Figure 7-41. This method does not require much strength to remove the SHCSs, and, because the dead-blow hammer and hex wrench apply an impulse, there is no tendency for the chuck to turn as it does when using a breaker bar. Three medium-strength blows will break most screws loose. Once loosened, the two SHCSs may be unscrewed with the hex wrench.

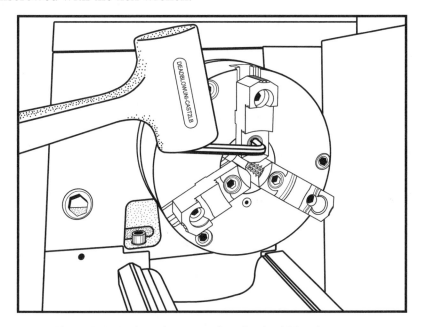

Figure 7-41. Using a hex wrench and a dead-blow hammer to
loosen the SHCSs on a two-piece reversible chuck jaw.

2. Even with the SHCSs removed, the top jaws are still gripped by the lower jaws. To break them free, the top jaws must be tapped loose with a dead-blow hammer as in Figures 7-42 and 7-43. The newer the chuck, the tighter the jaw fit. Tap gently on each side of the jaw while pulling it off with one hand until it comes out. And remember, *do not let the jaw fall onto the lathe ways*. The jaw and the ways can be damaged.

3. Figure 7-44 shows the top jaw removed from the chuck. Notice the number *one* on the chuck beneath the hand, and the number *one* on the side of the jaw itself. This matches the jaw position in the chuck. To avoid mix-ups, change only one jaw at a time. Because top jaws are ground in place for better accuracy, scrambling jaw locations will result in reduced centering accuracy.

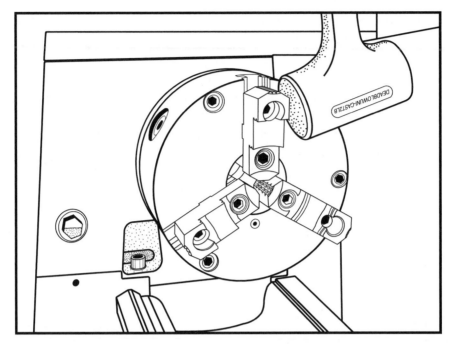

Figure 7-42. Alternately tapping on each side of the chuck jaw to free it. Top jaws on a new chuck may be very tight. Always use a soft-faced, dead-blow hammer, never a steel hammer.

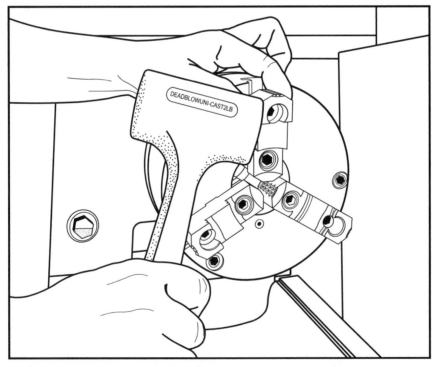

Figure 7-43. Alternately tapping on each side of the chuck jaw loosens the top jaw from the lower jaw. Hold onto the removable top jaw so it does not fall when it becomes free.

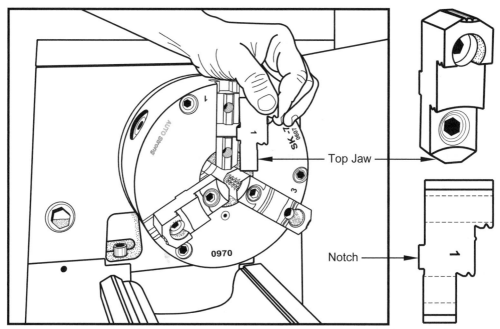

Figure 7-44. The lower chuck jaw face is visible when the top jaw is removed. The top jaw
has a projection in its base which fits snugly into a notch in the bottom jaw.

4.   To replace the jaws in the reversed position, turn the top jaw around a half
     turn and, using the dead-blow hammer, tap the jaw into place over the
     bottom jaw. Be sure you have the jaw correctly positioned before you start
     tapping. Once the jaws are correctly started into position, the SHCSs can
     pull them the rest of the way into position. See Figure 7-45.

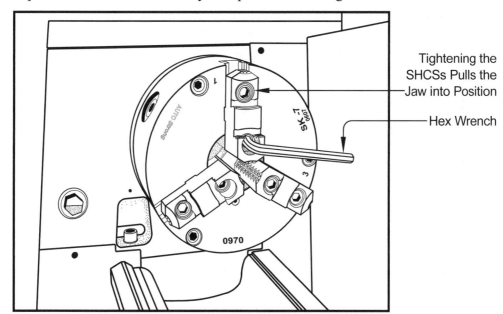

Figure 7-45. The hex-head wrench in place and ready to strike
with a dead-blow hammer to tighten the SHCSs.

Spindle Nose Designs

The lathe's *spindle nose* attaches a chuck to the spindle. The two most common spindle nose designs are the *threaded spindle nose mount*, common on small- and medium-sized lathes, and the *cam lock nose mount* found on industrial-grade lathes.

• *Threaded spindle nose mounts,* as shown in Figure 7-46, are inexpensive to manufacture compared with other chuck mounts. Although threaded spindle mounts allow the machinist to easily make his own faceplates, driveplates and backplates, threaded spindle mounts wear with use, increasing runout.

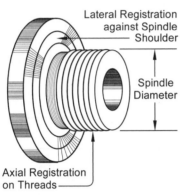

Figure 7-46. A threaded spindle nose mount, common on small- and medium-sized lathes, and a chart of its most common sizes.

Threaded Spindle Nose Mount Major Thread Diameter-Pitch (inches-threads/inch)
¾-16 NF (Sherline)
1-8 NC
1-10 Special
1⅛-12 (Whitworth)
1½-8 NS
1¾-8 NS
2¼-8 NS
2⅜-6 Special
2¾-8 NS

• The *Type D Series spindle mount,* also known as a *cam lock nose mount,* is the most popular non-threaded spindle mount today, and the standard on all full-sized industrial-grade lathes. See Figure 7-47. Although there are other excellent older spindle mount designs, like the *Long-Taper Key Type L* and the *American Standard Short-Taper*, the Type D Series is less expensive to manufacture and easier to use than these older designs and for this reason has become dominant. Chucks and mounting plates for all three spindle mounts are readily available.

The above three non-threaded spindle mount designs have several advantages over threaded spindle mounts:

-   The lathe spindle can be run in reverse, unlike threaded spindles which risk unscrewing themselves when run in reverse or stopping rapidly.

-   When subjected to instant spindle reverse or rapid braking, there is no risk of the chuck coming off the spindle. This is different from threaded spindle lathes which, even without reversing, run the risk of a chuck coming unscrewed if the motor is braked more rapidly than the chuck. The reason is that the kinetic energy stored in the chuck tends to keep the chuck rotating, and with the spindle turning more slowly than the chuck, the chuck will unscrew itself. Gradually reducing the spindle speed of a small, high-speed lathe like a Sherline is a better practice than simply turning off the motor.

- Type D spindle designs suffer less concentricity loss with wear than threaded spindles. See Figures 7-48 and 7-49 for mounting details.

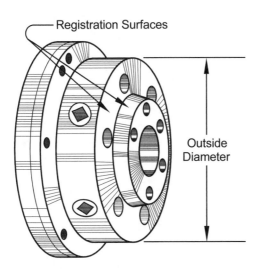

Spindle	Outside Diameter (in)
D1-3	$3\frac{5}{8}$
D1-4	$4\frac{3}{8}$
D1-5	$5\frac{3}{4}$
D1-6	$7\frac{1}{8}$
D1-8	$8\frac{7}{8}$
D1-11	$11\frac{3}{4}$

Figure 7-47. Cam lock Type D non-threaded spindle nose mount and size dimension chart.

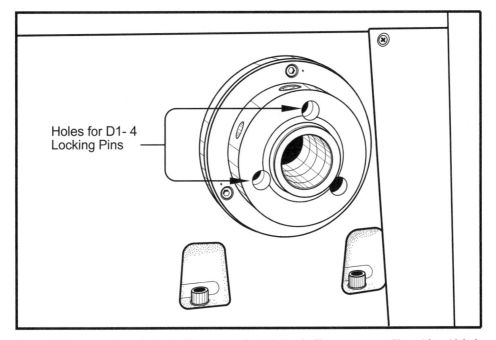

Figure 7-48. A non-threaded spindle mount, the D1-4 spindle mount on a Kent 13×40 lathe.

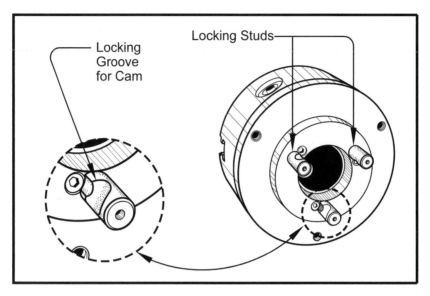

Figure 7-49. The chuck backplate of a D1-4 spindle mount
on a Kent 13 × 40 lathe. Notice the locking studs.

Taper Lengths

There are two main spindle nose taper lengths: The *short-taper*, or *Type A spindle nose* shown in Figure 7-50, and the *long-taper key*, or *Type L spindle nose* shown in Figure 7-51. These are both excellent older spindle mount designs, but they are no longer used on new lathes since the introduction of the cam lock spindle nose which is less expensive to manufacture and nearly as accurate. The long-taper key mount uses its large key to transmit torque from the lathe to its chuck, but uses the tapered cone to insure rigidity and maintain concentricity.

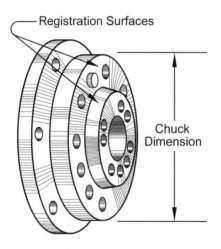

Spindle	Chuck Dimension (in)
A5	$3\frac{1}{4}$.
A6	$4\frac{3}{16}$
A8	$5\frac{1}{2}$
A11	$7\frac{3}{4}$
A15	$11\frac{1}{4}$
A20	$16\frac{1}{4}$

Figure 7-50. Short-taper, or Type A, spindle nose mount.

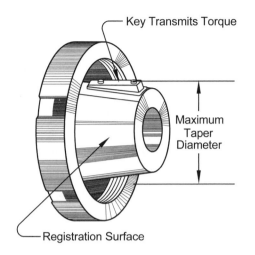

Spindle	Maximum Taper Diameter (in)
L00	$2^{3}/_{4}$
L0	$3^{1}/_{4}$
L1	$4^{1}/_{8}$
L2	$5^{1}/_{4}$
L3	$6^{1}/_{2}$

Figure 7-51. Long-taper key, or Type L, spindle nose mount.

Chuck Adapter Plates

Small chucks, like those for Sherline and Levin lathes, have integral spindle mounting threads cut into them. Larger chucks have flat backs and a series of mounting holes for an intermediate plate that bolts onto the back of the chuck. These plates, which adapt the chuck to a particular spindle mount design, go by many names: *adapter plates*, *chuck backs, backplates* or *chuck mounting plates*. They allow a single chuck design for a two-, three-, four- or six-jaw chuck to fit onto several different spindle mount designs by simply changing the chuck adapter plate. For example, most machinery catalogs offer backs to fit the four common spindle mount designs—threaded, cam lock, Type A short-taper and Type L long-taper—for 6- and 8-inch diameter chucks. Because these backs are available for out-of-production spindle mounts like the Type A and Type L, new chucks can easily be fitted for these spindles. Buying a chuck backplate to fit your lathe greatly simplifies making your own faceplate or driveplate because the most exacting and complicated machining of the project is already completed on the backplate when it is purchased.

Mounting a Chuck Adapter Plate onto a Chuck

Lathe adapter plates usually have a *boss* or raised step on their tailstock-facing side. This projection must be machined so it fits snugly into the recess on the chuck back. Here are the steps:

1. Check that the lathe is level, particularly front to back. If the lathe is not level, all cuts taken will be some form of cone and never a cylinder. To accurately level your lathe, use a precision level, not a carpenters' level.

2. Wipe all dirt off the spindle mount and the chuck adapter mounting surfaces.

3. Mount the chuck back onto the spindle.

4. Take a skim cut across the full face of the adapter plate. That is, both the face of the boss and the ring below the boss. This insures that the adapter plate face is perpendicular to the lathe axis.

5. The chuck plate has a boss which fits into the recess on the lathe chuck spindle-facing end. The recess on the chuck is usually tapered. Machine a taper on the adapter plate boss to fit into the recess on the chuck.

6. Bolt the lathe chuck to the adapter plate.

7. If the adapter plate diameter is larger than that of the lathe chuck, turn down the adapter plate diameter to match the chuck.

Figure 7-52 shows the modern adapter plate mounting method where the user reduces the diameter of the boss on the adapter plate in his lathe to fit into the factory-made cylindrical recess on the back of the chuck. Small tapered leads—short, steep bevels—are machined into both the boss on the adapter plate and the recess in the back of the chuck to make the parts assemble more easily. Alternatively, some machinists put a 5° taper on the boss and recess because it makes getting a perfect fit is easier. Both the boss face and the recess face may be machined to make the fit snug.

Figure 7-53 shows the traditional adapter plate mounting method where the user cuts the boss, or projection on the adapter plate, in the lathe to fit into the tapered recess machined in the back of the chuck by the factory. The adapter plate and chuck nest together and cannot shift. Four SHCSs in factory-drilled holes in the chuck secure the chuck to the adapter plate. The user may have to drill and tap the holes in the adapter plate during fitting.

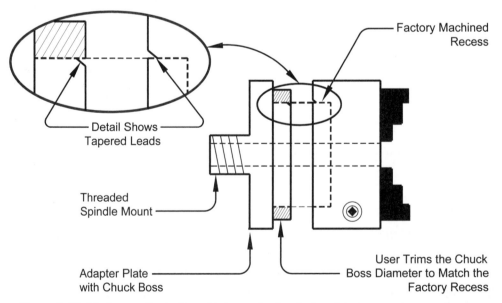

Figure 7-52. Modern method of machining a chuck adapter plate to mount a new chuck.

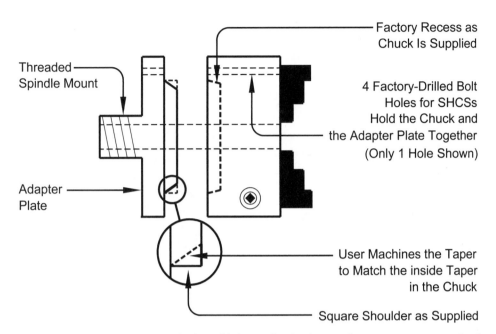

Threaded Spindle Mount

Factory Recess as Chuck Is Supplied

4 Factory-Drilled Bolt Holes for SHCSs Hold the Chuck and the Adapter Plate Together (Only 1 Hole Shown)

Adapter Plate

User Machines the Taper to Match the inside Taper in the Chuck

Square Shoulder as Supplied

Figure 7-53. Traditional method of machining a chuck adapter plate to mount a new chuck.

Mounting a D1-4 Chuck onto a Spindle

Chucks tend to be awkward and greasy so it is easy to lose your grip when mounting one—a catastrophe when you consider that a D1-4, 8-inch, three-jaw chuck weighs over 40 pounds. To protect yourself and the lathe ways from a dropped chuck, place some wood—a 6-inch wide piece of ½-inch plywood works well—across the ways below the spindle mount to give the chuck a platform on which to rest before attempting to mount it onto the spindle. Or better yet, use one of the chuck cradle designs in Figure 7-114 or 7-115 in the project section at the end of the chapter. The second design has handles to let you carry the chuck secured in its cradle. A well made chuck cradle supports and positions the chuck at the exact height of the chuck mount. This allows the cam lock pins on the chuck to slide into the matching holes of the D1-4 spindle mount while the chuck is still supported by the cradle.

With the D1-4 pins of the chuck backplate slipped into the spindle mount holes, press on the front of the chuck to close any gap between the spindle mount and the chuck backplate. This puts the D1-4 backplate mounting pins in position so the cams in the spindle mount can engage these pins to lock them in place. Use a ⅜-inch breaker bar, as in Figure 7-54, to turn the three square-drive locking cams on the spindle mount. You may also use a T-handle wrench to tighten the cams instead of the breaker bar. The T-handle is preferred as it will not pinch you like the breaker bar can. But sometimes the T-handle is too short. To lengthen a T-handle, see the project in Figure 7-112. Figure 7-55 shows how the cam locks the chuck to the spindle.

Note: There is a mark—an arrow or a line—on the square drive cam that indicates whether the cam is open or locked. On this particular cam lock mount, when the cams are locked, the indicating marks on the square socket drives are between the two Vs, from the 3 to 6 o'clock positions.

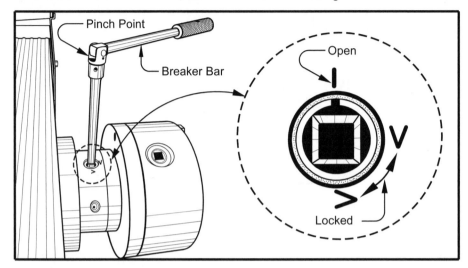

Figure 7-54. Tightening a D1-4 spindle mount backplate onto its spindle. The vertical notch at the 12 o'clock position shows that the cam lock socket is in the open position.

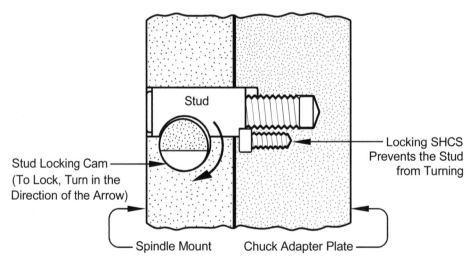

Figure 7-55. Cut view shows how the cam on the D1-4 spindle locks the stud on the chuck adapter plate into place on the spindle mount.

Chuck Care

When removing jaws from a three-jaw chuck and the scroll is exposed where the jaws sat, use this opportunity to clean debris from the scroll. Do this with a piece of balsa or other soft wood with its bottom end shaped like the scroll grooves, which are similar to an Acme thread. Turn the scroll with the chuck key so the scroll winds outward and the trash will be pushed out of the chuck.

Regrinding Three-Jaw Chucks

As three-jaw chucks are used, their runout increases from wear on their jaw work-holding faces, on the chuck jaw back teeth that engage the scroll, and from wear on the scroll itself. A tool post grinder on the lathe can regrind the chuck jaws and bring them back into symmetry. While the chuck jaw clamping surfaces are reground, the jaws must be put under load so that their back teeth fit snugly against the scroll and do not allow jaw movement during the grinding operation.

When grinding *internally* clamping jaws, which expand inside the work to clamp it, the jaws must be put under load in the same direction as when clamping *internally*. Anti-backlash chuck rings, sold in sets or shop-made, apply this load. See Figure 7-56.

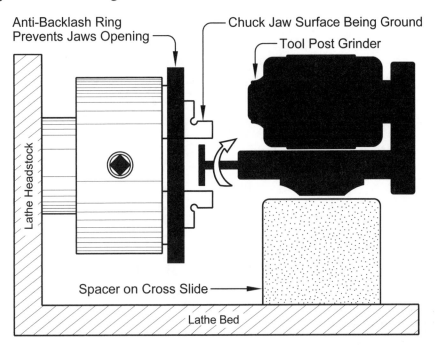

Figure 7-56. Tool post grinder on lathe cross slide set up to regrind chuck jaws.
Note the anti-backlash ring on the chuck jaws.

When grinding *externally* clamping chuck jaws, the jaws must be put under the same direction load as when clamping *externally*. Figure 7-57 (top) shows a steel plug positioned at the back of the jaws to put them under load. This figure also shows that wear is usually greatest at the front of the jaws and progressively less at the back. Figure 7-57 (middle) shows the jaws ground parallel by the tool post grinder. Because the tensioning plug is in the way, the back of the jaws cannot be ground by the tool post grinder and remain high. The jaws are removed from the chuck and the projecting, unground step is relieved. Now long stock can be run completely through the chuck as in Figure 7-57 (bottom) and remains centered.

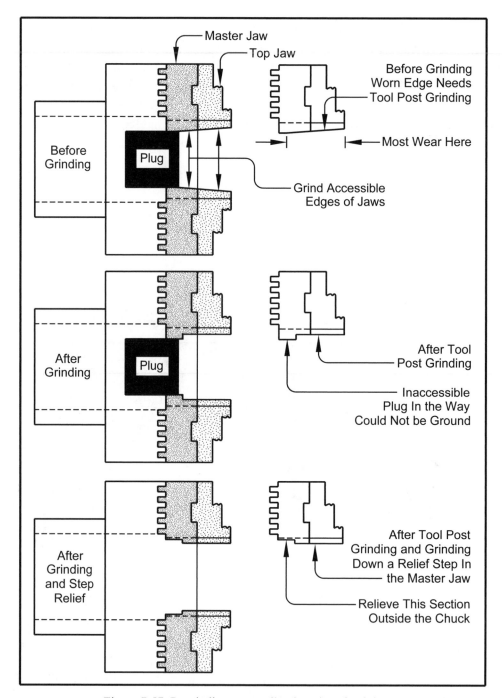

Figure 7-57. Regrinding externally clamping chuck jaws.

Because the scroll surfaces wear unevenly depending on the diameter at which the jaws are most often tightened, the most accuracy in regained when the jaws are reground while positioned *at the diameter* where runout is to be minimized. Although overall runout can only be improved, runout at the grinding diameter can be made as good as new.

Because recutting—or resurfacing—hardened chuck jaws involves interrupted cuts, neither HSS nor carbide cutters can be used. A tool post grinder must be used and the chuck turned under lathe power. Cover the lathe ways with paper taped in place to protect the ways from the grinding grit from the tool post grinder.

Centering Round Work in a Four-Jaw Independent Chuck

Here are the steps:

1. Begin by using the concentric rings on the chuck face to center the work by eye.

2. Set up the DTI as shown in Figure 7-58 (A).

3. Align any one of the chuck jaws with the axis of the DTI plunger and rotate the DTI scale to set it to zero. The black dot on the chuck illustration is to make it easy to keep track of the starting jaw.

4. Rotate the chuck exactly one-half turn, read the DTI dial and adjust these two opposite jaws by one-half the DTI reading to center the work. Use the DTI to make this adjustment as in Figure 7-58 (B). The work is now centered between these two jaws.

5. Rotate the chuck back and forth one-half turn to verify that the work is centered between these two jaws. If not, repeat Steps 1 and 2.

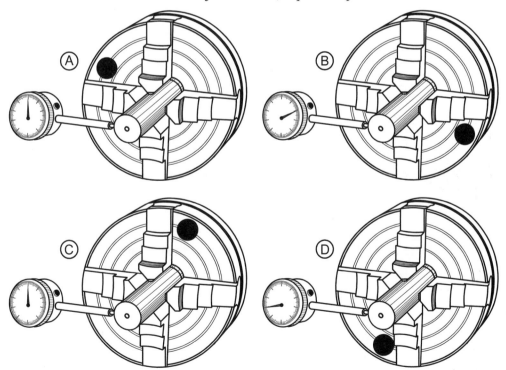

Figure 7–58. Steps to center round work in a four-jaw independent chuck. The large black dot is a reference point to show chuck rotation. On square bars, use the same centering process, but measure from the center of the bar's flats.

6. Rotate the chuck one-quarter turn in either direction to put a new chuck jaw parallel with the DTI probe, zero the DTI scale. See Figure 7-58 (C).

7. Rotate the chuck one-half turn in either direction, read the DTI, and adjust these two jaws one-half the DTI reading to center the work between these two jaws. See Figure 7-58 (D).

8. Verify that the work is centered by slowly turning the work through a complete turn while observing the DTI. The DTI needle should not move. Repeat Steps 4–7, if needed.

Alternative Centering Method

Another way to roughly center small stock in a four-jaw independent chuck involves a simple three-step process. First, grip the work in a drill chuck in the tailstock, second, push the tailstock holding the work into the open jaws of the chuck, and then, third, close the jaws to hold the work.

Removing & Replacing Work in a Chuck

When work must be removed from a four-jaw chuck for measurement or for inspection, mark one chuck jaw and the work where it touches this jaw with a Sharpie pen or china marker. Open only the master jaw and the jaw at the 9 o'clock position to remove the part. When the same part is re-inserted into the chuck, it will still be centered. See Figure 7-59.

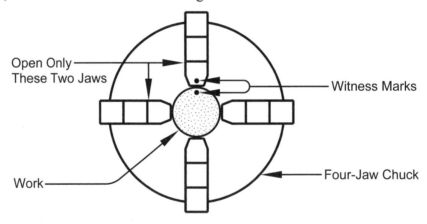

Figure 7-59. Marking the work and the four-jaw chuck jaw for
removing and replacing work without the need for recentering.

Protecting Work in the Chuck

Chuck jaws are usually hardened and most workpieces are not. As a result, workpieces become marked from clamping in the chuck jaws. This marking can be avoided by using copper, brass, aluminum or cardboard pads between the jaws and the workpiece. A convenient source of copper pads is copper tubing. Cut off a length of the tubing the depth of the chuck jaws, slit it open, and cut it into three curved segments to make clamping pads.

Chuck Spacers

Chuck spacers are used when clamping small, relatively thin parts in a three- or four-jaw chuck. See Figure 7-60. Spacers have two functions:

- Before the chuck jaws have been tightened on the work, a spacer prevents small work from falling though the hole in the back of the chuck jaws.

- To position the base of the workpiece *parallel* with the face of the chuck.

Spacers may be made of any metal or plastic, although aluminum is the most often used because it is easy to machine. Spacers should not be gripped by the chuck jaws. Their primary function is to rest against the chuck face when the work is being placed in the chuck. Sets of spacers are commercially available, but shop-made spacers are also popular and easy to make.

One or two parallels can be used to *position* the back of the workpiece parallel to the chuck face, but unlike chuck spacers, the parallel—or parallels—must be removed after the jaws are tightened. If not removed, the parallels will be flung out of the chuck with considerable force.

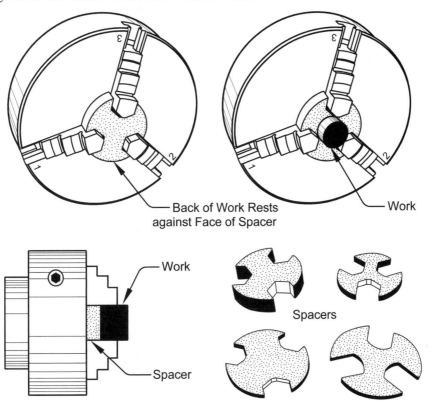

Figure 7-60. Spacers not only prevent short workpieces from slipping through the back of the chuck jaws, they insure that parts are clamped squarely against the chuck face.

Chuck Clamping Recommendations

Large forces of as much as one-hundred pounds are imposed on lathe workpieces from cutting tool pressure, so they must be clamped securely in chucks. If not securely clamped, physical damage to equipment, work and personnel may result. Figure 7-62 provides some work clamping guidelines.

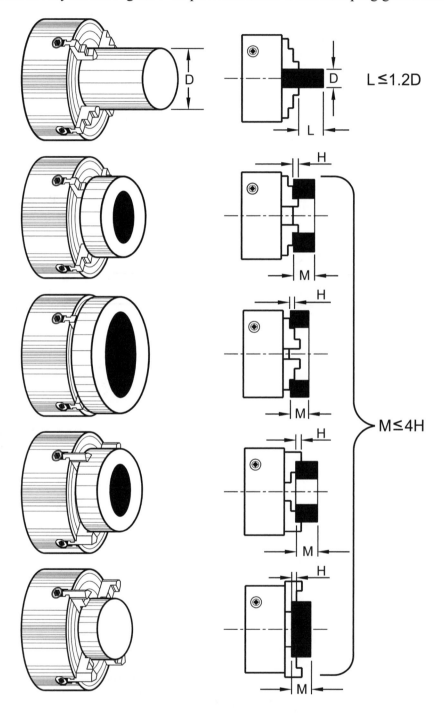

Figure 7-61. Clamping guidelines for holding chuck work in chucks 3–10 inches in diameter.

Handling Heavy Chucks

For safety, chucks larger than 8 inches in diameter should be moved with a chain hoist because they are very heavy and it is just too easy to lose control of a chuck during handling. Figure 7-62 shows a simple shop-made hoisting device to attach a chuck to a chain hoist. Following Steps 1–3, this device can prevent damage to the chuck, the lathe ways and the machinist.

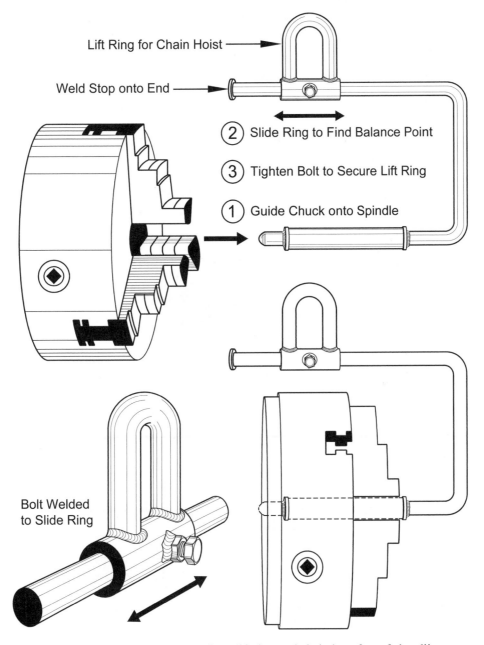

Lift Ring for Chain Hoist

Weld Stop onto End

2 Slide Ring to Find Balance Point

3 Tighten Bolt to Secure Lift Ring

1 Guide Chuck onto Spindle

Bolt Welded to Slide Ring

Figure 7-62. Larger chucks require a lift ring and chain host for safe handling.

Section VI – Collets

Collets

Collets, also called *spring collet chucks*, are the original three-jaw chuck. They are the wedge between the cutting tool and the tool holder. All chuck designs evolved from slit-sided tapered cylinders which, when forced into a tapered holder, collapse and grip the part. There are two different ways to close collets: the draw-in-to-close and the push-to-close methods. The method used depends on the location of the chuck on the lathe and the collet closer design.

Collet Terms

- *Collet type* refers to the shape and dimensions of the collet where the machine tool holds it. *Machinery's Handbook* lists more than eighty collet types, but the Type 5C, as shown in Figure 7-63, is the most common for full-sized lathes, followed by collet Types 16C and 3J for smaller lathes like South Bends. Both watchmakers' and Sherline lathes use Type WW collets which handle very small diameter work. See Figure 7-64.

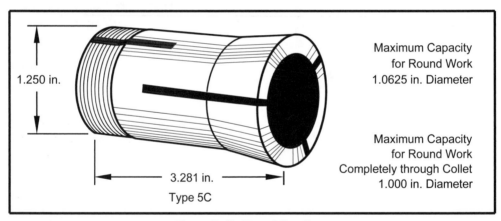

Figure 7-63. Type 5C collet.

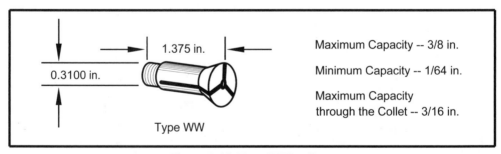

Figure 7-64. Type WW collet.

- *Collet design* refers to the shape and function of that part of the collet which holds the workpiece itself. The typical spring collet grips the outside of the workpiece, while expanding collet designs fit into the work to grip it.

Although this section uses Type 5C collets for examples of different collet designs, many other type collets have similar work-holding designs. Even the very small Sherline collets come in a number of these same designs.

The Four Most Common 5C Collet Designs

- *Round collets*, the most often used and the least expensive designs, are simple three-jaw collets for holding cylindrical work. With the exception of the *emergency collets* detailed below, round collets are steel that have been heat-treated to R_c 60 for wear and strength, then cylindrically ground for accuracy and a smooth finish. Round collets are readily available in both inch and metric sizes. Decimal collets in 0.001-inch diameter increments are available as special order items at a premium price. Number and letter size collets are also available.

- *Hexagonal* and *square collets* are both sized to hold standard dimensions of hex and square stock. Because hex collets hold hex stock so securely, they are particularly useful for making hex head screws and bolts.

- *Emergency collets*, also called *e-collets* and *soft collets*, are available in unhardened steel, brass and nylon. They are essentially round collets with unfinished bores. They have only a small starter hole in their centers so they can be bored to handle a particular job even when that size standard collet is not available. While an emergency collet will not wear as well as a hardened steel collet, it can produce several hundred parts. Every shop should have several emergency collets on hand. Figure 7-65 shows all four of the common collet designs.

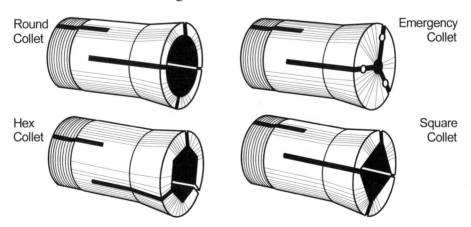

Figure 7-65. The four most common 5C collet designs.

Other Important Collet Designs

Figure 7-66 shows six additional collet designs:

- *Rectangular collets* hold rectangular stock and are special-order items.

- *Extended nose collets* can hold slightly larger work than standard round collets because they hold the work forward and outside of the spindle bore.

- *External expanding mandrel collets* are for workpieces with a hole on the turning axis. Some of these expanding mandrel collets are factory hardened, and others are supplied unhardened so the user can turn them to size to match the work.

- *Extended nose emergency collets* are supplied unhardened both with and without slits. The user modifies these collets to fit the workpiece.

- *Round serrated collets* offer greater gripping power than the more common smooth bore collets, but they are about three times more expensive and are relatively uncommon.

- *Chuck collets* hold work too large to fit inside a 5C collet—up to 6 inches in diameter. This design requires a tapered ring behind the collet which forces the collet closed when the collet closer is pulled tight. For clarity, this ring has been omitted from Figure 7-66 (bottom right).

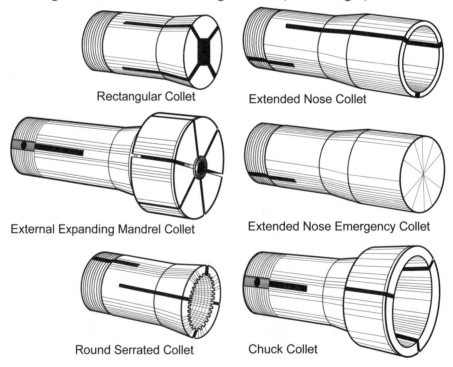

Figure 7-66. Other important collet designs.

5C Collet Size Ranges

Table 7-4 shows how each of the 5C collet designs has its own size range for workpieces.

Collet Description	Size Range
Round Fractional	$^1/_{64}$–$1^1/_{16}$ in., decimal, metric & fractional
Round Metric	0.5–27 mm inclusive by 0.5 mm increments
Hexagon Fractional	$^1/_{16}$–$^7/_8$ in. inclusive by $^1/_{64}$ in. increments
Square Fractional	$^3/_{64}$–$^3/_4$ in. inclusive by $^1/_{64}$ in. increments
Round Decimal	0.016–1.030 in. inclusive by 0.001 in. increments
Emergency	Steel, brass or nylon with $^1/_{16}$ in. pilot hole
Round Serrated Fractional	$^1/_4$–$1^1/_{64}$ in. inclusive by $^1/_{64}$ in. increments
Rectangular	$^1/_8 \times ^5/_{32}$ in. to $^5/_8 \times ^3/_4$ in. inclusive

Table 7-4. Type 5C collets and the size range of work they can hold.

Collet Advantages

Here are the advantages to using collets:

- Collets are self-centering and exert large clamping forces on the workpieces they hold.

- A quality 5C collet in a lathe with good spindle bearings will have less than 0.0005 inches of runout, and the collet will maintain this accuracy from part to part. With wear or abuse, though, collet runout will increase.

- Clamping forces are more evenly distributed around parts held in collets because there is more contact all the way around the part's periphery than when using a three- or four-jaw chuck. Also, when using a collet there is much less chance of marking a part or collapsing a thin-walled part than when using a chuck.

- The same part can be re-inserted into a collet later for other operations or adjustments with nearly the same concentricity as during its previous insertion.

- Because shifting a collet closer lever is faster than turning a T-wrench in a chuck, collets have a faster cycle time for inserting and removing parts than three- or four-jaw chucks.

- Turning, facing, threading, slitting and indexing can be performed on a part held in a collet though these operations require different machine tools. The part maintains positional accuracy because it remains in the collet for all of the different operations.

- Collets are much lighter in weight than full-sized chucks, so they are easier on the spindle bearings. They also accelerate and decelerate faster, an important consideration in a production setting.

- Centrifugical forces on chuck jaws tend to pull them open and reduce their clamping forces, but collets are much less affected by these forces.

- Brass, nylon or unhardened steel emergency collets are readily machined to hold irregular parts or to replace missing collet sizes.

- Collets work very well for holding cylindrical hardened parts such as dowel pins and SHCSs for turning or cutoff operations. Collets grip the parts all-around without damaging them.

- Nylon emergency collets can hold polished chrome-plated brass parts without leaving any clamping marks.

Collet Disadvantages

Here are the disadvantages to using collets:

- Round 5C collets cannot hold work larger than 1.0625 inches in diameter. The *inside hole* in the 5C collet is limited by the *outside diameter* of the collet itself. Refer back to Figure 7-63.

- Each collet has a small range of sizes it can clamp properly without damage to itself. A complete set of 65 round collets ($\frac{1}{16}$ through $1\frac{1}{16}$ inch by $\frac{1}{64}$ inch increments) is essential in a well-equipped shop.

- Collets work best for small, short, cylindrically-shaped parts of uniform size, not large asymmetrical parts, unless one end of the part has been turned down to fit into the collet.

Minimizing Collet Runout

The factors affecting runout are:

- A collet's runout, or TIR, is no better than the runout of the lathe spindle bearings themselves. The best chuck will not improve runout over that of the lathe spindle bearings. There is no point in using a 50 millionths of an inch runout precision collet in a lathe with poor or worn out bearings. The benefits of such a collet will only be visible with a precision tool room lathe with good bearings.

- Dirt in the collet bore, spindle nose and adapter, or between the collet and its holder increases runout. Always clean these surfaces before using a collet. Also, new collets must be cleaned before use.

- Collet dimensions must match the workpiece diameter, usually within ± 0.003 inches, or concentricity may be degraded. In general, the shorter the length of the part inside the collet, the greater the deviation from the collet's nominal diameter permissible without increasing TIR.

Collet Closer Designs

All collets require a mechanism to exert a closing force on them. Here are the most common:

- *Manual collet closers* – This traditional collet closer is a steel tube with internal threads on one end for gripping the collet and a handwheel on the other end for tightening the threads onto the collet. With the manual collet closer in Figure 7-67, pulling back on the collet draws it into the tapered spindle adapter, forcing the collet jaws tighter over the workpiece. Every cycle of putting work into and taking work out of the collet requires turning the handwheel. This type of collet closer is simple, reliable, and works well, but because it does not meet OSHA safety requirements, it is no longer produced for full-sized lathes in the US. Buyers of new lathes are required to purchase a lever-type collet closer for ten times the cost of a manual closer. Sherline lathes though, because of their small size, continue to use the manual closer design.

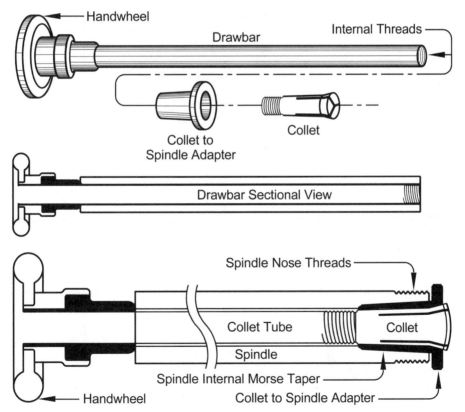

Figure 7-67. Manual collet closer on a lathe with a threaded spindle nose.

- *Lever-type collet closer* – Though this collet closer costs much more than a manual closer, the lever-type closer has many advantages. The fast and simple operation of this closer design is much better than a manual collet closer for production work because simply pushing the closing lever back and forth opens and closes the collet. See Figures 7-68 and 7-69. Once the closer is initially adjusted for the collet and the workpiece dimensions, no more turning of the closer is needed. Like the manual collet closer, the lever-type closer has rotating parts emerging from the left end of the spindle and poses no less a safety hazard than the manual closer.

Here is how a lever-type collet closer works:

1.   The collet closer tube shown in Figure 7-69 has internal threads on its right-hand end which grip the external threads on the back of the 5C collet. By turning the collar, these threads are adjusted to pull the collet closed to within ⅛ turn of being tight on the workpiece. This adjustment needs to be made only once for work of the same diameter.

2.   Pushing the actuating lever to the left pulls the cam spool to the left inside the collar though the ball bearing and associated linkage.

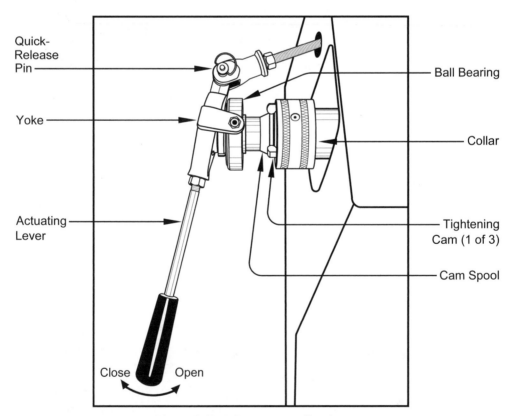

Figure 7-68. A lever-type collet closer.

3. When the cam spool moves to the left, ramps on it force three (or in some closer designs, four) cams inside the collar to pull the collet closer tube away from the spindle. This tightens the collet the remaining way down onto the work.

4. Pushing the collet actuating lever to the right moves the cam spool to the right, which releases pressure on the cams, opens the collet, and releases the workpiece.

5. The cam spool turns with the collet closer tube, but it slides from right to left with the actuating lever.

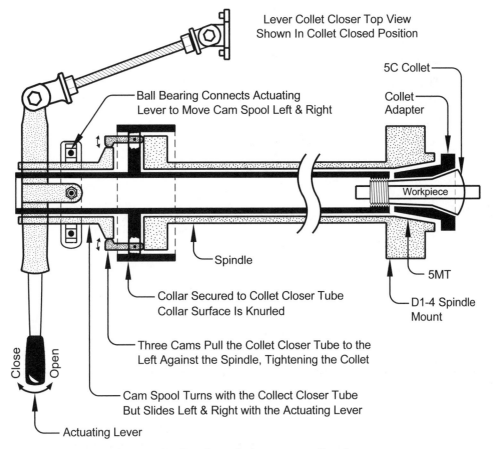

Figure 7-69. Cut view of a lever-type collet closer.

Collet Adapters

To hold a 5C collet in a lathe with a #5MT spindle requires an adapter sleeve which is normally furnished with each collet closer. There is a pin inside the adapter sleeve which drops into the groove on the side of the 5C collet to prevent the collet from turning in the adapter. The clock position of the spindle's internal pin is indicated by the location of the manufacturer's logo as in Figure 7-70. The pin inside the adapter and its matching groove on the collet must be aligned for the collet to enter the adapter. Instead of blindly turning the collet until the internal pin drops into its groove, note that the manufacturer's logo shows the clock position of the pin. If your collet adapter lacks such a logo or clocking mark, you may put one on the adapter with a hand-held grinder.

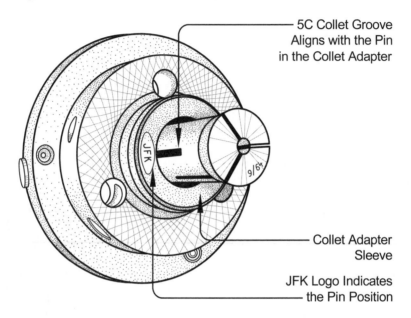

Figure 7-70. Manufacturer's logo indicates the clock position of the internal pin.

Collet Chucks

These chucks hold 5C collets *outside* the lathe spindle instead of *inside* it. Collet chucks eliminate the need for a manual or lever-type collet closer.

Here are some of the reasons for using a collet chuck:

- The lathe spindle internal diameter is too small to hold a 5C collet, but a collet of this diameter is required to hold the workpiece.

- Installing a collet chuck in a three- or four-jaw chuck is faster than installing a collet closer when swapping between different kinds of work.

- There is no available collet closer for your lathe.

- The workpiece needs to remain in the 5C collet chuck while other machining operations are performed in the milling machine or surface grinder.

- When the geometry of the lathe prevents cutting tool access close to the spindle; a collet chuck puts the work closer to the cutting tool. Many gap bed lathes have leadscrew and power drive components which limit carriage travel on the spindle end of the lathe.

There are two basic collet chuck designs:

- The first is collet chucks that are held in a three- or four-jaw chuck as in Figure 7-71. This design is a great time saver because the collet closer does not have to be installed, but the downside is that the runout of the chuck degrades the inherent concentricity of the collet.

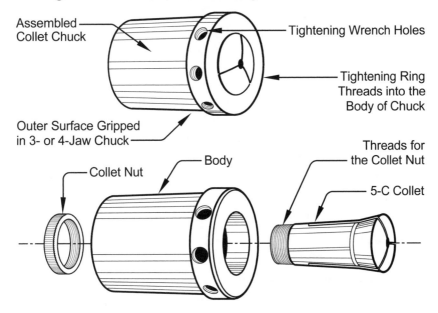

Figure 7-71. 5C collet chuck which fits in a three- or four-jaw chuck.

- The second design is collet chucks which mount onto a lathe adapter plate as in Figure 7-72. By using an adapter plate which mounts the collet chuck onto the spindle, runout can be reduced.

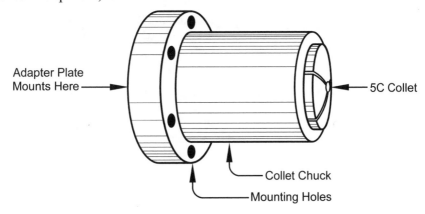

Figure 7-72. 5C collet chuck to be mounted on an adapter plate.

Collet chucks have greater runout than the same size collet installed inside the spindle because the runout of collets depends on several factors beyond the spindle and the spindle adapter. These factors are:

- The runout of the spindle mounting plate or the chuck holding the collet chuck.
- The runout of the collet chuck itself.
- The distance of the collet tip from the spindle bearings. The rule of thumb is, the farther the distance, the greater the runout is magnified. Often though, the loss of runout accuracy is not as important as the other reasons for choosing a collet chuck.

5C Chucks

These are 4-inch diameter three- and four-jaw chucks which have an R8 mount that fits into a 5C collet adapter just as a 5C collet would. See Figure 7-73. These chucks are a way of holding a workpiece on axis so many different operations may be performed on it. 5C chucks are used for work too large for a 5C collet—more than $1^1/_{16}$-inches diameter—or for when no suitable collet is available.

The advantages of 5C chucks:

- Just like 6-, 8- or 10-inch four-jaw chucks, workpieces other than round can be held in a 5C chuck's independent jaws.
- 5C chucks have the advantage that work can be machined in a lathe and then transferred to a milling machine or to a surface grinder while remaining in the chuck and still centered in the collet.

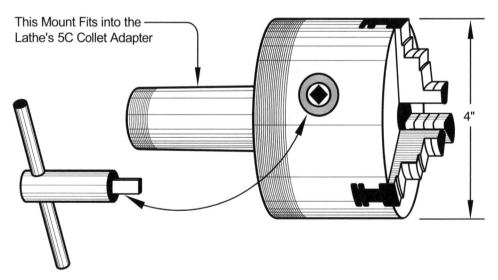

This Mount Fits into the
Lathe's 5C Collet Adapter

4"

Figure 7-73. A three-jaw 5C chuck with its key. Similar four-jaw chucks are also available.

Collet & Chuck Terminology

The terminology of collets and chucks can be confusing, so to clarify, let's review:

- A *collet to spindle adapter,* also called a *spindle adapter,* is a conical sleeve spacer that fits into the female Morse taper of the lathe spindle. It centers and holds a collet in its female cavity. See Figure 7-67.

- A *collet chuck* is a device to hold and close a collet. It either mounts on an adapter plate to mount on the lathe spindle or is held in the jaws of a three- or four-jaw chuck. It is a way to hold a collet in a lathe without using a collet closer and without putting the collet in the spindle. It is convenient either when there is no collet closer, the spindle diameter is too small to hold the needed collet, or when other operations must be performed while the work remains centered. See Figures 7-71 and 7-72.

- A *5C chuck* is a 4-inch diameter three- or four-jaw chuck that has a mount, or stub, that fits into a 5C collet adapter in the lathe spindle. The 5C chuck is an accurate and convenient way to hold small workpieces that would be too small to hold in the larger chucks used on a larger lathe. A 5C chuck allows work to remain centered and be removed for other operations in a milling machine or surface grinder. See Figure 7-73.

How to Bore an Emergency Collet

An emergency collet, as shown in Figure 7-74, is not hardened so it can be bored to the size needed. Here are the important steps to prepare an emergency collet for use:

1. Make certain that all of the spacer pins are in the face of the collet, then insert the collet into the lathe spindle with the drawbar in the full open position.

2. Adjust the collet closer until it closes on the pins, and then back off ⅛ to ¼ of a turn. Leave enough pressure on the collet so it is fully seated in the spindle, yet not as much force as you would use while holding a part for machining, and lock the drawbar in this position.

3. Close the collet. If you can pull the pins out, you should increase the chucking pressure until the pins cannot be removed.

4. Rough machine and finish ream the emergency collet bore to the chucking diameter of the workpiece to be held.

5. Remove the collet and deburr it.

6. Carefully clean the spindle and collet closer, and remount them.

7. Re-insert the emergency collet, then adjust the collet closer to insure proper gripping and the correct drawbar pressure to hold the workpiece.

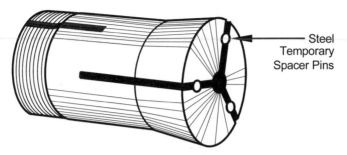

Figure 7-74. An unbored and unhardened emergency collet.

Extra-Long Stock

When a long piece of stock must pass though the collet and spindle and then out the left side of the headstock, it must be supported so it does not whip around and bend while turning. Usually a floor stand with a *yoke* does the job. When using extra-long stock for making many identical parts, rod or hex stock up to 20 feet long can be used if it is supported by several floor stands. Each part is machined in the collet and parted-off. The remaining rod stock is then pulled though the collet to machine the next part. An even safer alternative is to hold the extra-long stock inside a piece of PVC or ABS pipe. This will solidly support thin, flexible stock and prevent anyone from getting their clothing caught up in the rod or bar stock. See Figure 7-75.

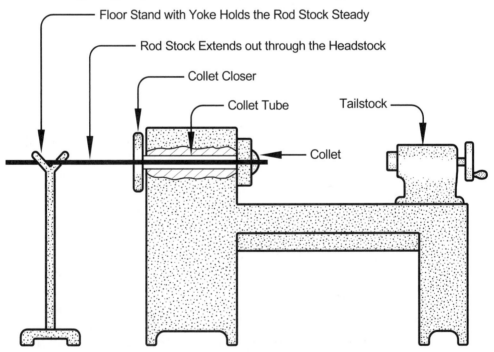

Figure 7-75. Extra-long rod stock passing through the headstock must be supported.

Section VII – Work Holding

Three-Jaw Universal Chucks

Three-jaw universal chucks hold three different workpiece shapes—rounds, triangles and hexes—without the centering step needed with a four-jaw chuck. See Figure 7-76 (top row). Square stock can be safely held in a three-jaw chuck by using a split ring to distribute the clamping forces on the work as shown in Figure 7-76 (bottom left). Eccentrics can also be turned with the help of a shop-made spider as in Figure 7-76 (bottom, middle and right). A spider is a spacer with legs that keeps a workpiece centered and makes it easy to position stock for cutting eccentrics.

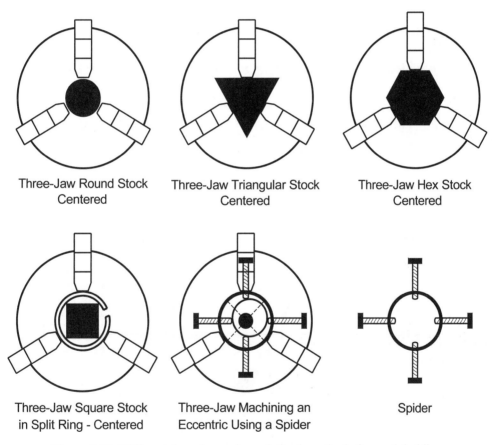

Three-Jaw Round Stock
Centered

Three-Jaw Triangular Stock
Centered

Three-Jaw Hex Stock
Centered

Three-Jaw Square Stock
in Split Ring - Centered

Three-Jaw Machining an
Eccentric Using a Spider

Spider

Figure 7-76. Different three-jaw universal chuck methods for work holding.

Mounting Square Stock in a Three-Jaw Chuck

When the workpiece and the turning forces will be too large for holding square work with a split ring, use the method shown in Figure 7-77.

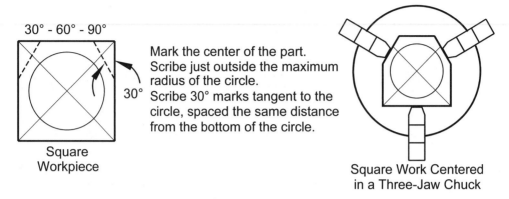

30° - 60° - 90°

Mark the center of the part.
Scribe just outside the maximum
radius of the circle.
30°   Scribe 30° marks tangent to the
circle, spaced the same distance
from the bottom of the circle.

Square
Workpiece

Square Work Centered
in a Three-Jaw Chuck

Figure 7-77. Securely mounting a square workpiece in a three-jaw chuck.

Cutting Eccentrics by Shifting the Workpiece

Although eccentrics are often cut using a four-jaw chuck, some eccentrics may be cut with a three-jaw chuck using a spacer—or shim—to shift the work center. See Figure 7-78. The fastest way to determine the shim height is to cut one and try it out. When turning many parts, it is a good idea to use a U-shaped shim, called a *spacing shoe*, which fits over one of the jaws instead of a spacer held by friction.

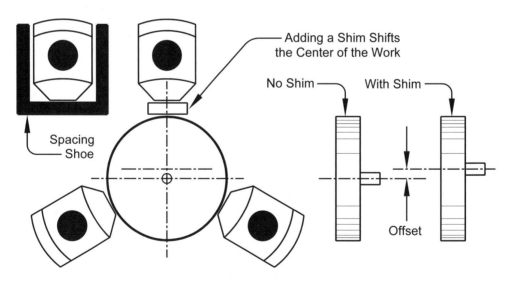

Adding a Shim Shifts
the Center of the Work

No Shim   With Shim

Spacing
Shoe

Offset

Figure 7-78. Adding a spacer to a jaw moves the center of the work with
respect to the lathe axis to cut an eccentric.

Four-Jaw Chucks

Four-jaw chucks are particularly well suited for holding square, rectangular and eccentric work as shown in Figure 7-79. Whenever precise centering or off-centering is needed, a four-jaw is usually the answer.

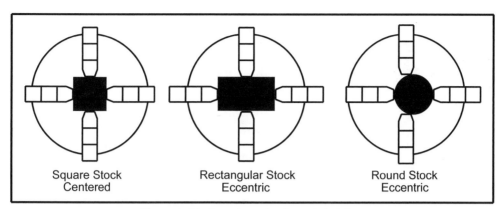

Figure 7-79. Four-jaw chuck work holding.

Using Chucks with Centers

Three- and four-jaw chucks are often used instead of a center in the spindle to provide more support for the work during turning. See Figure 7-80.

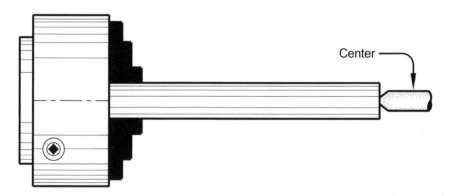

Figure 7-80. A chuck holding work rather than a center in the spindle.

Setting Up Steady Rests & Follower Rests

Positioning the jaws of a steady or follower rest can be done in either of two ways:

- If there is a tailstock-end center and a center hole in the workpiece, put the center in the work and adjust the steady rest so it is snug on the workpiece. Be sure to add lubrication to the fingers on the steady rest.

- With no tailstock-end center or center hole available, place the workpiece in a three-jaw chuck (or centered in a four-jaw chuck), slide the steady rest up close to the chuck, secure the steady to the lathe, then adjust the fingers on the steady against the work. Unfasten the steady rest from the lathe, position it on the tailstock end of the lathe, and lock it in position. The fingers are already adjusted to center the work. Again, be sure to lubricate the fingers. See Figure 7-81.

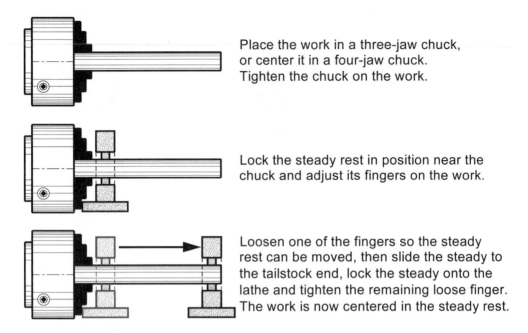

Place the work in a three-jaw chuck, or center it in a four-jaw chuck. Tighten the chuck on the work.

Lock the steady rest in position near the chuck and adjust its fingers on the work.

Loosen one of the fingers so the steady rest can be moved, then slide the steady to the tailstock end, lock the steady onto the lathe and tighten the remaining loose finger. The work is now centered in the steady rest.

Figure 7-81. Using a chuck to center work in a steady rest.

Friction Driving in the Lathe

Friction driving is when, using the tailstock and a live center, slightly oversized workpieces are squeezed between two metal back-up cylinders to hold the work for turning. For example, friction driving is a good solution if you require one or more metal, hard rubber or plastic discs with a diameter tolerance of ±0.001 inches. The workpiece material is supplied flat and must remain flat after cutting. Here are the steps to make this part:

1. Cut two metal back-up cylinders the same diameter as needed for the finished discs.

2. Center drill one of the cylinders.

3. Set up the work in the lathe as in Figure 7-82. When cutting more than one disc, use double-stick tape between the parts to keep them in place.

4. Reduce the diameter of the workpieces so they are slightly larger than the back-up cylinders. Then, set the lathe tool bit so it just clears the right-hand cylinder and "wipe" away the excess workpiece material. *Take light cuts.*

Friction driving works well whether the workpiece material is just a few thousandths of an inch thick to ¼-inch thick. It does not distort thin stock, works well with foil, and many identical discs can be cut at once. Rubber can also be trimmed, but be sure to allow for changes in part diameter caused by compression. This method does the work of an expensive punch and die set.

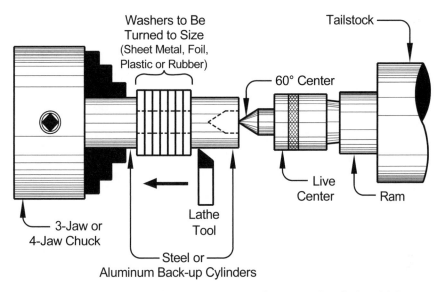

Figure 7-82. Cutting multiple discs to exact diameter using fiction driving.

Here's another example of friction driving: a workpiece must be turned which cannot be drilled for a mandrel and is too oversized to fit into the largest available chuck, so set up the work as shown in Figure 7-83. Apply enough axial force with the tailstock through the live center to keep the workpiece in place. The chuck jaws may be adjusted to minimize dishing of the work from these forces.

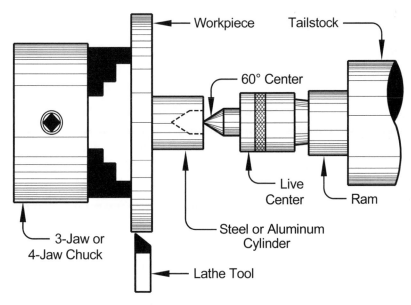

Figure 7-83. Turning oversized work with the chuck jaws
adjusted to help prevent the work from dishing.

A back-up cylinder may also be used as in Figure 7-84, but with the addition of abrasive cloth rubber-cemented to the cylinder face to increase friction. This prevents slippage and eliminates dishing.

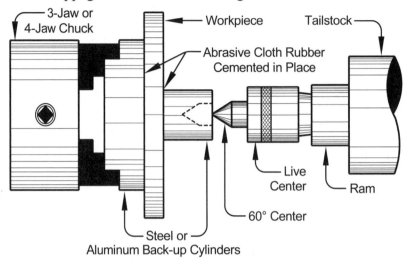

Figure 7-84. Turning oversized work with a large back-up cylinder to prevent dishing. Abrasive cloth glued to the back-up cylinder helps increase friction.

Section VIII – Turning Techniques

Cross-Feed Dial Movement

Figure 7-85 shows why you need to check your compound dial markings *before* turning down diameters:

- On American lathes, cross-feed dials indicate the *actual* tool distance moved; 10 thousandths on the dial removes 20 thousandths of an inch on the workpiece diameter. This requires the machinist to be constantly reminding himself that the actual tool movement distance is only half of the diameter reduction.

- On imported lathes, cross-feed dials indicate *half the actual* tool distance moved; so 20 thousandths on the cross-feed dial removes 20 thousandths of an inch on the workpiece diameter.

This difference in dial marking conventions can cause great confusion, particularly if you operate several machines with different cross-feed dials. Writing the cross-feed dial convention on or near the cross-feed readout is helpful. This difference between American and imported lathes does not apply to the lathes' compound where what you see on the dial is the movement you get on the compound.

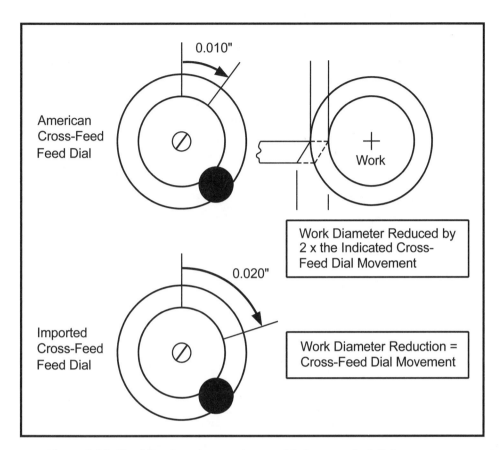

Figure 7-85. Checking American vs. imported lathe cross-feed dial movement.

Setting Lathe Tool Height

There are four ways to set the lathe tool height on center height:

- Using the tip of the cutting tool, pin a 6-inch steel rule between the tip of the tool and the workpiece. When the tool is exactly on center height, the rule will be vertical as in the middle drawing of Figure 7-86 (A).

- Place a dead center in the lathe tailstock or headstock as a reference, then adjust the lathe tool so its tip just touches the point of the center as in Figure 7-86 (B).

- Use a spool height gage, purchased or shop-made, on the cross slide as in Figure 7-86 (C). The gage indicates the tool height, so setting the lathe tool against the underside of the spool height gage sets your cutter to the proper height.

- Observe the *nubbin* left by a facing cut on the work. Using a test sample instead of the actual part is a good idea. When the lathe tool is at center height, there will be no nubbin remaining. See Figure 7-86 (D).

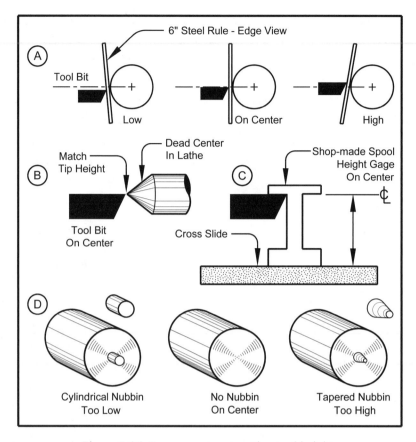

Figure 7-86. Four ways to set cutting tool height.

Shoulder Turning

There are several methods for turning shoulders:

- With the *two-step method* shown in Figure 7-87 (A), Step 1 starts by using a necking or grooving tool to cut the location of the shoulder, and then a cut is made to the depth of the final diameter. To finish, Step 2 uses a turning tool to remove the remaining oversize material on the right of the shoulder. The disadvantage of this method is that two different tools are used, which requires a tool change.

- The *single-tool shoulder-turning method* in Figure 7-87 (B) uses a zero-degree cutting angle to minimize cutting tool force on the workpiece. This method produces a shoulder with a small fillet.

- The *square-shoulder method* in Figure 7-87 (C) uses a pointed tool and a positive lead angle. For the best finish and fastest stock removal, an initial roughing cut, using methods A or B, is often used. The carriage longitudinal power feed cuts all but the last ¼ inch of the diameter of the shoulder. The last ¼ inch is fed by hand.

- The *additional square-shoulder method* shown in Figure 7-87 (D) uses a small flat ground on the leading edge or left side of the tool. This cuts a smoother finish without the "tree rings" that the method in Figure 7-87 (C) can produce.

- The *filleted-shoulder method* in Figure 7-87 (E) uses a round-nosed cutting tool to reduce the diameter and to cut the shoulder.

- The *two-tool method* in Figure 7-87 (F) shows another approach. Most of the diameter is cut with a round-nosed tool as in Figure 7-87 (B), and then the shoulder is finished with a nearly square-faced tool.

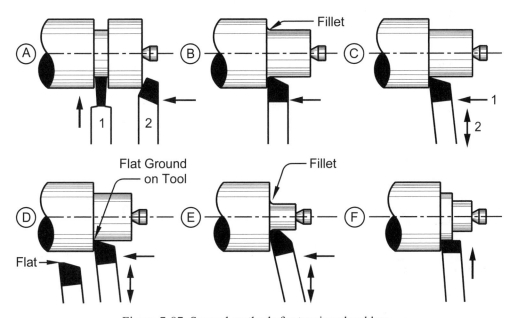

Figure 7-87. Several methods for turning shoulders.

Tip: When a workpiece is designed to have different diameters along its length, use the lathe tool to make light stab marks or rings at the shoulder locations. This will help you anticipate where the shoulders will go.

Boring Flat-Bottomed Holes

When held in the lathe tailstock, center-cutting end mills can cut perfect flat-bottomed holes. This is a good way to start a boring job because the milling cutter can be used to indicate the final bore depth. To make sure that the end mill can plunge cut, check to see if the end mill has a cutting edge on its bottom that *crosses* the centerline so on-center material will be cut and cleared. Some end mills have a center hole in both ends for use during sharpening, but these cannot cut a flat-bottomed hole.

Trepanning vs. Flycutting

Trepanning and *flycutting* describe two slightly different processes which produce similar results:

- *Trepanning* is the cutting out of a circle of material by removing a thin annular band of chips or waste material from the outer edge of the circle. A lathe cutter bit ground for plunge cutting is used for this task and the work rotates while the tool remains stationary. Most machinists perform trepanning in a lathe, usually with the work mounted on a faceplate. A sacrificial back-up of Masonite, aluminum or steel is used as shown in Figure 7-88. Because there are large cutting forces on the work, securely mounting the work is critical to success. Very often to insure a solid mount on the faceplate, a much larger piece of metal stock is used than is actually required for the part itself. Trepanning can be done on stock up to ½-inch thick, but the maximum trepanning depth is limited by the rigidity of the cutting tool.

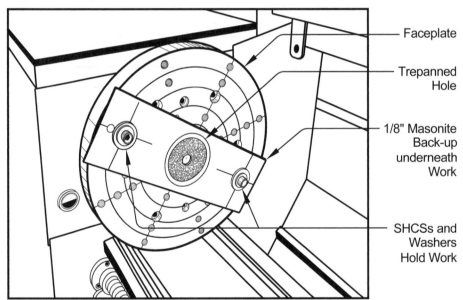

Faceplate

Trepanned
Hole

1/8" Masonite
Back-up
underneath
Work

SHCSs and
Washers
Hold Work

Figure 7-88. Trepanning on a faceplate. The Masonite back-up
or spacer material prevents damaging the faceplate.

- *Flycutting* also uses a cutting tool similar to a lathe cutter to remove a disc of material, but unlike the trepanning tool, the flycutting tool rotates and the work remains fixed. See Figure 7-89. Flycutting can be performed in either a drill press or a mill. Flycutters have a twist drill in their centers to provide a rigid pivot point, or center, to stabilize the cutting action. Circles removed by flycutters have a center hole remaining from the twist drill. Flycutting is usually performed on sheet metal ⅛ inch or less in thickness.

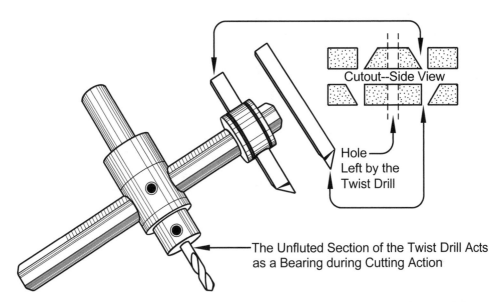

Figure 7-89. A flycutter cuts out a circle of material like a trepanning operation, but it leaves a center hole in the circle. Flycutters can be used in both drill presses and milling machines.

Although the tool pictured in Figure 7-89 is known as a *flycutter*, or *circle cutter,* another different milling machine tool used to produce a large, flat area on a part is also known as a *flycutter*. This tool, shown in Figure 8-85, is further discussed in Chapter 8 – Milling Machines.

Making a Bull Nose for Turning Pipe

A simple shop-made *bull nose,* also called a *cone adapter,* allows pipe to be turned between centers as shown in Figure 7-90. Here is the procedure for making a bull nose:

1. Place the short length of cylindrical stock for making the bull nose in a three-jaw chuck.

2. Center drill, then drill stepped holes in the stock to make boring the center cone easier.

3. Bore out a tapered hole, usually 60°, so the bull nose will fit onto the tailstock center. Either a live center or a dead center may be used with the bull nose.

4. With the bull nose still in the three-jaw chuck, cut the shoulder step.

5. Remove the bull nose from the chuck, turn it end-for-end and replace it in the chuck.

6. Turn the tapered end, which will fit into the pipe workpiece, into a 60° cone.

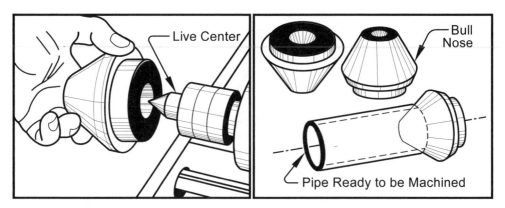

Figure 7-90. Turning a short length of steel cylindrical stock into a
bull nose makes holding pipe in the lathe easy and secure.

Setting a Compound Angle to Cut Morse Tapers

Taper attachments are desirable, but not necessary for accurately cutting male
Morse tapers. In lieu of a taper attachment, use a compound and a DTI to set
the cutting angle for the Morse taper. Here is how to make the set-up:

1. Place the MT between centers in the lathe. Live centers are preferred.

2. Mount the DTI on the compound so that it just touches the side of the MT.

3. Adjust the angle on the compound so that the dial indicator pointer does
    not move when the compound is moved back and forth across the taper.
    See Figure 7-91. The Morse taper cutting angle is now accurately set.

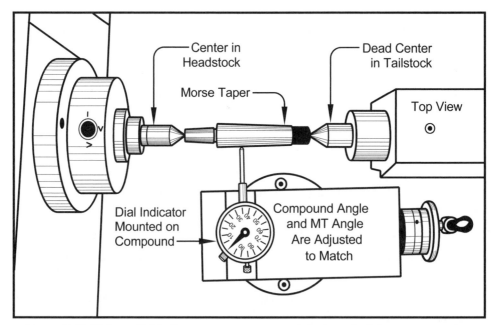

Figure 7-91. Using a dial indicator to set a compound angle to the Morse taper angle.

Centering Work in Four-Jaw Chucks

Clamp smaller round parts in a drill chuck in the lathe tailstock. This puts the work within ±0.010 inches of the lathe center axis. Slide the tailstock to the right end of the work until it fits into the four-jaw chuck, then close the chuck on the work.

Self-Locking Stub on a Shop-Made Mandrel

Sometimes work is held on a tapered mandrel or held onto a mandrel with a set screw and washer. Figure 7-92 shows how to make a self-locking mandrel that uses a dowel pin. There are a couple of advantages to this approach. First, the mandrel design provides complete access to one side of the work, and second, the work may be quickly mounted and dismounted. Here is how to make a self-locking mandrel:

1. Make the basic mandrel by milling or filing a flat on the proper sized steel round to hold your work. This flat must be parallel to the lathe axis.

2. Slide the work onto the mandrel.

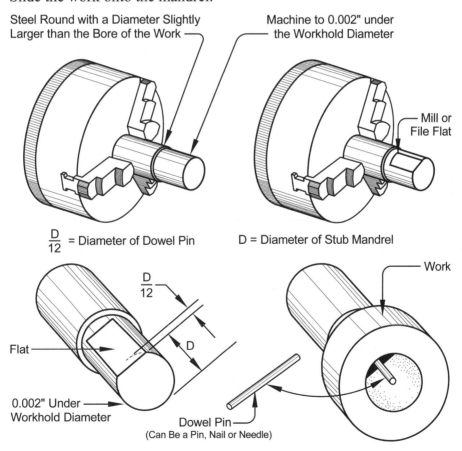

Figure 7-92. Self-locking stub on a shop-made mandrel.

3. Prepare the locking dowel pin by cutting it to length. It should be as long as the work is wide and $\frac{1}{12}$ the diameter of the mandrel.

4. Place the dowel pin between the work and the flat, and turn the work so it locks up on the mandrel and will not spin when in the lathe.

Cutting Thin-Walled Tubing to Length

Figure 7-93 shows how to cut thin-walled tubing to length squarely and accurately without crushing the tubing. Here are the steps:

1. Fill the inside of the tubing with a snug fitting metal or wooden mandrel. Aluminum is an excellent choice because it is easy to machine. The internal mandrel prevents the fragile tubing from collapsing under the cutting tool forces.

2. Place the thin-walled tubing with its mandrel in a three-jaw chuck. Use thin strips of copper, aluminum or cardboard between the chuck jaws and the tubing to avoid marking the tubing.

3. Apply cutting fluid and trim the tubing to length using a plunge cut with a cutoff tool. Do not try to cut the work to length by moving the carriage because the tubing is weak and will wrinkle.

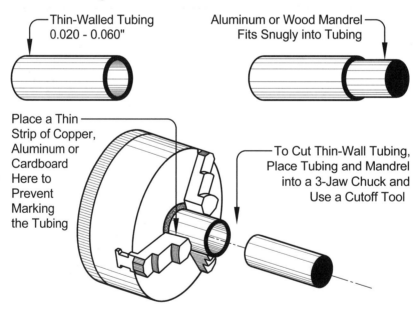

Figure 7-93. Thin-walled tubing may be cut without damage when supported internally on a mandrel that prevents it from collapsing.

Setting Offsets with Precision

Offsets for turning eccentrics in a four-jaw chuck can be set accurately using the method in Figure 7-94.

1. Lay out the offset for the eccentric by measuring from the center of the workpiece, and then use a radius-type combination center drill to mark the offset center. An alternative approach is to use a milling machine to set and drill this distance.

2. Place the work in a four-jaw chuck.

3. Insert an alignment rod as a test bar between the MT point in the tailstock and the offset center hole in the work. Snug up the tailstock so the test bar is secure, but does not bend.

4. Using a DTI, adjust the work position in the four-jaw chuck so that when the DTI is against the test bar it does not move as the work is turned by hand.

5. Machine the offset shaft with a cutoff tool.

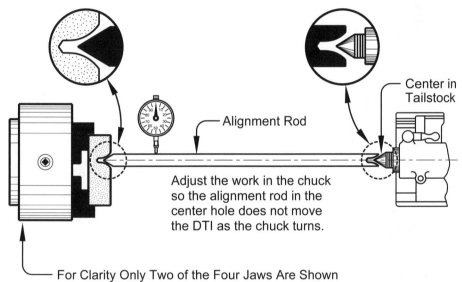

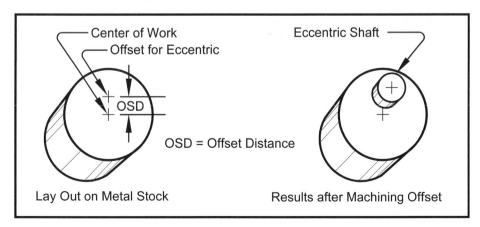

Figure 7-94. Using a test bar to set an offset.

Section IX – Sherline Lathe Tips

Handwheel Practice

When making the final finishing facing cut on a part, do not use the crank on the cross feed. Use both hands to turn the cross feed wheel so that the cross feed moves steadily across the work without slowing until the cut is complete. Using the crank will create distinctive "tree rings" on the face of the work wherever the tool slowed down during cranking.

Enlarging Sherline Tool Holders for ⅜-inch Cutters

The standard Sherline lathe tool holder is designed to hold $^3/_{16}$-inch square tool bits. While this size cutter is fine for most jobs, $^3/_8$-inch carbide cutters are sometimes needed. To make the conversion from $^3/_{16}$ to $^3/_8$ inch—which takes only a few minutes of milling time—modify the tool holder by cutting open the tool bit slot height to 0.600 inches, as in Figure 7-95, and chamfer the sharp edges.

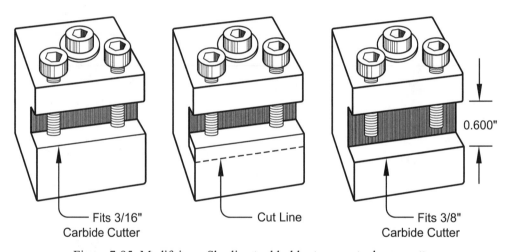

Figure 7-95. Modifying a Sherline tool holder to accept a larger cutter.

Making Soft-Tip Set Screws on a Sherline Lathe

A set screw with a soft tip of nylon, brass or Delrin is often needed to avoid damaging the shaft or threads against which it bears. Sometimes soft-tip set screws are used to provide adjustable friction drag on machine adjustments.

The simple shop-made fixture shown in Figure 7-96 can be used for end-drilling a small hex head screw, but here it is being used to make a soft-tip set screw. This is how it's done:

1. Start with a cup-type set screw. The dimple in the bottom end centers the drill and helps get drilling started.

2. Select a hex wrench that matches the hex socket on the set screw.

3. Cut off the L-handle of the hex wrench with an abrasive wheel, leaving a straight section of hex-shaped rod.

4. Place the hex rod in the Sherline lathe's three-jaw chuck.

5. Fit the hex set screw onto the cut off hex-shaped rod already in the Sherline lathe.

6. Using a HSS cobalt 135° twist drill in the tailstock drill chuck, set the spindle speed to 550 RPM, and drill out the pocket for the soft tip. Considerable force may be needed to initiate drilling.

7. Machine the soft tip insert slightly oversized to make it a force fit, and then press the soft tip into the hex set screw pocket.

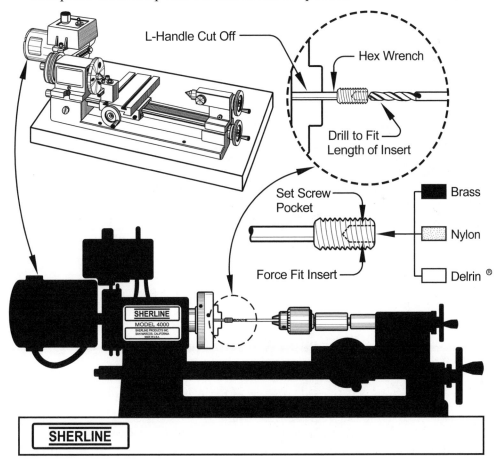

Figure 7-96. Drilling a hex head set screw to install a soft tip.

Adding a Steel Strip to a Sherline Lathe Base

To absorb vibration, mount these small lathes on a wooden base. Adding a strip of CRS on the back of the lathe mounting base provides a place to secure a magnetic base dial indicator. See Figure 7-97.

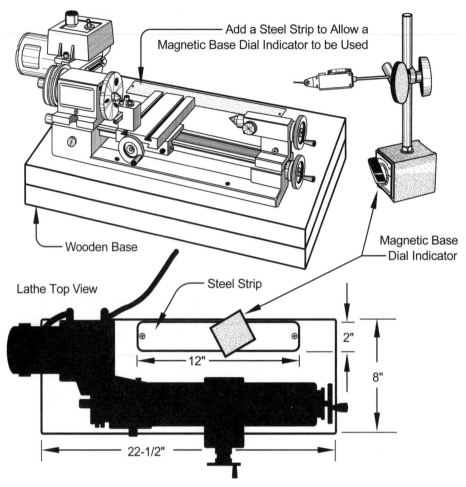

Add a Steel Strip to Allow a
Magnetic Base Dial Indicator to be Used

Wooden Base

Magnetic Base
Dial Indicator

Lathe Top View

Steel Strip

12"

2"

8"

22-1/2"

Figure 7-97. Adding a steel strip to the top of a wooden Sherline mounting
base makes it possible to use a magnetic base dial indicator.

Section X – Knurling

Applications

Knurling refers both to the process of applying knurls and the pattern rolled
on the part. Steel rollers, called *knurls*, apply these patterns which are usually
either a diamond pattern or a series of raised, parallel ridges. Knurling is a
plastic deformation and displacement process. As a result of the outward
displacement of the workpiece metal, there is a small increase in work
diameter, typically 10–25 thousandths of an inch, depending on the number of
teeth in the knurl and the knurl depth. Knurling is applied because it:

• Provides decorative or anti-slip surfaces onto tools, instruments and
  control surfaces.

- Repairs undersized shafts and oversized bores by increasing or decreasing their diameters with the metal displaced by knurling, respectively.

- Makes serrations and splines to lock cylindrical components together by pressing a slightly undersized part onto a slightly oversized shaft.

Although most knurling is done on cylindrical surfaces, it can also be applied to cone-shaped, tapered surfaces and on the ends of cylinders, usually to increase friction between components.

Processes

There are three approaches to applying knurling:

- *Bump knurling* is performed in the lathe using one or two knurls to apply the knurled pattern. Tool holders, like those in Figure 7-98 (top), force the knurls into the work, displacing surface metal to form a pattern. Because the knurls are applied on only one side of the work, bump knurling can:

  - Put large, potentially damaging asymmetrical forces on the lathe's spindle bearings. These forces can be as much as 10–15 times larger than those imposed by a typical cutting tool.

  - Bend and bow thin workpieces, making bumping impossible on long, slender work such as punches, scribers and screwdrivers.

  Using a live center in the right-hand side of the work as in Figure 7-98 (top left) reduces asymmetrical forces on the spindle bearings and also reduces work bending. If the workpiece is large enough in diameter to resist bending when held by the chuck and center, long work can be bumped without excessive wear on the lathe. Bump knurling works well on aluminum, particularly when the workpiece does not bend under knurling forces. Unless your lathe bearings are already worn out, or you can support the work with a live center, bumping is a poor practice.

- *Straddle* or *pinch knurling* is also performed in the lathe, but uses two diametrically opposed knurls to eliminate the asymmetrical forces by balancing the knurling wheel force on each side of the work. Because of these balanced forces, pinching can knurl thin, flexible work which would otherwise be impossible with bumping. See Figure 7-98 (bottom).

- *Roll knurling* is done by dedicated industrial machines which apply knurls in just seconds during 2–4 revolutions. Because these rolling machines have large, wide knurls and exert balanced forces on the work, even thin workpieces do not bend and knurl well. These machines are suited to rolling steel and stainless steel because they have hydraulic cylinders that squeeze the knurls together with *tons* of force. See Figure 7-99.

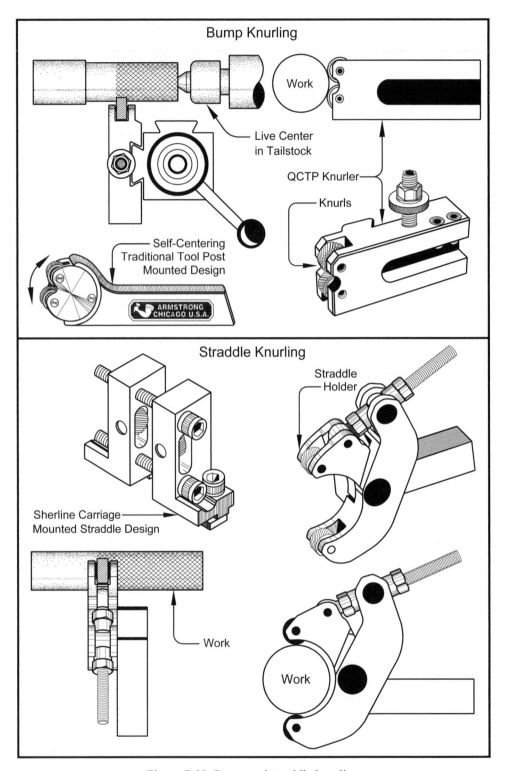

Figure 7-98. Bump and straddle knurling.

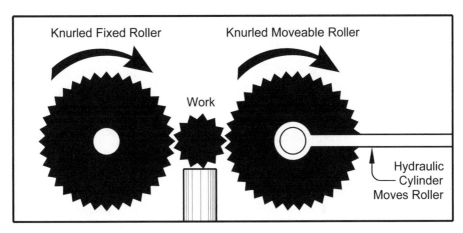

Figure 7-99. An industrial roll-knurling machine has two 6-inch diameter rollers each 5 inches long, a 5-hp motor and a hydraulic ram to squeeze the workpiece between its rollers.

Knurls

- *Materials* – In increasing order of cost and working life: HSS, HSS cobalt, HSS with TIN anti-wear coating, and powdered metal. HSS knurls are adequate for occasional, non-production knurling, but HSS cobalt (M48 with 9% cobalt) is necessary for stainless steel. Quality knurls are hardened to RH_c 62. Inexpensive knurls are milled and may be polished, but high-quality knurls are ground and lapped. The lapped surface finish produces a better knurl appearance and increases knurl life.

- *Dimensions* – There are a half-dozen common knurl sizes in industrial use in the US—plus metric sizes—but the two most common sizes are:

  - KN Series: ¾-inch diameter × ¼-inch wide × ¼-inch center hole.

  - KP Series: ¾-inch diameter × ⅜-inch wide × ¼-inch center hole.

- *Patterns* – There are two common patterns and one less common; all of which are available in a variety of pitches:

  - *Straight line knurl patterns* require one or two knurls. This pattern is often used on parts which will be pressed together. Although there are many pitches available, industrial tool catalogs often define coarse as 14 teeth/inch, medium as 21 teeth/inch and fine as 33 teeth/inch.

  - *Male diamond knurl patterns*, the most common pattern, consists of a series of raised pyramidal points which have an angle of 30º to the work axis and require both a left-hand knurl and a right-hand knurl.

  - *Female diamond knurl patterns*, a less common pattern, consists of a series of depressed pyramidal points with a 45º angle to the work axis. This pattern is applied using a single knurl.

- *Pitch* – The number of teeth on the knurl defines its pitch. There are three systems of pitch measurement:

  - *Circular pitch* is based on the number of teeth/inch (TPI) on the knurl. For left- and right-hand knurls the TPI is measured perpendicular to the teeth, not on the diameter.

  - *Diametrical pitch* is defined as the total number of teeth on the knurl divided by the nominal circumference of the knurl. Unlike gearing, only four standard diametrical pitches are used: 64, 96, 128 and 160. This means that knurls of 64 and 128 pitch should track properly for work diameters of any multiple of $1/64$ of an inch, and knurls of 96 and 160 pitch should track properly for work diameters that are multiples of $1/32$ of an inch in diameters from $3/32$–1 inch.

  - *Metric pitch* is the distance between knurl teeth tips in millimeters, ranging 0.3–3.0, usually in increments of 0.1 mm. Not all possible pitches are available as standard items. The Deutsches Institut für Normung—the German Institute for Standardization, similar to US ANSI—defines metric knurls in standard DIN 82.

- *Face* and *edge shapes* – There are three designs:

  - *Flat-face knurl with no edge chamfer*, as in Figure 7-100 (A), is the most basic, least costly knurl design. The sharp corners on the knurl edges wear rapidly, experience heavy tool loads and may break off during axial traversing. Still, these knurls work well for rolling a pattern the same width as the knurl and which requires no traversing.

  - *Flat-face knurls with a small chamfer on the wheel edges*, Figure 7-100 (B), may be used to roll a single band the same width as the knurl wheel or the knurl may be traversed along the work axis to extend the pattern over a larger area. This is the most common knurl design.

  - *Convex knurls,* Figure 7-100 (C), are for rolling long sections and feed better axially than flat-face knurls. Usually made from HSS cobalt with TIN coating, they are used in CNC machines, but work well in manual lathes too. The radiused edges of the wheels reduce the knurling forces both into and along the work compared with using a standard chamfered knurl. Also, because of the smaller surface area on first contact, these tools normally penetrate deeper into the workpiece on the initial revolution, which tends to reduce double tracking. They are designed only for axial feed to produce a knurl length wider than the wheel, not to make a single band the width of the knurl wheel.

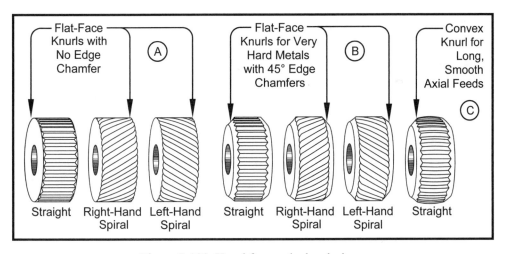

Figure 7-100. Knurl face and edge designs.

Tracking

When a knurl completes more than one revolution around a workpiece but leaves only one set of tooth impressions—that is, the knurl teeth drop precisely into the impressions made on the first revolution—the knurl is said to be *tracking properly*. See Figure 7-101 (left). A knurl tracks properly when a multiple of the number of teeth on the knurl fit on the circumference of the workpiece. This is very much like two gears of different diameters meshing properly.

If the circumference of the part being rolled is not an approximate multiple of the pitch of the knurl, the knurl may land somewhere between the two initial teeth causing the knurl to start a new row. This will cause *double tracking* or some other multiple of the initial pitch. See Figure 7-101 (right).

Getting proper tracking is the major task in knurling. Sometimes a greater infeed cures a tracking problem, sometimes the diameter of the work or the knurl must be adjusted, usually by plus or minus 5–10 thousandths of an inch.

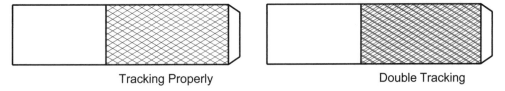

Tracking Properly   Double Tracking

Figure 7-101. Knurl tracking.

Due to the many variables involved in any knurling operation—speeds, feeds, lubricant, hardness of the workpiece, condition of the bearing pins—determining the proper blank diameters for circular pitch dies is a bit more difficult than knurling with diametrical pitch dies and usually involves some experimentation to get good results.

Determining the Workpiece Diameter

1. Beginning with a workpiece of a given diameter and a given knurl wheel, determine the closest workpiece diameter which will fit a *whole,* or *integral number,* of knurl teeth around its circumference.

2. Disengage the lathe spindle from the lathe motor, set the knurling tool holder perpendicular to the work so that the axle of the knurl is parallel with the work axis, and press the knurl wheel into the work.

3. Slowly turn the spindle by hand and observe whether the knurls track properly. If the knurls do track properly, proceed to knurling, if not, repeat this check in another spot on the same diameter workpiece, but with more pressure on the knurling tool. If proper tracking is not obtained, then remove 0.002–0.003 inches from the workpiece diameter and repeat until good tracking occurs. Because there are many factors that determine if a workpiece diameter and knurl combination will track properly, experimentation is usually needed.

Bump Knurling Procedure

1. Unless the workpiece is stiff and short, center drill the tailstock end of the work to accept a live center to reduce asymmetrical forces on the spindle and reduce work bending.

2. Place a small chamfer on the right-hand end of the work to provide an easy start for the knurling tool.

3. Adjust the knurling tool so it is *on* center height and *perpendicular* to the work. Using a scrap workpiece of the same diameter as the work, you can set the knurling tool on center by observing when both knurls leave equal imprints on the scrap as the tool post height is adjusted and the spindle is turned by hand. If using a knurling tool in a QCTP, as in Figure 7-98 (top right), snug up the QCTP, but do not tighten it, allowing the tool to float and to find its own center as it engages the work.

4. If possible, position the carriage to engage about ½–¼ of the knurl face on the end of the workpiece, but do not yet touch the work with the knurl.

5. Knurling may be performed at the same spindle speeds for turning with HSS tool bits, but to prevent possible seizing of the knurls on their pins, limit the maximum knurling speed to 150 SFM. Speeds of 50 SFM will produce better looking knurls on harder steels and stainless steels and extend knurl life.

6. Turn on the lathe and have light-weight lubricating, not cutting oil, at hand to flood the work surface.

7. Press the knurls into the work about ⅓–½ of the final knurl depth—typically 0.010–0.012 inches—and use the longitudinal feed to move the knurl across the work about 0.020 inches/revolution.

8. When the knurls reach the left end of the work, stop the lathe, reverse the carriage direction, restart the lathe, and increase the knurl depth. Do not withdraw the knurls from the work as their timing will be lost and the work ruined. Also, do not stop the lathe in the middle of a pass or the pattern will be uneven.

9. Continue the back and forth knurling sweeps until the knurls reach final depth. It is desirable to complete the knurls in as few passes as possible to avoid *over-rolling* which leads to the work flaking off bits of metal due to fatigue. In addition to the lubrication oil put on the work at the knurl, using a blast of compressed air following the knurl can remove metal flakes from future passes. Flaking is particularly a problem with aluminum workpieces.

10. The appearance of the workpiece can be improved by putting chamfers at the ends of the finished knurling.

11. If the knurls are too aggressive on your hands, use a wire brush, a light lathe filing, or turn off several thousandths of an inch in a lathe pass.

Straddle Knurling Procedure

1. Determine the correct workpiece diameter that tracks properly as in the bump knurling procedure above.

2. To center the knurler on the work, scribe a diameter line on the end of the workpiece and set the straddle knurls on these diameter marks.

3. Mark the cross-slide collar to indicate when the straddle knurler is centered on the work, then pull the knurler back.

4. Turn on the lathe, and gradually close up the straddle knurling tool opening to produce the final desired knurl depth in a single pass. Lock this adjustment, if possible, and turn off the lathe. If you plan to use this knurler later with the same diameter work, turn down a piece of round stock that just fits between the knurls. You can use this as a gage to set the tool to the proper diameter.

5. Place the work in the lathe, have the lubricating oil at hand, set the spindle speed and the horizontal feed, and again turn on the lathe.

6. When the lathe comes up to speed, advance the knurler onto the center of the work using the collar marks as guides and turn on the carriage feed. Keep adding lubrication oil.

7. Withdraw the knurler when the knurling is complete.

Cut Knurling

No discussion of knurling would be complete without the mention of *cut knurling* which uses sharp-edged knurls to actually cut away workpiece material like a milling tool. This process, popular outside the US, has these advantages:

- Cut knurling applies much lower force to the workpiece causing less bending of slender work and tubular parts than conventional knurling.

- Maintains the original workpiece diameter.

- Produces a very high quality knurl.

- Cuts workpiece metal so it does not cause work hardening, which can cause the tips of the knurl pattern to break off.

- Machines plastics and cast iron well, where conventional knurling, which depends on the work metal moving under knurl pressure, works poorly.

Cut knurling has these drawbacks:

- Cut knurling tool holders are several times more expensive than conventional knurling tool holders and cannot be used with conventional pressure knurls. Similarly, cut knurls are expensive and require special tool holders.

- Not suitable for knurling up to a shoulder due to the angular arrangement of the knurls.

- Cut knurls are usually offered in metric sizes because they are most often used outside of the US.

- Because cut knurls must be fed along the work, they are not suitable for making knurls only the width of the knurls themselves.

Section XI – Lathe Projects

Knock-Out Bar

Most lathes require a knock-out bar to remove the collet adapter, dead center and Morse taper reducer sleeves from the spindle. These items fit into the Morse taper inside the spindle. Since MTs are self-holding tapers and considerable force is applied on them while in use, they are well seated in the taper and only a tap on their back end through the spindle will release them.

The knock-out bar shown in Figure 7-102 is sized for a Kent 13×40 lathe, and is an excellent beginning lathe project. This shop-made knock-out bar requires turning, facing, drilling, boring and knurling, plus some hand tapping, yet requires little precision.

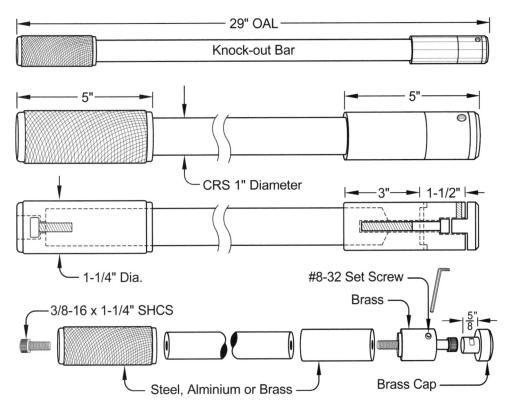

Figure 7-102. Knock-out bar with knurled handle and replaceable brass tip for removing collet adapters, centers and Morse taper sleeves from the lathe spindle.

Box Wrench Handle

Every time the QCTP is repositioned, the nut on the top of the QCTP T-bolt must be loosened and then retightened. This is done so frequently that most machinists keep a particular wrench handy for this purpose—a wrench with a handle so distinctive it is easy to find. This wrench is also a good beginning lathe project and a necessary tool. See Figure 7-103. Here is how to make it:

1. Cut a 1½-inch diameter aluminum round for the wrench handle. Make the round 1½ inches longer than the finished handle to leave a stub to be held in the lathe chuck during machining.

2. Center drill the right end of the handle for a live center, then, using a live center and a three-jaw chuck, knurl the handle from the right-hand end up to the chuck. Next, cut away the knurling to make any desired band(s).

3. Remove the live center, but leave the handle stub in the lathe chuck and taper the end of the aluminum handle. Using the existing center-drilled hole in the right-hand side of the handle, drill an undersized hole in the handle for the wrench to make a forced fit.

4. Using a cutoff tool bit, cut the handle away from its stub in the chuck.

5. Flip the handle end-for-end, place cardboard around the knurls so they are not damaged, and insert the handle in the lathe chuck, then round the end of the handle with a file or form tool.

6. Using a belt or disc sander, taper the end of the box wrench handle that will fit inside the aluminum handle. Apply a very gradual taper 2–3 inches long to the wrench handle and frequently check it for fit as you grind. Press the wrench into the handle.

7. Finally, add two #10-24 × ¼-inch set screws to secure the box wrench in its handle. Install the set screws 90° apart.

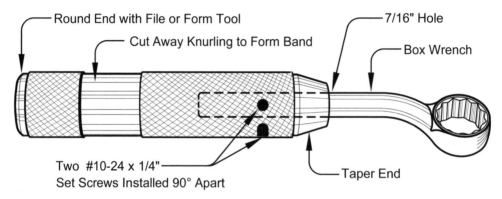

Figure 7-103. Adding a distinctive handle to the box wrench for the QCTP T-bolt nut.

Dedicated MT Center-Drill Holder

Although it is perfectly acceptable to make center holes with combination center drills held in a Jacobs drill chuck, a lot of time can be saved with the dedicated tool holders shown in Figure 7-104. These modified tool holders are readily made from Morse-taper-to-Jacobs-taper arbors. Here are the steps:

1. Install the MT-to-JT arbor in the lathe tailstock.

2. Install a collet adapter and collet in the lathe spindle.

3. Install a combination center drill in the collet.

4. Center drill the MT-to-JT arbor in the tailstock. It is not likely to be hardened and will drill easily, but first, check to verify that the arbor is not hardened.

5. Use a collet in the headstock to drill undersized for reaming, then ream to match the center drill diameter.

6. Drill and tap a side hole for a set screw to secure the center drill in place.

7. Grind a flat on the side of the combination center drill where the set screw will bear. This keeps the center drill from spinning under load.

8. Install the center drill, the place Locktite on the set screw and tighten it.

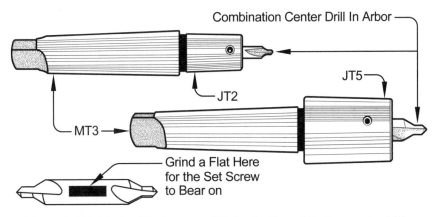

Figure 7-104. MT-to-JT arbors modified to hold combination center drills.
This modification avoids inserting center drills into the drill chuck.

Hex Wrench Handles

Many shops have more than one lathe and have sets of hex wrenches intended specifically for each machine. The simple aluminum handles in Figure 7-105 show which machine the wrenches belong with by the color of paint in their grooves. The handles also make the wrenches nicer to work with. Here are the steps to make these handles:

1. Using the aluminum round stock that best fits around the hex wrench, cut, center drill and drill a hole to hold the hex wrench. The hex wrench should fit snugly into this hole. Then, drill and tap for hex head set screws.

2. In a lathe, cut one or more grooves to hold paint to identify which machine the wrench belongs with. A matching paint dot on each lathe is helpful in a shop with many lathes.

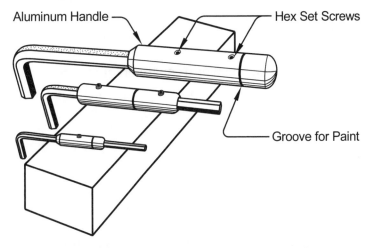

Figure 7-105. Color-coded handles on hex wrenches
identify which machine they belong with.

3. Round the end of the aluminum handle with a file or form tool.

4. Drill and tap holes for set screws in the handle. Insert the hex wrench in the handle and tighten the set screws. Small hex wrenches go completely though the handle and large wrenches go only into the end of the handle.

Making a Faceplate for a D1-4 Lathe Mount

It is easy to make a faceplate if you start with a purchased *adapter plate*, also called a *chuck back*. Making an adapter plate is a complex task with tight tolerances on its dimensions and should be reserved for experienced machinists. This technique for mounting a faceplate disc onto a D1-4 adapter plate uses dowel pins instead of the boss-and-recess method often used to mount chucks. Either of these methods works for faceplates. Figure 7-106 shows both the front and back sides of the purchased adapter plate. The body of the adapter plate is unhardened steel so it is easily machined. Here are the steps for mounting a faceplate disc onto a D1-4 adapter plate:

1. For the faceplate itself, choose a metal disc 12–12½-inches in diameter and about 1–1½-inches thick for a 13-inch lathe. Either steel or aluminum will work. Although aluminum is easier to machine, threads tapped into aluminum are not as strong as those in steel.

2. Two dowel pins ½-inch diameter and 2-inches long and six ⅜-16 SHCSs are needed.

3. Figure 7-106 (left) shows a D1-4 adapter plate as purchased. The ¾-inch high boss on the face of the adapter will not be used and must be removed. Install the adapter plate on the lathe and machine off the boss. Figure 7-109 (left) shows the adapter plate with the boss removed.

4. On a flat surface, place the adapter plate with its mounting studs up, scribe a diameter line, then mark and center punch the location for two ½-inch dowel pins as shown in Figure 7-107. These pins transfer the shear load from the faceplate disc to the adapter plate and prevent the bolts holding the disc and adapter plate together from going into shear.

5. Using an abrasive stone, clean up the surface of the disc that will face against the D1-4 adapter plate. Remove any dirt, dings or burrs so the disc will sit flat against the adapter plate and not rock when mounted.

6. Place the disc on the workbench clean side up and lay the D1-4 adapter plate over the disc with its studs up, then position the adapter plate so it is centered over the disc within $1/_{16}$ of an inch. You will have to use a ruler or combination square set at a given depth and go around and around the disc making adjustments to get the adapter plate centered on the disc. After the disc is centered, secure the two parts together with two large Kant Twist clamps. See Figure 7-108.

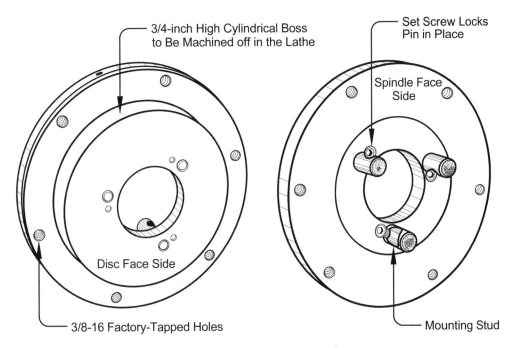

Figure 7-106. A purchased D1-4 lathe adapter plate—also called a chuck back—viewed from the front or tailstock end (left) and from the back or spindle end (right).

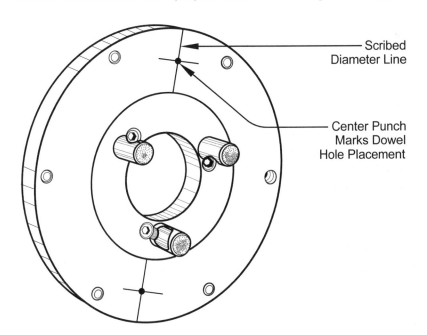

Figure 7-107. The D1-4 adapter plate with the holes for the ½-inch dowels marked and center punched.

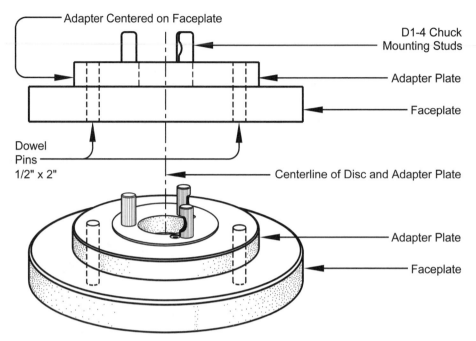

Figure 7-108. Centering the D1-4 adapter plate on the faceplate disc.

7. Step drill the two previously center-punched holes for the $\frac{1}{2}$-inch dowels. Center drill using a $\frac{1}{4}$-inch drill, then a $\frac{3}{8}$-inch drill, and finally a $\frac{31}{64}$-inch drill. This last drill leaves enough metal in the hole for the reamer to work properly.

8. Use the *undersized reamer,* which is 0.4990 inches diameter, for the $\frac{1}{2}$-inch dowel pins, and ream *both* holes all the way though both the disc and the adapter plate.

9. After drilling and reaming, but before unclamping, use a center punch to apply witness marks to the edge of the D1-4 adapter plate and the faceplate disc. This will insure the adapter plate and faceplate are centered and go together easily.

10. Ream *only* the dowel holes in the faceplate disc with the oversized $\frac{1}{2}$-inch reamer which is 0.501-inches in diameter. Do not ream the holes already reamed in the adapter plate.

11. Press a $\frac{1}{2}$-inch dowel into each of the undersized holes in the adapter plate. Because the dowel holes are undersized, you will need to tap the dowels with a hammer or press them into place with an arbor press. Apply lubricant to make them go in easier. The dowels installed in the adapter plate are shown in Figure 7-109.

12. Matching up the witness marks, slip the faceplate disc over the dowel pins already in the adapter plate and clamp the two parts together.

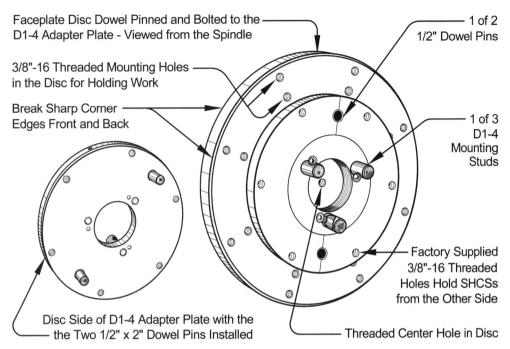

Faceplate Disc Dowel Pinned and Bolted to the
D1-4 Adapter Plate - Viewed from the Spindle

1 of 2
1/2" Dowel Pins

3/8"-16 Threaded Mounting Holes
in the Disc for Holding Work

Break Sharp Corner
Edges Front and Back

1 of 3
D1-4
Mounting
Studs

Factory Supplied
3/8"-16 Threaded
Holes Hold SHCSs
from the Other Side

Disc Side of D1-4 Adapter Plate with the
the Two 1/2" x 2" Dowel Pins Installed

Threaded Center Hole in Disc

Figure 7-109. D1-4 lathe adapter plate with boss removed and the ½-inch dowel pins
installed (left) and the adapter plate and faceplate disc bolted together (right).

13. Using a transfer punch, mark the location of the six $^3/_8$-16 threaded holes around the periphery of the adapter plate onto the disc. Separate the adapter plate and the disc, center drill, and then drill $^{25}/_{64}$-inch clearance holes in the disc for the six SHCSs which will hold the disc to the adapter plate. You will also need to countersink the bolt clearance holes to allow the SHCSs heads to drop below the surface of the disc. Use a $^5/_8$-inch drill to make each countersink 0.400 inches deep.

14. Decide on the pattern for the threaded mounting holes in the faceplate, mark their locations, center punch, center drill, and finally step drill for $^3/_8$-16 threads. Be sure to separate the aluminum faceplate disc from the adapter plate before drilling the disc for threaded mounting holes. Drill these holes all the way through the disc because blind holes accumulate debris which can be hard to remove. Tap these holes. A typical hole pattern is shown in Figure 7-110.

15. Assemble the adapter plate and faceplate on the two dowel pins, insert the six $^3/_8$-inch SHCSs finger tight, then finish tightening them with a hex wrench.

16. Put the fully assembled faceplate on your lathe, and turn the edge of the faceplate disc so it runs true. Also, break the sharp corners on the front and back edges of the disc.

17. Apply a series of concentric rings as a guide for centering work. Instead of using a sharply pointed lathe tool to make these rings, use a 60° lathe tool with the tip blunted to about $^{1}/_{16}$ inch. The resulting flat-bottomed grooves will not catch dirt as easily as V-grooves. See Figure 7-110.

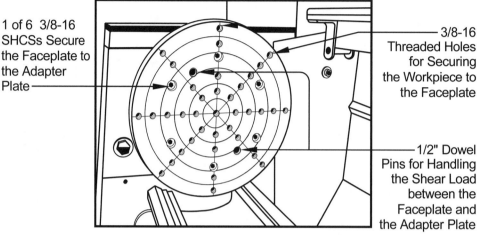

1 of 6 3/8-16 SHCSs Secure the Faceplate to the Adapter Plate

3/8-16 Threaded Holes for Securing the Workpiece to the Faceplate

1/2" Dowel Pins for Handling the Shear Load between the Faceplate and the Adapter Plate

Figure 7-110. Completed faceplate installed on the lathe.

Sliding Tool Tray

Having a tool tray on which to lay tools instead of placing them on the lathe ways is a must. Figure 7-111 shows a traditional sliding tool tray design made of wood. The bottom has two V-grooved slides which fit onto the lathe ways and keep the tray in place.

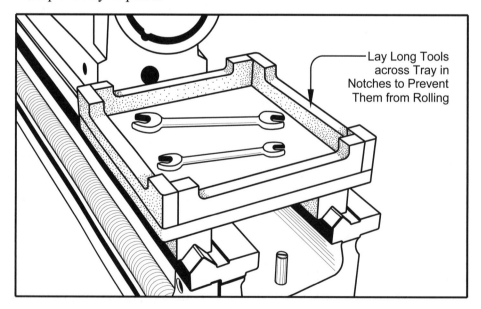

Lay Long Tools across Tray in Notches to Prevent Them from Rolling

Figure 7-111. Sliding tool tray keeps tools handy but avoids storing tools on the lathe ways.

Lengthening a Chuck's T-Handle

Frequently, when turning the T-wrench for the D1-4 spindle mount locking cams, the wrench is not long enough to clear the top of the lathe's headstock cover. The solution, beside buying another longer wrench, is to lengthen the one you have as shown in Figure 7-112.

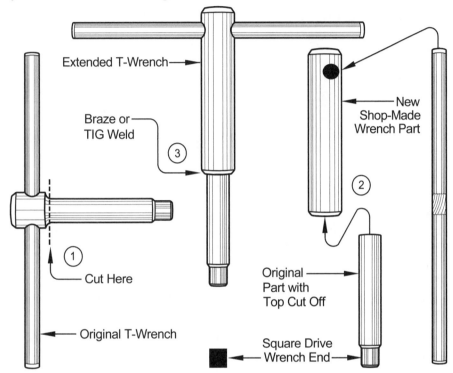

Figure 7-112. Lengthening the handle of a T-wrench.

To do this, follow these steps:

1. Cut the old wrench along the dotted line.
2. Machine the T-wrench extension.
3. Braze the old cut off piece to the new extension.

The advantage to this approach is that the original wrench is made from 4130 or 4140 steel and is much stronger than any CRS scraps you are likely to have around the shop. If using CRS, the square wrench end is likely to shear off or deform under load.

Crank Handles for Chuck Keys

Adding a crank handle to a chuck key saves a lot of hand-over-hand turning and is a good way to learn to use a radius cutting tool. See Figure 7-113. File or grind a flat on the side of the chuck key cross bar where the set screw bears to keep the crank handle locked in place.

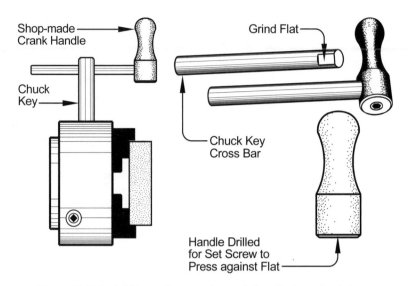

Figure 7-113. Adding a shop-made crank handle to a chuck key.

Chuck Cradles

While a simple wooden chuck cradle, such as the one in Figure 7-114, can be handy, the deluxe cradle in Figure 7-115 has some definite advantages:

- It has solid handles that will not slip out of your hands.

- It has two flip-over locks that prevent the chuck from tipping out of the cradle when the cradle is tilted.

- The bottom notches fit onto the ways and align the cradle with the lathe axis.

- The adjustable Delrin bumpers position the chuck so it effortlessly slides onto the spindle mount. The height of the bumpers is adjusted by drywall screws as shown in the bottom right of Figure 7-115.

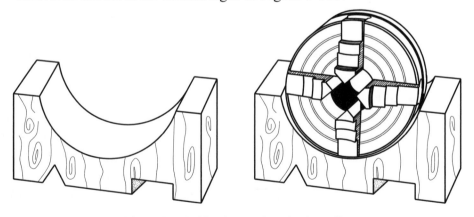

Figure 7-114. Simple wooden chuck cradle.

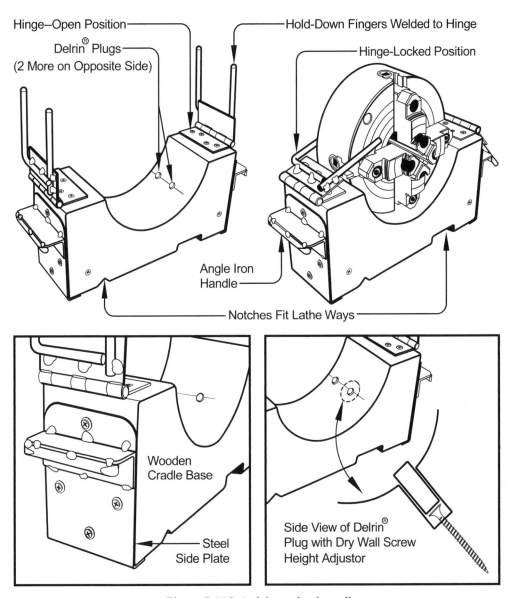

Hinge--Open Position

Delrin® Plugs
(2 More on Opposite Side)

Hold-Down Fingers Welded to Hinge

Hinge-Locked Position

Angle Iron
Handle

Notches Fit Lathe Ways

Wooden
Cradle Base

Steel
Side Plate

Side View of Delrin®
Plug with Dry Wall Screw
Height Adjustor

Figure 7-115. A deluxe chuck cradle.

Lazy Susan Drill Chuck & Center Holder

Drill chucks and lathe centers are used often and storing them on the right side of the lathe in a Lazy Susan tool holder is a very convenient place. A cylindrical fabric cover over the holder keeps condensation and dust off the tooling. The Lazy Susan tool holder in Figure 7-116 is made from a piece of scrap Corian supported on a Teflon bearing on a piece of square steel tubing. This tubing is welded to a piece of angle iron which is then bolted to the lathe pedestal casting. See Figure 7-117 (far right).

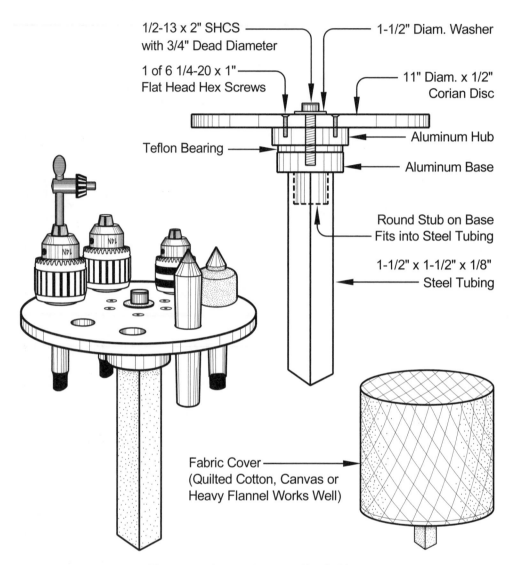

1/2-13 x 2" SHCS with 3/4" Dead Diameter

1-1/2" Diam. Washer

1 of 6 1/4-20 x 1" Flat Head Hex Screws

11" Diam. x 1/2" Corian Disc

Teflon Bearing

Aluminum Hub

Aluminum Base

Round Stub on Base Fits into Steel Tubing

1-1/2" x 1-1/2" x 1/8" Steel Tubing

Fabric Cover (Quilted Cotton, Canvas or Heavy Flannel Works Well)

Figure 7-116. Lazy Susan tooling holder.

Tool Holder Shelf for the Back of the Lathe

The steel shelf in Figure 7-117 places the QCTP tool holders in front of the machinist. The Lazy Susan steel tube, which is bolted to the lathe pedestal, supports the shelf on its right side. The left side of the shelf bolts to the lathe's electrical cabinet. Figure 5-26 shows how to locate the bolt holes to secure this shelf. The shelf is self-supporting and is independent of the lathe back-splash. The square tubing running underneath the shelf keeps it from sagging in the middle. The convenience of having QCTP tool holders right in front of you when working on the lathe is worth the effort to build this shelf.

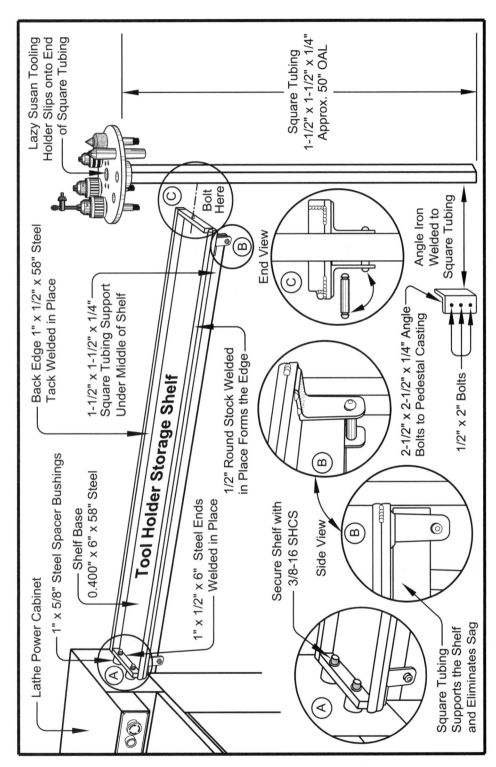

Figure 7-117. Lathe tool holder storage shelf.

Section XII – Lathe Safety

- *Always* wear safety glasses.

- Wear snug-fitting clothing, and remove ties, rings, necklaces and anything else that might pull you into the lathe. *Do not wear gloves.*

- *Never take your hands off the chuck key until it is out of the chuck.* This will prevent the dangerous and destructive event of starting the lathe with the chuck key in place.

- Keep a clear working area around your lathe. Round bars on the shop floor are a serious tripping hazard. Clean up grease and oil spills around your lathe. This will prevent tripping and falling into a running machine.

- Keep your face out of the plane of rotation of the chuck and the work.

- Do not attempt to brake a spinning chuck with your hand.

- Learn how to stop your machine quickly.

- When you put work into a chuck for the first time, either pull the chuck around a complete turn by hand or use the jog button to make sure that the work and chuck are free of obstructions.

- Do not lay tools across the lathe ways. Use a tool tray instead.

- Do not store tools on top of the lathe headstock without a provision to keep them from rolling or vibrating off.

- Always stop your lathe before cleaning it or before taking workpiece measurements.

- Do not attempt to use any machine tool without proper lighting.

- Using your fingers, always check that female Morse tapers are free of chips and dirt before inserting a male taper, but never do this while the lathe is under power.

- Lathes are top-heavy and can tip over on you. Get help when moving one.

- Never wear gloves or use rags to clean the workpiece or any part of a machine that is running.

- Never remove chips or turnings with your hands as these may cause nasty cuts. Chips may also be red-hot as they come off the work. Use a chip hook or pliers to move them to the trash. Be especially cautious of very long chips as they can be several feet in length and can pull you into the lathe if caught in the chuck or work. Remove small chips and turnings with a brush.

- Guards must be provided for belts, shafts, pulleys, gears and pinch points.

Chapter 8

Milling Machines

Every discovery contains an irrational element of creative intuition.

—Karl Popper

Introduction

Milling machines are the second most important machine tool in the shop. The Bridgeport-style vertical milling machine, also called a *turret mill* or a *knee-and-column mill,* and its miniature cousin, the Sherline milling machine, are among the most popular. There are more Bridgeport-style mills in use than all other designs combined because of their easy set-up, flexibility and cost-effectiveness. Although there are several small table-top mills available today, the many accessories available for the Sherline make it a good selection for this study. These smaller machines, often called *box mills*, lack the moveable quill of a full-sized Bridgeport, but they are an excellent choice for smaller work, smaller workshops and smaller budgets. See Figure 8-1.

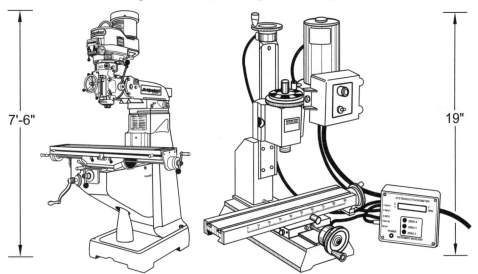

Figure 8-1. Bridgeport Series I Standard Milling Machine (left)
and Sherline Miniature Mill with DRO (right).

Lathes and mills are complementary machines. While lathes rotate the workpiece and produce a cylindrical cut, milling machines move work into a rotating cutter and make a straight-line cut. Lathes and mills are both capable of boring large-diameter holes, but mills are better at placing holes *anywhere* on the surface of the work. Although you can sometimes make do with just a lathe or a mill, a well-equipped shop needs both machines.

Milling Machine Evolution

Milling machines developed from *rotary files*, circular cutters with small file-like teeth that run in a lathe headstock. Rotary files date from the 1760s and were developed to reduce the time and effort of hand filing.

The early 1800s saw the first true milling machines. These machines used toothed rotary cutters turning on a horizontal axis and had table movement on the two horizontal axes, now called the X- and Y-axes. A drawback of these early milling machines was that they had no provision for vertical table movement and so the work had to be shimmed up to meet the cutter.

In the mid-1800s, John R. Brown of Brown and Sharp, introduced the *universal milling machine.* This was a distinct improvement because its milling table swiveled around the vertical axis *and* had vertical table movement. A swiveling table allowed the cutting of helices with the table leadscrew geared to an indexing head, a giant step forward in cutting tool, drill and gear manufacturing. Also, the vertical table movement made for faster set-ups.

The early years of the 20th century ushered in more innovation in the form of *anti-backlash leadscrew nuts* that permitted coordinate positioning to 0.001 inches or better from a single reference point. This important development allowed parts to be made directly from prints rather than from jigs. By the 1930s, hydraulic tracer milling machines could make multiple parts by copying from a template. These two developments, coördinate positioning and pattern tracing, laid the groundwork for CNC machining, which began in the 1950s. The further refinement of horizontal milling machines led to the near extinction of shapers and planers since most of their work is now better done on a milling machine.

The Bridgeport Design

Another important development came in the 1930s when Rudolph Bannow and Magnus Wahlstrom brought out the Bridgeport vertical milling machine. Though traditional horizontal milling machines have higher metal removal rates, the Bridgeport design offers quicker set-up time, economy and versatility. Because of this versatility, there are more Bridgeport-style mills in existence today than any other milling machine design. Traditional horizontal mills are now usually reserved for production applications where high metal removal rates on identical parts are needed, not for prototypes and short runs.

The Bridgeport-style vertical machine offers many advantages over older horizontal milling machine designs:

- The biggest advantage is the quill's ability to advance and retract the cutter easily *without* cranking to raise and lower the milling table. This speeds production and reduces operator fatigue. The retractable quill lets the machinist quickly withdraw the tool to clear chips from a hole or to check its progress. Also, tactile feedback through the quill feed handle or handwheel tells the machinist how the tool is cutting and lets him optimize the feed rate with less danger of tool breakage. Vertical table movement is still available for high-accuracy depth adjustment or when more axial force on the tool is required.

- The second largest advantage is the Bridgeport's ability to make angle cuts. With the horizontal milling machine, either the milling cutter is made on an angle or the work must be positioned at an angle to the spindle axis. With the Bridgeport machine the operator merely needs to tilt the spindle to make an angle cut. Of course, with the Bridgeport you can also use an angled cutter or mount the work on an angle.

- Vertical milling machines must use smaller cutting tools than horizontal mills because they have smaller, less rigid castings and lower horsepower motors. Still, vertical milling machines can accomplish the same end results as horizontal mills, just more slowly. Bridgeport-style milling machines usually have 1–5-hp motors and smaller castings than most horizontal mills, which often have 20–50-hp motors. Because of this, Bridgeports generally cost less.

- Vertical milling machines—with their gearing located *inside* the head— are less complex than horizontal machines because the one-piece head eliminates the complicated gearing of horizontal milling machines.

- Bridgeport-style mills provide better visibility of the end mill cutter.

In the last two decades, digital readouts (DROs) and CNC controls have been added to Bridgeport-style mills. With their additional capabilities, these machines can now engrave—drive the tool to cut numbers and letters in various sizes and fonts—cut radii and angles without a rotary table, make islands, pockets, and cut ellipses and frames. Entering the position, diameter and number of holes automates cutting a bolt-hole pattern; the system does the math. The computer can also automatically compensate for the reduced diameter of resharpened milling cutters, saving time and money, and improving accuracy. In addition, the computer control systems can be manually programmed through their control panels, use stored programs, "learn" new tasks by memorizing a series of manual operations as the operator makes the first part, or accept files from CAD programs.

Section I – Milling Machine Design

Castings

A Bridgeport-style milling machine has nearly a dozen iron castings. Over time the dimensional stability of these castings is critical for machine accuracy. Because several of these castings are quite large, during production the outermost cast metal cools more rapidly than the internal metal, setting up internal stresses. These residual stresses gradually even out with time, but warp the castings in the process. This is why castings cannot be machined too soon after they are poured or bad things will happen.

The traditional method used to eliminate residual stress was to pour the castings, let them age outdoors in the weather for a year, then machine them. Bridgeport, as well as Rolls Royce, followed this practice. Twelve months of natural temperature cycling gave the cast iron a chance to work out its internal stresses and become dimensionally stable. Today, many quality machine builders use Meehanite castings, which are made according to a licensed process. By adding proprietary materials to the molten cast iron, solidification occurs with fewer internal stresses. These castings are dimensionally stable and ready to machine immediately. Machines made with the Meehanite process carry the logo in Figure 8-2 on the top front of the base casting. Poorer quality machines which do not use this process may experience dimensional changes in the first year or so of their lives.

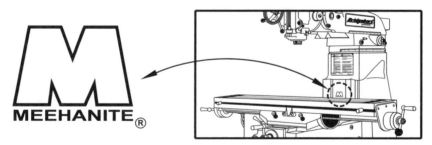

Figure 8-2. The Meehanite logo is found on quality machine tool castings.

When comparing different mills, always consider their weight. Milling puts large forces on machine castings, which can deflect the cutting tool out of alignment. When machine builders put more cast iron into their machines, rigidity and accuracy usually improve. One rough way to check a mill's rigidity is to place a DTI on the milling table with the DTI's foot against the spindle, then lean against the table or head and observe the indicator's deflection. It should not deflect more than a fraction of one-thousandth of an inch. Smaller Bridgeport-style mills weigh in at 1650 lbs, larger manually-operated versions at 2800 lbs, and the CNC-equipped mills at nearly 4000 lbs. Heavier machines, because of their larger and more rigid castings, can use larger horsepower motors and can take larger cuts before chatter begins. Also, these machines can take large accurate cuts because of their rigid frames.

Table Size

Although a few of the small Bridgeport-style mills have 8×36-inch tables—that is, 8-inches wide and 36-inches long—full-size Bridgeport-style mills begin at 9×49 inches and go up to 10×50. Many CNC versions are 12×50.

Horsepower

Motor horsepower has gradually increased over the years with the evolution of the Bridgeport-style mill. Early mills had ¼-hp motors, very small when you consider that a home vacuum cleaner has about 2 hp. Later mills went to 1 hp, then 2 hp, and today are mostly 3 and 5 hp. Eventually, even a low-power mill will get the job done, but a more powerful machine will get the job done quicker.

Spindle Speed Control

Early Bridgeport-style mills had belts and pulleys that produced eight spindle speeds—four in direct drive and four in backgear. To change spindle speed with this arrangement, the mill had to be stopped and the drive belt shifted from one pulley to another.

The next mill improvement, *variable-speed heads*, changed the spindle speed by using variable width pulleys. These pulleys have V-grooved sheaves in which the groove width can be mechanically increased or decreased, allowing the belt to ride in the groove at various diameters, effectively changing the pulley diameter—and the spindle speed.

The latest mill improvement is the *variable frequency drive (VFD)*. VFDs are small—a 3-hp unit is the size of a shoebox—and their cost continues to decline. Many machinists who use older three-phase machines can set their drive belts to medium speed, attach a VFD, and enjoy the benefits of this time-saving technology. See Figure 8-3.

VFDs have many advantages:

- Variable frequency drives eliminate the confusing practice of running the spindle motor backward to get the spindle to turn forward when in backgear, as with the traditional Bridgeport-style design. With VFDs, forward is forward and backward is backward in direct drive or in backgear.

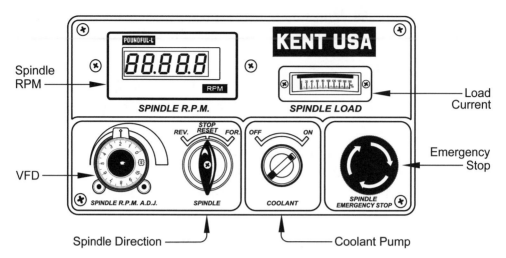

Figure 8-3. A Kent milling machine power panel.

- VFDs have infinitely variable speeds with a digital readout.

- Spindle speeds as low as 10 RPM are possible for tapping and reaming under power.

- Instant spindle reverse permits tap threading.

- Because of electronic spindle braking, the machinist does not have to wait for the spindle to coast to a stop.

- VFDs operate on single- or three-phase power without changing out the motor.

- Most VFDs have an analog current output which allows the motor current to be displayed on a 0–10 volt voltmeter. When the lathe motor current increases, ammeters show that the cutting tool is dull.

Spindle Designs

Nearly all Bridgeport-style mills use an R8 spindle. The popularity of this design has made R8 collets low cost and widely available. Some heavier machines, such as the Italian SAMIA and the larger CNC Kent mills, have NMTB Series-40, -50 and -60 spindles. These larger spindles are necessary because these machines have beefier castings, more horsepower, and must transmit more torque to the tools than the smaller Bridgeport-style mills.

Milling Machine Table Axes

The Bridgeport milling machine has three axes:

- *X-axis*, or *table travel,* is the left-right table movement.

- *Y-axis*, or *saddle travel*, is the in-out table movement with reference to the vertical column.

- *Z-axis*, or *knee travel*, is the up-down table movement. Both the quill and the tool also move along this axis. See Figure 8–4.

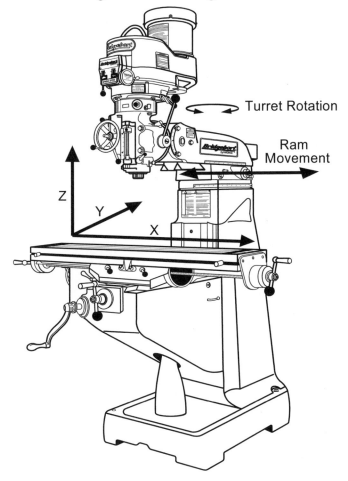

Figure 8-4. The X-Y-Z arrow heads show the positive direction of the milling machine axes.

Digital Readout (DRO) Designs

To position the spindle over the milling table, the original Bridgeport mills had only graduated collars on the X-, Y- and Z-axis cranks. Next, mechanical and optical systems were developed to allow measurements to 0.0001 inch, but these systems were more like extended-range micrometers than the digital readouts of today. These older systems did not provide a simple, direct readout. With the age of electronics, came the digital readouts common today.

Digital readouts may be divided into four classes:

- *Single-axis DROs* are most often used on the milling machine quill. They can be set to zero or to any other figure at any point, which makes it easy to take accurate cuts without doing additional math. These simple battery-powered, self-contained DROs, as shown in Figure 8-5, are really specially adapted digital calipers. They provide the z-axis accuracy of the milling table without the need to crank the table up and down. This saves a lot of wear and tear on both the table screw and the machinist because, even without the weight of work on it, the table weighs several hundred pounds and requires considerable cranking force to raise.

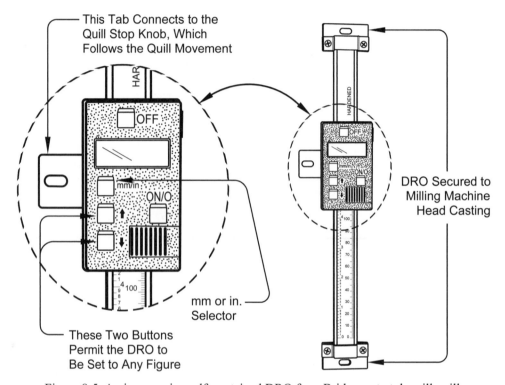

Figure 8-5. An inexpensive self-contained DRO for a Bridgeport-style mill quill.

- *Two-axis DROs* are the most common of these devices and show the position of the x- and y-axes. These two-axis systems have two *linear encoders,* or distance sensors, one between the knee and the saddle for the y-axis and another sensor between the saddle and the table for the x-axis.

- *Three-axis DROs* show the table position with respect to all three axes using one position sensor on each axis. These systems do not reflect the position of the quill.

- *Three-axis DROs with z-axis coupling* have a fourth position sensor on the quill. This takes into account the quill position with respect to the table height and does the math between their motions to show their *relative distance.* For example, if both the table and the quill move down the same amount, the readout will show zero *relative* movement. See Figure 8-6.

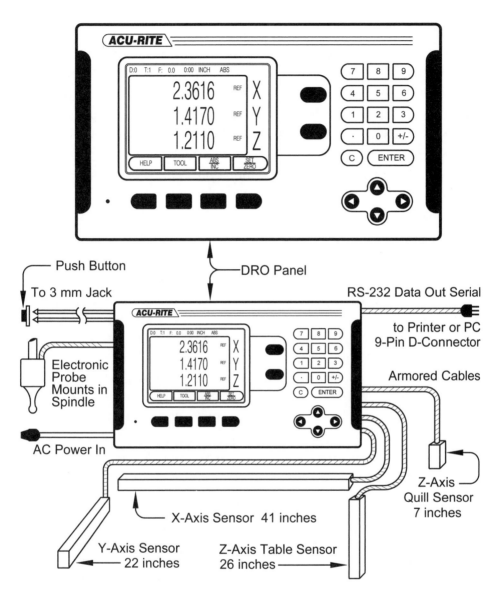

Figure 8-6. Three-axis DRO for a Bridgeport-style milling machine with a z-axis coupling.

DRO Resolution

DRO resolution runs 0.0005–0.001 inches for inexpensive systems, to 0.0002 inches for typical machine shop systems, and to 0.00002 inches for tool room systems. Inside the DRO, sensor phototransistors detect and count lines at 5μ (5 millionths of a meter) intervals on a glass scale to measure distance. The scales and electronics are under protective steel covers. One sensor bar is required on each axis.

Basic DRO Functions

A basic DRO performs the following functions:

- Displays distance in either inch or metric units at the push of a button. This function makes it easy to work from prints in either measurement unit without converting between the two systems.

- The axes can be set anywhere on the table by zeroing the display. Usually the axes zero-reference points are set at the corner of the workpiece for the X- and Y-axes and on the top surface of the workpiece for the z-axis.

- The DRO can display either the *absolute position* of the spindle over the milling table or the *distance-to-go* to complete a cut.

Other DRO Functions

In addition to displaying the position of the spindle relative to the milling table, industrial-grade DROs have other valuable functions:

- The *near-zero warning display* is a bar graph that shows when the readout is above, below or exactly zero. This feature makes it easy for the machinist to move the table to the zero position without watching the individual numerical digits go to zero. Using a near-zero warning is more accurate and less fatiguing for the operator.

- The *power-failure recovery* feature allows the last position before a power failure to be recaptured. In addition, it can find the last power-on table position even if someone turns the table cranks during the power outage.

- The *bolt-hole pattern layout function* needs only the number of holes, their starting angle, and the pattern diameter to be entered. The operator moves the table so the DRO shows zero on both axes and drills the first hole, then calls for the next hole and repeats the cycle until all of the holes are drilled. The DRO display in Figure 8-7 (right) shows the hole pattern layout, and the display in Figure 8-7 (left) shows the hole pattern data.

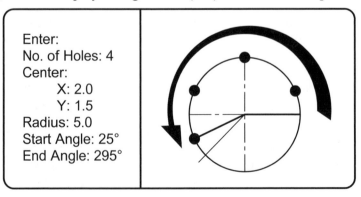

Figure 8-7. Bolt-hole pattern layout function.

- The *scale function* shrinks parts down to $0.1 \times$ or up to $10 \times$ the input dimensions. A negative number in the scale function produces a mirror image of the original part.

- The *hole-pattern layout function* is similar to the bolt-hole pattern layout function except that this function is for holes placed in rectangular rows and columns as in Figure 8-8.

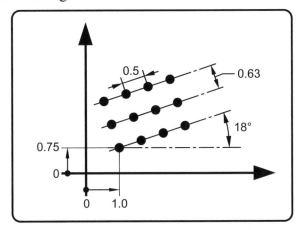

Figure 8-8. Hole-pattern layout function.

- The *edge-probing function* enables the DRO axes to be set to any convenient reference point on the part. Usually edges are chosen for reference. There are three ways to perform this function:

  - Locate the edge of the part—the reference point—with an edge finder, then zero the DRO for that axis. Repeat for all other axes. The edge finder used for this may be a traditional mechanical, an electronic or a laser edge finder. The DRO takes into account the diameter of the edge-finder tip when setting the axis to the reference edge. For more on edge finders, see Section III of this chapter, Measuring & Locating.

  - An electronic probe senses the edge of the part and sends a "set axis to zero" signal to the DRO when the point of the probe touches the part.

  - With a milling cutter in the spindle, the machinist probes the edge of the work and sets the DRO to zero by pressing a button on the DRO panel when the edge is found.

- The *remote-switch function* transmits digital data for the table position via the RS-232 serial port when the machinist closes an external circuit. This can be done with a push button or a foot switch. This data then goes to a printer or a PC. Using this function, the dimensions of the part may be measured and recorded.

- The *tool-table function* stores the diameter and length of 16 tools, usually end mills. Also, it stores the diameter of the edge finder in the tool table eliminating the need for the machinist to do arithmetic. The DRO does the math for him.

- The *tool-compensation function* allows the machinist to enter the part dimensions directly from the work print. The displayed *distance-to-go* is automatically lengthened or shortened by the value of the tool radius stored electronically in the tool table. See Figure 8-9.

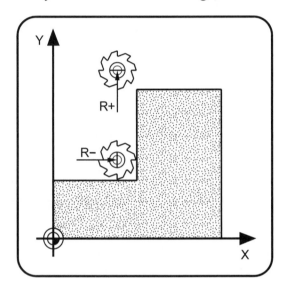

Figure 8-9. DRO tool-compensation function.

- The *½ function* locates the mid-point between two edges. Touching each side of the work with a tool or center finder and then pressing a function key on the DRO provides the answer.

- The *center-of-circle function* locates the center when given the diameter of the circle and three points on its radius are probed. This is useful for drilling center holes in cylinders or rounds.

Power Feeds

The motor which drives a milling machine axis leadscrew is known as a *power feed*. This accessory can be installed in about an hour by an experienced machinist. As shown in Figure 8-10, a milling machine power feed consists of:

- A high-torque DC motor.

- A power supply, speed control and direction lever for the DC motor.

- Reduction gears, which transmit motor torque to the milling machine table leadscrew with a typical 72:1 reduction. Within the same enclosure is a mechanism to disconnect the motor and gearing from the leadscrew when the motor is turned off. This permits easy manual cranking.

- Power feeds also have *rapids*, that is, a push button on the power feed housing which turns on the drive motor at its highest speed. This is used to position the table, not to move the table when milling or drilling. The rapids are a valuable feature because it reduces operator fatigue and speeds up production.

Warning: Exercise caution when using the rapids because the inertia of the power drive and leadscrew can carry the table some distance after the rapids push-button is released. This motion can cause the tool to crash into the work or the milling table.

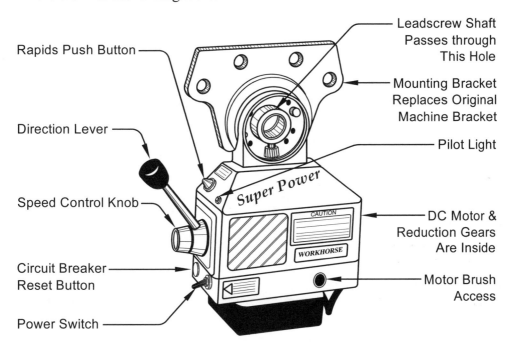

Figure 8-10. Side view of a milling machine power feed.

- A limit switch on the axis of *each* power feed. This switch is a precaution so if the machinist fails to turn off the power feed motor at the end of the table travel, the leadscrew and power drive are not damaged. The limit switch interrupts the electric power to the motor. See Figure 8-11.

Adding a *power feed* to a mill has a couple of advantages:

- Table movement is more uniform than hand-leadscrew cranking, so the finish on the work is more smooth and uniform.

- Using a power feed eliminates the physical effort required to turn the leadscrew cranks which, in turn, reduces operator fatigue. This is a major issue on the z-, or vertical, axis since it requires much more torque than the other two axes. The fatigue factor becomes especially important during boring and heavy drilling operations where many up-and-down cycles are needed and the power feed in the machine head cannot be used.

When only one power feed is purchased, it is usually installed on the x-axis to ensure long, even cuts. The next axis to receive a power feed is the z-axis because it requires so much torque to move the table up and down that it can be exhausting. Since y-axis movement is relatively short, this is usually the last choice of axis to receive a power feed.

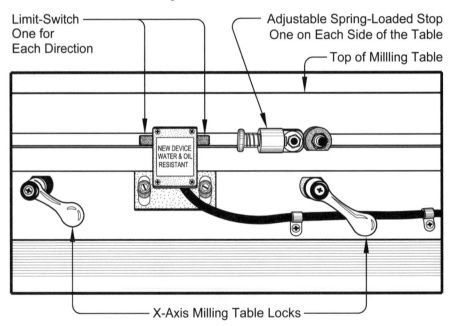

Figure 8-11. Limit switches on power feeds prevent damage to the mill and to the power drive.

Power feeds are rated at 90–150 in-lb continuous torque, but can develop upwards of 200 in-lb peak torque. Figure 8-12 shows a common pinch point that occurs when a power feed with a crank is installed. Replacing the original crank with a handwheel eliminates this pinch hazard. Handwheels with a fold-away crank handle are routinely used to avoid the machinist being spanked by a spinning crank handle.

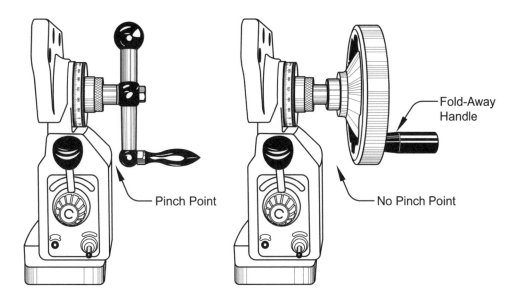

Figure 8-12. Milling machine longitudinal (X-axis) power feed installation creates a
dangerous pinch point removed by installing a handwheel in place of the original crank.

Milling Machine Lubrication Systems & Wear

When properly cleaned, lubricated and protected, industrial-grade machine
tools can last for decades. In fact, they are likely to become commercially
obsolete *before* they wear out. Lubrication is critical to minimizing wear and
maximizing the service lives of machine tools.

Full-sized milling machines have built-in lubrication systems that distribute
oil under pressure to the ways and leadscrews. The most basic lubrication
system, known as a *one-shot lube system*, is meant to be used once or twice a
shift. It consist of:

- A hand-actuated pressure pump.

- An oil reservoir.

- A lubrication distribution manifold and the associated piping.

More modern, advanced systems have motor-driven pumps on timers which
automatically deliver way oil at preset intervals of motor operation.

Aside from rust, the dust from grinding operations is the most destructive
substance to tools, followed by the chips from machining cast iron. As a
precaution, use paper coverings, such as brown wrapping paper or paper
grocery bags taped in place over the ways and carriage to keep these abrasive
materials from getting on machine components.

*Warning: Do not use rags as a covering because they can be pulled into
cutters and drag your hand into the lathe with them.*

Section II – Setting up a New Milling Machine

Introduction

Here are the major steps for setting up a new milling machine:

- *Location considerations* – Adequate clearance is essential around a full-sized milling machine to allow for side-to-side table movement and access to the electrical box and to the cutting fluid sump. Overhead clearance is also an issue since many modern milling machines, like the Kent (USA) 3- and 5-horsepower milling machines, are 84-inches tall and may have trouble being moved under beams, light fixtures and wiring. Sometimes a tall mill can be installed between ceiling beams with the motor poking up between them. The motor can be tipped 45° to get the mill in place.

- *Leveling* – Unlike lathes, milling machines are not as sensitive to leveling because their vertical ways are on one large single casting which makes them less susceptible to warpage or twisting from uneven support. However, careful leveling of the milling machine is helpful. A level can be used to check whether a workpiece is parallel to the mill table.

- *Cosmoline degreasing* – All cosmoline must be removed on the initial set-up because it dries out with age and will become much harder to remove. Kerosene or mineral spirits are the least hazardous degreasing agents and least likely to damage the milling machine paint finishes.

- *Check lubrication* – Typical Bridgeport-type mills have several points to check for proper lubrication:

  - The oil reservoir for the one-shot lubrication system usually requires several pints of oil.

  - On many mills, the Zerk grease fitting on the z-axis leadscrew requires a grease gun for lubrication.

  - The milling head spindle bearings usually have 2–3 snap-cap oilers and each requires a few drops of oil.

  - Some older Bridgeport mills have several Zerk fittings on the middle front face of the milling table. These fittings are there to apply oil to the ways with a special high-pressure oiler, not for grease. Putting grease in these fittings will require disassembling the milling table from the saddle to clean out the grease.

  - The lengths of leadscrews not reached by the one-shot lubrication system should have oil applied with a brush.

  - Wipe down the milling table with way oil.

- *Power and grounding* – For 1- and 1½-hp motors, whenever the wiring cost of bringing 220 volts to the milling machine motor is not excessive, the motor should be wired to run on 220 volts because there will be less voltage drop in the lines, which can reduce the machine's power. Larger motors *must* be run on 220 volts.

- *Blanking off the sump* – If a coolant pump will not be used, blank off the sump under the mill because the oils and hand-applied cutting fluids will accumulate there and eventually turn rancid. Although cutting speeds and feeds can be greatly increased with cutting fluid flooding, the mess it creates may not be worth the additional speed.

- *Installing lights* – Getting adequate light on the spindle area of a mill is often a problem, but there are low-cost halogen lights on 2-foot booms that are perfect for mounting on the milling machine casting. For the mounting location, refer to Figure 1-15.

- *Power strips* – In addition to 220 volts needed for the mill motor, 120 volts are needed for the DRO, the power feed motors and the halogen lights. By mounting a power strip onto the back of the milling machine casting, a single switch can control power to all these items.

- *Limit switch stops on the power feeds* – Check to see that the limit switch stops are set to prevent the table from moving to extreme positions where damage will occur to the power feed or leadscrew.

- *Aligning, or tramming, the head* – Check the head alignment and, if necessary, make the spindle perpendicular to the table. (For more details, see *Machine Shop Essentials by Frank Marlow, Chapter 8 – Milling Operations*.)

- *Prepare and install the milling vise* – Remove all burrs from the vise casting, clean away cosmoline and lubricate with way oil, then align the fixed vise jaw with the milling machine's x-axis.

Marking the Spindle Locking Pin Location

The R8 and similar collets engage a locking pin inside the spindle bore. This pin enters a groove in the side of the collet. The pin and groove arrangement insures that the collet remains stationary while the drawbar is tightened. See Figure 8-13. The taper on the front side of the collet provides most of the force locking the collet to the spindle when it is in use. It is helpful to add a small alignment dot near the mouth of the spindle bore to indicate where to position the R8 collet groove so it easily slides into the locking pin inside the spindle bore. Make this dot on the spindle by using a hand grinder with a carbide burr. Using an alignment dot eliminates the need to turn the collet in the spindle bore until the locking pin is found.

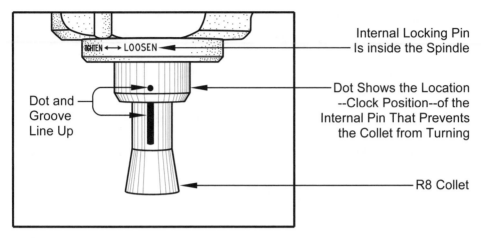

Figured 8-13. The dot shows the proper alignment for the
collet to engage the locking pin in the spindle bore.

Preparing the Milling Vise T-Bolts

Examine the T-bolts furnished with the milling vise. The majority of these T-bolts are ½-inch in diameter, although most Bridgeport-style milling machines have table slots that accommodate ⅝-inch bolts. If your vise comes with square-based ½-inch T-bolts, as in Figure 8-14 (left), consider upgrading these bolts to the ⅝-inch T-based T-bolts shown in Figure 8-14 (right). These larger T-based bolts are less likely to crack out a section of your T-slot when pulled up tight. Also, these larger bolts distribute the load over a greater area.

Before using them, go over the vise T-bolts with a medium file to remove any raised seam lines remaining from forging. It is important to make sure that the bearing area is flat. Whether or not you decide to upgrade the milling vise bolts, be sure to place hardened washers under their nuts. Hardened washers prevent the nut from digging into, or *coining*, the clamping surface on the vise which causes a loss of tension and a reduction in holding power. Without hardened washers, the milling vise gradually shifts out of alignment.

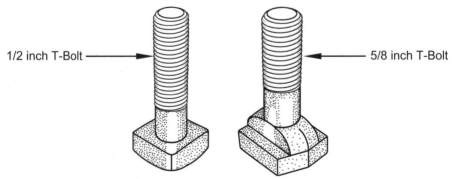

Figure 8-14. Square-based T-bolt (left) and stronger T-based T-bolt (right).

Preparing the Milling Vise for Use

A fresh-from-the-carton milling vise is not yet ready for use. To make it ready, follow these steps:

1. Remove all the cosmoline preservative using kerosene or mineral spirits, a brush and paper towels.

2. With a file, remove all the burrs that may be found on the edges of the base casting. If these sharp burrs remain when the vise is installed, they will damage the milling table. Remember, most milling tables are not hardened.

3. Unbolt the jaws from their jaw blocks, flush out the bolt holes to remove the cosmoline, and clean up the bolts too.

4. The jaws and jaw blocks may have razor edges. Remove these with emery cloth backed by a strip of metal. Only remove metal from the edges, never touch the jaw faces. Usually only a 3–5 thousandths of an inch chamfer is needed so the vise edges do not cut you. The bolt holes on the jaws should also be checked for burrs.

5. To keep rust away, spray all parts of the vise with LPS-1 greaseless lubricant.

6. Place the vise on the milling table and insert *one* T-bolt in the bolt slot, place a hardened washer over the T-bolt threads, screw on the nut, and tighten it.

7. Put two T-slot clamps on the side of the vise without the T-bolt, leaving room for flycutter access to the bolt groove. You will see why in Step 8.

8. Many milling vises have paint where the hardened washers on the T-bolts bear. Remove this paint and flatten the bearing area using a flycutter. Try an 800 RPM spindle speed and take a series of light cuts until you can see the area for the washer is flat and free of paint. See Figure 8-15.

9. Repeat steps 6–8 for the other side of the vise.

10. Install the missing T-bolt, hardened washer and nut.

11. Most milling vises are installed with the fixed jaw parallel to the x-axis of the milling machine. Make this alignment by indicating in—using a dial indicator—to align the fixed jaw with the machine axis. (For more on this, see *Machine Shop Essentials by Frank Marlow, Chapter 8 – Milling Operations*.)

12. Pull up the nut with an over-length box wrench. Do not attempt to tighten these bolts with an open-end wrench since it may slip off and surprise your knuckles.

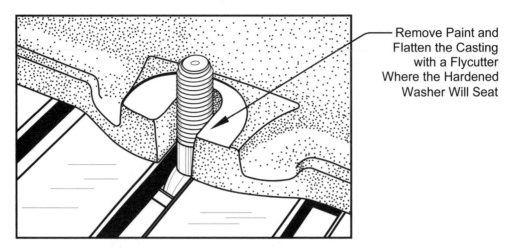

Remove Paint and
Flatten the Casting
with a Flycutter
Where the Hardened
Washer Will Seat

Figure 8-15. T-bolt and machined flats on a milling vise.

13. Full-size milling machine vises are sold with the tightening handle, or vise crank, shown in Figure 8-16 (bottom). While this style handle provides great leverage, it is a good idea to remove it from the vise before using the mill. When less clamping force is needed, as on smaller parts, the aftermarket vise crank in Figure 8-16 (top) is a better choice. This vise crank is small enough to be left in place when the mill is in use and much faster for moving the jaw than the original handle.

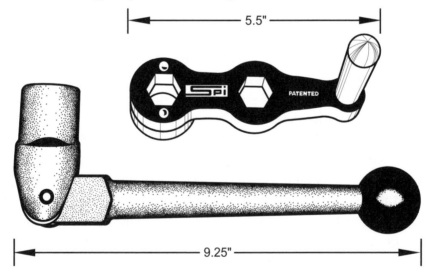

Figure 8-16. Aftermarket milling vise crank (top) and original vise crank (bottom).

The short aftermarket crank also avoids the problem shown in Figure 8-17 where the milling vise handle gets trapped in the Y-axis ways when the power feed is in use. This can damage the vise screw, the vise, and even damage the mill's leadscrew—a very expensive mishap.

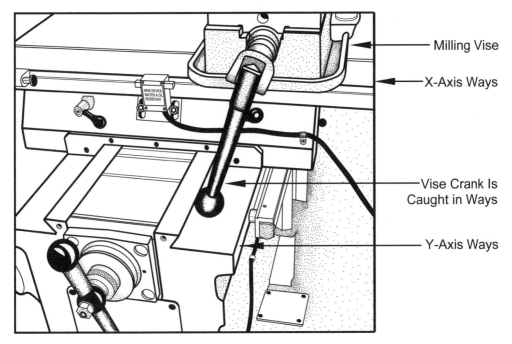

- Milling Vise
- X-Axis Ways
- Vise Crank Is Caught in Ways
- Y-Axis Ways

Figure 8-17. A standard factory-supplied milling vise crank caught and locked in the Y-axis ways and about to do serious damage to the vise and the Y-axis leadscrew and its nut.

Milling Table Covers

There are three reasons to use *milling table covers*:

- To prevent damage caused by dropping tools on the milling table.
- To keep chips out of the T-bolt grooves.
- To reduce the chances of rust. Using a cover allows the machinist to keep the table oiled without making an oily, chip-filled mess.

There are commercial milling table covers made of neoprene sheet rubber, and there are shop-made substitutes made from toolbox drawer liners or from vinyl floor runners, which are cheaper. Both types work equally well. Figure 8-18 shows a shop-made table cover. Also, there are commercially available plastic strips to fill in the T-bolt grooves and keep chips out, but these do not protect the table from damage.

To make the vinyl table cover, start by placing the vinyl material on a wood or chipboard cutting surface and mark the cutting line. Next, clamp a straight edge on the cut line using welding Vise-Grips or large clamps, then, using a mat knife, make the cut. More than one cutting pass may be needed to get all the way through the vinyl. After attaching a wood strip that fits into the T-slots, your shop-made table cover is complete.

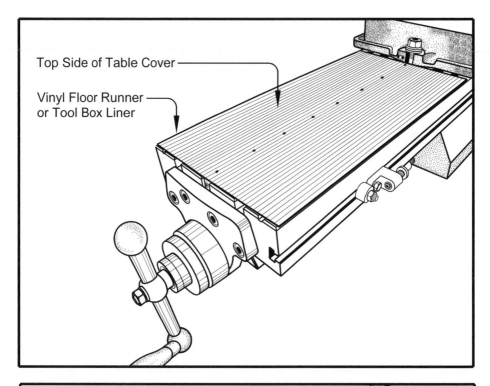

Top Side of Table Cover

Vinyl Floor Runner
or Tool Box Liner

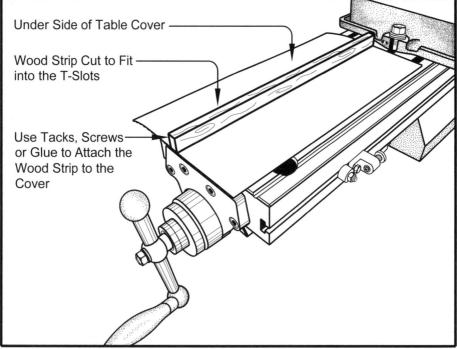

Under Side of Table Cover

Wood Strip Cut to Fit
into the T-Slots

Use Tacks, Screws
or Glue to Attach the
Wood Strip to the
Cover

Figure 8-18. Shop-made vinyl milling table cover keeps chips
out of the T-slots, protects the ways, and simplifies clean-up.

Section III – Measuring & Locating

Edge Finders

There are three common tools used for locating an edge on a workpiece so a DRO can be set to that edge:

- *Mechanical edge finders*, Figure 8-19 (A), are the traditional edge-locating tools. But, because they must be used while the spindle is turning, they may mark the work during contact. Mechanical edge finders cannot be used to locate scribe lines or center-punch marks.

- *Electronic edge finders,* Figure 8-19 (B), have an internal battery and a lamp or LED which illuminates when the sensor touches metal. They work only with conductive workpiece materials, not plastics. Electronic edge finders are used with the spindle stopped. Like the traditional mechanical edge finders, electronic edge finders cannot locate scribe lines or center-punch marks.

- *Laser edge finders*, also called *laser center finders,* Figure 8-19 (C), are red solid state laser pointers aligned with the spindle axis to project a spot of light on the workpiece. They work with metals and non-metals with the spindle stopped. For accuracy, polarizing filters are often used to reduce the size of the locating light spot, but these filters also reduce beam intensity so much that the spot is hard to see in normal shop light levels. Black plastics and anodized parts create additional problems as the red light spot is difficult to see on dark-colored work. Laser edge finders *can* locate scribe lines and center-punch marks.

Table 8-1 summarizes edge finder characteristics.

Centering Device	Typical Accuracy* (inches)	Comments
Mechanical Edge Finder	± 0.0002	Spindle must be turning. Cannot locate lines or center-punch marks.
Electronic Edge Finder	± 0.0005	Spindle must be stopped. Part must be conductive, not plastic. Cannot locate lines or center-punch marks.
Laser Edge Finder	± 0.002	Spindle must be stopped. Needs low ambient light level to see red spot. Sensitive to user technique and judgment. Excellent for locating over center-punch marks.

* With an experienced user taking reasonable care and time.

Table 8-1. Edge finder characteristics and accuracy.

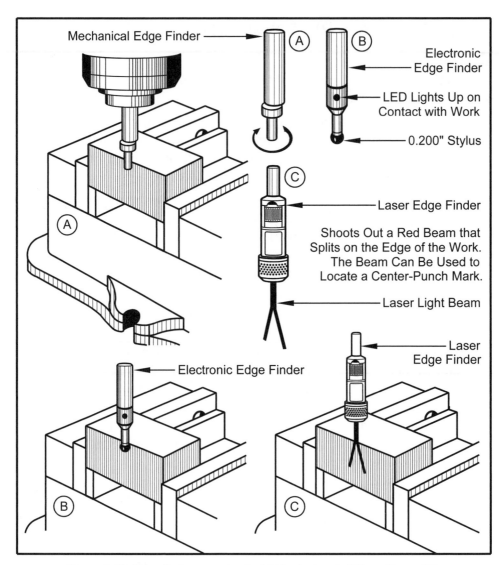

Figure 8-19. Edge finders: mechanical (A), electronic (B), and laser (C).

How to Hold a Dial Indicator

There are several good ways to hold a dial indicator, and each method has its own pluses and minuses. No one method works for all set-ups.

- *In the spindle in a collet* is the simplest way to hold a dial indicator. This method works fine for aligning work with a mill axis, but cannot be used for centering work. To allow a dial indicator to fit into several different size collets, many machinists use the shop-made adapter, called a *stepped spindle bushing*, shown in Figure 8-20. To make this bushing, a ¾-inch piece of CRS round stock is turned down in steps, and then a ⅜-inch hole is center drilled and reamed. This stepped spindle bushing reduces the number of times a collet must be changed out from one size to hold the cutting tool to another size to hold the dial indicator, and then changed back again to the cutting tool collet. An annoying and time-consuming process.

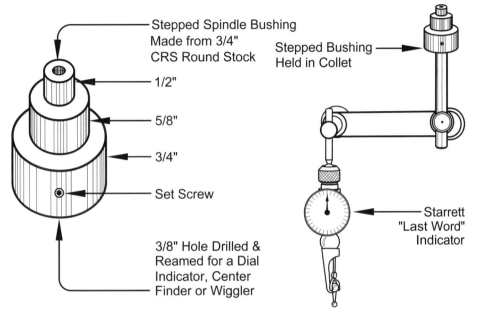

Figure 8-20. A shop-made stepped spindle bushing allows a dial
indicator to fit into several different sized collets.

- *Indicol universal dial indicator holders,* Figure 8-21, clamp directly onto the outside of the mill spindle. While this method of holding a DTI may be used for aligning a vise or workpiece with a mill axis, the principal function of the indicol holder is to align the axis of a round workpiece with the mill spindle axis.

Here is how it is done:

1. Disconnect the motor from the spindle so that the spindle turns freely and easily by hand. On Bridgeport-style milling machines, setting the HI-LO SPEED CONTROL LEVER to the NEUTRAL position does this.

2. Clamp the indicol dial indicator holder onto the lower end of the mill spindle.

3. Adjust the table position so that the DTI shows about half its scale deflection and is not pinned at one end of its scale.

4. While slowly turning the spindle by hand, adjust the X- and Y-axes leadscrews so that the DTI remains steady and does not fluctuate as the DTI rotates around the workpiece.

5.   The spindle and workpiece are coaxial when the DTI does not move
     during spindle rotation.

The dial indicator on the indicol can align cylindrical work under the spindle
axis or the fixed vise jaw to the X- or Y axis. Because the indicol clamps
around the spindle instead of inside a collet in the spindle, the milling cutter
can remain in place while the indicol and dial indicator is used.

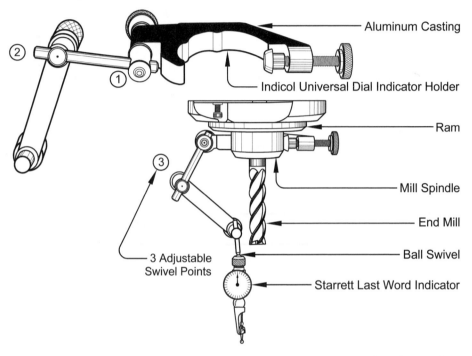

Figure 8-21. The indicol universal dial indicator holder clamps onto the mill spindle.
Notice the three adjustable swivel points.

- *Coaxial centering indicators,* Figure 8-22, work like an indicol except
  with the spindle turning under motor power. As does the indicol holder,
  they center cylindrical workpieces and holes in workpieces under the
  spindle. Coaxial centering indicators center work much faster than an
  indicol, but are more costly. Here is how to use one:

  1.   Lower the milling table—or raise the quill—so that the bottom end of
       the centering indicator does not touch the workpiece.

  2.   Install a coaxial centering indicator into a collet, and then install a
       centering probe into the bottom end of the indicator.

  3.   Install the stabilizer rod by screwing it into the side of the centering
       indicator. This rod prevents the indicator from spinning while the
       spindle rotates. Machinists often install a magnetic indicator base on
       the mill table to stop the stabilizer rod from spinning.

4. Center the spindle over a hole in the workpiece, as in Figure 8-22 (left), or over a cylindrical workpiece, as in Figure 8-22 (right).

5. Raise the table, or lower the quill, so the centering probe rests on the face of the work.

6. Set the mill for a spindle speed for 200 RPM and turn on the mill. Adjust the table position, and when the indicator needle remains stationary, the work is centered.

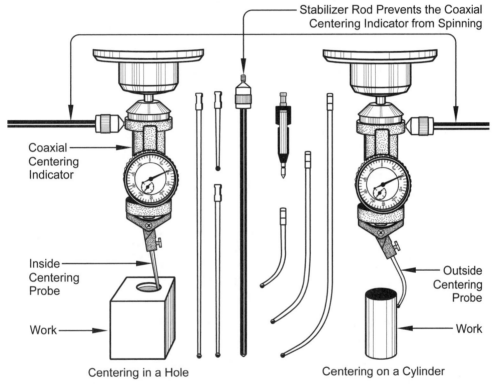

Figure 8-22. A coaxial centering indicator makes centering work in the mill fast and easy.

Finding the Center of an Existing Hole

Figure 8-23 (left) shows a ball-end wiggler for centering the spindle over an existing hole. Use a ball end slightly larger than the hole to be centered on, turn the spindle on to 500 RPM and adjust the milling machine table position so that the ball end does not move as it is repeatedly engaged with the hole opening and pulled clear of it.

Locating Center-Punch Marks & Scribed Lines

There are three ways to position the spindle over center-punch marks:

- With a *wiggler pointer*, as shown in Figure 8-23 (right). Wigglers locate holes, center-punch marks and lines ± 0.003 inches.

- The center-punch mark can be found using the laser edge finder shown in Figure 8-19 (C).

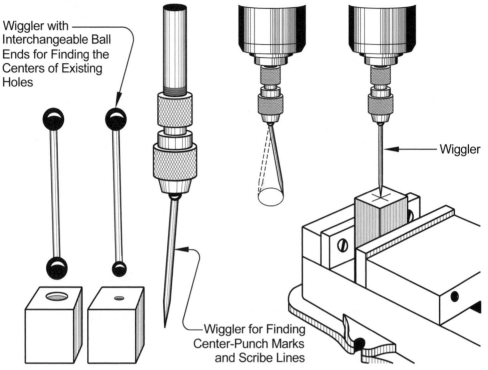

Wiggler with Interchangeable Ball Ends for Finding the Centers of Existing Holes

Wiggler

Wiggler for Finding Center-Punch Marks and Scribe Lines

Figure 8-23. A wiggler with two interchangeable ball ends for locating holes (left) and a wiggler with a pointed end for finding scribe lines or center-punch marks (right).

- The center-punch mark can also be located using a drill in the spindle. The center-punch mark is axially positioned when the drill drops into the punch mark without flexing to either side of the punch mark. See Figure 8-24. On smaller twist drills, you can see the drill deflect when it touches the sides of the center-punch mark. On larger drills, when the drill enters the center-punch mark, you can feel it through the quill handle. Check the center location by observing the drill at two positions 90° apart.

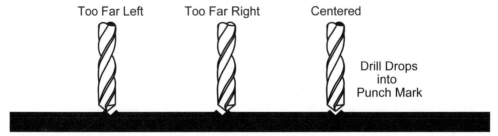

Too Far Left   Too Far Right   Centered

Drill Drops into Punch Mark

Figure 8-24. You can see small drills flex when they touch the sides of a center-punch mark, and you can feel larger drills drop into the center-punch mark.

Fast Rotary Table Alignment

Rotary tables can be quickly aligned to the mill spindle axis within 0.005 inches by making the centering tool in Figure 8–25. The tool's small diameter shank fits a standard collet size, and its large diameter is 0.002-inch under the diameter of the rotary table's center hole. To align the rotary table:

1. Using T-slot bolts, fasten the rotary table to the milling table, positioning the rotary table in its approximately correct location.

2. Mount the collet to hold the shop-made centering tool, insert the tool, and tighten the collet.

3. Apply light downward pressure on the quill feed handle so that the centering tool touches the edge of the hole in the center of the rotary table.

4. Move the table back and forth while observing the centering tool.

5. When the spindle and rotary table are coaxial, the centering tool will drop into the center hole. Alignment is now complete. Set the DRO (or table collars) to zero.

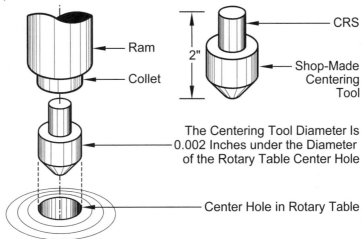

Ram

Collet

2"

CRS

Shop-Made Centering Tool

The Centering Tool Diameter Is 0.002 Inches under the Diameter of the Rotary Table Center Hole

Center Hole in Rotary Table

Figure 8–25. Shop-made centering tool quickly aligns a rotary table.

Section IV – Clamping & Work Holding

Milling Vise

A milling vise and parallels are the most common work-holding devices used in the mill. With them work can be quickly set up and securely held. The back, or fixed jaw, of the vise is usually aligned with a machine axis, typically the x-axis. Because of this, the vise jaw is already parallel and there is no need to *indicate in* the work as would be needed if the work were secured to the milling table with strap clamps in the T-slots. For work-holding examples, see Figure 8-26.

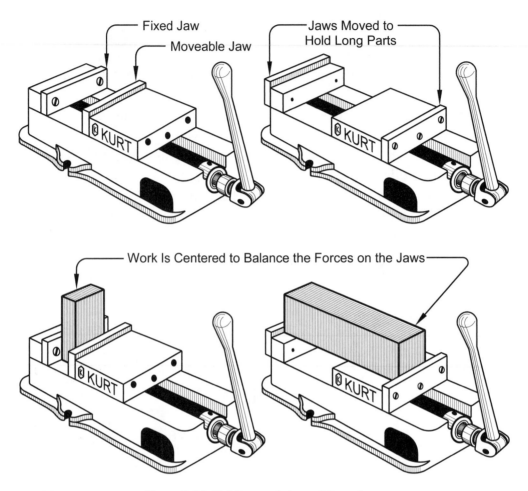

Figure 8-26. Holding work in a milling vise.

Here are some tips for properly using a milling vise:

*   Always use the fixed vise jaw—usually the one on the opposite side of the milling table away from the operator—as the reference point. Make the most critical cuts going *toward* the fixed jaw because the fixed jaw is used to align the vise with the X-axis of the mill and because the fixed jaw is more rigid than the moveable jaw.

*   Use spacers to balance the force on the vise jaws when work must be held off center. To resist cutting forces, support all work by placing it on the floor of the vise opening or on parallels. Figure 8-27 shows correct and incorrect milling vise practices.

*   See the most common work-holding techniques in the milling vise shown in Figure 8-28.

Correct   Incorrect

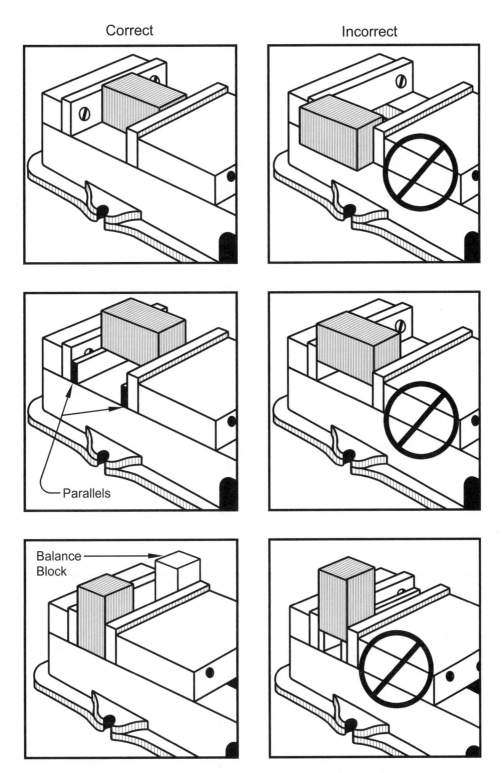

Figure 8-27. Correct and incorrect milling vise practice.

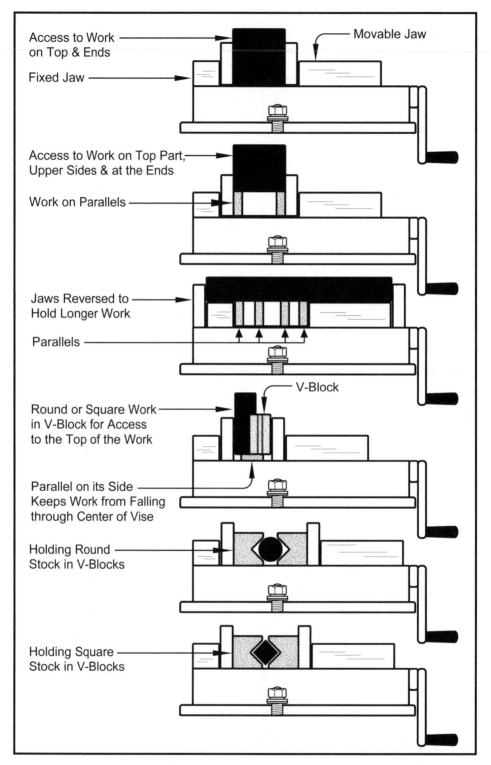

Figure 8-28. Work-holding techniques in the milling vise.

- Placing a piece of copy paper or a cardboard shim (not corrugated) between the work and the milling vise jaws improves the vise's grip and prevents marring the work. The paper or cardboard shim acts as a clutch, applying force evenly all across the jaws, even when the work is slightly out of parallel. Put the shim against the moveable jaw, not the fixed one. This keeps the work against the reference face of the fixed jaw.

- When the thickness of the work is the same as the thickness of one or two parallels, add a cardboard shim in front of the moveable jaw to allow the jaws to grip the work. See Figure 8-29.

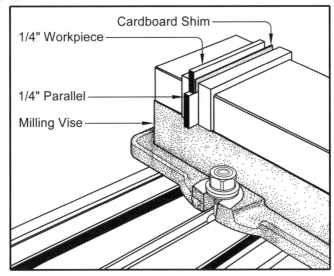

Figure 8-29. Adding a cardboard or copy paper shim to hold the work securely.

- When work is too wide to be supported by one parallel, yet not wide enough for two, place one parallel diagonally under the work as shown in Figure 8-30.

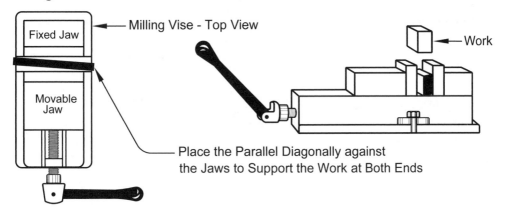

Figure 8-30. Placing a milling parallel diagonally under work for solid support.

Milling Vise with Crutches

Milling table *crutches* are spacers that are usually shop-made of steel or aluminum and are the same height as the distance of the ways or floor of the milling vise is above the milling table. They support the ends of long workpieces so that the work does not bend or wiggle when subjected to machining loads. See Figure 8-31. Most jobs need strap clamps to secure the work onto the crutches. While some jobs benefit from custom-made crutches that have integral clamps, many crutches are secured with T-bolts that go through a hole countersunk inside the crutch base.

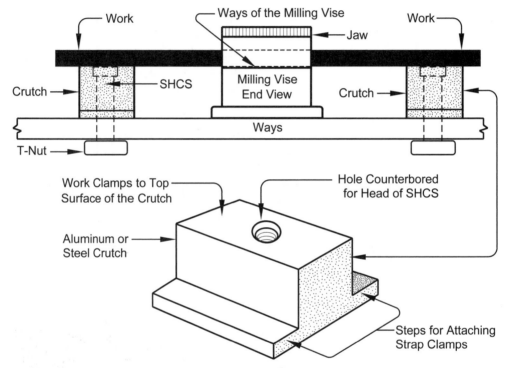

Figure 8-31. Crutches make the work more rigid, allowing long, continuous cuts to be made. The strap clamps normally used in a set-up like this are not shown in this drawing.

Milling Vise Clamping Technique

Here are the typical steps to secure work in a milling vise:

1. Open up the vise jaws to get access to the interior of the vise.
2. Remove all chips and debris to insure that the work—or the parallels—sit flat on the bottom floor of the milling vise and that the work lies flat against the jaw faces.
3. When using two parallels, place one parallel against each vise jaw and set the workpiece on top of the parallels.
4. Close and snug up the vise on the work.

5. Because the moveable jaw tends to raise the work slightly upon tightening, use a lead dead-blow or soft-faced hammer to strike the top of the work to insure it is fully seated on the parallels.

6. Attempt to push out each parallel with your fingers. They should not move, but be trapped between the bottom of the vise and the work. If they do move, the parallels are not secure and the work does not lie flat. Check for dirty work or faces out of parallel, then repeat the hammering process.

7. Tighten the vise. Considerable torque is usually applied.

Milling with Two Vises

When many long workpieces are to be machined, using two or more milling vises together may be the best strategy. See Figure 8-32. But, be aware that, as they come from the factory, no two milling vises are exactly the same height from their bases to the top of their ways and it is necessary to even them out before use. To make them a uniform height is simple. First, remove their jaws, then flip the vises upside down on their jaw blocks and Blanchard grind their bases. Some shops send all of their milling vises out for grinding at the same time so they will all be identical, and therefore, interchangeable.

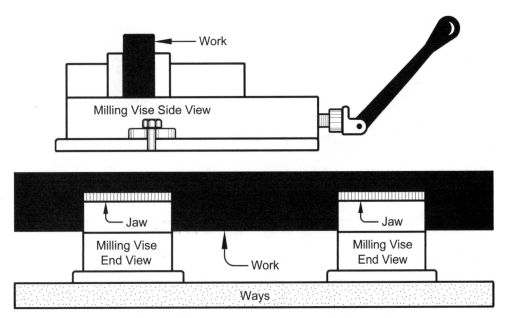

Figure 8-32. Two milling vises can speed jobs with long workpieces.

Extension Bars

Extension bars are used to make long work more rigid. See Figure 8-33. Sandwiching the work between two CRS bars which are longer than the milling vise jaws adds four capabilities:

- Milling cuts can be taken which are much longer than the width of the milling vise jaws, but it may be necessary to add Kant-Twist™ clamps or welding-type Vise-Grips to the outboard ends of the sandwich.

- If the cut takes place at or just below the top of the extension bars, very thin stock, even sheet metal, can be cut accurately and without damage.

- Many stacked sheets of work can be cut at the same time and trimmed to exactly the same size in a single cut with an end mill. This saves time and money. Although the milling machine is not a replacement for a hydraulic- or foot-powered metal shear, for smaller work, it can make smooth, straight, precise cuts.

- Adding a 45° bevel to the top outside edges of the CRS bar stock extensions provides better work visibility as well as clearance for bevel cutters.

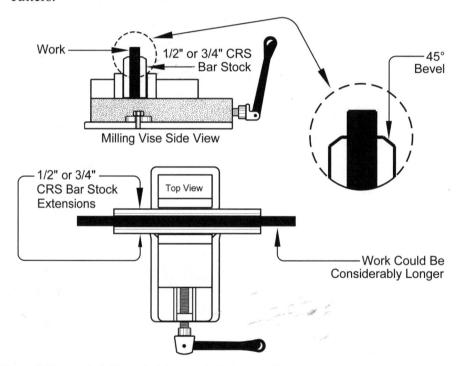

Figure 8-33. Sandwiching work between CRS extension bars makes the work more rigid. Using this extension bar method, thin stock may be trimmed to exact dimensions.

Cutting a Series of Slots in Metal Angle

Figure 8-34 shows how to cut multiple slots into a leg of steel or aluminum angle. Cutting from left to right, when all the slots have been cut in the section of the angle clamped between the CRS bars, the milling cutter will end up in the last slot on the right of the work which is fully supported between the extension bars. Now, raise the quill, move the table, and lower the milling cutter into the far left-side slot, raise the cutter, open the vise, and move the work to the left so the cutter fits into the last slot cut. You have just indexed the work so that the next slot to be cut will be at the same starting point and at the same incremental distance on the DRO as the already cut slots.

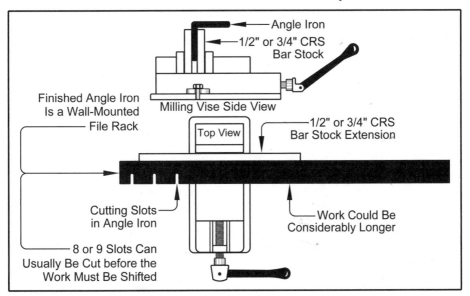

Figure 8-34. Using CRS extensions to add rigidity to a long piece of aluminum angle allows the cutting of more slots before the work must be moved to the next position.

Making Angle Cuts in a Milling Vise

There are many techniques for holding work in a vise to cut angles:

- The simplest method is to clamp the workpiece at an angle in the milling vise, but the lack of solid support requires taking light cuts or the workpiece can be thrown from the vise. Also, accurately setting the angle in the vise is difficult. Always try to make milling cuts perpendicular to the face of the vise jaws. See Figure 8-35 (A). Cutting perpendicular to the vise jaws is more secure than taking cuts parallel to the jaws.

- A milling parallel, as in Figure 8-35(B), can be used to set a cut line scribed on the workpiece parallel with the vise jaws.

- Clamping the workpiece at an angle in the milling vise using a pair of *milling angles* is much more accurate than clamping work without them. Milling angles also improve support and hold the part at the same angle every time. Mill angles are commercially available or can be shop-made. Figures 8-36 (C) and (D) show one milling angle placed against the fixed jaw and the other angle placed against the moveable jaw. The three notches in the milling angle are for holding large, medium and small workpieces.

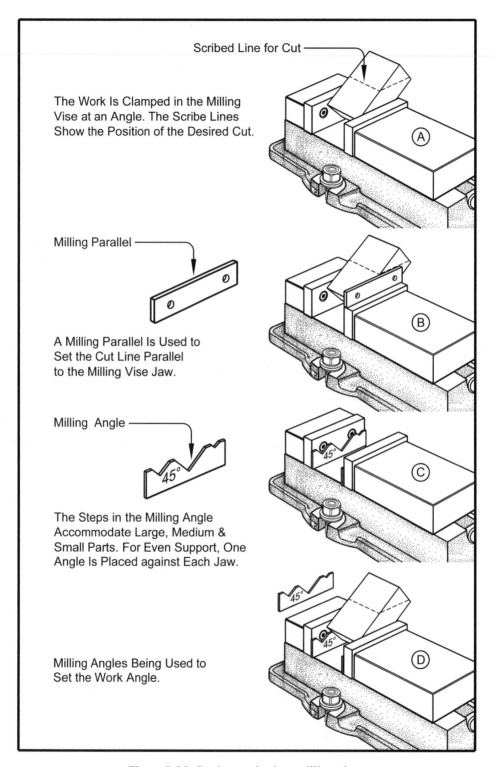

Scribed Line for Cut

The Work Is Clamped in the Milling Vise at an Angle. The Scribe Lines Show the Position of the Desired Cut.

Ⓐ

Milling Parallel

A Milling Parallel Is Used to Set the Cut Line Parallel to the Milling Vise Jaw.

Ⓑ

Milling Angle

The Steps in the Milling Angle Accommodate Large, Medium & Small Parts. For Even Support, One Angle Is Placed against Each Jaw.

Ⓒ

Milling Angles Being Used to Set the Work Angle.

Ⓓ

Figure 8-35. Cutting angles in a milling vise.

- Using a *milling angle plate* and a purchased *angle standard*, as in Figure 8-36, is another way to make an angle cut in the milling vise. A dial test indicator is mounted on the spindle or in the milling head and its foot runs along the angle standard. To copy the angle standard, the table is adjusted until the dial indicator shows no movement. Work can be clamped directly to the milling angle plate or a vise can be secured to the angle plate and the work in the vise. This milling angle plate is for light duty and will not take heavy cuts or the drilling of large holes.

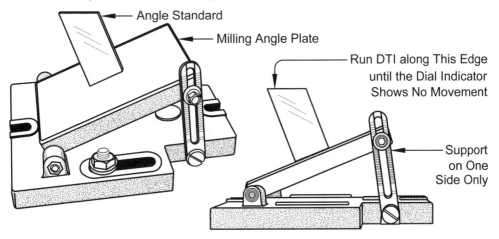

Figure 8-36. Setting an angle on a milling angle plate.

- Figure 8-37 shows a Sherline angle plate, sometimes called a *tilting table*. Work can be clamped to this plate or a vise secured to the angle plate. The Sherline angle plate has predrilled holes for mounting work with strap clamps. This simple design works well because the angle plate is supported on both sides. Taking larger cuts is limited only by tool chatter, not by angle plate rigidity.

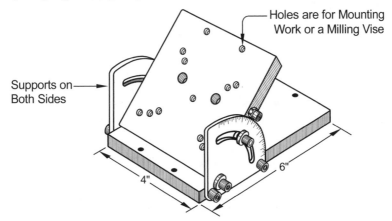

Figure 8-37. Small Sherline angle plate has predrilled holes for mounting work.

Other Vise Designs

- The *toolmakers' grinding vise* in Figure 8-38 is ideal for precise cuts on smaller work. Unlike the standard milling vise, its clamping screw is at 45° to the faces of the vise. Because of this design, the clamping jaw does not pull upward on the work when it is tightened. A grinding vise is perfect for small rush jobs because it avoids the need to disturb set-ups in the milling machine's full-size milling vise.

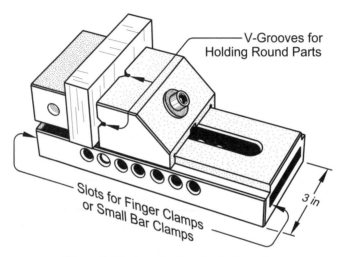

Figure 8-38. A toolmakers' grinding vise.

- Although the *two-piece milling vise* in Figure 8-39 seems like a great idea for holding extra-long work, when properly tightened, a two-piece milling vise can *bend* the milling table and the work into an arc. See Figure 8-40. This not only degrades accuracy, it can damage the milling table. Two-piece milling vises look good in catalogs, but are usually a poor choice and should be avoided.

Figure 8-39. The two-piece milling vise bolts to the milling table.

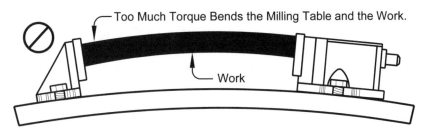

Figure 8-40. The result of over-tightening a two-piece vise on the milling table.

Strap Clamps & T-Bolts

After the milling vise, the combination of strap clamps and T-bolts is the second most common work-holding method in the milling machine. Strap clamps and T-bolts easily hold large or non-rectangular work, but they require additional time to align the work to the milling machine axis. Figure 8-41 shows the correct use of strap clamps and T-bolts in conjunction with step blocks. It also shows the incorrect use. The strap clamp, sometimes called a step or bar clamp, has three parts: the clamping strap, the fastener, and the end support.

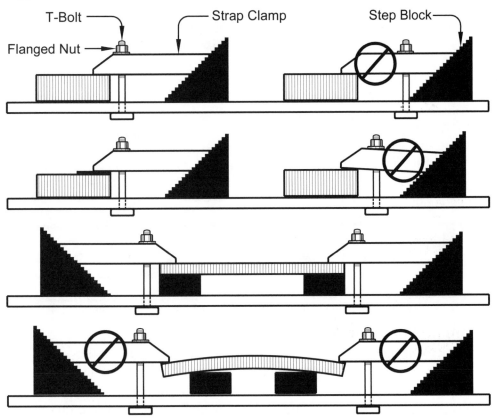

Figure 8-41. Good and bad practices for strap clamps and T-bolts used with step blocks.

Using Strap Clamps in Milling Table T-Slots

Because the ways on the milling table are parallel to the x-axis of the machine, placing round stock in them automatically aligns work with the x-axis. Figure 8-42 shows a typical set-up for holding round stock.

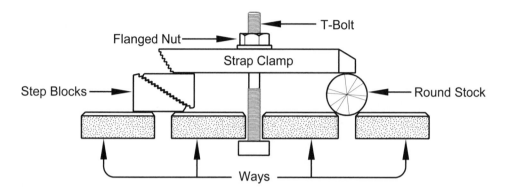

Figure 8-42. Securing round stock in a T-slot with a strap or bar clamp.
The milling table T-slots are parallel with the x-axis.

Figure 8-43 shows how changing the step-block orientation changes the height increments. This allows for a more accurate clamping set-up. Ideally, the step blocks should be set to make the strap clamp level.

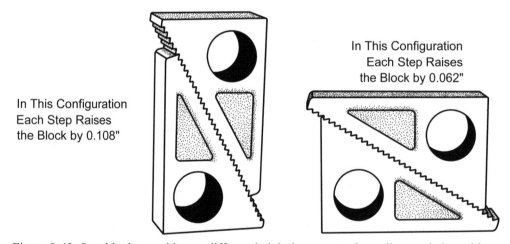

Figure 8-43. Step blocks provide two different height increments depending on their position.

Clamping Forces on Strap Clamps

The typical Bridgeport-style mill has three T-slots that allow the use of ⅝-inch diameter T-bolts, but most machinists use only smaller ½-inch diameter T-bolts (or T-nuts and stud bolts). Table 8-2 shows how upgrading to ⅝-inch T-bolts provides 60% more clamping force, which is good practice on milling vises, rotary tables, and angle plates.

Stud Size	Recommended Torque* (ft.-lbs.)	Clamping Force (lbs.)	Tensile Force in Stud (lbs.)
⅜-16	16	1300	2600
½-13	33	2300	4600
⅝-11	77	3700	7400

*Clean, dry clamping stud or T-bolt, torqued to 33% of its 100 ksi yield strength with a 2:1 lever ratio.

Table 8-2. Torque and clamping forces on strap clamps.

Securing Strap Clamps

The strap clamps in Figure 8-44 can be secured to the milling table with:

- T-bolts which slide into the T-slots in the milling table. These T-bolts are not normally furnished with mill clamping sets because of their cost. Buying an assortment of different length clamping studs and a few T-nuts is much less expensive than furnishing a set of T-bolts in a variety of lengths. But in their favor, quality T-bolts are forged with rolled threads versus clamping studs which can have weaker cut threads. Budget T-nuts have a similar drawback. They are often machined from bar stock, while quality T-nuts are forged.

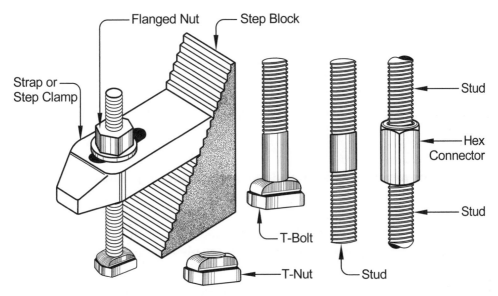

Figure 8-44. Strap clamp and clamping hardware.

- T-nuts plus clamping studs in the T-slots of the milling table also work well to secure strap clamps. This T-nut and clamping stud arrangement has an advantage over T-bolts because clamping studs can be lengthened for holding larger work by joining the studs with hex connectors.

Preventing Milling Table Damage

Milling table damage can be prevented if the bottom end of the clamping stud is *not* allowed to go all the way through the T-nut when the stud is being tightened. To assure that this costly accident does not happen, the last few threads in the bottom of the T-nut are either left incomplete or purposely damaged by crushing them to form a stop. Inspect all of your T-nuts to insure that studs cannot go through the bottom. If a stud does go though the bottom of a T-nut, the stud can act as a jack and crack out a section of the milling table as shown in Figure 8-45. This table damage is not repairable. Only an expensive milling table replacement will put you back in business. There are three different ways to avoid this problem: first, use only T-bolts in the T-slots, second, make sure that your T-nuts have a stop in the bottom threads, and third, if you find a T-nut with complete threads, place a plug weld in the bottom of the T-nut with a stud in place, effectively converting the two parts into a one-piece T-bolt. Converting a portion of all your T-nuts and studs into T-bolts will help avoid an expensive "crack-out." Use clamping studs only for when extending T-bolts with hex-connector nuts.

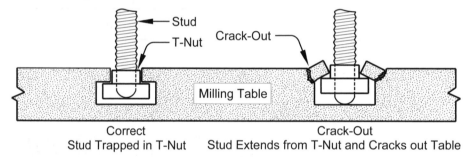

Figure 8-45. Studs passing through T-nuts may damage the milling table.

Collet Blocks

Collet blocks are square or hexagonal steel tooling fixtures which provide a simple, quick means of holding and indexing work. See Figure 8-46 (A & B). When the blocks are held on a different face, the work is indexed to that same angle, as in Figure 8-46 (C). Figure 8-46 (D) shows a collet block in a milling vise, the most common way to hold collet blocks for milling. Figure 8-46 (E) shows a simple way to cut hex flats on a bolt made from round stock.

Hexagonal collet blocks are ideal for making hex head bolts or for cutting triangles by using every other flat on the hexagonal block. Square collet blocks work well for cutting wrenching flats on round stock. Also, when a job requires milling a square cut onto round or hex stock, this is the tool for holding the work. Collet blocks are also useful when cutting slots into opposite sides of round stock or tubing such as the hose clamp wire applicator in the top of Figure 9-76.

While either a rotary table, indexing head, or a spin indexer could be used instead of a collet block, these costly tools require much more set-up time to clamp and locate them at each position. Though collet blocks are simple, inexpensive tools, they are extremely useful, and for small work, they are nearly fool proof.

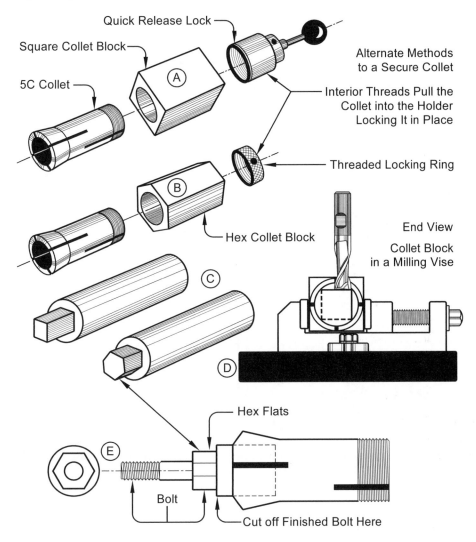

Figure 8-46. Collet blocks are easy to use, and for many jobs, faster than indexing heads.

Applying Wrenching Flats to Clamping Studs

Quality clamping studs have wrenching flats as shown in Figure 8-47. These flats allow studs to be tightened into their T-nuts, effectively making up a T-bolt. Make sure that the studs do not penetrate through the bottom of the T-nut when tightened. When nuts against the bar clamp are loosened or unscrewed, the clamping studs often unscrew from their T-nuts as well, which is very annoying. This is less likely to happen if there are wrenching flats on the clamping stud because the flats allow the stud to be tightened more securely.

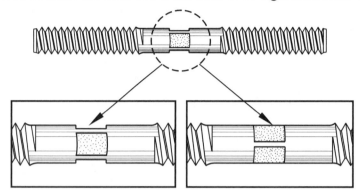

Figure 8-47. Wrenching flats on clamping studs.

Wrenching flats are easily applied to clamping studs using a ⅜-inch end mill with the clamping studs held in a collet block, as in Figure 8-48. One cut with each turn of the collet block applies the flats. Adjust the cut depth of the end mill so the distance between the flats fits a ⅜-inch open-end wrench.

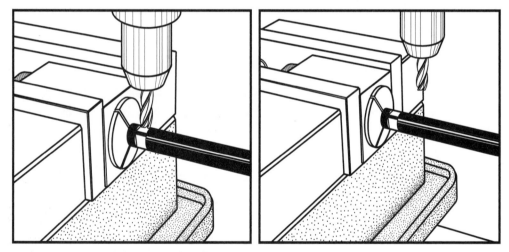

Figure 8-48. Applying wrenching flats on a clamping stud with the stud in a collet block.

Knife-Edge Clamps

Knife-edge clamps are used on irregular workpieces, especially those with no square sides on which to clamp such as pyramids, trapezoids and parallelograms. Take light cuts since work held in these clamps is not nearly as secure as work held directly in vise jaws. Taking milling cuts perpendicular to the vise jaws imposes lower forces on the clamps than cuts taken parallel with the vise jaws. See Figure 8-49.

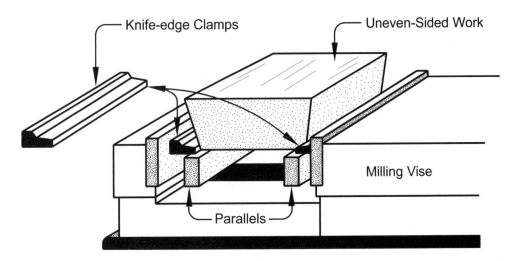

Figure 8-49. Knife-edge clamps securing uneven-sided work in a milling vise.

Edge Clamping with Cam Clamps

Cam clamps, such as the Mitee-Bite clamps in Figure 8-50, are handy for when step clamps cannot be used because they would be in the way of the cutter on the top of the workpiece, such as on thin stock.

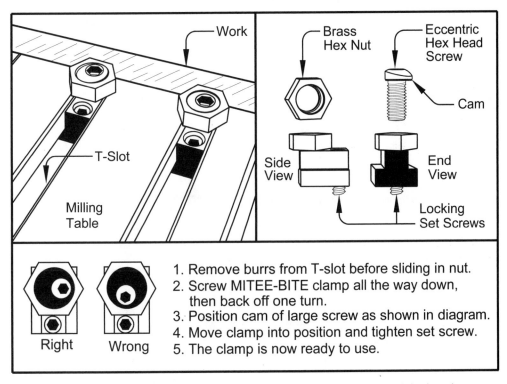

Figure 8-50. Mitee-Bite cam clamps are useful for holding thinner stock by its edges.

There are several necessary precautions when using cam clamps:

- Take light cuts because these clamps do not hold nearly as well as step clamps. Too heavy a cut will send the work flying and you to the emergency room. Also, do not make interrupted cuts.

- If possible, cam clamps should be positioned in pairs opposite one another. When all clamps are tightened to the same torque—best done with a torque wrench—excellent clamping results.

- When cam clamps are used on an aluminum workpiece, the lateral forces they exert will dish or bow the work upward, making precise cuts impossible. Cam clamps work much better on steel.

Angle Plate Clamping

Clamping milling work to an angle plate, as in Figure 8-51, offers several advantages over holding work in a vise alone:

- Angle plates can hold taller and larger work than a milling vise.

- By adding C-clamps and spacers, irregular work can be held.

- As with a milling table, slotted angle plates use T-bolts to secure work.

- Angle plates provide access to the workpiece top and most of one side.

- Work can be accurately positioned at an angle and securely held.

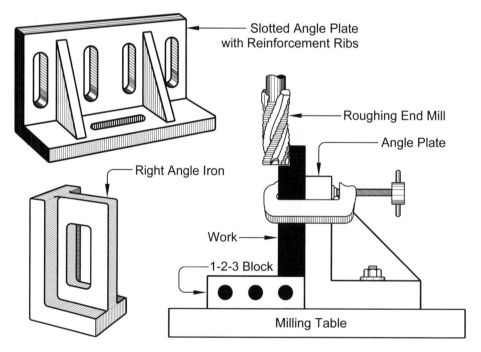

Figure 8-51. Two types of angle plates with reinforcing ribs (left)
and a side view of an angle plate with work clamped to it (right).

- When the same part will be machined many times, the angle plate can be drilled and tapped for custom clamping points. This is possible because angle plates are not usually hardened.

- Spacers can be placed under the work to provide vertical support against cutting tool forces. Clamps holding the work to the plate must be placed close to where the cutting tool forces will be.

Because milling cutters can push poorly clamped work out of place—damaging for both the work and the machinist—use clamping studs and strap clamps placed in the slots of the angle plate to rigidly hold the work against the angle plate. Kant Twist or large C-clamps may also be used to secure work against the angle plate. In the case of clamps, more is better.

Indexing Work with a Mill Stop

Mill stops are as useful as they are simple. They clamp into the milling machine's T-slots with T-bolts. Together, the fixed jaw of the milling vise and the mill stop provide complete, accurate, and repeatable positioning for work.

Using a mill stop allows work to be removed for inspection and measurement, then accurately replaced for more machining. When multiple workpieces are machined, they can all be placed in the identical position in the milling vise and the DRO settings will remain accurate. When work needs symmetrical cuts, like matching beveled edges, the work can be rotated one-half turn and the other side cut without resetting the milling table for cut depth. A real time-saver. See Figure 8-52. For smaller work, there are milling stops which clamp directly onto the jaws of the milling vise.

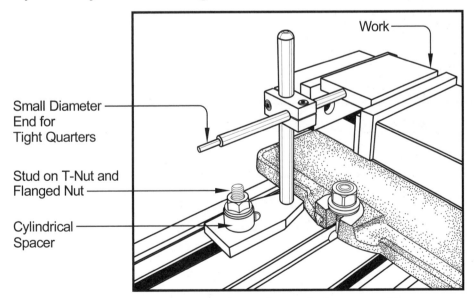

Figure 8-52. The mill stop locates the part in exactly the same position.

Making a mill stop is a good first milling machine project because it requires drilling, slotting, facing, edge trimming and rounding, reaming, and threading. For instructions, see Section XI in this chapter – Milling Machine Projects.

Section V – End Mills

Introduction

While more than a half-dozen different cutting tools can be used in milling machines, end mills are by far the most common. A look inside an industrial tool distributor's catalog reveals the dizzying array of end mills available. This wide selection provides the optimum cutter to match each job. However, for non-production milling in CRS or aluminum, most uncoated HSS end mills will prove satisfactory. For faster cuts and long production runs, more expensive end mills are necessary, especially when working with harder materials such as alloy and tool steels.

End Mill Designs

* *Two-flute end mills* – End mills remove more workpiece material with each revolution from soft materials like aluminum and plastic than from harder materials like steel. Because of this, additional room for metal cuttings *between* the flutes, called *chip clearance* or *chip-carrying capacity*, is required if the cutter is to take the largest cuts possible. The larger chip clearance capacity of a two-flute end mill makes higher feed rates—and higher metal removal rates—possible in soft materials. Although a four-flute end mill works fine in soft materials, its feed rate will be lower due to its smaller chip clearance capacity. In most cases, with soft materials a two-flute end mill is the optimum choice. Two-flute end mills are also ideal when a plunge cut is needed. In addition, they hold slot diameter better than end mills that have more flutes. See Figure 8-53.

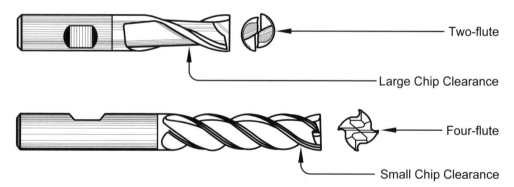

Figure 8-53. The number of end mill flutes determines their chip clearance capacity.

- *Four-flute end mills* – These milling cutters have more rigidity than two-flute end mills and more cutting edges. This means more cuts between sharpening. In general, on ferrous metals four-flute end mills leave a smoother surface finish than two-flute end mills. Use four-flute end mills on steel, stainless steel, and titanium. Because on hard materials only a small amount of workpiece material is removed on each flute pass, the chip clearance between the four flutes is adequate for the highest feeds possible without jamming the flutes with chips.

- *Three-* and *five-flute end mills* – These milling cutters have more rigidity than two-flute end mills and can take larger cuts with less flexing, but these end mills require special tools or fixtures to measure their diameters. This is a major drawback because when end mills are resharpened, their diameters change and the new diameters must be precisely measured in order to make accurate cuts. Sometimes three- and five-flute end mills eliminate the resonant vibrations that two- and four-flute end mills can produce. This vibration can result in a rough surface finish. The elimination of resonant vibrations allows 3- and 5-flute end mills to operate at higher spindle speeds and to produce a better surface finish.

- *End mill designs for Bridgeport-style mills* – The most common end mills are ⅛–¾ inches in diameter. Smaller end mills are available, but are not a good choice in this application because the highest spindle speeds of the Bridgeport are much slower than the optimum speeds for smaller end mills. End mills larger than ¾-inch diameter are expensive and require high torque, so when large areas of metal must be smoothed, a facecutter with carbide inserts or a flycutter is usually a better choice.

- *Extended-length end mills* – When a standard length end mill makes a cut beyond the depth of its flutes, the sides of the cutter rubbing against the work leave *heeling marks,* like shoe scuff marks, an undesirable condition. Extended-length cutters solve this problem because they have longer flutes, and therefore, do not leave heeling marks. However, simply using longer flutes does not mean that a deep cut can be made in a single pass.

- *Non-center-cutting end mills* – Not all end mills can be used for plunge cutting because they are not center-cutting, meaning that a flute does not *extend* across the *centerline axis* of the cutter to remove material from this area. Some end mills have a center hole in both of their ends, which makes them easy to sharpen because they can be placed between centers, but these same center holes are what prevents plunge cutting. But there is a workaround, to use these end mills for plunge cutting requires only a starting twist-drill hole just slightly larger than the area cut away from the mill's center. See Figure 8-54.

- *Plunge-cutting end mills* – These are end mills that can make plunge cuts. They have a flute that *extends* across the *centerline axis* of the cutter to remove material from this area. See Figure 8-54 (top three end mills).

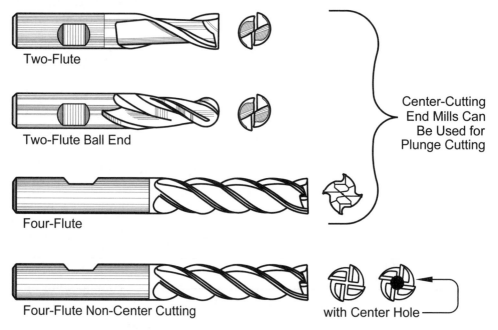

Figure 8-54. Plunge-cutting end mills have at least one flute that extends to the centerline axis of the cutter to cut material at the center of the hole bottom.

- *Ball-end cutters* – These end mills, shown in Figures 8-54 (second from top), cost more to purchase and to sharpen than conventional end mills. Still, they are excellent for aluminum and have many uses:

  - Making plunge cuts.

  - Applying a chamfered or fluted edge.

  - Applying a rounded inside corner to reduce stress concentrations.

  - Drilling round-bottom holes.

  - Forming a slot with a round bottom.

  - Making a three-dimensional contour, usually under CNC control.

  - Machining die cavities.

The chip clearing capacity of ball-end milling cutters is not as good as that of square-end milling cutters. This can adversely affect surface finish. Here are two ways to improve the surface finish when using ball-end cutters:

- When ball-end mill cutters are used to cut a round-bottom inside corner, leave 0.030 inches to finish the corner. Plan on three 0.010-inch cuts and use the first two to adjust the feed and speed so you will get a smooth surface finish with the third and final pass.

- Use compressed air on the cutter to remove chips and always use climb milling for aluminum.

• *Roughing end mills,* also called *hogging* or *corn cob cutters* – These cutters remove up to three times as much metal as conventional end mills and the small chips they make are easy to remove with cutting fluid or compressed air. Roughing end mills are most commonly used in production shops, especially those with powerful CNC milling machines which produce so many chips when using regular end mills that removing them is a problem. Typically, roughing end mills remove most of the metal and a conventional end mill finishes the job, leaving a smooth finish. Roughing end mills are excellent in Bridgeport-type mills because they require much less spindle power than regular end mills to remove the same volume of metal. See Figure 8-55.

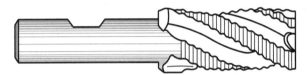

Figure 8-55. Roughing end mills remove more metal
and produce more easily removed small chips.

End Mill Materials

There are four major choices in end mill materials:

• *High-speed steel cutters (HSS or M7 tool steel)* is the least expensive, most common end mill metal. HSS end mills are suitable for most jobs in non-production shops, and these cutters are easily sharpened.

• *HSS cobalt steel cutters (M42 with 8% cobalt)* cost more than HSS end mills, but when cutting hard materials, they last much longer than HSS cutters. Cobalt steel cutters are excellent for cast iron where sand particles from the casting process are embedded in the casting's surface and rapidly dull HSS end mills. Cobalt cutters work well on hard metals like tool steels.

• *Solid carbide cutters* have a couple of advantages over HSS and HSS cobalt cutters. First, they offer exceptional wear resistance, and second, they are stiffer so they deflect less under load. This reduces or eliminates side-wall taper. And, because carbide softens at a much higher temperature than HSS, speeds and feeds 2–3 times higher than HSS end mills are common. However, carbide is shock-sensitive and is easily shattered or chipped if the set-up and machine are not rigid. Unless you are cutting tool steels and very hard materials, solid carbide end mills are not usually the best choice in a non-production shop. Solid carbide cutters are easily damaged in handling and storage, so keep them in plastic tubing, protective vinyl mesh netting, or in hot-dip wax to prevent fractured edges. Also, they can shatter or chip if dropped.

- *Carbide insert cutters* have a couple of important advantages over HSS and HSS cobalt end mills:

  - First, they do not need expensive resharpening, only the replacement of their carbide inserts which cost only a few dollars each.

  - Second, when the inserts become worn, they can be replaced without removing the tool from the spindle. And, because the carbide inserts have uniform dimensions, all DRO readings for the part's dimensions remain unchanged *after* the insert change.

Figure 8-56 shows three carbide insert cutters. None of these are suitable for plunge cutting. The square insert on the left has four cutting edges, the round insert in the center may be rotated three times, and the triangular cutter on the right has three cutting edges. These multiple edges extend the useful life of the inserts and reduce machining costs. Carbide insert cutters are particularly well suited to hard or abrasive materials like tool steel, cast iron and glass-filled plastics. The cutters in Figure 8-56 can be divided into two types. The left and center cutters are *form cutters* used for outside chamfered edges and inside bottom radii, respectively. The insert cutter on the right is a *slot cutter*.

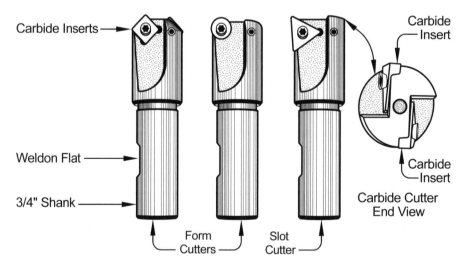

Figure 8-56. End mills with carbide insert cutters. Each of these cutters holds two inserts.

Shop-Made Carbide Cutters

Inexpensive, durable and resharpenable end mills and flycutters can be easily made by TIG welding a brazed carbide lathe tool bit to a dowel pin or a CRS shank using nickel stainless steel welding rod. This welding rod should meet or exceed 120,000 psi tensile strength. By choosing the outside diameter of the shank to be twice the nominal size of the lathe tool, the carbide cutter is at the exact center height with the CRS shank for welding. After welding, the brazed carbide lathe tool is trimmed to length in a bandsaw or with an abrasive disc, and finally, the remaining lathe tool shank is ground for proper clearance as it swings around its arc. Despite their being single-lip cutters, these shop-made cutters—a type of end mill—produce a fine surface finish on steel and aluminum. These 45° form tools will easily cut a chamfer on R_c 60 steel. Other cutter angles can be made by altering the cone angle on the CRS round. The shoulder on the cutter shank prevents the shank from slipping up into the collet or tool holder under cutting forces and it also insures repeatability. See Figure 8-57.

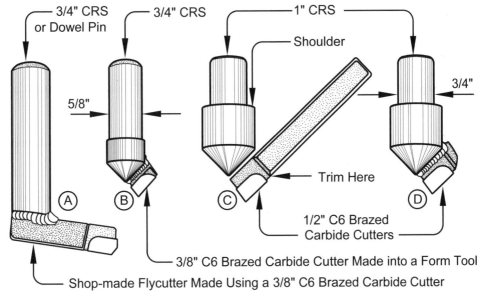

Figure 8-57. Shop-made cutters made by TIG welding brazed carbide lathe tool bits to CRS shanks. Flycutter (A), form tools (B & D) and cutter and shank set up for welding (C).

End Mill Operations

Here are some of the most common end mill operations:

- *Facing* applies a flat, smooth surface by using only the *end* of the cutter. See Figure 8-58 (A) This is a good way to bring a relatively narrow edge to dimension. Facing leaves an excellent surface finish when used for only a few back and forth cutting passes, but end milling is usually too slow for smoothing large areas. For large areas, flycutters and insert end mills are a better choice. A properly sharpened flycutter with a very slow feed will produce a fine finish. Because the 4–6 carbide inserts in a facing mill can never be set to *exactly* the same length, the finish they produce will not be as smooth as that of a flycutter.

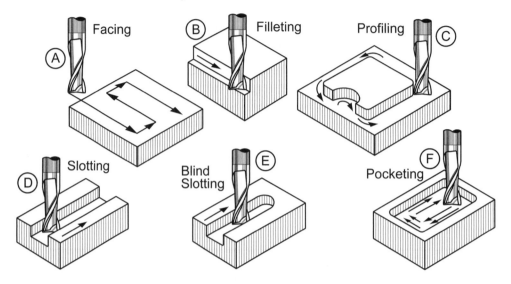

Figure 8-58. Common end mill operations.

- *Filleting* cuts a step into the work using the side flutes of the cutter. See Figure 8-58 (B).

- *Profiling* uses the end of the cutter to make a projecting island. It cuts a fillet on all corners of the work. See Figure 8-58 (C).

- *Slotting* and *blind slotting* applies a slot in either a single horizontal cut or in a series of side-by-side horizontal cuts. This is best done by first making a series of plunge cuts which are then connected with one or more horizontal passes. This technique is easier on the cutter and mainly dulls only the end of the mill, which is more easily resharpened than the side flutes.

  Slots cut in tubing are started by fist drilling a starter hole, then using the side of the cutter to make the slot. When cutting slots in thin materials, place a piece of wood, plywood or Masonite on the milling table below the work, then clamp the work to the milling table. This prevents damage to the table. See figure 8-58 (D & E).

- *Pocketing* removes material from a sunken, enclosed area. Usually the end of the cutter plunges into the work to begin the pocket and the side flutes cut away the remaining material. Removing chips with a vacuum cleaner or compressed air provides a smoother finish because the chips are not redrawn under the cutter and scratch the work. See Figure 8-58 (F).

- *Windowing* is similar to pocketing except that the pocket has no bottom, making the work resemble a window frame. See Figure 8-61 for more on windowing.

Causes of Swirl Marks & Poor Finishes

There are three causes of these problems when using a milling cutter:

- A dull cutter.
- Cut too heavy for the feed.
- Speed too low for the feed.

Guidelines for Maximum End Mill Cuts

Taking too heavy a cut has four possible adverse effects:

- The end mill may snap.
- The vertical sidewall may be *drafted,* which means that the sidewall is tapered and not parallel to the spindle axis. Too heavy a cut results in this tapered sidewall because the milling cutter bends under cutting forces.
- The surface finish may be rougher than when lighter cuts are taken.
- Tool life may be greatly shortened.

Figure 8-59 shows some good practice guidelines for end mill cuts.

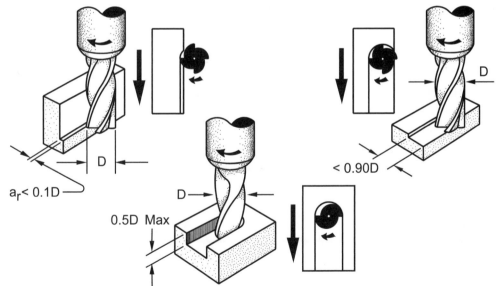

Figure 8-59. Good practice guidelines for cut depth limits on milling cutters when cutting steel. Double the depth of these cuts for aluminum.

Trimming the End of a Plate

A common use of an end mill is to trim the edge of a plate. The fastest method is to use an end mill slightly wider than the plate, but if a smaller end mill must be used, make the cuts as in Figure 8-60 for steel and in the reverse direction for aluminum. For steel, the side of the cutter performs conventional milling—a counterclockwise path—and for aluminum, to get a better finish, the side of the cutter performs climb milling—a clockwise path.

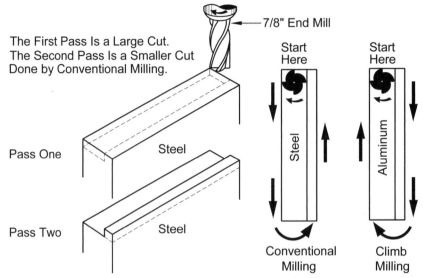

Figure 8-60. Trimming a plate with an end mill.

Cutting a Window in a Steel Plate

Here are the four steps for cutting a window as shown in Figure 8-61:

1. Scribe the final (finished) cut line of the window, and then scribe an inner window $\frac{1}{16}$ of an inch inside the final cut line. This second line is for the rough cut. The radius of the end mill used for the final cut will be the corner radius of the window.

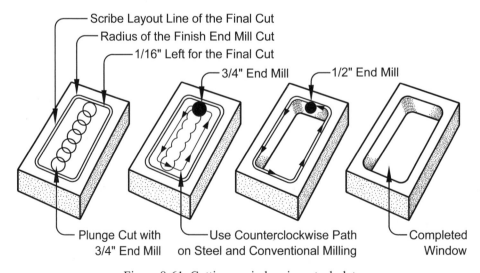

Figure 8-61. Cutting a window in a steel plate.

2. Use the largest available end mill—¾ inch is used in the example—to plunge cut along the centerline. This quickly removes the most metal.

3. With the same large cutter, remove the rest of the metal up to the inner scribe line. For steel, use a counterclockwise pattern and conventional milling. (Again, for a better finish when cutting aluminum, use a clockwise pattern and climb milling.)

4. To make corners with a ¼-inch radius, make the final cutting circuit with a ½-in end mill.

End Mill Slotting

Cutting a slot in a single end-mill pass cuts one side of the slot with conventional milling and the other side with climb milling. This leaves one sidewall rougher than the other and also results in a slot width which is slightly wider than the end mill. Cutting oversized slots is not normally a good thing. Making two passes with a cutter slightly smaller than the desired slot cuts both sides of the slot smoothly since each side is cut with climb milling and results in a slot of the correct width. See Figure 8-62.

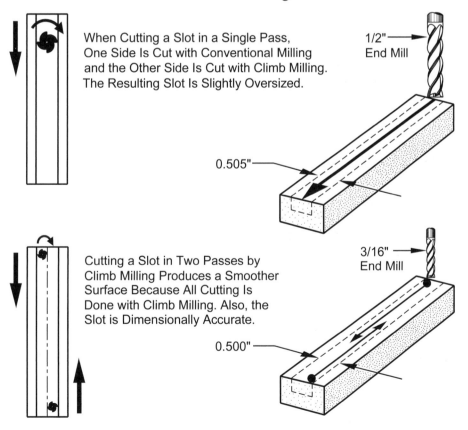

Figure 8-62. Cutting a slot in one or two passes. A two-pass cut results in smoother sidewalls in aluminum and better control of the slot width in any material.

Milling Cutter Rules of Thumb

- Use the shortest possible end mills to avoid bending them and cutting tapered, or drafted, instead of straight walls.

- Make aggressive cuts undersized and then take several light cuts to bring the work to size. *Clearcutting*—taking a second or third pass with the same cut depth—allows the end mill to remove metal missed on the earlier pass or passes due to the end mill bending away from the work under load. Any time the length of the side of the end mill is three or more times larger than the end mill diameter, clearcutting will be needed.

- Cutters with more flutes leave a smoother surface finish than those with fewer flutes.

- Use roughing end mills and older end mills for the initial cuts, then use newer end mills for the finishing cuts.

- When workpiece metal welds itself to the cutter, there are three causes: the spindle RPM is too high, the feed is too high, or the cut is too big.

- Aluminum can weld itself to HSS cutters and sometimes be very hard to remove mechanically. Immersion of the welded cutter into a sodium hydroxide (lye) solution will remove the aluminum without damaging the cutter. Drano, which is mostly sodium hydroxide, will work too. Soak the cutter in a glass or plastic container, *not aluminum*, and do not breath the fumes. In a short time, the aluminum welded to the cutter will dissolve in a rapid boiling reaction. Rinse and dry the cutter before storage.

- Use conventional milling for all metals except aluminum.

A Shop-Made Tool Holder for Small End Mills

Although R8 collets for holding ⅛-inch diameter drills, reamers and end mills are readily available, a shop-made tool holder not only provides a longer reach than a collet, it also provides excellent concentricity and better work visibility. This simple shop-made tool holder is excellent for smaller drills and end mills for which R8 collets are not available. See Figure 8-63.

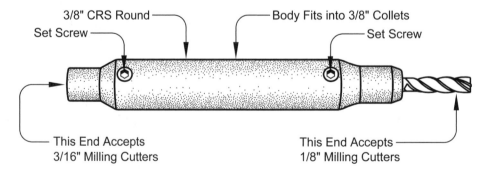

Figure 8-63. A shop-made tool holder extends the reach of small milling cutters.

To make this tool holder, start with a ⅜-inch diameter CRS round. This round stock will be very close to its nominal diameter and will not require any OD turning. While holding the round in a collet in the lathe, center drill, drill and ream to size. Next, drill and tap holes for set screws as shown in Figure 8-63. Finally, cut tapers on both ends to provide better access to the work and visibility for the machinist.

Corner-Rounding End Mills

Because the corner-rounding end mill in Figure 8-64 (left) removes the most metal with the inside corner of its flutes, this section of the end mill wears rapidly, causing the need to frequently resharpen the cutter, which shortens the cutter's life. However, there is a simple solution to extending the life of the cutter. Use the 45° shop-made single-flute cutter shown in Figure 8-64 (right) to start the corner-rounding cut. This cutter removes the outside corner metal that would cause the most wear on the corner-rounding mill. For instructions on making this cutter, see Figure 9-77.

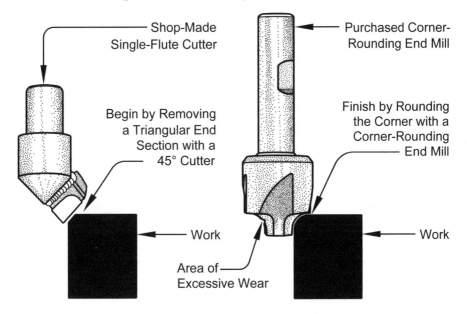

Figure 8-64. A corner-rounding end mill wears rapidly and unevenly where it removes the most metal. Cutting a chamfer with a single-flute cutter first, reduces wear on the end mill.

Handling End Mill Limitations

An end mill cannot produce a corner pocket like that shown in Figure 8-65 (left). This type of machining can only be done with EDM and is relatively expensive versus milling. Here is a work-around: first, drill a clearance relief hole in the corner that extends slightly below the floor of the pocket, then mill the faces of the pocket. The result is shown in Figure 8-65 (bottom row). The square-cornered part now fits into the pocket.

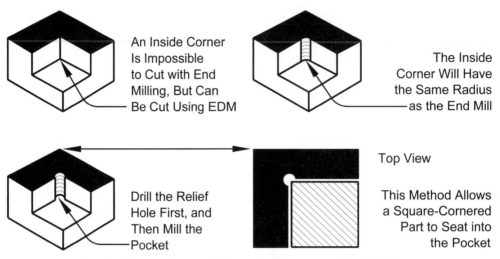

Figure 8-65. A work-around for end mill corner cutting limitations.

Squaring Up Stock

Here are the steps for *squaring up stock* in the mill:

1. Using a file, disc or belt sander first, remove any chips, burrs or dirt from the work that might prevent the stock from seating. Since the work in our example is roughly rectangular, we placed it in the vise horizontally, adding spacer(s) as needed to clamp the work rigidly as in Figure 8-66 (A). Now, take one or more light cuts with a flycutter, face mill, or end mill. When using a flycutter, set the tool to approach the work so cutting forces are against the *fixed* vise jaw. Should the work be too small to project above the jaws of the milling vise, use a pair of parallels to raise the work. With this step completed, Side 1 of the work is now flat.

2. Remove the work and deburr it. Rotate it 90° counterclockwise so only the just-flattened face is against the fixed vise jaw, then reclamp the work and make the cuts needed to smooth Side 2, Figure 8-66 (B).

3. Remove the work and deburr it using a triangular scraper or a 3M wheel. Rotate it 90° counterclockwise and smooth Side 3, Figure 8-66 (C).

4. Remove the work, deburr it, rotate it 90° counterclockwise and smooth Side 4, Figure 8-66 (D). The four sides of the workpiece are now square.

5. To square up the ends, deburr the part and secure it in the vise vertically, placing it against the fixed vise jaw, as in Figure 8-66 (E). Use a spacer between the moveable jaw of the milling vise and the work to clear the milling parallel on the base of the milling vise. If the part is too long to be stable, place it in the vise horizontally and machine its ends square, as in Figure 8-66 (F). An alternative is to clamp or bolt the work to a right angle plate. (Refer to Figure 8-51.) Deburr the work, and when finished, check the work for squareness.

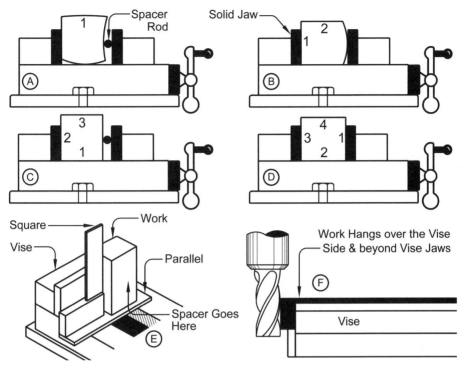

Figure 8-66. Squaring up stock.

Section VI – Drilling

Holding Twist Drills

As Table 8-3 shows, there are many ways to hold drills in a milling machine.

Drill Design	Holder	Comment
Twist Drill	R8 Collet	The R8 collet holds the drill with excellent concentricity and it allows the drill to spin if stalled, preventing damage to the drill and the mill. Holding a drill in a collet instead of a drill chuck saves more than 3 inches of vertical clearance to the table, which may be critical on tall work. The drawback is that a collet size to match the drill may not be available.
	Drill Chuck	Fits all drills within its diameter range.
	End Mill Tool Holder	The set screws prevent the drill from spinning in the tool holder avoiding a snapped drill—a potentially dangerous situation.
MT Shank Twist Drill	R8-to-MT Adapter	The shank end of the MT prevents the tool from spinning in the holder if stalled. Use only when the extra long flutes of an MT drill are needed. Otherwise, use a S&D drill in a chuck or a collet.

Table 8-3. Methods for holding twist drills in a milling machine.

Many machinists turn down the shanks of several different sizes of twist drills to fit into one collet size. For example, if you had a project with both tap holes and clearance holes for $^3/_8$-inch bolts, you might use a $^5/_{16}$-inch collet to hold a $^5/_{16}$-inch tap drill and a $^3/_8$-inch clearance drill which has had its shank reduced to a $^5/_{16}$-inch diameter.

Silver & Deming vs. Morse Taper Shank Drills

There are a couple of factors that determine which drill design is the better choice to use in the milling machine:

- For deep holes, Morse taper drills have longer flutes and are the better choice. But, because the MT cannot slip and must turn with the spindle, if the drill hangs up, something will break—usually the drill itself or the spindle key. See Figure 8-67 (bottom).

- For shallower holes, where shorter flutes can suffice, S&D drills are the better choice. If these drills hang up, they will spin whether in a drill chuck or a collet. In addition, because the OAL of the S&D drills is much shorter than an MT drill of the same diameter, much less repetitive up-and-down table travel is needed and much time and z-axis table cranking will be saved. S&D drills also use up less vertical clearance space between the spindle and the milling table. See Figure 8-67 (top).

Silver & Deming reduced-shank twist drills with $^1/_2$-inch diameter shanks, in drill diameters from $^1/_2$–$1^1/_2$ inches in $^1/_{64}$-inch diameter increments, are commonly found in most shops. Larger S&D twist drills have $^3/_4$-inch shanks and some of these are made with three flats cut on the sides of their shanks for added slip resistance, but see the caution below.

Morse taper drill sets in the same diameters as S&D drills are also common and most shops have both drill types. Also, most shops invest in an R8-to-MT3 adapter because the shop already owns a set of MT3 shank drills for use in a lathe tailstock, and for the cost of one R8-to-MT3 adapter, the entire set of MT drills can be used in the mill.

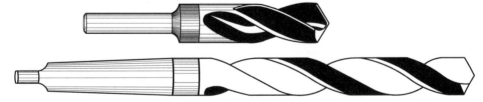

Figure 8-67. Silver & Deming reduced-shank drill (top) and
Morse taper twist drill (bottom). Both drills are the same diameter.

Caution: Adding flats on an S&D drill and mounting it in a milling machine tool holder eliminates the advantage of the collet or drill chuck because an S&D drill with flats held in a tool holder will not spin if the drill hangs up. Do not add flats unless you like seeing pieces of drill bit fly around the shop. Also, replacing a sheared-off key in the milling machine quill is a big job.

Extra-Long Combination Center Drills

Just as the shorter Silver & Deming drills reduce the need for z-axis table travel to get the drill in and out of the spindle, an extra-long combination center drill also reduces this movement by putting the working point of the center drill at about the same height as the twist drills that will be used next. Figure 8-68 compares the lengths of a standard and an extra-long ⅜-inch diameter № 4½ combination drill.

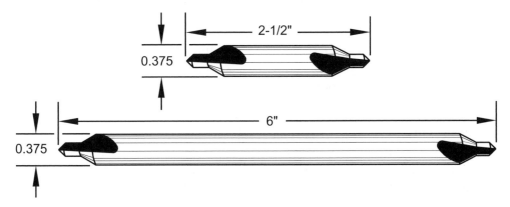

Figure 8-68. Two № 4½ combination drills: standard length (top) and extra long (bottom).

If you don't have center drills long enough for your job, using the shop-made center-drill extension in Figure 8-69 is a good solution. Made from CRS round stock, this shop-made extension will also reduce the need for up-and-down table movement when changing from a jobber-length drill to a regular—and relatively short—center drill and back. This is because the center drill extension can be made so that the overall length of the extension with the center drill is the same total length as the jobber drill in use.

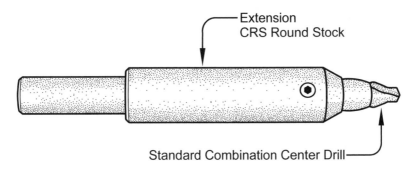

Figure 8-69. Shop-made center-drill extension holds a combination center drill at about the same distance from the milling head as an extra-long center drill.

Section VII – Boring

Advantages of Boring

Making holes with boring heads has many advantages over using twist drills, hole saws or spade drills:

- More accurate hole positioning, often within a few thousandths of an inch.

- Better roundness, or axial symmetry.

- Better sidewall smoothness.

- More accurate final diameter, often within one-thousandth of an inch. Even higher tolerances are possible with special boring heads.

- Larger maximum diameter holes are possible. On the same size milling machine, much larger holes may be bored than drilled. In steel, for example, many Bridgeport-style mills can drill one-inch diameter holes with a twist drill, but they can bore 14-inch diameter holes.

- Boring can correct the location and drift of an existing hole.

These advantages are possible because boring is done with a *single-point tool* that is always the same distance from the bore axis. Boring is the milling machine operation most closely related to turning a cylinder in a lathe, an operation that also uses a single-point tool and results in excellent symmetry and diameter control. While a twist drill tends to drift to the side of its sharper flute because the sharper flute cuts more freely, a boring head does not suffer from this drift problem. See Figure 8-70 (left).

An existing off-center hole can be corrected by reboring it, but this off-center problem *cannot* be corrected by redrilling because the twist drill used for this will follow the path of the existing off-center hole. Correction with a boring head is possible only because a single-point tool can remove more stock from one side of a hole than from the other. See Figure 8-70 (right).

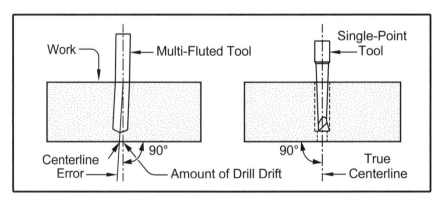

Figure 8-70. A twist drill drifting to the side of the sharpest flute (left),
and a boring head correcting the location and drift of an existing hole (right).

In Figure 8-71 the centerline distance between the holes is not correct. But, by simply dialing in the correct centerline distance, the hole can be rebored to its true position. However, this operation can only be successful if there is sufficient stock remaining in the hole for a 100% clean-up.

Sometimes a two-step correction process is needed. To do this, first rebore the hole oversized with the correct center location, then insert a bushing to bring the hole to the proper diameter. The bushing may be a press fit or secured with Locktite. An alternative method is to use a bushing with an undersized ID. Insert the bushing as above and then rebore the hole in place.

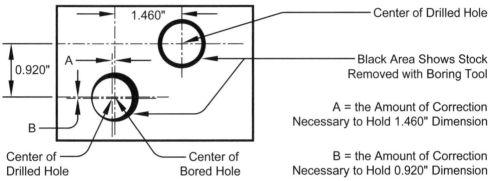

Figure 8-71. Correcting the center position of a hole by boring.

Disadvantages of Boring

Boring is an inherently slow, labor-intensive process in which relatively small cuts are made at low feed rates, typically 0.003 in/rev, then the mill must be stopped and the boring head tool extended before another cut is taken. Normally, the cut depths in steel are 50–250 thousandths of an inch.

While a twist drill requires only selection and insertion into the milling machine, a boring head requires much more of the machinist's attention before use. First, the shape and sharpness of the boring bar must be checked and corrected, if needed, because the smoothness of bored holes is sensitive to tool shape and sharpness. Second, the tool offset, or position relative to the rotational axis, must be monitored and continuously increased to reach the final diameter. Many cycles of bore, stop the spindle, measure the bore, increase the boring head diameter, and repeat are needed.

Limitations of Boring Bars

The common limitation of boring bars is the depth-to-width ratio of the hole:

• 3:1 ratios are easy and trouble free, but 5:1 ratios can be made with care.

• 8:1 ratios are common with special chatter-free boring bars like Criterion's Cridex Damping Bar, which has a spring-loaded weight inside the tool end to absorb and eliminate chatter, making holes of up to 12:1 ratios possible.

Boring Heads

A boring head consists of three major components:

- The *body* has a female dovetail cut into it which holds the male dovetail of the bar holder. There are three set screws on the side of the body. The center set screw clamps the bar holder into the dovetails and prevents the bar from moving under cutting load. The two outside set screws snug up the dovetails to remove backlash. These two outside set screws can also be securely tightened, although it is not usually necessary. See Figure 8-72.

    Boring head sizes are specified by the diameter of the body. Bridgeport-style mills usually use 2-inch, 3-inch, or 4-inch boring heads. Some boring heads have an integral R8 shank, while many others, like those from Criterion, have separate *arbors*, also called *shanks,* which screw onto the body using right-hand threads. For more on this, see Left-Hand vs. Right-Hand Boring Bars, Figure 8-80.

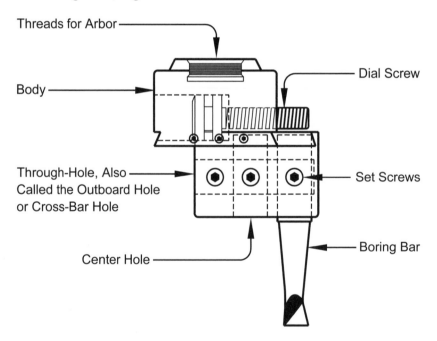

Figure 8-72. Boring head schematic.

- The *bar holder* has three hole positions for holding the boring bar, which does the metal cutting. Each boring bar position has a set screw to lock the bar in place. The center hole has the least offset from the tool axis and bores the smallest holes. The hole position on the outside bottom of the bar holder bores medium-size holes. On the outside of the bar holder, the *through-hole*, also called the *outboard hole* or *cross-bar hole*, holds the boring bar horizontally where it can cut the largest diameter holes.

- The *dial screw* adjusts the offset between the bar holder and the boring head body by indicating the increments of the leadscrew rotation. This offset determines the diameter of the bore cut. The dial screw is calibrated in thousandths of an inch increments of hole diameter. Moving the dial by 0.001 inches increases the hole diameter by that distance.

See Figures 8-73 and 8-74.

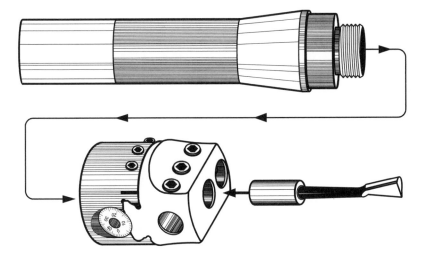

Figure 8-73. Criterion boring head, its arbor, or shank, and a boring bar.

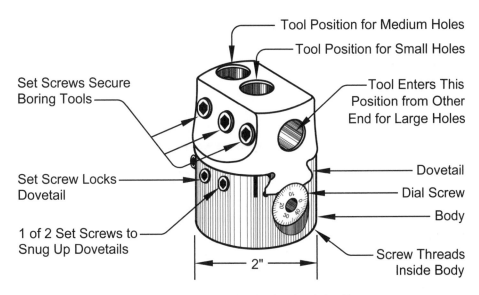

Figure 8-74. Criterion boring head detail.

Sherline boring heads are similar to the Criterion boring head, only smaller. Also, they do not have a cross-bar hole. See Figure 8-75.

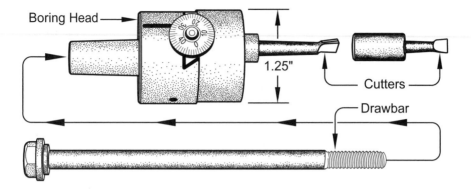

Figure 8-75. Sherline miniature boring head, drawbar and cutters.

Figure 8-76 shows typical boring head set-ups which use both left-hand and right-hand boring bars.

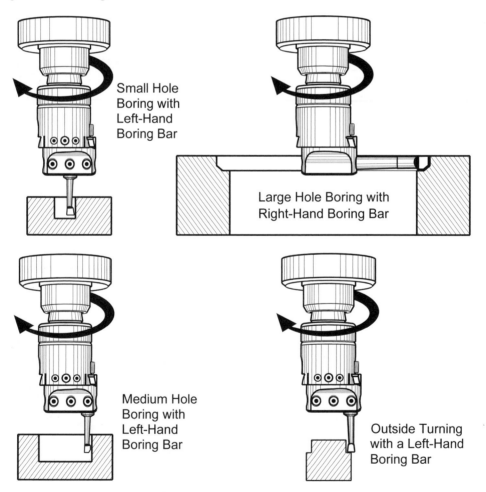

Figure 8-76. Boring heads and several different set-ups.

Factors for Successful Boring

Boring precision holes is performed under much different conditions than encountered under conventional lathe turning because of the much greater springiness and flexibility of the boring head, its shank and the boring bar.

There are five major factors to consider when boring:

- *Tool overhang* is that unsupported section of a boring bar or tool that extends out of the boring head. To determine the overhang, we take the ratio of the diameter of the bar to the unsupported length of the bar. A workable ratio is about 1:4.5 and the majority of commercial boring bars have this ratio. Doubling the unsupported length of the bar increases its deflection under the same load by a factor of eight, so boring bar overhang ratios are very important. To reduce overhang:

  - Use as large a shank or adapter as possible and insert it into the milling machine spindle with the boring head as close to the spindle bearings as possible.

  - Use the largest diameter boring bar that will do the job and still permit adequate chip disposal. Also, use the largest diameter boring head that will fit the job since this will reduce boring bar length and overhang. For example, you could use a boring head with a 2-inch diameter body to bore a 6-inch diameter hole, but a boring head with a 3-inch diameter body would be a better choice because the boring bar required would be shorter, and thus stiffer.

  - Given a choice between a steel boring bar and a solid carbide boring bar, choose the carbide one because it is more rigid.

  - If you are making your own boring bar, either use the same diameter cross section for its full length or taper down towards the cutting tool end. Putting the larger cross section at the boring head end produces greater stiffness. In other words, do not put the fat end of the bar at the cutting tool end.

- *Tool geometry* is critical to tool performance, and it is much more critical in boring than in turning. Match the cutting tool angles, particularly the clearance and rake angles, to the workpiece material. For HSS tool angles, consult *Machine Shop Essentials,* by Frank Marlow, Table A-1 in the Appendix or *Machinery's Handbook.* For carbide tool angles, check with their manufacturers.

  Caution: Do not enter the cut in the hand-fed mode and allow the tool to bounce at the bore entrance. Carbide boring tools are hard, but very brittle, and chip easily. Also, do not drag them back out of the bore on the completion of a cut. This will leave a helical scratch mark inside the bore.

Another important aspect of tool geometry is the tool's lead angle. Here are a few lead angle rules of thumb:

- Use *positive* and *zero lead angles* when boring to a shoulder or into a blind hole.

- Use *negative lead angles* only in a *through* bore or when boring into a relief at the bottom of a bore, never on blind holes. Although negative lead angles require more tool pressure, they produce a finer finish.

- Applying a *nick-off* to the zero lead cutter, as discussed in *Chapter 7 – Lathes*, Figure 7-29, reduces stress on the tool when starting a cut and provides better support to the tool tip under load. See Figure 8-77.

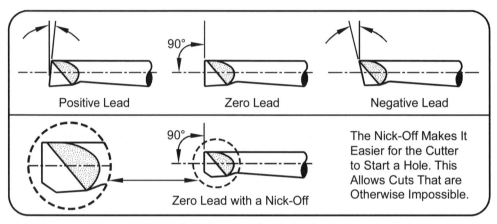

Figure 8-77. Lead angles on boring bars.

- *Speeds and feeds* must be matched to the work material. Consult *Machinery's Handbook* for a starting point and fine tune the speeds and feeds with a sample part. Record the results for later reference. Keeping a logbook of speed and feed combinations that produce good results will save a lot of time later. In boring, the *surface feet per minute (SFM)* is more critical in reducing tool chatter than the *feed per revolution*. Heavy feeds will distort parts with thin walls and prevent a symmetrical bore. Take note of the cut smoothness, the nature of the chips, and the sound of the machine and boring bar. With experience, these factors will tell you when the speed and feed are properly set.

Although the quill power feed is usually used for boring, many mills are equipped with a power feed on the z-axis. This provides an infinite range of quill feed rates, not just the three available on the Bridgeport milling machine. Installation of this z-axis power feed allows the machinist to adjust the boring head feed rate for the best possible surface finish. Now the machinist has control of both feed and speed while boring.

- *On-center cutting tool location* is important because:

    - *Above center cutting tool location,* when the clearance is excessive under the boring tool while the top rake is negative, is a very undesirable condition which can cause chatter. See Figure 8-78 (A).

    - *Exact center tool location* is the correct position for the most efficient performance, good clearance and free cutting. See Figure 8-78 (B).

    - *Below center tool location* causes all clearance on the cutting tool to be lost. This makes the tool drag on the work, producing poor results. See Figure 8-78 (C).

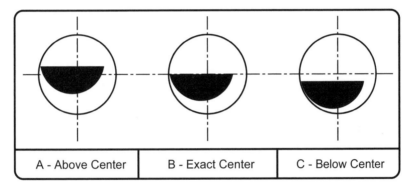

Figure 8-78. Tool location affects both the accuracy and wall quality of the hole.

Tool center height also affects the depth-of-cut accuracy. In addition to better tool performance when the cutting edge is on the centerline, dial accuracy improves. Because tool advancement is measured by graduated leadscrews that are usually in increments of 0.001, accuracy can only be obtained with the cutting edge on the exact centerline. See Figure 8-79.

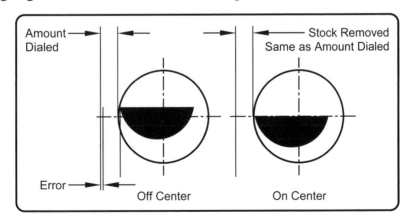

Figure 8-79. An off-center tool height affects cutting accuracy, introducing error into the dial screw offset adjustments.

- *Chip control* and *cutting fluid* affect the finish. Blind bores require chips to be removed with compressed air, vacuum cleaning, or by stopping the boring process and manually removing the chips. Leaving too many chips in the bore prevents a smooth wall finish because the chips are pulled under the cutter and mar the work. When possible, flood the bore with cutting fluid to keep the tool and the work cool, and to help remove chips.

Left-Hand vs. Right-Hand Boring Bars

The most common boring bar sets are *left-handed*. See Figure 8-80 (left). In a tool holder, these cutters can perform boring in a lathe or a milling machine. When the boring bar projects from one of the bottom holes of the boring head, the mill spindle turns forward, clockwise as viewed from above.

Left-Hand Boring Bar (Same as Standard Lathe Boring Tool)

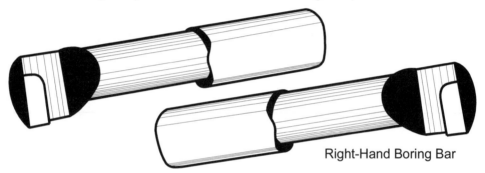

Right-Hand Boring Bar

Figure 8-80. Left- and right-hand boring bars with brazed carbide cutters.

When boring large holes with the boring bar in the through-hole, also called the outboard-hole or cross-bar hole, the milling machine spindle must run in reverse, counterclockwise, for the boring bar tool to cut. This arrangement poses two possible complications:

- The most popular boring head design today is the Criterion-type with right-hand threads between its separate shank and body. Running the spindle in reverse tends to unscrew these two parts—potentially a serious safety problem.

- Having to run the mill spindle in two directions depending on the tool location makes it easy to make costly mistakes that can damage both the tool and the work.

The best solution to this problem is to use only right-handed boring bars in the through-holes in Criterion-type heads, and run the spindle forward at all times. But then another problem arises, right-handed boring bars are less common and not offered by all tool suppliers. If you do decide to use left-handed boring bars in side through-holes, try to make sure that the boring-bar shank and body do not unscrew. To do this, carefully clean the body-to-shank threads and apply permanent Locktite. When need be, the boring bar shank can be removed with a heat gun.

Tips for Successful Boring

- The cutting edge of the boring tool must be on the centerline.

- Tool sharpness for boring is more critical than for OD turning in the lathe.

- Keep tool overhang to a minimum.

- Use a power feed whenever available to give your bore a more uniform wall finish.

- When using carbide, avoid reversing or stopping the spindle in the middle of a cut. This can cause the tool to chip or break.

- Avoid *bottoming-out* in a blind hole. A boring tool is not designed for end cutting.

- When the boring head reaches the bottom of the bore on the finish cut, do not leave the spindle turning and withdraw the head. This will cause the tool to leave a helical gouge mark on the finished cut. Instead, stop the spindle, position the boring bar parallel to one of the machine table axes, and move the milling table so the boring bar moves away from the finished wall surface. The tool can then be withdrawn.

- Plan the final cut so there is 5–10 thousandths of an inch remaining. It is much easier to take a precise larger cut than to make a precise final cut of 0.001–0.002 inches. The reason for this is *springback*. That is, the flexibility of the tool, work, and set-up which requires a minimum tool pressure to remove metal. Too small a cut will only burnish the work, not cut it. Remember that the boring head and tool always have springback. This is seen when a second cutting pass is made with the same boring bar offset. The second pass has less springback, and so cuts additional material.

- Make allowances for *springback* when taking a heavy cut. Remember, additional material will be removed on the finish cut even though an additional adjustment has not been made.

- When setting the boring bar offset with the dial screw, remove backlash by backing down the dial screw and then coming up to the desired dimension. Turning the dial screw back and forth a short way to set a new diameter without first removing the backlash will cause inaccuracies.

- When boring thin tubing there will sometimes be tool chatter which causes the tubing to ring like a bell. One solution is to wrap the accessible portion of the tubing with bicycle tire inner tubing or with duct tape. This will often damp out the chatter.

Step-by-Step Procedure for Boring

Here are the steps to bore a 3-inch diameter hole in a one-inch thick plate of 1018 carbon steel:

1. Paint the workpiece surface with layout fluid and mark the position of the center of the hole to be bored. Next, mark the hole with a prick punch, followed by a center punch.

2. Although not essential, it is often helpful to scribe a circle marking the outside diameter of the bore to be made around the center-punch mark. This shows your progress toward the final diameter.

3. To avoid drilling into the milling table, secure the workpiece in a milling vise either on parallels or clamped on the milling table and supported on spacers. A common problem is not leaving enough clearance for the parallels or spacers, which results in the boring bar cutting into them.

4. After identifying the hole center location, position the milling machine spindle over it.

5. Step drill a starting hole. Begin with a center drill, then move on to a ¼-inch twist drill, followed by a ½-inch twist drill, and finally use a 2½-inch S&D ¾-inch shank twist drill. In general, you want to make the largest starting hole possible that will leave about ¼-inch of stock remaining for the boring bar to cut. This ¼-inch of remaining metal stock gives you the chance to set the proper speed and feed to produce a smooth finish on the final bore. After the right combination of speed and feed is known for the situation, you can leave less remaining stock the next time.

6. Install the boring bar into the boring head and tighten the spindle drawbar to pull up the boring head into the mill spindle. A 2-inch boring head would be a good choice for this job, with the boring bar placed in the bottom outside bar-holder location.

7. Adjust the spindle speed for about 300–350 RPM. This speed will provide about 100 SFM.

8. Set the power spindle feed for 0.003 in/rev.

9. Position the micrometer depth-stop nut on the milling machine to stop the power feed after the boring head reaches full cut depth; for this job, 1.1 inches from the top of the work.

10. Set the boring head offset for an initial cut of ⅛ inch per side using the scribed circle to set the boring bar radius.

11. Use the lever or crank feed to bring the boring bar down to the work, and then engage the automatic feed.

—

12. Withdraw the boring head, and repeat the same cut. This is called *clearcutting* and it will remove just the whisper of metal not cut on the initial pass due to springback.

13. Measure the bore, determine the remaining depth of cut, and increment the boring bar to make the final cut. Until you have experience with this particular workpiece and set-up, it is a good idea to make several small cuts to "sneak up" on the final diameter. Repeat Steps 11–13 until the final bore diameter is reached.

Automatic Boring Heads

Two common operations that a manually adjusted boring head cannot do by itself are cutting an O-ring groove and facing the annular surface area around a bore. For these jobs, an automatic boring head is needed. Here is how it's done:

- To cut O-ring grooves, the boring bar is set to clear the sidewalls of the bore, and the boring head is lowered into the bore to the point where the groove is to be applied. While the spindle is turning, the machinist grasps the knurled ring on the boring head. When the machinist holds this knurled ring and keeps it from turning with the boring head, the boring head's internal mechanism moves the bar outward 0.003 in/rev until the cutter reaches the final depth preset on the head. See Figure 8-81 (top).

- To face an area around a bore, the machinist grasps the knurled ring on the automatic boring head and the head's internal mechanism moves the boring bar outward 0.003 in/rev to complete the facing. See Figure 8-81 (bottom).

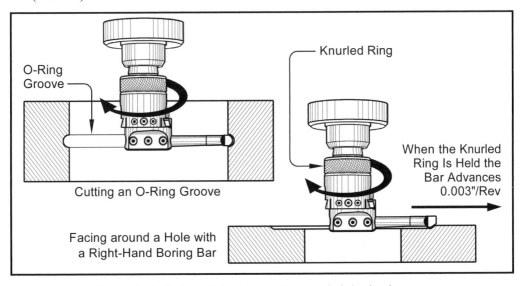

Figure 8-81. Automatic boring heads move their boring bars
a set distance outward with each spindle revolution.

Another O-Ring Groove Cutting Method

Here is a way to cut O-ring grooves without an automatic boring head using a manual boring head and a rotary table. See Figure 8-82. Because the boring bar is shorter than the bore radius, the boring head can be lowered into the bore and the milling table off set to cut the groove as the rotary table turns. The spindle turns clockwise and the rotary table turns counterclockwise. While O-ring grooves can also be cut in a lathe, sometimes the work is too large to fit in the available lathe and this approach is used.

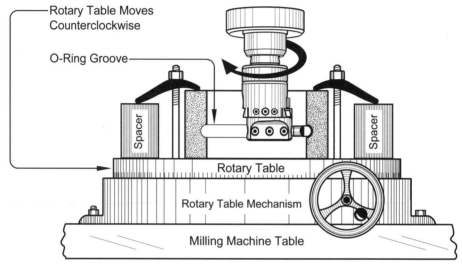

Figure 8-82. Cutting an O-ring groove with a manual boring head and a rotary table

Setting Boring Heads to Diameter

Here is a method to accurately set boring bar offset that uses a spindex and a height gage:

1. First, the centerline height of the spindex must be determined. Once it is known, it can be marked on the spindex and need not be measured again. Insert a dowel pin into the spindex 5C collet and measure the height of the top of the dowel with a height gage. See Figure 8-83 (top).

2. Place the boring head shank into the 5C collet in the spindex, snug up the collet, and adjust the boring bar height for the desired bore diameter. See Figure 8-83 (bottom).

Because the boring head and boring bar have springback, the *exact* boring bar offset cannot be known until the springback of this particular boring head and bar combination and of this particular workpiece material is determined. This is done by experiment. Once known, the boring head can later be set to this diameter to make the same size bore any number of times—a great time saver. Also, if the same diameter hole is to be bored many times, a boring head may be set to the desired bore and put aside for later use.

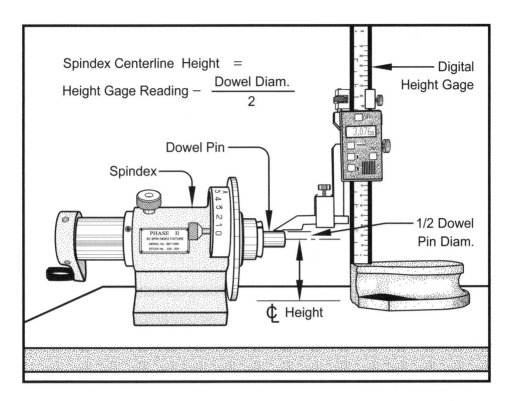

Spindex Centerline Height =

Height Gage Reading − $\dfrac{\text{Dowel Diam.}}{2}$

Dowel Pin

Spindex

Digital
Height Gage

1/2 Dowel
Pin Diam.

₵ Height

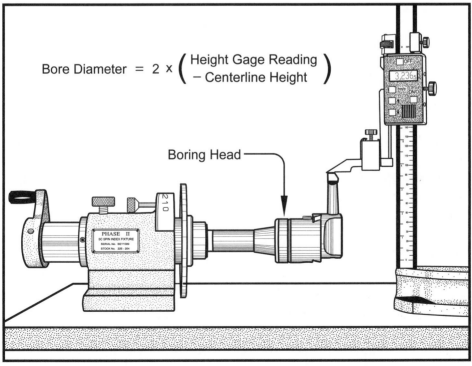

Bore Diameter = 2 × $\left(\begin{array}{c}\text{Height Gage Reading} \\ \text{− Centerline Height}\end{array}\right)$

Boring Head

Figure 8-83. Measuring the centerline height with a spindex (top) and
setting the boring head diameter with a height gage (bottom).

Section VIII – Face Mills & Flycutters

Face Mills

Face mills flatten and smooth large areas of a workpiece parallel with the cutter face. These cutters run from ¾–3-inches in diameter and have from 1–6 carbide inserts, depending on their diameter. With their multiple carbide inserts, the larger diameter cutters remove metal rapidly and can leave a very fine surface finish. Also, because they have large chip clearance pockets, they can take aggressive cuts and utilize the full power of 3–5-hp Bridgeport-style milling machines. See Figure 8-84.

Tip: When face milling using a power feed, leave the power feed engaged until the entire face mill clears the work. If the work is manually moved before the back half of the face mill has a chance to pass over the work at the same speed as the rest of the work, the finish of this last section will be different.

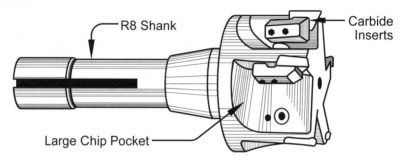

Figure 8-84. A 3-inch diameter face mill with five carbide inserts on an R8 shank.

Flycutters

Like face mills, flycutters also flatten and smooth large areas. Although most flycutters sweep a circle of 4–5 inches in a Bridgeport-style mill, larger flycutters can sweep circles up to 12 inches in diameter. Larger flycutters hold a single brazed carbide or HSS tool bit and in a single pass are capable of flattening a much larger area than a face mill, but much more slowly. Using a power feed with flycutters insures an even feed and a smooth surface finish.

Tip: Should you decide to purchase a budget import flycutter, remove the three set screws holding the cutter in place, go outside your shop, and throw them as far as you can, then replace them with US-made set screws that are properly heat treated. Doing this will prevent rounding the set screw sockets when you tighten them with a hex wrench and the subsequent problem of removing defective set screws. After this minor upgrade, the budget import flycutter will be an acceptable tool. See Figure 8-85 which shows the "nick-off" discussed in Chapter 7, Figure 7-29—this time on a flycutter.

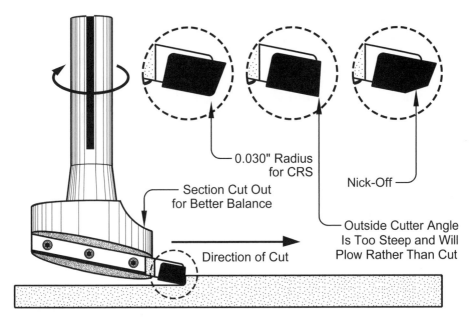

0.030" Radius
for CRS

Nick-Off

Section Cut Out
for Better Balance

Outside Cutter Angle
Is Too Steep and Will
Plow Rather Than Cut

Direction of Cut

Figure 8-85. This flycutter, on an R8 shank for a Bridgeport-style milling machine, has a 2½-inch diameter head and holds a ⅜-inch brazed carbide cutter. The cutting tool angle is critical to fast cutting and a smooth finish.

Figure 8-86 shows two Sherline flycutter designs; on the left with a brazed carbide cutter, and on the right with a carbide insert cutter that can cut up to a sidewall.

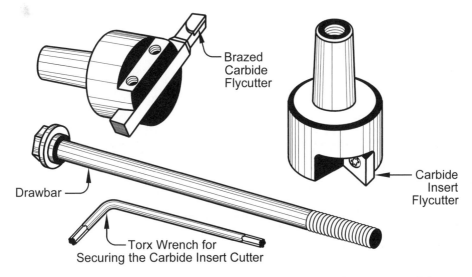

Brazed
Carbide
Flycutter

Carbide
Insert
Flycutter

Drawbar

Torx Wrench for
Securing the Carbide Insert Cutter

Figure 8-86. Two Sherline flycutters with their drawbar. The Torx wrench is for the screw securing the carbide insert on the right-hand flycutter.

Although the flycutter's speed and feed influence work surface smoothness, there are five other determining factors:

- *Milling head adjustment* – When the milling head is tilted slightly in the direction of cutter motion, the flycutter only cuts on its forestroke, leaving a series of cutting arcs concave to the direction of motion. See Figure 8-87 (bottom). However, when the spindle is *exactly* perpendicular to the work, the flycutter cuts on *both* the forestroke and the backstroke resulting in arcs facing both directions. See Figure 8-87 (top). Although not as visually attractive as single-arc cuts, double-arc cuts are slightly flatter and are an indication of perfect vertical head alignment.

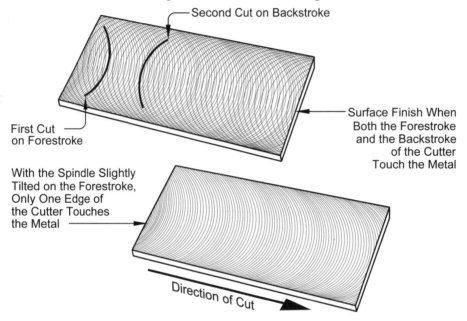

Figure 8-87. Milling head alignment affects flycutter surface finish.

- *Cutting tool outside angle* – Unless the cutting tool outside angle is ground *greater* than 90°, the cutting tool will *plough* the work. That is, the cutter tip will push the cutter down into the work with a wedging action and raise metal ahead of itself. This makes the surface finish unacceptable.

- *Cutting tool tip radius* – Whether using an HSS or a carbide bit, tool tip radius is an important factor in determining surface smoothness. A sharp point on the cutter leaves a more pronounced cutter path mark, while a tip with a greater radius leaves a more shallow mark and is often more desirable. Again, refer to Figure 8-85. On hard materials, though, cutters with radiused tips tend to *skate* rather than dig into the work and remove metal. There is a balance between removing the most metal and achieving the best surface finish—a balance that depends on this radius. A small diamond dresser can add a tip radius to both HSS and carbide cutters. Experiment to find the radius that works best for your job.

- *Table feed rate* – In addition to the usual spindle speed and depth of cut settings that determine how a tool cuts, the table feed rate determines the distance between cuts. Faster feeds leave cutter marks farther apart, resulting in a more rippled surface.

- *Flycutter radius vs. work width* – The flycutter radius should be set to extend about ⅛-inch beyond each edge of the work as in Figure 8-88. This allows the cutter to make a gradual angled entry onto the work. When the cutting circle is too large, the tool re-enters the work at nearly a right angle which shocks the tool, the work, and the spindle bearings. Also, when the circle is too large, the cutter pushes up the entering edge rather than cutting it.

  Try these settings as a starting point for a fine finish on CRS: 0.030-inch radiused tip on the cutter, 3-inch diameter cutter sweep, 1000 RPM, 0.010-inch cut depth and 2–5 in/min (IPM) feed rate. On aluminum, use a little kerosene for a better finish.

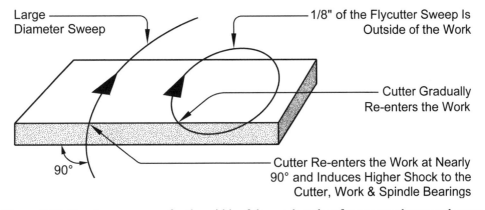

Figure 8-88. Too large a sweep for the width of the work makes for a more abrupt tool entry.

Section IX – Quill Feed Methods

Introduction

As stated earlier, for more than seventy years the Bridgeport-style milling machine has been the most popular, most-produced mill design in the world. Its versatile and clever quill feed mechanism is a key reason for this. Not only does the head mechanism offer three ways to downfeed the quill—with the quill feed lever, the manual feed handwheel, or the power feed—it also provides an automatic depth stop to kick out the power feed at the bottom and top of the quill stroke *and* it provides a very precise depth stop for its manual feed. These are a lot of great features for a relatively inexpensive machine tool. Together they allow the machinist to match the mill to the work, saving time, cost and effort.

Quill Feed Lever

The *quill feed lever* is on the right-hand side of the milling machine head. Pulling down this lever lowers the quill through a rack and pinion mechanism inside the head. *Remember to release the quill lock before attempting to move the quill.* See Figure 8-89 (center right).

Using the quill feed lever allows the machinist to *feel* how the tool is cutting and adjust the feed pressure accordingly. The disadvantage to using the quill feed lever is that pulling the lever down from the 12 to the 6 o'clock position—where there is the best feel—moves the quill down only 1½ inches. To move the quill its full 5 inches of travel, the lever must make more than one and a half complete revolutions. This is awkward and reduces sensitivity to the tool, particularly when going counterclockwise from the 6 to the 12 o'clock position. In general, the quill feed lever works best when short quill movement, maximum feel, and light force on the tool are needed, or when precise depth control is required as described below.

Manual Feed Handwheel

The *manual feed handwheel*, located on the left-hand side of the milling machine head casting, provides:

- Positive depth control, since the quill moves *only* when the handwheel is turned. This makes it easy to drill or bore to a precise depth and not overshoot it. This positive depth control prevents a twist drill or an end mill from pulling itself into the work, a real possibility when using the quill feed lever.

- A much greater mechanical advantage than the quill feed lever. While pulling the quill feed lever down one-half turn lowers the quill 1½ inches, the manual feed handwheel turns 13 revolutions to move the quill the same distance—a 7:1 mechanical advantage.

- The feel—through the handwheel—of how the tool is cutting. This makes the manual feed handwheel a good choice for drilling holes of up to ⅜-inch diameter in steel.

Because the quill feed lever moves when the quill does, for safety, remove the quill feed lever when operating the quill with the manual feed handwheel. The handwheel applies considerable force to the lever and you may be pinched or the lever may become entangled in the DRO support arm. Also, be aware that unless it is removed, the handwheel turns with the power feed and is a hazard to fingers.

The manual feed handwheel can be set in any one of its three positions:

- Pushed in connects the manual feed handwheel so it can move the quill.

- Pulled out about ⅜ of an inch from its innermost position lets the handwheel remain on the shaft, but spin freely.
- Pulled completely off the shaft for safety when the power feed is used.

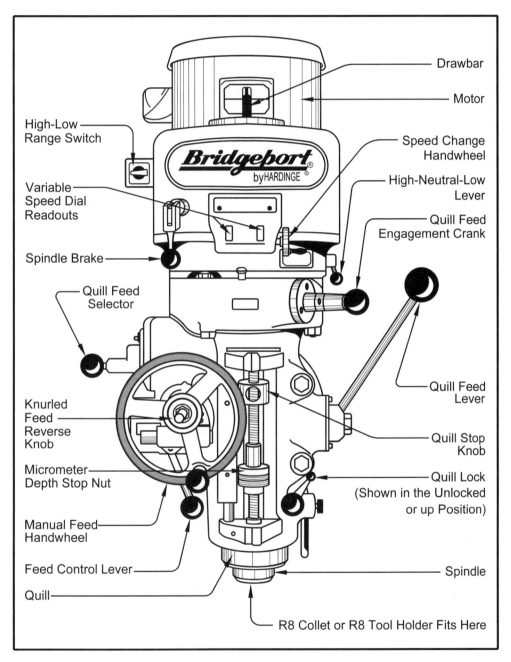

Figure 8-89. Bridgeport milling machine head.

The Quill Power Feed

The *quill power feed* provides a smooth, even vertical feed when drilling, reaming or boring and replaces a lot of the machinist's effort with machine power. This machine function is particularly useful when boring because the steady, even feed results in a smooth bore wall. Figure 8-90 shows details of the quill power feed mechanism.

Using the quill power feed requires setting the micrometer depth stop nut and the actuation of four controls. Here are the steps:

1. Set the *micrometer depth stop nut* to determine how far down the quill will move.

2. Swing the *quill feed engagement crank* to the 3 o'clock position by turning it counterclockwise from its normal—and disconnected—position at 9 o'clock. Do this with the spindle stopped. You may need to wiggle the spindle to allow the gears to mesh. Although you will do no damage to the feed mechanism by turning the quill feed engagement crank clockwise, the worm gear that takes power from the spindle to drive the power feed will not be engaged. When finished using the quill power feed, turn the quill feed engagement crank back to the 9 o'clock position to save wear on the gear train. Again, do this procedure with the spindle stopped.

3. Set the *quill feed selector* to the rate of quill advance required: either 1.5, 3.0, or 6.0 thousandths of an inch/spindle revolution. The small lever on the quill feed selector mounts on the left side of the milling head and is more easily moved with the spindle turning.

4. The knurled *feed reverse knob* projects through the center of the manual feed handwheel and determines the direction of quill movement. Push in the feed reverse knob, that is, away from yourself, to set the feed for downward quill movement.

5. Swing the *feed control lever* on the lower left-hand side of the head casting by pushing it to the right. This lever locks the quill power drive to its gear train and drives the quill downward. When engaged, it will remain in gear until one of four events occurs:

   - You manually disengage the gear train by flipping the feed control lever to the left.

   - The quill reaches full preset depth as determined by the micrometer depth stop nut. When the quill stop knob, which is fastened to the quill, contacts the micrometer depth stop nut, two things happen: the nut pushes down on the micrometer screw and the micrometer screw disengages the feed control lever. This is often called the *throwout* or *kickout function*.

- When the quill, moving upward, reaches its fully retracted position, the quill stop knob pushes against the safety pin and disengages the feed control lever. This function eliminates the need for the operator to shut off the power feed to avoid damaging the mill when the reverse quill feed is used to retract the quill.

- The safety overload trips from excessive tool pressure on the quill.

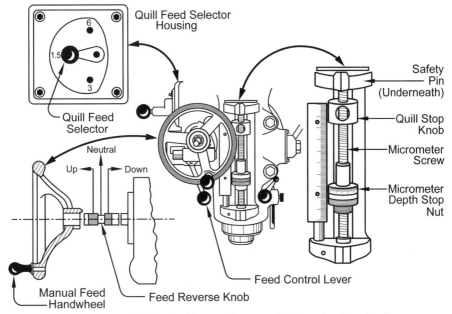

Figure 8-90. Milling machine quill power feed mechanism details.

Important Quill Power Feed Details

- The feed reverse knob can be moved in and out to any position with the spindle turning and the power feed control lever engaged. If you pushed in the knob, making the quill go down to the end of its stroke, and now you want the quill to come back up, pull out the feed reverse knob. Note that you will pass through a *neutral setting* when reversing quill direction.

- When the feed control lever is engaged and the feed reverse knob is set in the neutral position, the quill maintains its position and remains locked in place. Either move the feed reverse knob to change quill direction, or disengage the feed control lever to free the quill.

- The feed reverse knob positions for the quill movement directions—UP-NEUTRAL-DOWN—are correct for when the spindle is running forward, or clockwise. See Figure 8-90 (bottom left). However, if the spindle direction is reversed, these directions are reversed. Using a left-hand drill or an end mill calls for running the spindle in reverse.

- Whenever the feed control lever is engaged—that is, when either the handwheel or the power feed is in use—the *feed overload clutch* will throwout, or trip, the feed control lever to the disconnect position. This clutch is set to trip at 200-pounds of force on the spindle. This is preset at the factory and should not be tampered with. When using twist drills larger than ⅜ inch, lock the quill, then use the table feed to apply a larger axial drilling force—a force which would otherwise trip the feed overload clutch.

- When a quill stop is used with the power feed to halt the downward motion of the quill at the end of its stroke, the machinist should not leave the mill unattended. Sometimes small chips, particularly aluminum chips coated with cutting fluid, get into the trip mechanism causing it to fail with unpleasant and expensive results.

Depth Stop Accuracy

The 5-inch vertical scale to the left of the micrometer screw is useful for making *rough* depth stop settings. Each revolution of the micrometer depth stop nut changes the depth stop by 0.050 inches. There are additional calibration marks for each one thousandth of an inch around the nut itself. These calibrations are not absolute, they depend on the tool length and the work height.

Although the micrometer depth stop nut is set the same way for all three feed methods, its behavior and accuracy is very different when used with the quill feed control lever or with the power feed.

When used with the quill feed control lever, the micrometer depth stop nut is accurate and repeatable to within one-thousandth of an inch. However, when used with the power feed, the accuracy of the depth stop degrades and is repeatable only within several thousandths of an inch. This is because when the power feed is engaged, the micrometer screw is raised slightly to cock the throwout mechanism so it can be tripped by contact between the quill stop knob and the micrometer depth stop nut. Since this linkage will not trip out at exactly the same depth each time, do not use the power feed when precise depth control is needed. The purpose of the power feed is to make the cut *near* the final depth and then finish the rest of the cut under manual control.

Quill Stops

There are three types of quill stops:

- The permanent *micrometer depth stop nut* on the micrometer screw defines the bottom of the quill stroke.

- *Clip-on quill stops*, shown in Figure 8-91, are less accurate than the micrometer depth stop nut, but clip-on quill stops are helpful when there are several tools performing operations with different depths of quill movement. For example, a hole is drilled, and then a clip-on quill stop is attached to limit the quill depth for countersinking the hole. While performing this operation, the micrometer depth stop nut remains in place for the next hole. Although clip-on quill stops are commercially available, they can be shop-made.

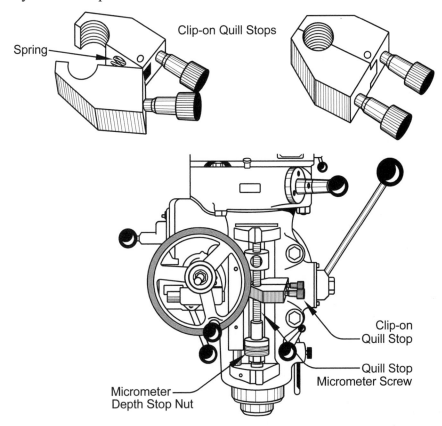

Figure 8-91. Clip-on quill stops open and closed (top) and a clip-on quill stop on the quill stop micrometer screw (bottom).

- *Hand-held depth cut spacers*, Figure 8-92, are simply a length of rod or bar stock. The machinist holds the spacer against the micrometer nut, pulls down on the quill feed lever until the quill stop knob contacts the top of the spacer, and then locks the quill in place. The spacer remains in position and the depth of the quill is set accurately and repeatably. When different stops are needed, use several spacers, one for each depth of quill movement. It's a good idea when several spacers are used to mark or color code them to help avoid errors.

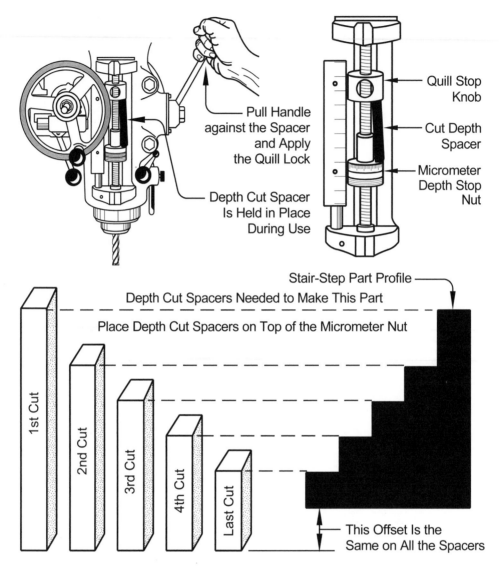

Figure 8-92. Using spacers between the quill stop knob and the micrometer depth stop nut (top) for a series of precise depth cuts (bottom).

Precision Depth Stop Techniques

Mold makers and instrument makers, who require the most cut-depth accuracy from Bridgeport-style mills, use the quill feed lever in conjunction with feeler gages and the micrometer depth stop nut as in Figure 8-93. Here is how to use the three components together:

1. Engage the table locks on the z-axis and snug up the table locks of the x- and y-axes to prevent minor table movements.

2. Mill or bore to about 0.030 inches of the final cut depth using either the manual or power feed.

3. Lower the quill so the cutting tool lightly touches the work and apply the quill lock.

4. Insert a feeler gage, or series of gage leaves, to make a total thickness of 0.020 inches between the top of the micrometer depth stop nut and the bottom of the quill stop knob. Snug up the micrometer depth stop nut.

5. Pull the quill feed lever down onto the feeler gage and lock the quill in place.

6. Remove the gage leaves and make a test cut.

7. Measure the part to determine the exact distance-to-go.

8. Put together another set of gage leaves to make up the final distance.

When used with feeler gages, the micrometer depth stop nut is more accurate than the table vertical feed. It is nearly impossible to move the table just one-thousandth of an inch with the z-axis table crank, but easy and certain with the micrometer depth stop nut and a feeler gage. In fact, milling cuts to within 0.0005 are possible using this feeler gage method. But, be aware that any time the milling table is moved there is some inaccuracy caused by the z-axis gibs, the oil on the ways, and the leadscrew mechanism.

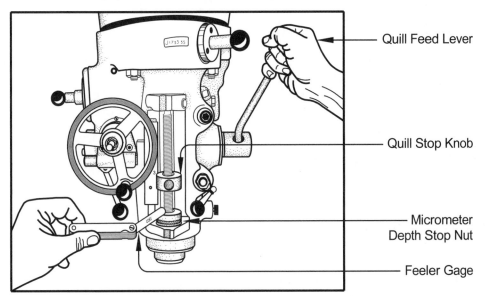

Quill Feed Lever

Quill Stop Knob

Micrometer Depth Stop Nut

Feeler Gage

Figure 8-93. Using a feeler gage with the micrometer depth stop nut.

Clearcutting with the Micrometer Depth Stop Nut

Use *clearcutting* when large drills or form cutters are used which are too large for the rigidity and power of a machine. If allowed an unrestricted cut, these drills or cutters are likely to dive into the work—a situation that makes clearcutting necessary. Here's how this is done:

1. Set the micrometer depth stop nut to restrict the tool cut depth to 0.002–0.005 inches.

2. Pull the feed handle down so the quill stop knob bumps the stop nut. You may want to move the tool in and out several times to insure that the tool has reached the final depth allowed by the micrometer depth stop nut and that the cutter has removed all the metal it can.

3. Using your left thumb, advance the micrometer depth stop nut 0.002–0.005 inches as shown in Figure 8-94 and repeat Step 1.

4. Take additional clearcutting passes to finish the entire cut.

See Section X of this chapter for more on clearcutting.

Tip: On many Bridgeport-style milling machines it is necessary to put a rubber band on the quill lock to hold it in the up, or unlocked position, as it has a tendency to drop down and lock the quill.

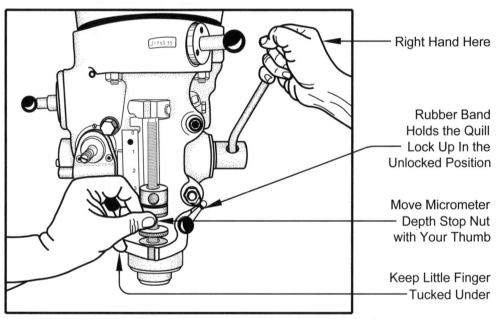

Right Hand Here

Rubber Band Holds the Quill Lock Up In the Unlocked Position

Move Micrometer Depth Stop Nut with Your Thumb

Keep Little Finger Tucked Under

Figure 8-94. Clearcutting set-up using the micrometer depth stop nut.

Installing Tools on the Drawbar

Here are the steps:

1. Insert a collet into the spindle, and slowly rotate the collet until the groove in the collet fits onto the spindle key and the collet pushes up into the spindle.

2. Finger tighten the drawbar a few turns into the collet to hold it in the spindle.

3. Holding the cutting tool in a rag to avoid cuts, insert the cutting tool into the collet and hold it there until the drawbar is tightened enough with your fingers so that, when released, the tool does not drop out of the collet.

4. Apply the spindle brake and use a box wrench, not an open wrench, to snug up the drawbar. Only 5–10 ft-lbs of force are necessary.

When removing a tool from a collet, remember to hold the tool so it does not drop out of the collet when the drawbar tension is released. When a tool drops out of a collet and strikes the floor or the milling table, the end of a flute can chip off and ruin the tool.

Conventional & Climb Milling

The rule for when to use conventional or climb milling is simple: Use conventional milling on all materials except for aluminum, copper, lead, zinc and soft brass, where climb milling produces a better finish. See Figure 8-95.

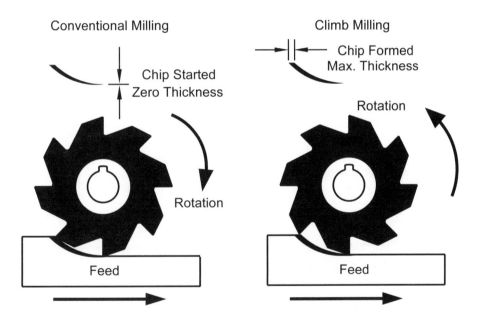

Figure 8-95. The mechanics of conventional and climb milling.

Climb milling produces a better finish on these soft metals because the chips are dropped behind the cutter which reduces the cutting of the chips a second time as the cutter enters new material. Recutting chips damages the finish of newly cut surfaces.

Climb milling has a major downside caused by the following sequence of events:

1. As the milling table moves to the right to bring the work in contact with the cutter, backlash between the leadscrew nut and the leadscrew appears on the left side of the leadscrew/leadscrew nut pair. See Figure 8-96 (top).

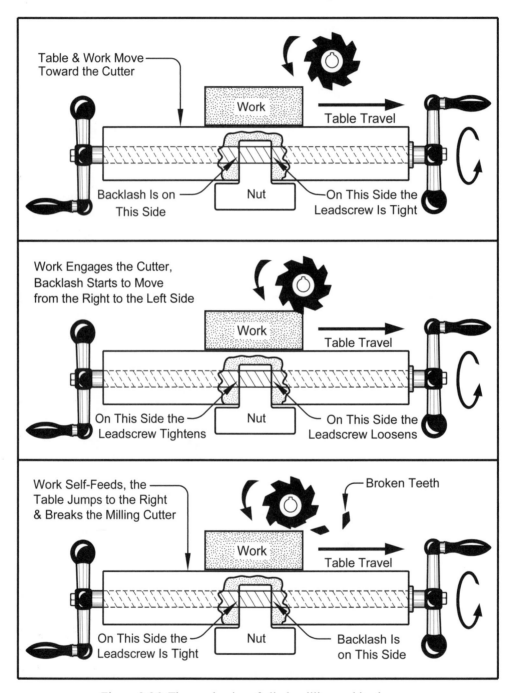

Figure 8-96. The mechanics of climb milling and its danger.

2. The cutter engages the work and begins its cut with the table feed rate set to allow a proper depth cut. See Figure 8-96 (middle).

3. Rotation of the cutter tends to draw the work farther under the cutter. And the milling table, which was being pushed under the work by the leadscrew, is now pulled under the cutter. As a result, the work begins to self-feed to the right. Backlash, initially on the left side of the leadscrew nut, moves to the right side of the leadscrew nut under self-feeding forces. This causes the table to jump farther to the right and the cutter suddenly takes an even greater bite. Depending on the amount of backlash, the cut depth can become excessive enough to rip the teeth from the cutter. This is the danger of climb milling. See Figure 8-96 (bottom). If the milling machine has backlash eliminators, climb milling may be possible. However, except for aluminum and other soft metals, it is not advisable as it is not worth the risk of breaking a cutter. Climb milling does produce a smoother finish than conventional milling on these metals because these soft metals cut differently than harder metals like steel, which does not benefit from climb milling.

Section X – Milling Examples

Clearcutting Aluminum Auto Engine Cylinder Tops

The aluminum head of a sports car engine, damaged by a flying connecting rod, has been repaired by TIG welding. The domed original shape of the cylinder top must be recut into the repaired area of TIG filler metal.

To do this job, first, a special dome-shaped milling cutter is shop-made. Here is how:

1. Turn the milling cutter base in the lathe, and mill turning flats as shown in Figure 8-97 (top left).

2. The actual cutter will be the purchased HSS cutoff tool shown in Figure 8-97 (top right). Mill a slot ⅛-inch deep—the same width as the cutoff tool—across the top face of the cutter base as in Figure 8-97 (top middle). This slot, or *center retention groove*, will locate the cutter accurately on the diameter and resist cutting torque. Note that the cutoff tool will be installed inverted.

3. Cut a cardstock or sheet metal template to the shape of an undamaged engine cylinder dome. Use this template and a bench or pedestal grinder to grind the lathe cutoff tool into this dome shape. Figure 8-97 (top right). Grind for only 2–3 seconds before dipping the tool in water. The tool is furnished hardened so if any part of it turns blue, you have annealed that section of the steel and must start over with a new cutoff tool.

4. After the cutoff tool is shaped into the dome, bevel the top of the cutter so the cutting edges face opposite directions as in figure 8-97 (bottom right). When the cutter is completed, slide it down into the retention groove.

5. Make the aluminum *blade-support blocks* shown in Figure 8-97 (bottom left and center), and bolt them to the cutter base. Then install the two set screws in the blade-support blocks and tighten the set screws so they press against the cutter, pinning it against the blade-support blocks.

6. Install the completed dome-shaped milling cutter in a milling tool holder and set the mill spindle speed to 100 RPM. Using bar clamps, secure the damaged engine head to the milling table with the center of the engine dome under the spindle axis. This precise location may be determined by measuring the distance between *existing,* undamaged domes and then transferring this measurement to find the center of the dome to be cut.

7. Just pushing the cutter into the work will cause the cutter to take too big a bite and both the cutter and work are likely to be damaged. For this job, clearcutting is essential. To begin, set the micrometer quill stop to limit the quill's downward motion to 0.005 inch—that is, between the full up and the full down position so the quill moves only 5 thousandths of an inch.

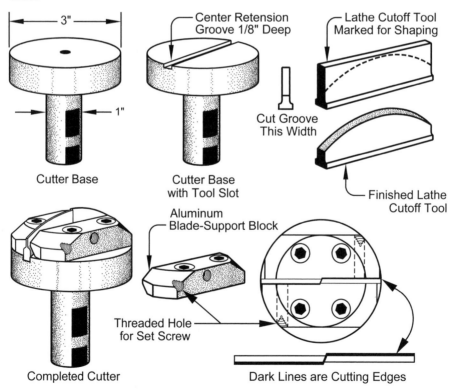

Figure 8-97. This shop-made milling cutter works well when clearcutting.

8. Pull the quill up with the spindle lever and lock it in place. This is done because the pull-up springs on many mills are not strong enough to keep their spindles in the fully up position.

9. Raise the milling table so the dome-shaped milling cutter just clears the work, then slowly pull down on the spindle lever until it reaches the full 5 thousandths of an inch cut depth. The micrometer depth stop nut prevents the tool from self-feeding and becoming over-powered.

10. Repeat Steps 8 and 9 until the dome-shaped cylinder head is completely cut and matches the original.

Using a Hole Saw to Remove a Half-Plug

A half-cylinder shaped slug needs to be removed from the edge of a 1¾-inch thick piece of hot-rolled steel. Although this job could be done with a boring head, it would take a long time. But, using the HSS hole saw in Figure 8-98 and running at 300 RPM with plenty of cutting oil, the job took only 20 minutes. The reason it took so little time was because the hole saw turns only an annular, or donut-shaped, ring of metal into chips instead of the entire half-plug. This technique not only saves time and money, it leaves a half-round plug which can be used elsewhere.

While the sides of the cut were relatively smooth, if a better finish was required, a slightly undersized hole saw could have been used to make the first cut, followed by a boring head to bring the finish cut to precise dimensions with a very smooth wall.

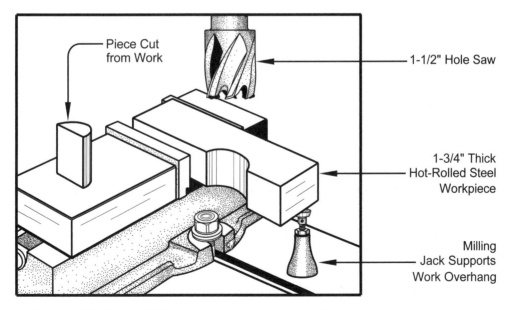

Figure 8-98. Using a HSS hole saw to remove a half-cylinder section from a steel bar.

Repairing Broken Gear Teeth without an Indexing Head

Here is a repair procedure for replacing broken gear teeth:

1. Remove all dirt and grease from the gear with a solvent such as spray carburetor cleaner or brake cleaner.

2. Use a TIG torch to apply filler metal to replace the broken gear teeth. Make the teeth slightly larger than their final size to provide enough metal stock for machining. Use filler metal which is "hard as welded."

3. TIG weld a brazed carbide lathe tool bit to a dowel pin or to a length of CRS round stock to form the shop-made flycutter in Figure 8-99.

4. Use a green wheel to shape the flycutter to match a pair of existing good teeth on the gear.

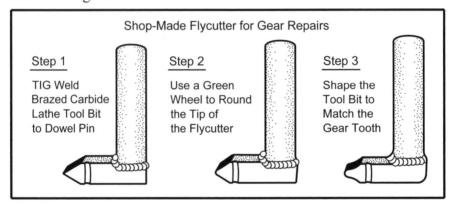

Figure 8-99. Making a shaped flycutter from a brazed carbide lathe tool bit.

5. Secure the damaged gear in a milling vise as in Figure 8-100. Note the three registration points. This clamping arrangement not only holds the gear rigidly, the milling vise jaws support the gear on its axle and keep the centerline height of the gear constant as it is rotated. The end of the milling stop uses a good tooth on the gear to index—or register—the tooth to be repaired.

6. In a series of small cuts, approximately 5–10 thousandths each, use the shop-made flycutter to recut the profile of the damaged teeth.

7. Paint the newly recut gear teeth with layout fluid, then secure the mating gear in a lathe.

8. Run the lathe at low speed, and holding the repaired gear on an axel, mesh the repaired gear against the mating gear for about 30 seconds.

9. The areas of bare metal showing through the layout fluid reveal the high spots on the new teeth. Use a diamond file in an air file to remove these high spots.

Repeat Steps 7–9 until the new teeth mesh properly and show even wear.

A further refinement of this repair is to install the repaired gear in its transmission and add a grinding compound such as Clover-brand medium, then allow the gears to mesh until they quiet down—usually just a few minutes. This allows the high spots on the repaired gear to be ground down to better mesh with its mate. It is remarkable how quiet the gears become. The transmission must then be torn down, and completely flushed to remove all of the abrasive, and the shaft seals must also be replaced. The quite smoothness of the gears is worth this extra work.

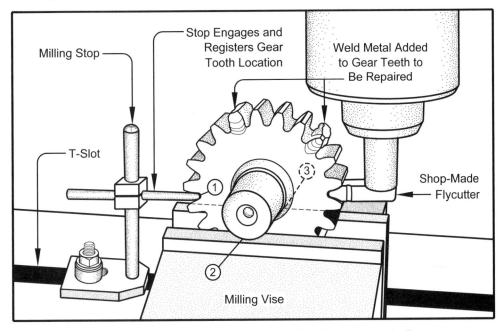

Figure 8-100. Reshaping a damaged gear tooth with a shop-made flycutter.

Slitting Saws

There are a few things to remember to get excellent results with a slitting saw:

1. Running a slitting saw backwards, that is, with the teeth in the wrong direction, instantly destroys the saw. Be sure that the teeth point in the direction the spindle turns, usually clockwise as viewed from above.

2. The work must be held rigidly. Collet blocks, as in Figure 8-101—where two slits at 90° angles are being applied to a workpiece—not only hold work securely, they easily index the work with little chance of error. A square collet block holds the work for one or two cuts, and a hexagonal collet block holds the work for three or six cuts.

3. Begin with a low spindle speed, say 50–100 RPM, and a light feed and observe how the cutting proceeds, then boost the speed and feed.

4. Except on cast iron, always use lubricant.

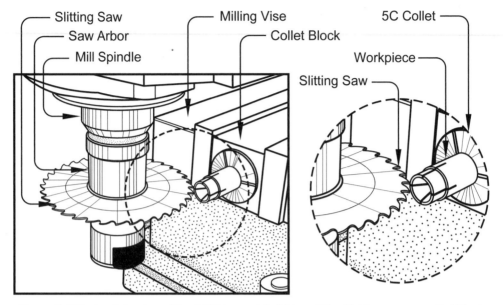

Figure 8-101. Applying two slits at 90° to work held in a 5C collet in a square collet block.

Section XI – Milling Machine Projects

Shop-Made Milling Stop

Figures 8-102 and 8-103 show a good milling machine project for beginners. Because the two ⅜- and ⅝-inch rounds used in the shop-made milling stop are CRS, their diameters are within one-thousandth of an inch of their nominal size and will slide nicely through holes reamed with an oversized reamer. The threaded holes for the ¼-20 SHCSs are countersunk for appearance.

Here are the steps to make the milling stop:

1. Cut the following parts to length and remove all burrs and sharp edges:

    -   Cut a piece of ⅝-inch CRS round stock 7½ inches long. Square one end in the lathe and round-off the other to form the vertical post.

    -   Cut a piece of ⅜-inch CRS round stock to 7 inches. Square one end and step the other.

    -   Cut a piece of 1 × 1 × ½-inch CRS bar stock for the cross clamp.

    -   Cut a piece of 2 × 5 × ½-inch CRS bar stock for the base.

    -   Cut a piece of 1¼ × ½-inch CRS round stock to form the cylindrical spacer needed to raise the flanged nut to the height of the threads on the stud. See Figure 8-103. This spacer is needed because the stud does not have threads along its entire length.

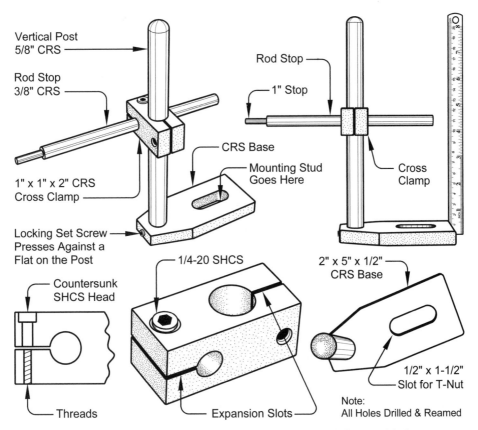

Figure 8-102. A shop-made mill stop assembled and disassembled.

2. Mill a $^1/_4$-inch wide $\times$ $^1/_2$-inch long flat on the square end of the vertical post for the locking set screw to bear on.

3. On the base, plunge cut the slot for the mounting stud using a $^1/_2$-inch end mill. Mill the slot slightly wider than $^1/_2$ inch so the $^1/_2$-inch diameter stud which fits through this slot will not bind.

4. Also, on the base shown in Figure 8-102, center punch and drill a $^{19}/_{32}$-inch hole for the vertical post, then ream the hole to $^5/_8$ inch. Drill and tap a #7 hole and tap it for a $^1/_4$-20 thread to hold the post locking set screw.

5. Drill a $^{19}/_{32}$-inch hole and a $^{11}/_{32}$-inch hole in two different sides of the cross clamp. Ream these holes for $^5/_8$- and $^3/_8$-inch diameters.

6. Cut expansion slots in the two cross-clamp holes with a bandsaw.

7. Find and center punch the location for the two $^1/_4$-20 cross-clamp screws, then drill with a #7 drill all the way through the cross clamp and tap the holes just beyond the half-way point. Drill a $^1/_4$-inch clearance hole for the screw threads and countersink the hole for the screw head.

8. Assemble the parts and the milling stop is finished.

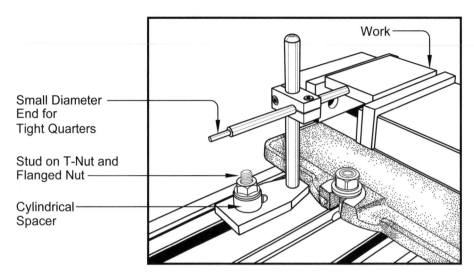

Figure 8-103. Shop-made mill stop in use showing the cylindrical spacer needed.

Chip Shield

A chip shield of polycarbonate or acrylic mounted on a magnetic indicator base helps contain chips but, more importantly, keeps chips from hitting the machinist. When positioned properly, the shield provides an excellent view of the milling process with complete safety. See Figures 8-104 and 8-105. The chip shield must be positioned low on the milling table so that chips do not slip under the lower edge of the shield and reach the magnet base. Placing the magnetic base inside a plastic bag makes chip removal simple. Just remove the base from the bag and the chips will fall away.

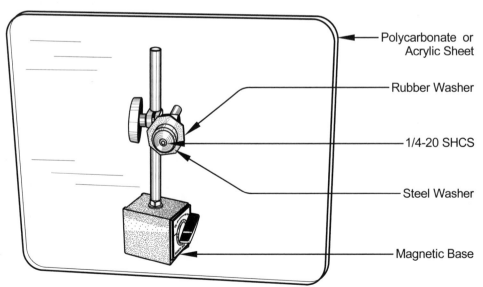

Figure 8-104. A Lexan chip shield mounted on a dial indicator magnetic stand.

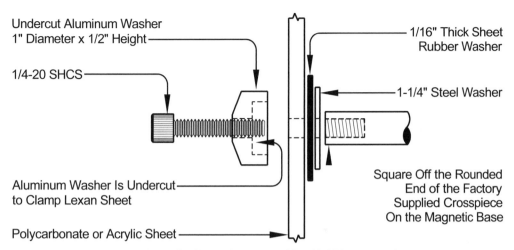

Undercut Aluminum Washer
1" Diameter x 1/2" Height

1/4-20 SHCS

1/16" Thick Sheet
Rubber Washer

1-1/4" Steel Washer

Aluminum Washer Is Undercut
to Clamp Lexan Sheet

Square Off the Rounded
End of the Factory
Supplied Crosspiece
On the Magnetic Base

Polycarbonate or Acrylic Sheet

Figure 8-105. Detail of how the Lexan chip shield is mounted on an
inexpensive magnetic base. The Lexan is easily drilled with a twist drill.

Sump Covers

Many Bridgeport-style mills have a cutting fluid sump cast into their base. An electric pump picks up the cutting fluid from the sump and moves it to the cutting area. Gravity returns the fluid from the milling table to the sump. Many machinists in small or prototype shops choose not to use this cutting fluid pumping system because the oil creates a mess in the shop and will turn rancid if not maintained. In a production setting, though, continuous flow of cutting fluid is important, especially when cutting hard, exotic materials.

There are two openings in the base of the mill below the milling table that allow the cutting fluid to return into the sump. If the sump is not going to be used, the return openings in the base should be blocked off with flat metal covers and gaskets so that oil drippings do not accumulate in the sump. This is needed even if a cutting fluid pumping system is not used because there will always be some oil dripping onto the base casting from the automatic oiler and from fluids applied by hand, and it is easier to cover the drain holes in the base casting than to clean the rough casting surfaces inside the sump.

Spur Driver & Center for Turning Wood

This tool makes it easy to turn wood or other soft materials in a metal lathe. It consists of two parts: a spur driver, which fits into a collet or chuck, and a tailstock center. On both the spur driver and the tailstock the work is supported with hardened centers made from dowel pins, but the tailstock center also has a sharpened ring which digs into the workpiece. This ring provides additional lateral support and prevents the center point from splitting the work. Because no part of the workpiece is *inside* a chuck or collet, the entire length of the work is accessible to the turning tool.

Here is how to make the tool in Figure 8-106:

1. Materials required: One 4½-inch length of 1-inch CRS round stock, two ¼ × 1½-inch dowel pins, and three #10-24 × ¼-inch set screws.

2. Apply 60° points to the two dowel pins using a carbide tool with a nick-off. Hold the dowels in a collet and set the lathe speed to 600 RPM.

3. Cut the 1-inch CRS round into two 2-inch lengths and face all ends.

4. Center drill and drill a ¼-inch hole in one end of each CRS round.

5. Turn down one-half the length of the tailstock, also called the tailstock center bearing, to ½-inch diameter. Then, center drill, step drill, and drill the spur driver to create a ½-inch hole so the two parts can fit into each other for storage. Chamfer both ends of these parts. Figure 8-106 (A & B).

6. Drill three #25 holes as in Figure 8-106, and tap them for the #10-24 set screws. Two set screws hold the dowel pin centers in place, and the third holds the spur driver and tailstock center together when they are stored.

7. Grind a double-sided HSS cutter as in Figure 7-23, then use it to apply the double-bevel cup to the tailstock center as shown in Figure 7-24.

8. Enlarge the ¼-inch hole in the spur driver to ⅜-inch diameter with a ⅜-inch depth to provide clearance when cutting the spurs.

9. Place the spur driver in a 1-inch collet and place the collet in a square collet block. Pull up the nut on the collet block.

10. Paint the end of the spur driver with layout fluid, hold the work in a collet block, and using a height gage, using the center head on your square, scribe two diameters on the 1-inch round 90° apart. See Figure 8-107 (A).

11. Lower the height gage to 0.075-inch below the diameter of the 1-inch round and scribe a line at the 3 o'clock position on the face of the spur driver. Turn the collet block 90° and scribe the next spur. Using this method, define all four relief ends of each spur. See Figure 8-107 (B). Do not remove the driver from the collet block.

12. Place the collet block in a milling vise and, using the scribed lines defining the spurs, cut each spur to a depth of 0.200-inch with a ¾-inch diameter milling cutter. Figure 8-107 (C).

13. To harden the spurs, use an oxyacetylene torch to heat the spurs cherry red, and then plunge them into room temperature tempering oil. Support the part while torch heating on a loop of stainless steel wire so the part heats evenly. Repeat for the tailstock center's double-beveled cup edges.

14. When the spur driver and tailstock center cool to room temperature, clean and polish the hardened edges of these parts down to shiny metal so heat oxide formation can be observed during tempering.

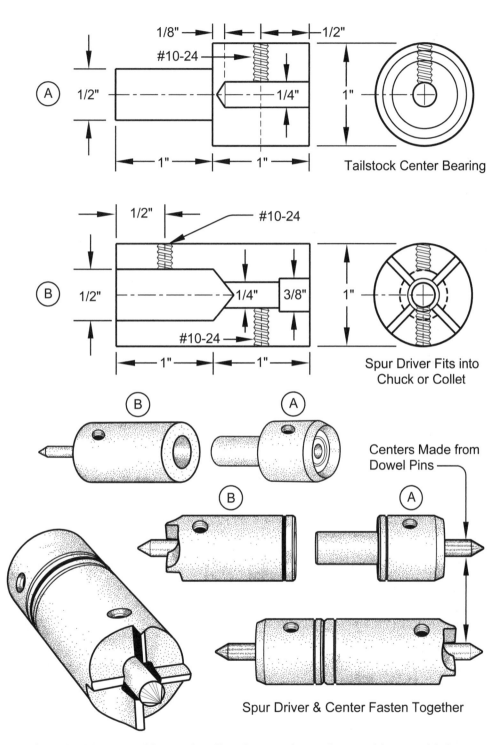

Figure 8-106. A spur driver and a tailstock center for turning wood in a metal lathe.

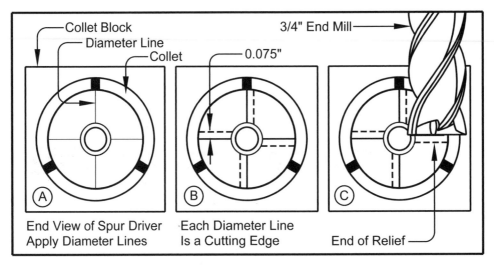

Figure 8-107. Holding the spur driver in a square collet block and cutting its spurs.

15. Again, support the spur driver on a stainless steel loop of wire and, with an oxyacetylene torch, begin heating the part on the end opposite the spurs. As the heat moves forward, the spurs will turn straw color. Remove the heat and allow the part to air cool. Do not plunge in water or oil. The spurs have now been hardened and tempered. Repeat for the tailstock center's double-beveled cup edges.

16. Using a Dremel tool and an abrasive stone, apply a 20–30° bevel to each of the spurs so they can dig into the work as it turns counterclockwise as viewed from the tailstock.

Section XII – Milling Machine Safety

Good Practices

- Many milling operations generate large volumes of hot flying metal chips, so wear safety glasses with full eye coverage and use chip shields to allow close observation of the work without the hazard of flying chips. Using chip guards makes clean-up easier too.

- Cutting tools have sharp edges, so to avoid being cut when installing them, handle them with a rag.

- Allow the spindle to come to a complete stop before attempting to take a measurement.

- Always keep your head out of the plane of tool rotation. This reduces the chance of being struck by flying cutter parts.

- This sounds obvious, but is worth repeating, while the machine is in operation, keep your fingers away from the cutting tools.

Chapter 9

Machine Shop Problem Solving

Most people don't recognize opportunity
because it's usually disguised as hard work.

—Unknown

Introduction

Being aware of existing devices and solutions forms the basis of intelligent problem solving—a skill that all good machinists need. This chapter will help with that goal by first, demonstrating several dozen shop techniques, repair methods and shop-made tools for solving specific problems, and second, by presenting an assortment of mechanical components, mechanisms, and alternate construction methods that any machinist will find useful.

Section I – Layout & Machining Techniques

How to Lay Out a Bolt-Hole Pattern Using Chords

Although circular bolt-hole patterns are usually drilled using a rotary table or the x-y coordinates on a milling machine, sometimes there is a need to lay out a bolt-hole pattern without the use of these tools. This can be done accurately using *chords*—the line which joins the end points of an arc or two points on a circle. Here is how to lay out a 6-inch diameter pattern of 7 bolt holes:

1. Locate the center of the bolt-hole pattern, center punch it, and scribe the 6-inch bolt diameter circle using one leg of the divider in the punch mark.

2. Mark and prick punch the initial bolt-hole location, which is usually at the 12 o'clock position.

3. Look up the chord length for a 7-hole pattern in *Machinery's Handbook*. You'll find it is 0.433993, rounded to 0.4339 inches for a 1-inch circle, or $6 \times 0.4339 = 2.6034$ inches for the chord of a 6-inch circle.

4. Set your dividers to 2.603 inches, put one divider point in the initial hole punch mark, and step off the remaining hole points. See Figure 9-1 (top).

If the hole pattern needs to have the top two holes perpendicular to the vertical—flat on top—look up the chord for a 14-hole pattern. Next, multiply this chord number by the diameter of the circle and step off 14 points beginning at the top vertical point, or 12 o'clock position. Then use alternate points to make the 7-hole pattern as shown in Figure 9-1 (bottom).

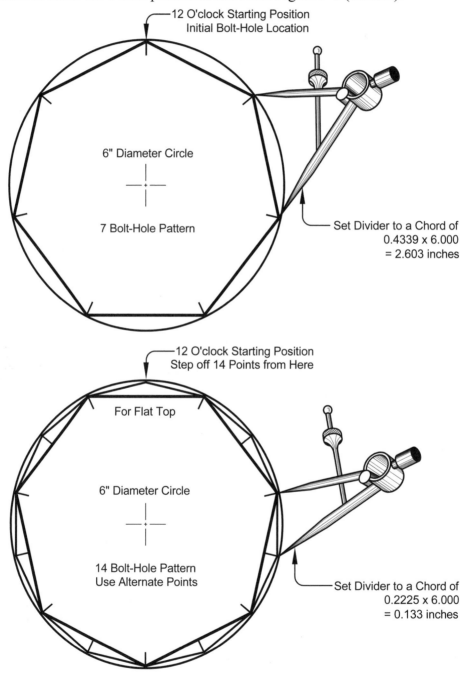

Figure 9-1. Laying out a 6-inch diameter 7 bolt-hole pattern using chords.

Boring vs. Turning

When one existing cylindrical part must fit into a hole in a second part, and that hole is yet to be made, there are two alternative methods, or as Tony Soprano would say, "We can do this the easy way, or we can do this the hard way."

1. Drill the second part to the correct size hole. This is a good idea, but likely not possible because the cylindrical shaft diameter does not match any of the drills on hand, so instead the hole must be bored to size. This is the hard way.

2. The easy way is to drill the hole in the second part with an available drill, and then turn the cylindrical part down to size to match the drilled hole. Drilling is always faster and easier than boring. See Figure 9-2.

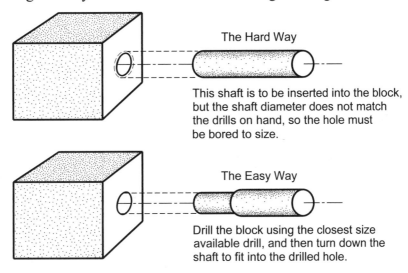

The Hard Way

This shaft is to be inserted into the block, but the shaft diameter does not match the drills on hand, so the hole must be bored to size.

The Easy Way

Drill the block using the closest size available drill, and then turn down the shaft to fit into the drilled hole.

Figure 9-2. Boring vs. turning when fitting together two parts.

Broaching a Single Keyway

Here is the procedure for broaching a single keyway in an arbor press:

1. Select the broach and choose the bushing which matches the workpiece hole diameter and hole length. To cut a full-length keyway groove, the bushing must be as long as the length of the hole in the work.

2. Insert the bushing into the work, and insert the broach into the bushing. Then place the work in the arbor press so the ram of the arbor press bears on the top of the broach. Make sure that the broach is perpendicular to the work and the arbor ram face. At this and all later steps, add cutting fluid to the broach teeth, sides and back.

3. With the arbor press, force the broach through the work. Use smooth, even pressure on the broach and do not stop in the middle of a stroke. As the

broach completes its cutting stroke and exits the bottom of the work, catch the broach so it does not fall and get dinged. Never pull the broach backwards up through the keyway. This dulls the broach teeth.

4. Clear the chips from the broach.

5. Again insert the broach into the top of the bushing and place one or more L-shaped shims behind the broach in the keyway. The shims move the broach deeper into the keyway to make the next cut.

6. Repeat the downward cutting stroke, catching the broach as it emerges from the work. Remember, do not allow the broach to drop onto the floor.

7. Repeat Steps 5 and 6 until the keyway is the required depth, Figure 9-3.

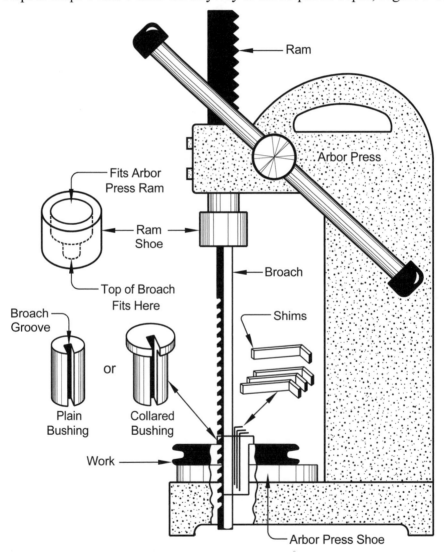

Figure 9-3. Cutting a keyway with a broach in an arbor press.

Hundreds of pounds of force are applied to the broach to make it cut. Broaches for cutting extra-long keyways advance their teeth 0.030–0.035 inches along a 9-inch length, instead of the more usual 0.050-inch advance. This reduces the force on the broach when a long keyway engages many teeth at once. If you are broaching in a hydraulic press, which is required for wide broaches and extra-long keyways, monitor the pressure gage on the hydraulic press cylinder to insure that the broach is not jammed and you are not applying excessive force to the broach. Too much force can snap the broach and send pieces of it flying around the shop.

Lubricants for Broaching
See Table 9-1.

Workpiece Material	Lubricants
Aluminum	Kerosene or aluminum tapping fluid
Brass	Dry, but lube back of broach in bushing
Bronze	Oil
Cast Iron	Dry, but lube back of broach in bushing
Steel	Cutting oil

Table 9-1. Cutting lubricants for broaching. With all broaching materials, lubricate the back of the broach bushing where the broach slides.

Broaching Trouble Shooting
The most common broaching problems are the result either of misalignment, lack of lubricant, dull broaches, using the wrong tool, or using the wrong size broach. Here are the solutions to these problems:

- Proper alignment of the arbor press ram, broach and bushing are critical to avoiding drift, deflection, and breakage of the broach. Take the time to get the ram shoe, broach and bushing carefully aligned.

- Apply lubricant to all four sides of the broach as it enters the bushing, not just on the cutting teeth.

- Make sure that your broach is sharp. A dull broach is subject to high cutting forces and may snap.

- Use the right tool. Good practice is to use a ram shoe that positions the broach against the face of the arbor press ram. This reduces the chances of deflection. On larger or extra-long broaches, use a hydraulic press to get the force needed.

- Extra-long keyways require extra-long broaches, shims and bushings. There is a maximum and minimum length cut for each broach which is specified by its manufacturer. Two or more workpieces may be stacked to establish the minimum length of cut.

- And remember, never attempt to broach any material harder than Rockwell R_c35. Metals with higher Rockwell numbers are harder than the broach and will not be cut, and they will damage the broach.

Why Shaft Key Metal Should Not Be Upgraded

As equipment wears, the torque transmitted by shaft keys often increases. Because keys are in shear, they fracture along the line between the shaft and the load. To work around this problem, some well-meaning maintenance man may decide that to stop key breakage, he need only make the key of stronger material than the original one, so he replaces the original steel key with one of 4130 steel. Though keys of this high-strength alloy can be made from shanks of brazed tungsten carbide lathe tool bits, it is not a good idea. When this new key is put under load, it does not shear; it tears the keyway out of the shaft—ruining the shaft. Keys are not only devices to connect shafts with their loads, they are mechanical fuses. Do not upgrade the shaft key metal.

Indexing for Broaching Two Keyways at 90°

On larger machines, two keyways and two keys are needed to transfer the torque and are usually placed at 90° with respect to each other. This technique is shown in Figure 9-4. Notice that you will need a large-collared broach bushing to complete this task. (See Figure 9-5 for details on making this bushing.) Here is how to broach two keyways at 90° to each other:

1. Insert the large-collared broaching bushing into the gear or pulley.
2. Clamp the bushing so it does not turn inside the work and drill a ⅛-inch hole through the bushing and into the work using Hole A in Figure 9-4 as a guide. This hole in the work needs only to be deep enough to secure a dowel pin.
3. Insert a ⅛-inch dowel pin into Hole A.
4. With the dowel pin in this hole, place the work and the bushing into the arbor press and broach the first keyway.
5. Remove the ⅛-dowel pin, turn the bushing a quarter turn, and insert the dowel pin into Hole B. You now have the broach accurately positioned for the second keyway.
6. Broach the second keyway.
7. Remove the dowel pin and collar bushing. The keyways are done.

As long as the broaching collar holes are 90° to each other, the broached keyways will be too. While this job required locating only two keyways, this same method could be used to locate keyways at more than two angles.

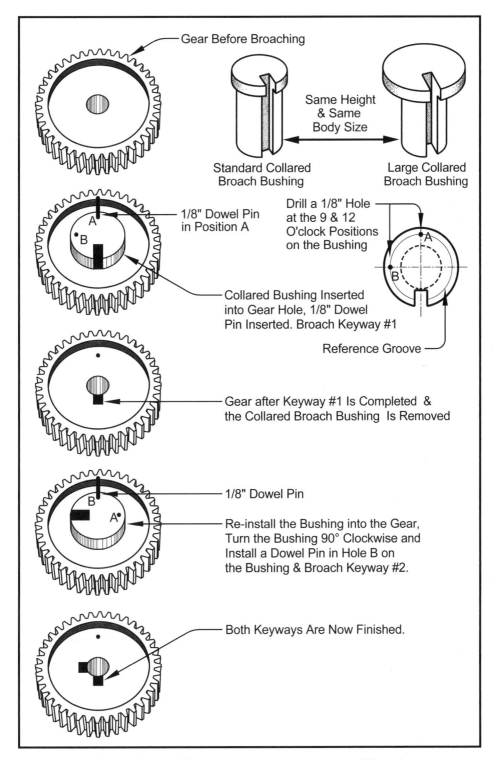

Gear Before Broaching

Same Height
& Same
Body Size

Standard Collared
Broach Bushing

Large Collared
Broach Bushing

1/8" Dowel Pin
in Position A

Drill a 1/8" Hole
at the 9 & 12
O'clock Positions
on the Bushing

Collared Bushing Inserted
into Gear Hole, 1/8" Dowel
Pin Inserted. Broach Keyway #1

Reference Groove

Gear after Keyway #1 Is Completed &
the Collared Broach Bushing Is Removed

1/8" Dowel Pin

Re-install the Bushing into the Gear,
Turn the Bushing 90° Clockwise and
Install a Dowel Pin in Hole B on
the Bushing & Broach Keyway #2.

Both Keyways Are Now Finished.

Figure 9-4. Broaching two keyways into a gear at a 90° angle.

Making an Indexing Collared Broach Bushing

A rotary table or an indexing head makes it easy to accurately locate the indexing holes in a broach bushing. But, if you don't have access to these tools, there is another way to make this part. Here are the steps:

1. Make the bushing with the oversized collar and broached slot as shown in both Figures 9-4 and 9-5.

2. Put the collar in a lathe and "stab" a fine reference groove on the circle where the indexing holes will be drilled. This groove must be positioned only accurately enough to provide sufficient metal around the holes to make them strong drill guides and leave enough clearance around the gear hole so it does not weaken the gear hub.

3. Put the bushing collar in a suitable collet, and then insert the collet into a square collet block. Position the keyway groove in the bushing at the 6 o'clock position. By eye is close enough. On this job, the collet block does the accurate indexing.

4. Place the collet block against the fixed jaw of the milling machine vise.

5. Use a mill stop to locate the position of the collet block in the vise. Lightly tighten the milling vise.

6. Prepare the milling machine to drill a ⅛-inch hole.

7. Find the left-right center of the collet block, as in Figure 9-5 (bottom right), and lock the table. Position the milling table to center drill, then drill a ⅛-inch hole on the top, or 12 o'clock position, of the stabbed reference groove.

8. Open the vise, turn the collet block 90°, and drill the second hole at the 9 o'clock position. The indexing collet is now complete. The accuracy of this method does not depend on how worn the milling machine is or whether you have a DRO.

It's a good idea to drill a third ⅛-inch hole on the *other* side of the broaching slot, or 3 o'clock position, just in case you need to place a keyway on the right-hand side of the first keyway. This would occur if there were other complications on the shaft being broached.

The way a milling machine stop is used to make this part demonstrates the usefulness of this simple device. A milling machine stop not only eliminates repeated set-ups, it increases accuracy without any additional time penalties. Making a milling machine stop would be an excellent project for a first-time milling machine owner.

Refer back to Figures 8-102 and 8-103 in Chapter 8 – Milling Machines for how to make a milling machine stop.

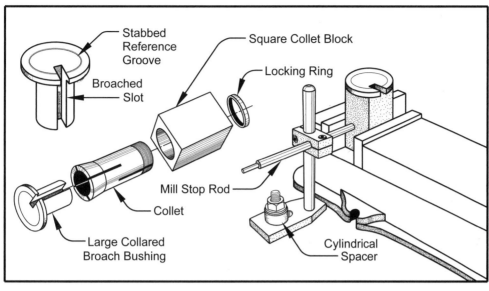

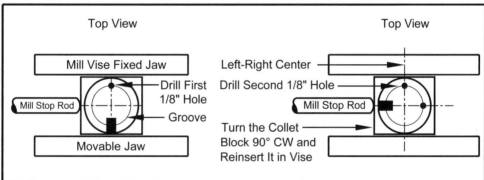

Figure 9-5. Making an indexing collared broach bushing with a
collet block and without using a rotary table or indexing head.

Sacrificial Centers

Sacrificial centers are usually one-time use items made of steel. They serve
two purposes:

- When turning a shaft with a damaged center, using a sacrificial center
  provides a way to produce an accurate new center. To use a sacrificial
  center, bore its center to snugly fit the workpiece shaft and put a 60°
  center hole in its other end. See Figure 9-6 (A). Some machinists put a ½°
  taper in the walls of the bored hole to help insure perfect centering.
  Making a sacrificial center is much faster than repairing an existing
  damaged center, particularly if the workpiece shaft is hardened. Make the
  sacrificial center out of CRS.

- When pressing bearings in and out with an arbor or hydraulic press, a sacrificial center over the end of the workpiece shaft prevents damage to the shaft center hole during pressing and insures that the ram forces are axially aligned with the shaft to prevent the workpiece from binding. See Figure 9-6 (B).

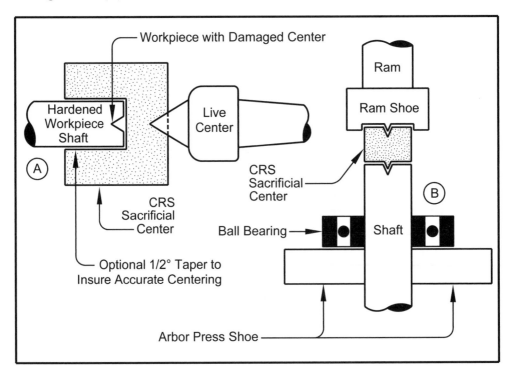

Figure 9-6. Sacrificial centers are useful in lathes when repairing workpieces with damaged centers and in arbor presses to prevent shaft damage when pressing bearings in and out.

Increasing the Diameter of an Existing Hole

When the diameter of an existing hole must be enlarged with a spade bit or metal-cutting hole saw, and there is no center workpiece material in which to center the drill or hole saw, the solution is to make a drill guide to surround the hole. This drill guide solves the problem of locating the center of the workpiece. For the spade bit, make the drill guide out of wood, and for the hole saw, make the drill guide out of steel or aluminum.

Carefully center the guide around the hole and clamp it securely to the workpiece, then enlarge the hole with the spade bit or hole saw.

Figure 9-7 shows the drill guide set-ups for both the spade bit and the hole saw.

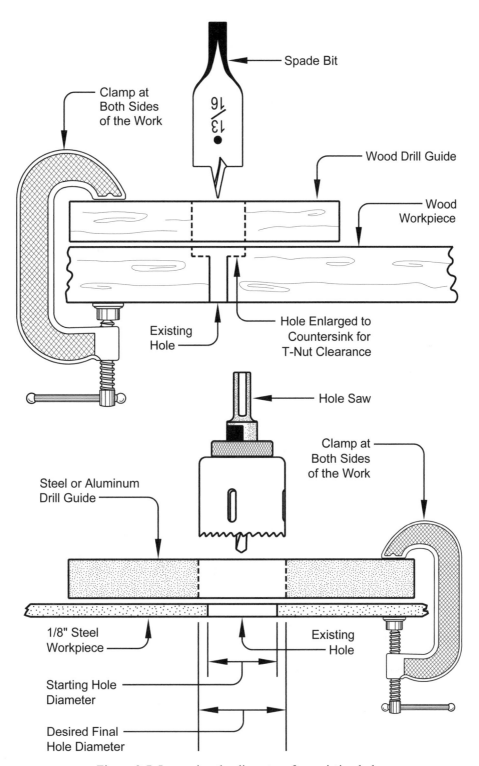

Figure 9-7. Increasing the diameter of an existing hole.

Cutting Perfect Half-Cylinders

You cannot make complete half-cylinders by drilling or boring a hole into a workpiece and then cutting it in half because the saw kerf removes a slice of the cylinder, as in the top of Figure 9-8. There is, though, an easy solution. Here are the steps:

1. Cut the workpiece in half. This removes the kerf before the hole is drilled.

2. Add dowel pins to insure proper part alignment during machining and after separation, and clamp the halves together. See Figure 9-8 (bottom).

3. Consider putting springs in the dowel pin holes before inserting the dowel pins to help separate the halves if they are to be repeatedly opened.

4. Mark the hole location, then drill or bore the hole.

Perfect half-cylinders are particularly useful for holding thin-walled tubing during machining without damaging the tubing. To do this, make the cylinder hole *slightly smaller* than the tubing diameter.

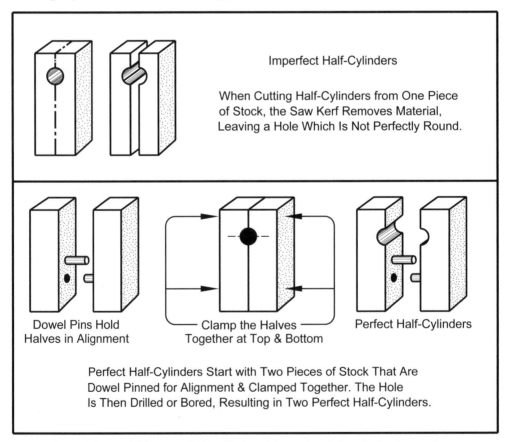

Figure 9-8. Machining two half-cylinders. The optional dowel pins insure that the two halves can be reassembled in perfect alignment after being opened.

Adding Hardened Steel to a Shop-Made Weld Bend Test Fixture

Figure 9-9 shows a shop-made weld bend test fixture which can also serve as a hardened V-block because of the addition of hardened steel rods which support the bending. Figure 9-10 has step-by-step instructions.

This weld bend test fixture is easy to make for the following three reasons:

- By using hardened steel in only critical areas of the fixture, the benefits of hardened steel can be gained without having to work with a large amount of difficult-to-machine hardened steel.

- In the base, the bedding areas for the hardened steel rods are easily made by drilling, reaming, and then cutting away unneeded material, as in Figure 9-10 (bottom two rows).

- Multiple identical fixture bases can be made by machining a long bar through Step 4 of Figure 9-10, then bandsawing the bar into two or more fixture bases.

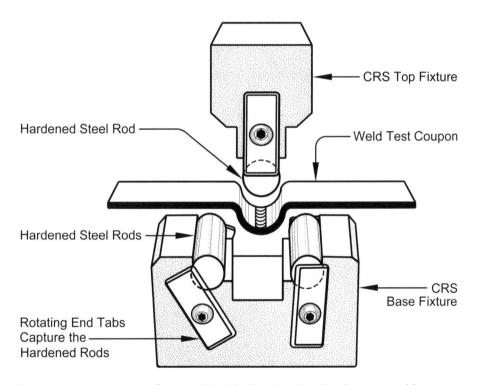

Figure 9-9. Weld bend test fixture with added hardened steel rods to test weld coupons.

Should they become worn, the hardened steel rods are easy to replace by rotating the end tabs on the CRS base fixture, removing the old rods, and sliding in a new pair.

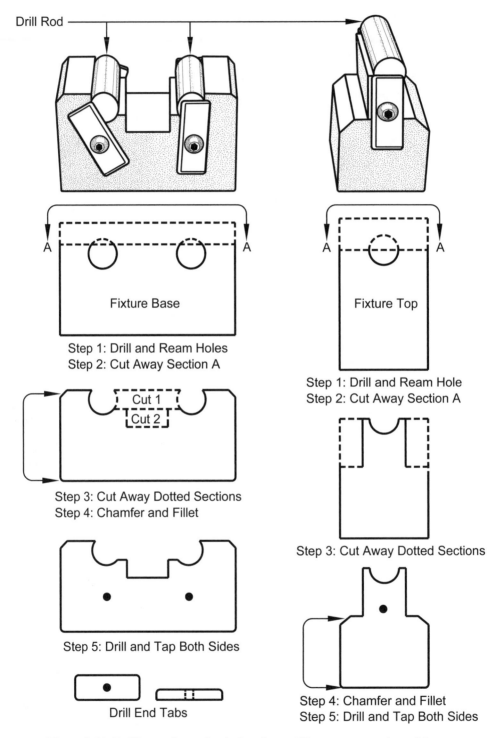

Drill Rod

Fixture Base

Step 1: Drill and Ream Holes
Step 2: Cut Away Section A

Cut 1
Cut 2

Step 3: Cut Away Dotted Sections
Step 4: Chamfer and Fillet

Step 5: Drill and Tap Both Sides

Drill End Tabs

Fixture Top

Step 1: Drill and Ream Hole
Step 2: Cut Away Section A

Step 3: Cut Away Dotted Sections

Step 4: Chamfer and Fillet
Step 5: Drill and Tap Both Sides

Figure 9-10. Drilling and reaming holes, then milling away a portion of the workpiece captures the hardened rods. The holes and rods are parallel.

Several different materials can be used to make the hardened steel rods, and there are several ways to cut them to length:

- Purchase drill blanks, reamer blanks, or dowel pins which are all sold hardened, and cut them with an abrasive wheel.

- Use O-1 HSS drill rod, which is sold unhardened in 3-foot lengths, and cut it to size using either a lathe with a cutoff tool, a hacksaw, or an abrasive wheel. Then, harden the rod by heating it to red, quenching it in oil, and drawing it to a straw oxide color.

- Recycle discarded mold core-pins or reamer shanks, which are hardened as used, and cut them to length with an abrasive wheel.

Steel Marking Stamps on Critical Surfaces

Many times parts, tools, or molds must be steel stamped or be engraved with identifying letters and numbers, but the roughness of these markings can disturb the smoothness of the part. To avoid this, cut a shallow milled pocket in the part where the stamping or engraving can go without projecting above the part's smooth surface. See Figure 9-11.

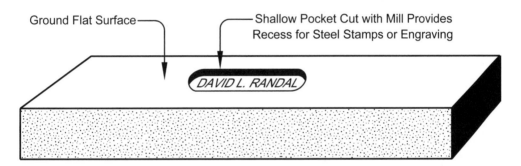

Figure 9-11. A recessed pocket keeps stamped or engraved letters below a critical surface.

Repair Plugs

Moldmakers often use repair plugs to hide mistakes, to seal unneeded holes, or to eliminate damaged sections. Here is how to make a repair plug:

1. Drill, then bore a hole for the plug with a step in it to give the plug a place to seat. See Figure 9-12.

2. Turn a snug-fitting plug for the hole with a matching step. This step will keep the plug in place while being installed and later resist forces against it when in use.

3. Along the seam line between the plug and the hole, mark, prick punch, center punch, drill, tap threads and counterbore for two SHCSs.

4. Insert the plug and screw in the two SHCSs.

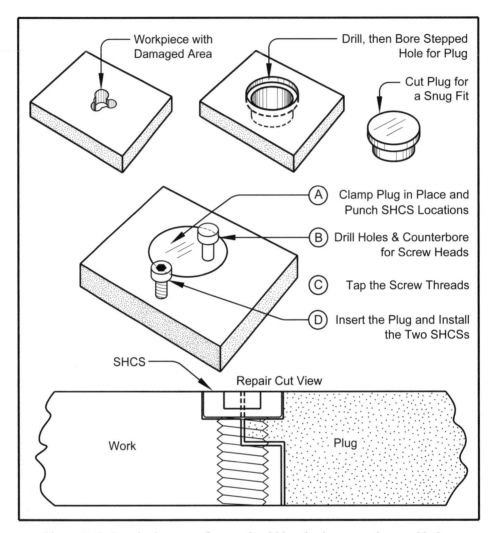

Figure 9-12. Repair plugs are often used to hide mistakes, to seal unused holes, and to remove markings or defects from valuable parts.

Plugs for Installing Lift Rings

Many machine parts require the addition of threads for installing a lift ring. If the part is hardened, though it can be drilled with a carbide drill, it *cannot* be tapped for threads. The solution is to drill a hole, insert a threaded plug into the hole and weld the plug in place. Now there are threads where they are needed. Here is how it's done:

1. At a balance point, drill a hole in the part to be lifted.

2. Make a threaded plug to fit into the drilled hole. It should be made from a high grade of steel, such as 4130 or 4140. A readily available source of suitable steel is the shank of a Grade 5 or a Grade 8 bolt. To use one, put the bolt shank in a lathe, turn a section to size, then drill and tap it.

3. Chamfer the edge of the hole in the part and the edge of the lift ring insert plug. These chamfers give the final weld bead a place to go. Though it is best to chamfer both the plug and the hole as in Figure 9-13 (bottom left), sometimes only the lift ring insert plug can be chamfered, as in Figure 9-13 (bottom right).

4. Weld around the bottom of the threaded hole so that any bolts in these threads cannot act as a jack to force the insert plug out of its hole.

5. Weld the insert into the hole and screw in a purchased lift ring.

Because lift rings with the same stub threads are available in several stub lengths—for example ¾-, 1-, and 1¼-inch lengths—a stub can be longer than a plug is deep. If this happens, add spacer washers or the screw will act as a jack and place an additional load on the weld holding the plug in place. This added load—beyond the weight of the part—may lead to load release.

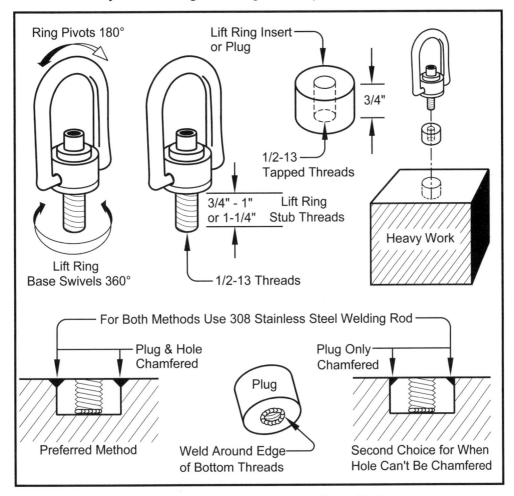

Figure 9-13. Making an insert for installing a lift ring.

Texturing Punches

Durable texturing punches for steel are easily made by using a file as a pattern source. Texturing improves handgrip and appearance. Here are the steps for making a texturing punch:

1. File or grind the tip end of an O-1 steel punch blank flat and smooth.
2. Using an oxyacetylene torch, bring the O-1 blank to red hot.
3. Place the tip end of the O-1 punch blank on the file teeth which have the desired pattern. With a ball-peen hammer, strike the punch blank *only* once.
4. Quench the punch's newly-patterned end in motor oil, swirling the punch to achieve even cooling.
5. Reheat the punch and draw the patterned-end temper to a straw oxide color.

Should the pattern transfer be unsatisfactory, the punch may be reground and restruck on the file.

Tip: The pattern transferred depends on the size of the file teeth, whether the file is single-cut or double-cut and, in the case of double-cut files, *where* on the file the transfer strike is made. See Figure 9-14.

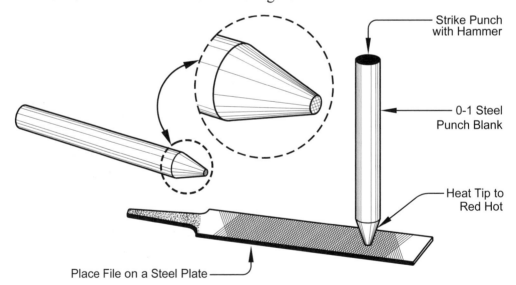

Figure 9-14. Making a texturing punch.

Punching

When using an *Osborne punch*, sometimes called a *saddlers' punch*, to cut thin work, always use a piece of wood to support the work. Place the wood grain in a vertical position because punching into the end grain produces the sharpest, best-defined cuts. See Figure 9-15.

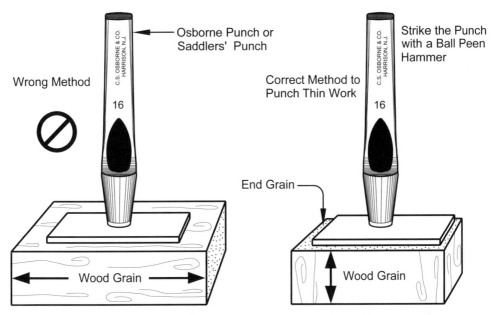

Figure 9-15. Osborne punches produce a cleaner hole
when an end-grain wood block supports the work.

Tightening Threaded Shafts

When a shaft has threads on both ends, and the threads at the far end must be tightened without marring the shaft, this is done using the *two-nuts-and-a-washer method* shown in Figure 9-16. Turning the outermost nut on the right end of the shaft turns the entire shaft.

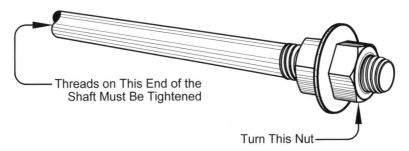

Figure 9-16. Using the two-nuts-and-a-washer method to
tighten a threaded shaft without damaging the shaft.

Making Holes in Spring Steel & Hacksaw Blades

Spring steel and hacksaw blades are difficult to put holes through because they are hardened, but this task can easily be done if you know how. Here are two methods:

- Drilling holes – Set the drill press to its slowest speed, place an aluminum block under the spring steel for a heat sink so the steel will not be annealed, and using an HSS cobalt drill with a 135° point, drill the work. Be sure to apply cutting fluid. Considerable drill pressure may be needed to get the drilling started. Remove the burrs around the hole. Step drill holes over ⅜ inch.

• Making holes with a TIG torch – Figure 9-17 shows an unusual method which rapidly produces smooth, round, burr-free holes.

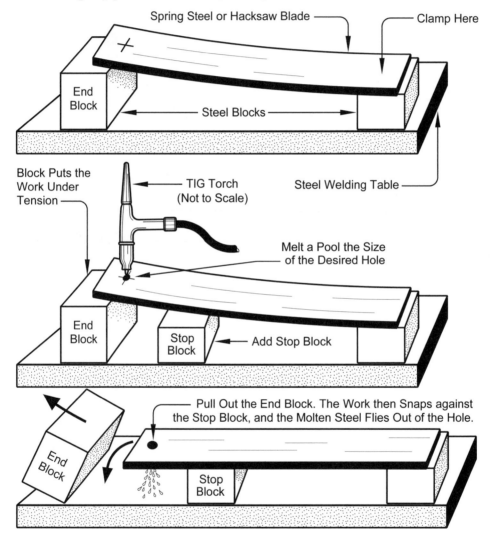

Figure 9-17. Using a TIG torch to make holes in spring steel or hacksaw blades.

Stretching Metal to Flatten Parts

Metal that has been distorted can be stretched so it will once again lie flat. For example, Figure 9-18 (top row) shows a small machine part—a sewing machine needle plate insert—that has been fractured and repaired with TIG welds. In this repair, metal was added to the "fingers" of the needle plate and now the plate no longer lies flat, a critical issue with this part. The solution is simple and fast—stretch the part slightly and the fingers will once again lie flat as in Figure 9-18 (bottom right). To do this, place a row of center-punch marks along the outer edges of the part. These punches stretch the part's outer edges enough to allow the repaired section to fall into its proper place.

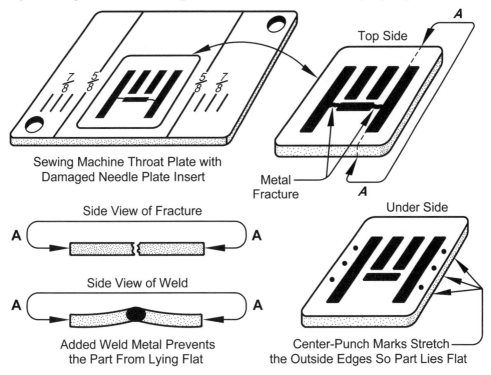

Figure 9-18. Stretching a section of work to flatten it.

Trimming Vinyl & Rubber

Many times rubber or vinyl sheet is glued to the metal base of a device to prevent the base from marring the surface it sits on or to prevent the base from sliding. Here is a simple method to trim the sheet vinyl or rubber after it has been glued to the base:

1. Use a router with a carbide bit intended for trimming laminate as in Figure 9-19. These bits have a small ball bearing on their lower end to guide the bit along the work edge. This technique is fast and produces professional results.

2. The best router action occurs when the bit is cutting upward as it leaves the work as in conventional—not climb—milling. Since router bits turn clockwise as viewed from above, you will want to go around the work in a counterclockwise direction.

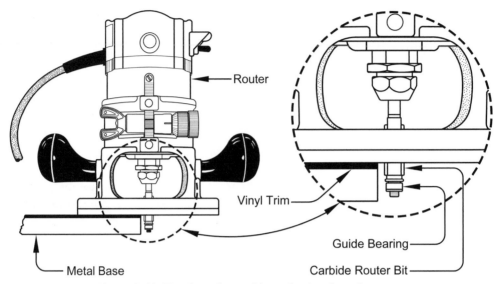

Figure 9-19. To edge a base with professional results, use a
router laminate trimming bit to trim the rubber or vinyl.

Whitney Punch Guides

Whitney punches and their imported clones are useful tools for putting small
holes in thin stock quickly and without burrs. If a series of hole patterns must
be punched, Figure 9-20 shows a two-step method to get the job done quickly
and accurately:

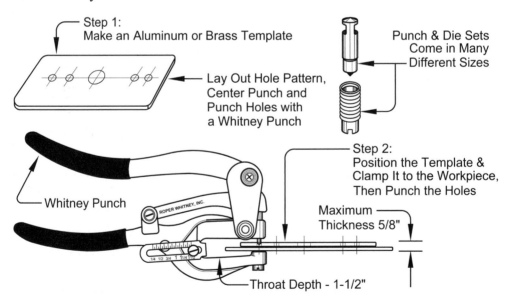

Figure 9-20. Making a hole layout template for a Whitney punch.

1. First, using thin metal—aluminum or brass—make a template and lay out
   the hole pattern on it, center punch, and then punch the holes in the

template with a Whitney punch. Because these punches have a center projection, you can locate the punch exactly on the center-punch mark.

2. Next, clamp the finished template in place and punch, then repeat this step for each set of holes needed. The template guides the Whitney punch to position the holes in the correct positions.

Section II – Threaded Fasteners

Introduction

Though there are hundreds of different sizes of fasteners available, most machinists find that they never have the size they need. This section presents some work-arounds for this common shop problem.

Shortening Screws & Bolts

There are many ways to shorten screws and bolts:

- *Hacksaws* work fine, but they leave a rough end that must be finished. The unwanted threads—since we don't care if they are damaged—can be clamped in a vise to secure the screw or bolt while sawing.

- *Bandsaws* are much faster than hacksaws for cutting screws and bolts, and they leave a smoother end. Bandsaws can cut hardened fasteners such as SHCSs, but because these fasteners have a hex-head socket, they will not lie flat on the bandsaw table. Also, they have a tendency to spin against the saw blade. To stop them from spinning, use a wood cradle to hold the screws and bolts as in Figure 9-21.

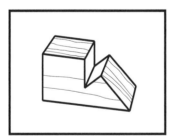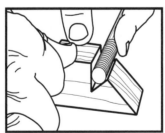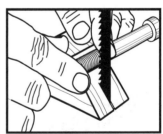

Figure 9-21. Using a wood cradle for bandsawing a SHCS. The wedge-shape of the cradle prevents the bolt from spinning when contacting the saw blade.

- *Multi-purpose pliers*, such as those in Figure 9-22, cut fasteners made of brass, aluminum and plastic. They do not work well on steel fasteners. If the thread-end of the fastener is screwed into the threads of the multi-purpose pliers, withdrawing the fastener through these threads straightens the end threads. No additional dressing is needed. The side of the multi-purpose pliers with the stamped markings is the side that the fastener should enter.

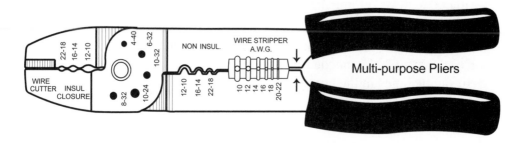

Figure 9-22. Multi-purpose pliers cut fasteners made of brass, aluminum and plastic.

- *Bolt cutters* and *nippers* cut plastic, brass, stainless steel and unhardened steel fasteners, but they leave a rough and jagged thread end. These tools are generally not a good choice when other methods are available.

- *Bolt shears* are perfect for when many hardened fasteners such as SHCSs must be cut. Figure 9-23 shows the parts needed to be cut to fabricate the shop-made bolt shears in Figure 9-25. Figure 9-24 has the step-by-step diagram, and written instructions follow the completed shears in Figure 9-25. With this easy-to-use shears, a single strike with a 5-pound hammer severs a bolt cleanly. The hard-face alloy welding rod, which is added to the inside edges of the bolt-shearing hole, is the key to the shears' strength and effectiveness.

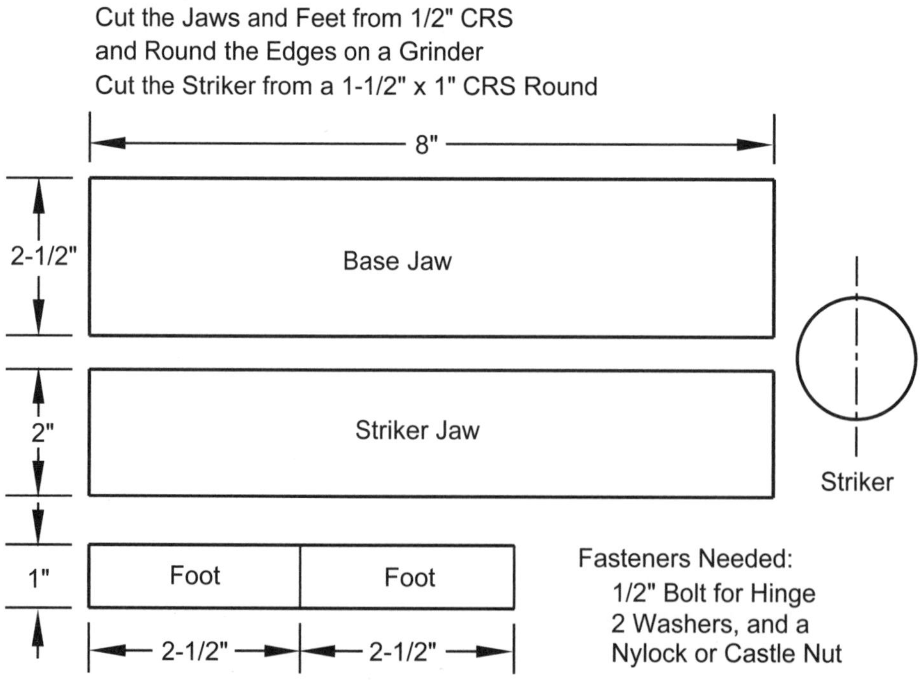

Cut the Jaws and Feet from 1/2" CRS
and Round the Edges on a Grinder
Cut the Striker from a 1-1/2" x 1" CRS Round

|←——————————— 8" ———————————→|

2-1/2"   Base Jaw

2"   Striker Jaw   Striker

1"   Foot   Foot   Fasteners Needed:
                                       1/2" Bolt for Hinge
   |←— 2-1/2" —→|←— 2-1/2" —→| 2 Washers, and a
                                       Nylock or Castle Nut

Figure 9-23. Parts needed to make the bolt shears shown in Figure 9-25.

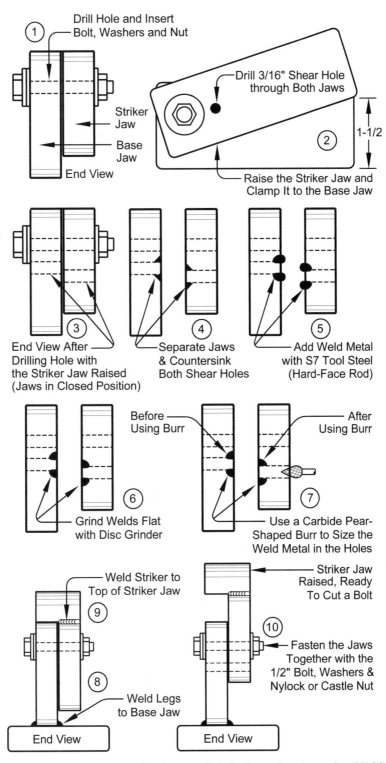

Figure 9-24. Steps to make the shop-made bolt shears for shortening SHCSs.

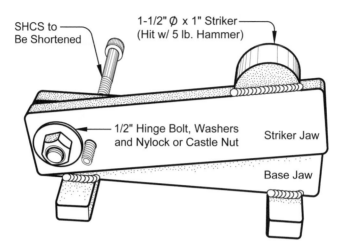

Figure 9-25. The completed bolt shears.

1. Prepare the CRS parts:

    - Cut the two sides or jaws, one $2\frac{1}{2} \times 8 \times \frac{1}{2}$ inch, one $2 \times 8 \times \frac{1}{2}$ inch and cut the two feet which are $1 \times 2\frac{1}{2} \times \frac{1}{2}$ inch.

    - Cut a half-cylinder from a $1\frac{1}{2}$-inch long $\times$ 1-inch CRS round for the striker.

2. Clamp the two sides, or jaws, of the bolt shears together, drill the hole for the $\frac{1}{2}$-inch hinge bolt, insert the bolt, add washers, and put on the nylock or castle nut.

3. Open the two sides of the bolt shear so the jaws are off-set by about $1\frac{1}{2}$-inch, clamp the sides together, and drill a shear hole for the bolts to be cut—a $\frac{3}{16}$-inch hole is used in this example. Drill the $\frac{3}{16}$-inch hole through both sides of the shear jaws at the same time so they will align properly.

4. Separate the two sides of the bolt shears and countersink the inside faces of both $\frac{3}{16}$-inch shear holes.

5. Using a TIG torch, add S-7 tool steel hard-face rod to the countersunk areas.

6. With a belt or disc grinder, grind the faces of the two shear holes flat.

7. Weld the feet to the base jaw positioning them as in Figure 9-25.

8. Run a $\frac{3}{16}$-inch pear-shaped carbide burr through the shear holes.

9. Weld the CRS striking half-cylinder to the top of the striker jaw as shown on the finished bolt shears in Figure 9-25.

10. Fasten the two jaws together with the $\frac{1}{2}$-inch hinge bolt, washers, and nylock or castle nut.

To shorten a fastener in the bolt shears, open the jaws, insert the fastener though the two holes in the shear jaws, place the shears on a solid surface and hit the striker with a 5-pound hammer. This bolt shears works because the severing faces are hard-as-welded and because the shock load is imposed on hardened SHCSs. These shears will not work as well on stainless steel fasteners of the same size as the fasteners will deform rather than fracture.

- *Abrasive wheels* are a good choice for shortening steel and hardened fasteners. These wheels leave fasteners with a relatively smooth end, needing only minor thread dressing.

- *Fixture for shortening smaller SHCSs* – The shop-made fixture for trimming small SHCSs in Figure 9-26 (top) can be made of steel or aluminum. The step in the face of the fixture insures that fasteners are all cut to the same length when the fixture is inserted against the jaws of a chuck. With this fixture, use a cutoff lathe tool with lubricant to cut the screw, then put a new chamfer on the end of the screw threads.

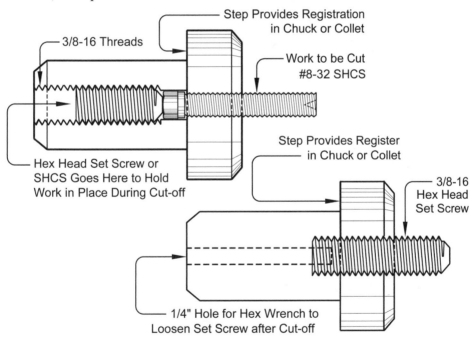

Figure 9-26. Fixture for trimming SHCSs (top) and set screws (bottom).

- *Fixture for shortening hex head set screws* – A variation of the fixture in the top of Figure 9-26, this shop-made fixture uses a step in the hole inside the fixture so the hex screw does not become unscrewed by cutoff tool forces. Cut the screw with a lathe cutoff tool using lubricant and put a new chamfer on the end of the screw. See Figure 9-26 (bottom).

- *Fixture for shortening larger SHCSs* – This fixture is made from a split bushing which holds the SHCSs in either a three-jaw chuck or in a collet without damaging the screw threads. See Figure 9-27. Shortening is done with a carbide lathe tool. Be sure to put a new chamfer on the end of the threads.

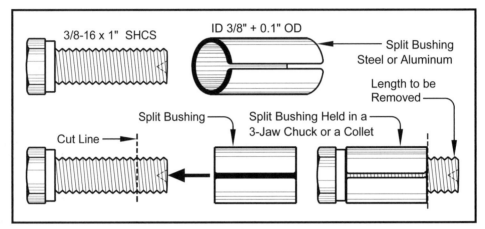

Figure 9-27. A split bushing makes easy work of trimming SHCSs in the lathe.

Permanently Securing a Bolt to a Plate

When a bolt must never come off a plate, try either of the two welding methods in Figure 9-28.

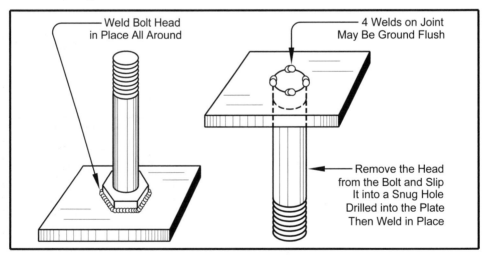

Figure 9-28. Two methods for securing a bolt to a plate that use MIG or TIG welds.

Marking Bolts

When bolts must be easily identified, fill the hollow depression in the bolt head with paint as in Figure 9-29. This method was popular with automakers to mark bolts that had been checked or replaced.

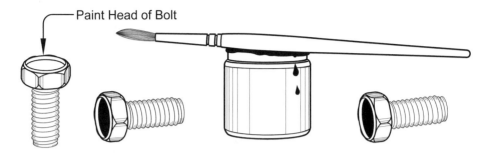

Figure 9-29. Paint in the bolt-head depression identifies the bolt as checked or replaced.

Bolt Locking Method

When a bolt must lock in place, yet also must be removable, try the method shown in Figure 9-30. It uses a notch cut out of the bolt head which locks up against a SHCS. This example is the center bolt of a tilt table that holds work for milling.

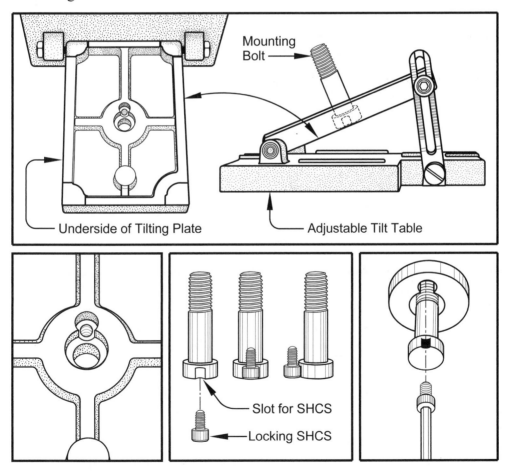

Figure 9-30. A removable locking bolt.

Section III – Repair Methods

Splicing Nichrome Wire

Nichrome resistance wire, which is used in heating elements and for foam cutters, can be repaired by splicing the broken ends together with stainless steel repair tubing as shown in Figure 9-31. Bend over the short wire ends and crimp the tubing. The wire cutters on Vise-Grip pliers are perfect for this job because they crimp more than they cut, and that is what's needed here.

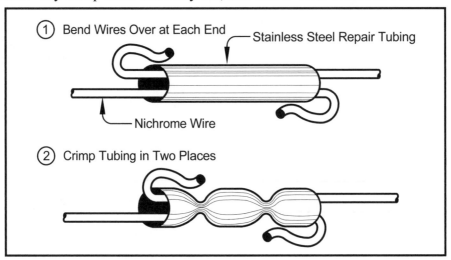

Figure 9-31. Repairing broken Nichrome wire with stainless steel repair tubing.

Stubbing Out Shafts

When the keyways on a large machine have been torn out of the shaft, and the shaft and the machine are too expensive to replace, the shaft can be repaired by machining off the damaged end section and adding on a new repair stub.

Here are the steps:

1. Machine the replacement repair stub shown in Figure 9-32 (right). The rounded corners at the bottom of the stub reduce stress concentrations.

2. Place the damaged shaft in a lathe with a steady rest supporting the shaft on the lathe tailstock end. This arrangement provides access to the damaged end of the shaft.

3. Center the shaft in the steady rest using a DTI.

4. Remove the damaged section of the shaft using a cutoff tool and lubricant. Alternatively, the damaged section may be cut off with a bandsaw before going into the lathe.

5. Prepare the shaft's damaged end for its new stub by boring a center hole and chamfering its edges to help the stub slide into place. To provide a

space for trapped air when the stub goes in, the hole is made deeper than the end of the stub. The corners at the bottom of the hole are also rounded to reduce stress concentrations. See Figure 9-32 (left).

6. Bevel both the outer diameter of the repair shaft and the damaged shaft to allow for a weld which will hold the new stub in place.

7. Remove the damaged shaft from the lathe and block it up to secure the new stub. Hold and position the shaft so the new stub can be driven in with a sledge hammer.

8. Heat the damaged shaft with one or two oxyacetylene rosebud torches while cooling the repair stub in dry ice. Once the heated and cooled parts are put into position, the repair stub must be driven into place without delay.

9. While one machinist inserts the repair stub into the shaft hole and holds it in position, one or two other machinists drive the repair stub into place with sledge hammers. The repair stub is larger than the shaft so that if the repair stub is not perfectly seated, it can still be turned down to match the outer diameter of the original shaft.

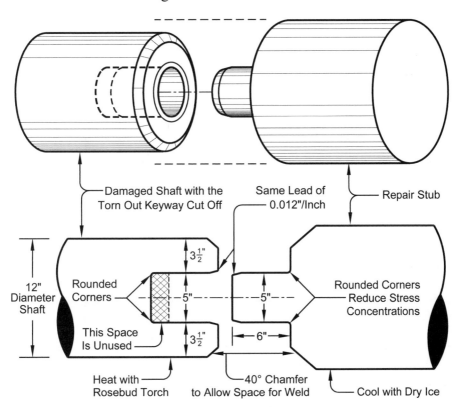

Figure 9-32. When a keyway is torn out of a machinery shaft, by making a repair stub, a new shaft end can be added and a new keyway cut.

10. The stub and original shafts are tack welded at the 3, 6, 9, and 12 o'clock positions. Next, the shafts are welded all-around and then turned down so that the two shafts are the same diameter.

11. Cut the new keyway or keyways in the new stub.

Thread Repair Tools

There are two ways damaged threads can be repaired. One method cuts away damaged thread metal that is not within the thread profile. This is easy to perform, but weakens the threads. The other method actually moves the damaged thread metal back into place and does *not* remove metal or weaken the threads. The following list details which tool does what.

- *Repair dies*, also called *rethreading dies* – There are a couple issues with these tools:

  - There are usually two differences between repair dies and threading dies: the purpose of threading dies is to cut threads initially, while the purpose of repair dies is to fix damaged threads. Repair dies are often made in square or hex outlines so that they can be turned with a socket, box or an open-end wrench in tight quarters where the long handles of a die wrench will not fit. But, as part of the endless dumbing-down, cheapening, and rationalization of products, repair dies are now being marketed as *threading dies* although repair dies cannot be adjusted for wear or tweaked for a particular thread OD because they lack adjustment screws. Also, because they are shaped to accommodate open-end wrenches and socket wrenches, many repair dies will not fit into a conventional die wrench. See Figure 9-33.

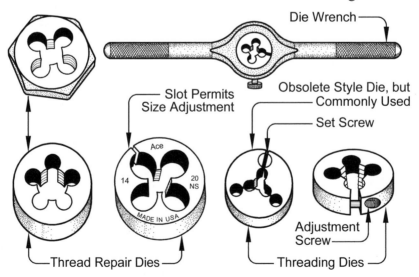

Figure 9-33.Thread repair dies, threading dies and a die wrench.

- Repair dies and threading dies should be used for repairing damaged threads only when the threads are too small to use other, better repair methods, or the right tools are not available. Both of these dies cut away thread areas outside the proper thread profile, weakening them. But these dies *are* excellent for cleaning dirt and paint out of undamaged threads.

- *Thread Repair Files* – The two most common repair files for inch-based threads are shown in Figure 9-34. Similar files are available for pipe and metric threads. Compact for field repairs, each file has eight thread pitches. Start the thread file ahead of the damaged area and use the existing good threads to guide it into the damaged threads. These files must be used carefully or they will cause more damage than they repair.

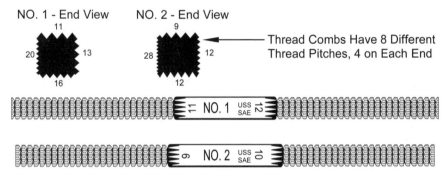

Figure 9-34. Thread repair files from Reiff & Nestor Co.
File № 1 has teeth for 11, 12, 13, 14, 16, 18, 20 and 24 threads/inch.
File № 2 has teeth for 9,10, 12, 16, 20, 27, 28 and 32 threads/inch.

- *Universal Thread File* or *Thread Repair Comb* – This tool, shown in Figure 9-35, looks like a file but it both files and pulls threads back into place. One size fits all 60° threads, inch or metric. This tool is more forgiving than the thread repair files pictured in Figure 9-34 and does less damage than a three-cornered file.

Figure 9-35. Thread repair comb.

- *OD Thread Repair Chasers* – The thread repair chaser shown in Figure 9-36 (left) has two hardened tines which fit into the threads. If the threads are not too badly damaged, this tool will *push* the threads back into position, reforming them. Thread repair chasers have a couple advantages:

- They handle a wide range of thread diameters and work on both inch and metric threads.

- They produce better results than a thread file for threads with light damage, and using them requires much less skill.

The heavy-duty repair chaser in Figure 9-36 (right) is often the best choice of all tools for threads larger than 24 threads/inch because it has a rigid frame, a large handle, and can remove damaged thread metal. To provide the proper relief for the comb to work, the chaser must only be turned clockwise. If the damaged threads can be rotated, this tool can be used in tight quarters. To use, rotate the tool one-quarter turn in one direction, then rotate the tool *and thread shaft* one-quarter turn in the other direction and repeat. The chaser carries 6 different combs, each with 4 thread sizes. Use these tools with heavy cutting oil. Do *not* use these thread repair tools on machines under power.

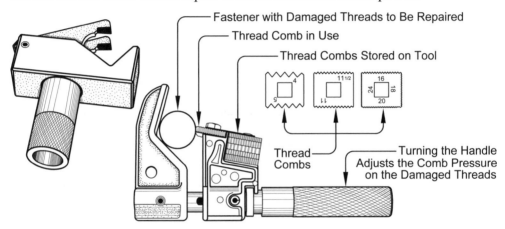

Figure 9-36. OD thread repair chasers, light duty (left) and heavy duty (right).

- *ID Thread Repair Chasers* – These tools, shown in Figure 9-37, are more difficult to use than the OD thread chasers above. ID thread repair chasers require more physical strength to keep the combs working and the tool on the thread diameter.

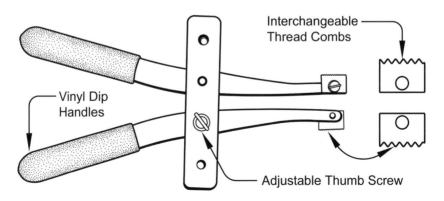

Figure 9-37. ID thread repair chasers.

Other than a thread tap, this is the only alternative for ID thread repair. Replaceable combs are available in both inch and metric threads. This tool removes thread metal and weakens threads.

- *Thread Reforming Tool* – Figure 9-38 shows the only other thread repair tool that moves threads back into place. Threads as hard as 50 R_C can be restored with this shop-made tool. This thread reformer does not seem to have a commercial version.

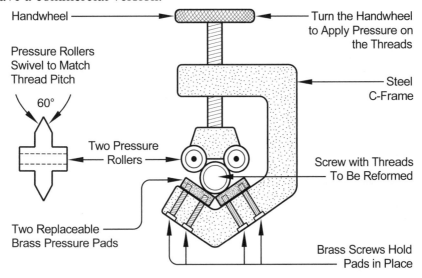

Figure 9-38. Shop-made thread reforming tool.

- *Thread Repair Chisels* – These chisels, shown in Figure 9-39, do not remove metal, they move it back into place and reshape it by using the undamaged—or repaired—threads as a guide. The diameter of the arc on these chisels must be 20–30% larger than the diameter of the threads to be repaired, and the chisels's cutting edge must be stoned off so that the chisel point never reaches the thread root. Because the chisels have a 60° included angle that matches that of the threads, they fit snugly between the thread walls of undamaged threads. Most machinists make themselves a set of four chisels to fit most thread diameters. Figure 9-74 in the section on shop-made tools later in this chapter shows how to make these thread repair chisels from cold chisels.

To use one of these chisels, support the rod, shaft or bolt to be repaired on a set of wooden V-blocks to prevent further thread damage while you perform repairs. Place the chisel ¼ turn away from the damage and tap the chisel as you walk it into the damaged area. Alternatively, you can have someone else slowly rotate the threads while you keep the chisel vertical and tap it. You will need to perform several passes to move all of the damaged threads into place.

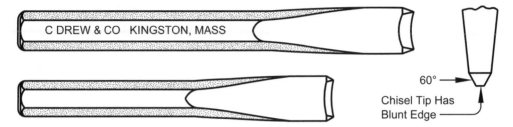

Figure 9-39. Thread repair chisels.

Replacing Gaskets

When a gasket needs to be made from roll or sheet goods, and a pattern is needed to cut it, place paper over the existing gasket face and make a rubbing with a soft pencil to transfer the pattern. This paper pattern is then used to cut the new gasket. See Figure 9-40.

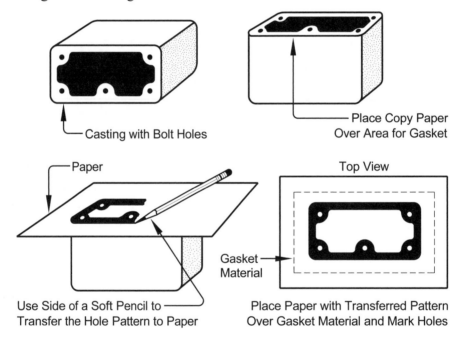

Figure 9-40. Obtaining a gasket pattern by making a pencil rubbing.

Gasket Compounds

Although some applications require traditional gasket materials, many original manufacturers now use formed-in-place silicone rubber gaskets. With this method no patterns are required, just apply a bead of the silicone rubber where the gasket should go and press the parts together. Do not pull up the bolts too tightly or the uncured compound will be squeezed out. Most gasket compounds cure overnight at room temperature.

Gasket-forming compounds offer many advantages, they:

- Eliminate gasket cutting.

- Fill voids of up to 0.25 inches.

- Are insensitive to gasket interface flatness.

- Work well with flimsy sheet metal covers where uneven bolting forces and poor fit-up tend to cause leaks with solid gaskets.

- Flex with temperature changes at the gasket interface and maintain a seal.

- Come in tubes like toothpaste for small jobs and in cartridges for use in caulking guns for large jobs.

- Eliminate the need to stock gaskets.

Two important considerations in selecting a gasket compound are:

- The maximum and minimum temperatures on the work.

- Their chemical compatibility with gasoline, oil or other potentially active solvents which may come in contact with the gasket.

Section IV – Adding Security

Vandal-Resistant vs. Tamper-Proof Screws & Bolts

Over the last decade, as screw-head design patents expired and screw manufacturing moved off-shore, many more manufacturers have entered the vandal and tamper-proof fastener business. With this increase in suppliers, the availability of the bits needed to remove tamper-proof screws has increased as well. Now that local hardware and budget tool stores are selling sets of these bits for the price of a cup of coffee, what were once *tamper-proof* screws have now sadly become merely *vandal-resistant* screws.

Many screw designs including Torx-pin, six lobe-pin, hex-pin, Allen-pin, drilled spanner, Triwing and Phillps-pin and other designs have been compromised by these changes. Now, more tamper-resistant designs must be used for genuine security.

New Security Screw-Head Designs

Bryce Fastener, in Gilbert, Arizona, offers three new screw-head designs that provide increased security over the older, and now compromised, designs. See Figure 9-41.

In order of increasing security and cost, here are three Bryce fasteners:

- *Penta-Plus* screws and bits are more secure than other tamper-proof screws because the bits are sold only to registered users and are not for sale on the open market.

- *Key-Lok* screws and bits are a big step up the security scale because each user receives his own registered unique head design and matching bits. There are millions of *Key-Lok* head designs and they are secure because no other manufacturer makes them or supplies bits for them.

- *Key-Rex* screws and bits offer even more security because not only does each user receive his own registered screw head design and matching bits, the screw head design is more complex than the *Key-Lok* design.

A full array of these Bryce fasteners are available:

- #3-56 to ⅝-11 inch, or M2–M12 metric sizes.

- Both button and flat head machine screws, as well as sheet metal screws.

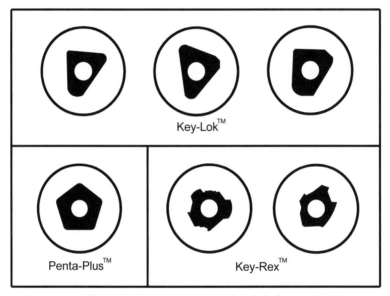

Figure 9-41. Security screw head designs.

Additional Ways to Improve Screw & Bolt Security

Here are several old machinist tricks that frustrate the average criminal:

- Drive a slightly oversized ball bearing into the hex depression of a hex head screw or bolt. Although this method retards the removal of button-head cap screws because pliers slide off their heads and cannot get a grip, countersunk SHCSs with ball bearings in their hex holes are very difficult to remove. See Figure 9-42.

- Adding Locktite to threads adds another level of difficulty in screw or bolt removal. Screws and bolts secured with red Locktite can only be removed by heating them to destroy the adhesive bond of the Locktite.

- Using fasteners with left-handed threads always presents another challenge to their removal by vandals.

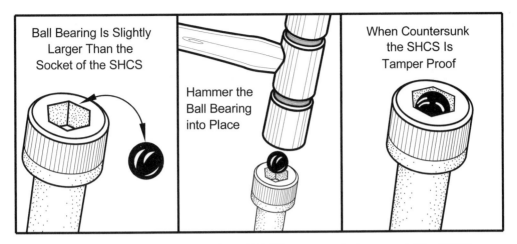

Figure 9-42. Blocking the hex socket of SHCSs prevents their removal. The SHCSs must be countersunk to prevent the use of pliers to remove them.

Security Nuts

When the nut end of a security fastener is accessible to the public, *Penta* nuts are a good choice. Because of their cone shape and the fact that these fasteners are hardened, pliers and Vise-Grips slide right off their sloping sides, preventing their removal. See Figure 9-43.

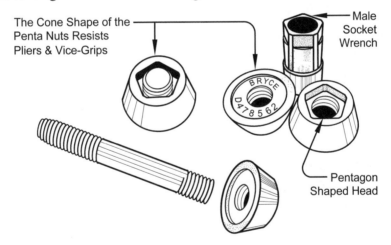

Figure 9-43. Penta nuts.

Snap-Off Head Bolts

This hex-head, one-time-use security bolt is nearly as secure as a weld. The bolt is installed in a countersunk hole, and when tightened, the bolt head snaps off just below the surface of the workpiece making the fastener inaccessible. With this design of security bolt, when the head snaps off, it is automatically tightened to the proper torque. To make it *really* permanent, place a plug weld over the top of the snapped-off fastener.

Many times it is important to have an indication that a fastener has been tampered with, and this snap-off bolt does just that. Also, because of its unique design, if a vandal or thief somehow manages to remove this bolt, he will not have a matching replacement, an obvious clue that someone has been tampering. See Figure 9-44.

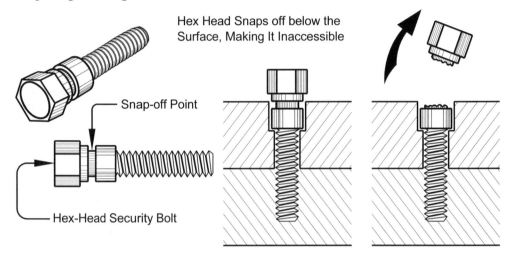

Figure 9-44. Hex-head security bolts with snap-off heads.
The heads are easy to snap off, but the bolts are difficult to remove.

If for some reason you need to remove a snap-off security bolt, there are two different methods:

• TIG weld a shaft to the stub in the countersunk hole and apply Vise-Grip pliers to the new shaft to unscrew the bolt.

• Use a bolt disintegrator—an EDM machine dedicated to removing broken bolts and taps.

Since these methods are conspicuous to employ—sparks and flames—and require equipment that most thieves do not carry around with them, snap-off head bolts are very secure.

Securing Cylindrical Assemblies

Using a roll pin in a blind hole, as shown in Figure 9-45, provides some tamper resistance, but using a dowel pin in a blind hole is even more secure because dowel pins are hardened and much more difficult to remove or drill out.

Tip: Be careful when installing dowel pins in a blind hole. If there is no path for air trapped at the bottom of the hole to escape, the dowel can shoot back out with considerable force. Applying a small flat to the side of the dowel pin with a disc or belt sander solves this problem.

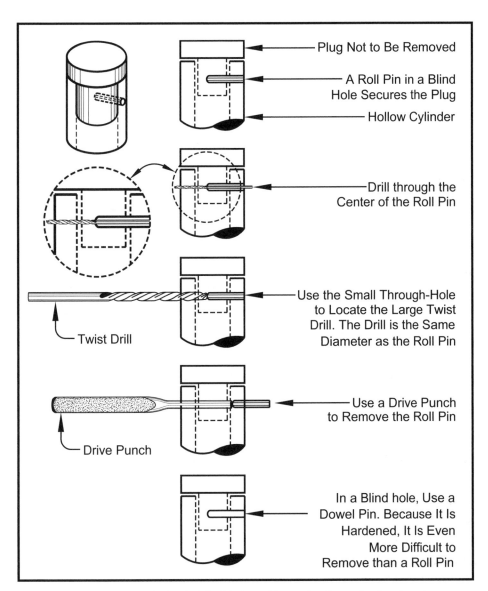

Figure 9-45. Roll pins in blind holes add security, but using hardened
dowel pins in blind holes increases the difficulty of removing the pin even more.

Securing Nuts

Preventing the removal of nuts from threaded fasteners is a common requirement. Figure 9-46 shows four ways to do this:

- Use a steel wedge to secure the nut.
- Mushroom over the end of the bolt itself.
- Weld the nut in place.
- Apply a weld bead at the end of the bolt.

Use a Steel Wedge to Secure the Nut

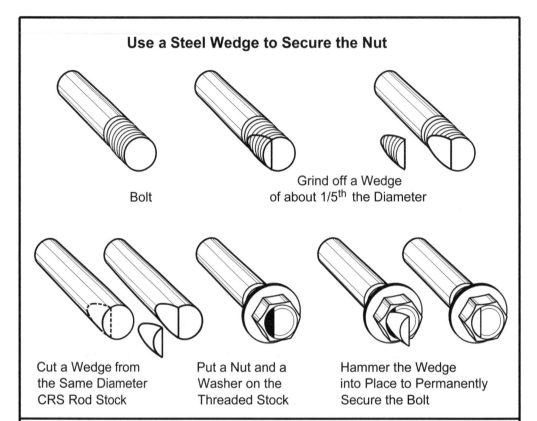

Bolt

Grind off a Wedge
of about 1/5th the Diameter

Cut a Wedge from
the Same Diameter
CRS Rod Stock

Put a Nut and a
Washer on the
Threaded Stock

Hammer the Wedge
into Place to Permanently
Secure the Bolt

Mushroom Over the End of the Bolt to Secure the Nut

 To Secure a Nut on a Shaft
without the Use of Electric
Welding, First Cut 2 Slots on
the End of the Bolt, then

 Heat the End of the
Threads to Dull Red
and Hammer them
into a Mushroom

Weld the Nut in Place

 To Prevent Movement of
a Nut, Apply a Weld Bead
to the Threads and the Nut

Weld the End of a Bolt

 To Prevent Nut Removal
but Still Allow Adjustment,
Apply a Weld Bead to
the End of the Bolt

Figure 9-46. Several methods of securing nuts.

All but the last method for securing nuts are permanent and require the destruction of the nut and the fastener for removal. The first method is used by a major pump manufacturer to prevent customer tampering.

Subtle Workpiece Marking

Because the same part may be worked on by several different machinists or even several different shops, many machinists inconspicuously mark the section of the part they repaired. This avoids the question of who did the repairs. To do this, marking punches can be made from drive pin punches of ⅛-inch diameter or less which are modified to produce a distinctive mark. A machinist usually only reveals his marking code when a customer suggests that his work was done by another or vice versa. See Figure 9-47.

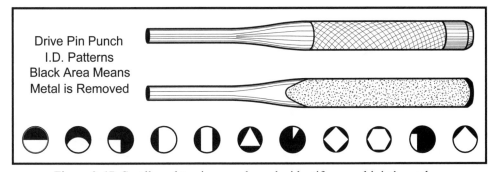

Figure 9-47. Small unobtrusive punch marks identify a machinist's work.

Section V – Shop-Made or Modified Tools

Lead Hammer Mold

This mold for making lead hammers was welded from two steel pipe reducer adapters, a pipe nipple, and a heavy-duty welded gate hinge. A length of iron pipe goes through the pipe nipple and then lead is poured in though the side hole. See Figure 9-48.

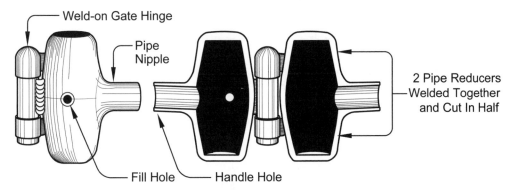

Figure 9-48. Mold for making lead hammers.

To prevent the lead from tinning the steel mold and sticking to it, either dust the mold with chalk dust or soot the mold with an oxyacetylene torch. Should the mold leak lead through its seams, put one or two sheets of copy paper between the mold halves for a seal. The molten lead will burn away the interior paper and fill the mold, but the seal will hold.

Molds for Lead Pads & Rod Stock

Machine shops often need to make aluminum molds for casting lead pads and lead rod stock for solder. Since lead does not adhere to aluminum, no release agent is needed to get the lead out of the molds, but the molds must have 1–2° sloping sides, called *draft*, and no undercuts or the rods will not release from the molds. See Figure 9-49.

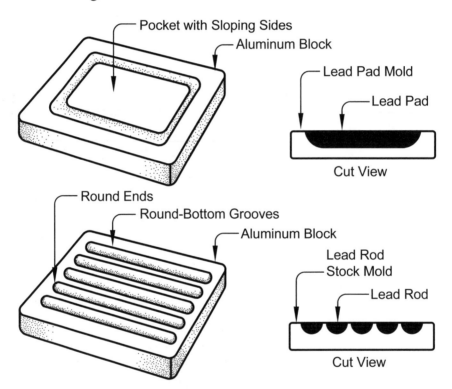

Figure 9-49. Aluminum molds for lead pads and rod stock.
These molds are normally much longer than those pictured.

Driving Hex-Head Fasteners

Tightening or loosening large numbers of hex-head fasteners can be made easy by adapting a hex wrench to do the job. Start with a hex wrench of the proper size, then cut off the bent "L" portion with a grinder or cutoff wheel and use the straight section in a variable-speed reversible drill as shown in Figure 9-50.

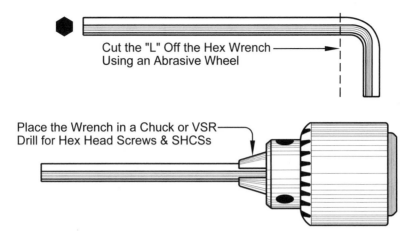

Figure 9-50. A hex wrench in the chuck of a variable-speed reversible drill makes short work of tightening or loosening hex fasteners.

Pin Vises

Pin vises have many sizes and uses, and in most shops they are underutilized. The function of a pin vise is to *hold* items too small for human hands to grasp. Here are some examples of what a pin vise can hold:

- *Diamond burrs* – Useful for small adjustments in metal, ceramic or glass, diamond burrs are rubbed or wiped across the surface to be reduced, taking off just a small amount of material. Using a burr in a pin vise rather than in a high-speed grinder is a much less aggressive way to use burrs.

- *Twist drills* – In a pin vise, twist drills are used to deburr larger holes when a countersink of the proper size is not available.

- *Small taps* – When applying threads, small taps used in a pin vise provide a sensitive feel. This reduces the chance of snapping off a tap in the work.

- *Gage pins* – Used for checking a hole size.

- *Small tapered* and *dowel pin reamers* – These reamers require handles larger than their own small stubby shanks. Pin vises are perfect for holding these reamers.

- *Swiss needle* and *diamond files* – These files are usually sold with vinyl handles or no handles at all. The vinyl-dip handle coatings must be removed from Swiss needle files in order to fit them into the chuck of a pin vise. Remove the vinyl with a mat or utility knife. Because most Swiss needle file shapes must be held at a specific orientation to the work, many machinists install the file in the pin vise and then grind a small flat on the front of the vise. This modification allows the machinist to *feel* the position of the file. See Figure 9-51.

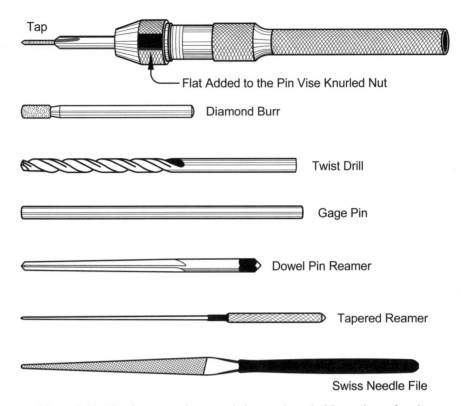

Tap

Flat Added to the Pin Vise Knurled Nut

Diamond Burr

Twist Drill

Gage Pin

Dowel Pin Reamer

Tapered Reamer

Swiss Needle File

Figure 9-51. Pin vises come in several sizes and can hold a variety of tools.

Sharpening Nippers

Dulled steel nipper blades are easy to sharpen with silicon carbide paper wrapped around a mandrel. Pull the silicon carbide paper so it is tight around the mandrel and slide the mandrel back and forth along the nipper's cutting edge. See Figure 9-52.

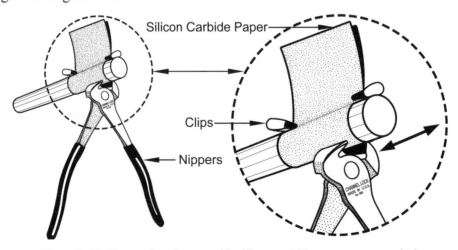

Silicon Carbide Paper

Clips

Nippers

Figure 9-52. Sharpening nippers with silicon carbide paper on a mandrel.

Carpenters' Square Alignment

While a carpenters' square is a relatively crude measurement tool compared with an engineers' square, for very large work it may be the only tool of the proper size. But before use, check its alignment. If it is out of square, follow the steps in Figure 9-53 to correct the alignment. The only tools you'll need for this are a round-nosed punch, a ball-peen hammer, a straight edge and a pencil.

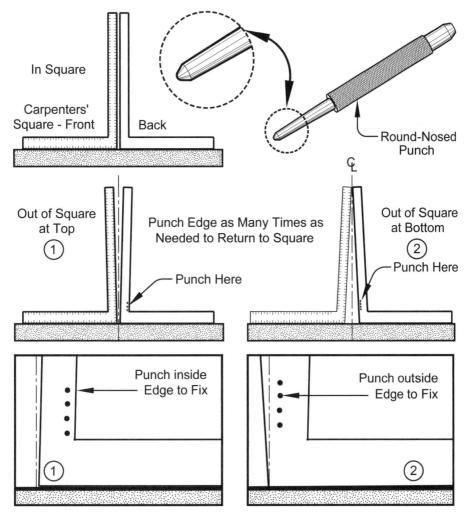

Figure 9-53. Checking and correcting the alignment of a carpenters' square.

Air Wrench Attachments

Air wrenches turn reamers, taps, large drills and countersinks at low speeds with high torque. To connect attachments to an air wrench, use either chucks adapted to the air wrenches' square drive, or square-drive adapters welded directly to the tool. Both choices work well.

To make an adapter between the air wrench square drive and the attachment, begin with an impact socket wrench that fits the square drive on the air wrench. Put the socket in the three-jaw chuck of a lathe, and using a carbide tool, cut off the end of the socket which holds a nut or bolt. Now you have an adapter ready to be TIG welded or brazed onto the air wrench attachment. Imported air wrenches are inexpensive and reasonably durable, but because they usually cannot be repaired, they are disposable. See Figure 9-54.

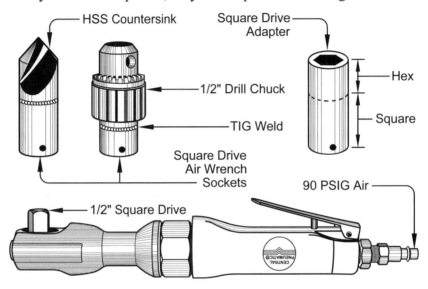

Figure 9-54. Air wrench alone (bottom), HSS countersink (top left) and drill chuck with square drive adapter (top right).

Angle Blocks

Large aluminum shop-made angle blocks, though they are not hardened, are handy for making custom fixtures for milling, soldering, brazing and welding. Tapped holes in the blocks are for mounting work. See Figure 9-55.

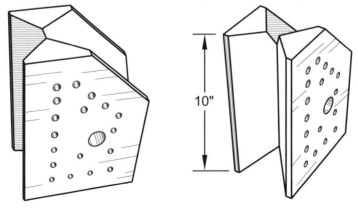

Figure 9-55. Shop-made aluminum angle blocks with tapped mounting holes.

Angle Gage

A simple, but accurate, shop-made angle gage appears in Figure 9-56. Using this gage, angles can be set or measured. Here is the formula:

The unknown angle = {tan^{-1} (caliper measurement − 0.1875) / 6}

In other words, the unknown angle is the angle whose tangent is equal to the caliper measurement less 0.1875 (to compensate for the diameter of the dowel pins) divided by 6. Using the inverse tangent function on a scientific calculator is the fastest way to determine this angle.

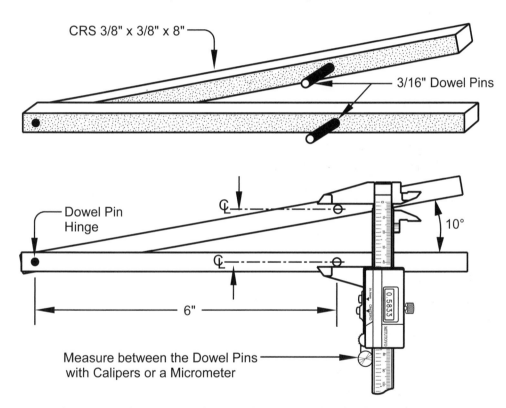

CRS 3/8" x 3/8" x 8"

3/16" Dowel Pins

Dowel Pin Hinge

10°

6"

Measure between the Dowel Pins with Calipers or a Micrometer

0.5833

Figure 9-56. Shop-made angle gage alone (top) and with calipers (bottom).

Micrometer Bridge

A shop-made *micrometer bridge* provides support for a depth micrometer so measurements that would otherwise be hard to make become simple and accurate. This long, rectangular bridge is approximately 1½-inches wide and about 12-inches long, but the size can vary according to your needs. The bridge can be machined in one piece or in two pieces fastened together. See Figure 9-57.

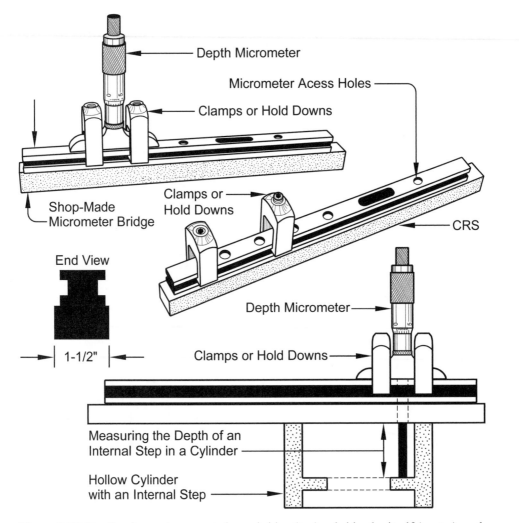

Figure 9-57. Depth micrometer mounted on a bridge (top), a bridge by itself (center), and the schematic shown measuring the depth of an internal step in a cylinder (bottom).

Hole Diameter Measuring Tool

Figure 9-58 shows another simple shop-made tool. This one is a fixture used for measuring the diameter of small holes with dial or digital calipers. The following steps explain how to use this tool:

1. Insert the tapered rod into its sleeve.

2. Push the end of the tapered rod into the hole of unknown size until the rod can go no farther.

3. Lock the sleeve against the tapered rod using the SHCS.

4. Remove the tool from the hole and measure the base of the rod extending from the sleeve with a dial caliper. This is the hole diameter.

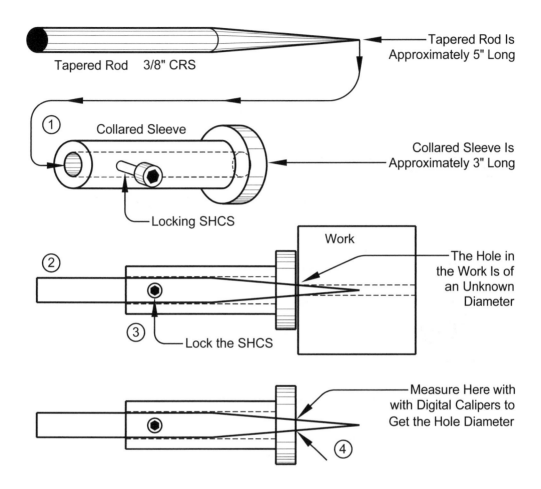

Figure 9-58. Shop-made hole diameter measuring tool.

Brass- or Bronze-Jawed Padded Pliers

There are two methods for making these padded-jaw pliers. Method 1 uses a brass insert brazed to the jaws and Method 2 uses silicon bronze TIG weld filler metal applied to line the jaws. But, before beginning either approach, the jaws of the pliers need to be ground down to make room for the new jaw material. This step must be done or the pliers will not close properly. See Figure 9-59.

Notice that the edges of the new added jaw metal are slightly rounded so that when the pliers are used to bend materials such as piano wire, high stresses at the bend point are not induced. High stress at a single point can lead to cracking and failure, while a long, gradual bend will not causes stresses. Padded-jaw pliers can also be used to straighten threaded rods without damaging them.

Making Padded-Jaw Pliers - Method 1

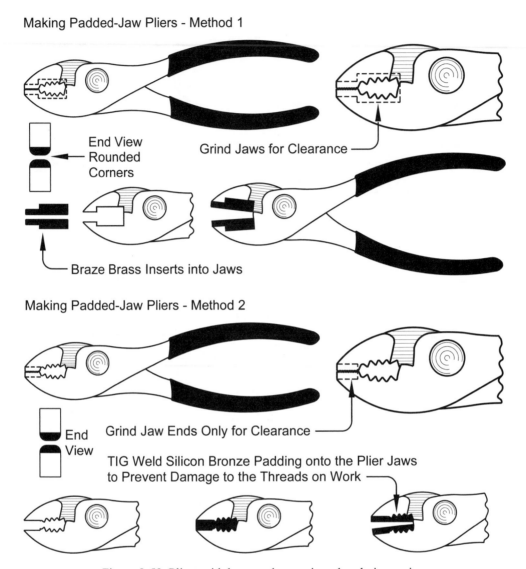

Figure 9-59. Pliers with brass or bronze jaws bend piano wire
and straighten bent threaded rods without damaging the threads.

Shop-Made Diamond Dresser for Grinding Wheels

Figure 9-60 shows a design for an easy-to-make diamond wheel dresser. Except for the knurled aluminum knob on the dresser screw, all the metal stock is CRS.

The tip of the factory-supplied steel shaft, which holds the mounted ⅓-carat dressing diamond, is cut off, and then a step is turned on the end of the short shaft which holds the diamond so it can be soldered to its diamond dresser screw. The dressing fixture itself is made in three pieces: the base, the guide rail, and the diamond mounting bar.

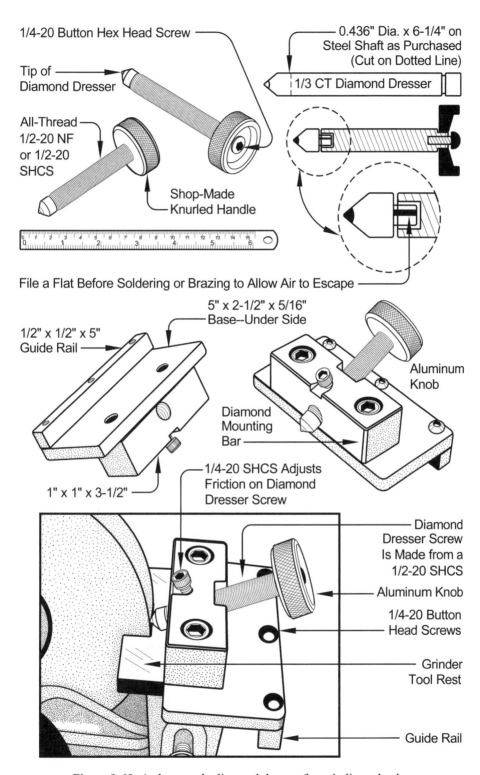

1/4-20 Button Hex Head Screw

Tip of Diamond Dresser

All-Thread 1/2-20 NF or 1/2-20 SHCS

Shop-Made Knurled Handle

0.436" Dia. x 6-1/4" on Steel Shaft as Purchased (Cut on Dotted Line)

1/3 CT Diamond Dresser

File a Flat Before Soldering or Brazing to Allow Air to Escape

5" x 2-1/2" x 5/16" Base--Under Side

1/2" x 1/2" x 5" Guide Rail

Aluminum Knob

Diamond Mounting Bar

1" x 1" x 3-1/2"

1/4-20 SHCS Adjusts Friction on Diamond Dresser Screw

Diamond Dresser Screw Is Made from a 1/2-20 SHCS

Aluminum Knob

1/4-20 Button Head Screws

Grinder Tool Rest

Guide Rail

Figure 9-60. A shop-made diamond dresser for grinding wheels.

Securing Magnets

The neodynium magnets in Figure 9-61 support up to 1300 times their own weight and are many times used to replace weaker and less expensive samarium-cobalt magnets. Neodynium magnets are available as cubes, discs, cylinders, blocks, spheres, bars and rings. Most of these magnets are nickel plated to protect their soft compressed metal powder. Many machinists find them useful for holding soft vise jaws and milling machine parallels in place. Here are three good methods for securing these disc-shaped magnets to soft jaws:

- *Press-fit into a slightly undersized hole* – This is a good method if the proper size twist drill is available.

- *Press-fit into a slightly oversized hole* – Using a piece of copper wire as a shim secures the magnet. You may adjust the thickness of the wire shim by flattening it with a hammer. When the magnet is pressed into place, cut off the protruding wire length with diagonal wire cutters or a nipper.

- *Fill a slightly oversized hole with 5-minute epoxy* – Press the magnet in place and wipe off the excess epoxy which flows out the sides of the hole. This method can also be used to secure magnets in parallels. Do not use epoxy filled with magnetic materials since it will cluster around the magnet.

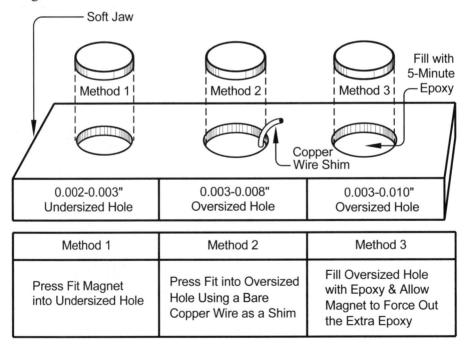

Method 1	Method 2	Method 3
Press Fit Magnet into Undersized Hole	Press Fit into Oversized Hole Using a Bare Copper Wire as a Shim	Fill Oversized Hole with Epoxy & Allow Magnet to Force Out the Extra Epoxy

Figure 9-61.Three ways to secure disc magnets into metal parts.

Roll-Pin Punches

There are three different tools used to drive roll pins out of work without damaging either the work, the holes for the roll pins, or the pins themselves:

- Commercial roll-pin drive punches
- Shop-made step punches
- Dowel pins

All of these methods work fine when the removal tool and the roll pin sizes are matched, but if the proper size of commercial roll-pin punch, shown in Figure 9-62 (top), is not available, and more than one pin must be removed, using the durable shop-made punch in Figure 9-62 (middle) is a good alternative. This punch can be made from O-1 steel, then hardened and tempered. If you are driving an installed roll pin out using a dowel pin, chamfer the tip of the dowel pin and reduce the dowel pin diameter slightly with emery cloth in the lathe so the punch will slip in and out of the hole easily. See Figure 9-62 (bottom).

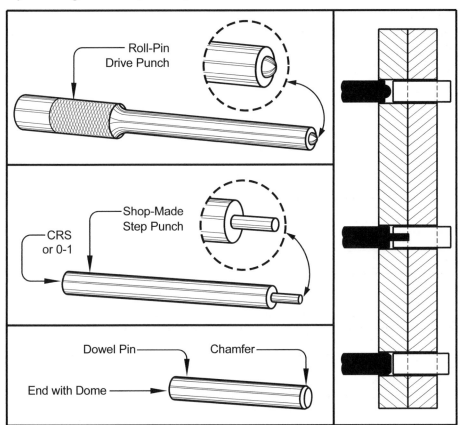

Figure 9-62. Three tools for removing a roll pin without
damage to the work, the hole or the roll pin.

Shop-made Scrapers

Shop-made scrapers are easily made from old screwdrivers and carbide lathe cutting tool inserts as shown in Figure 9-63. To make these scrapers:

1. Check the hardness of the screwdriver shaft with a file at the point where the screw driver tip will be cut off. If the file bites into the shaft and cuts it, the shaft is soft enough to cut, drill and tap, so proceed to Step 5. Otherwise, the screwdriver shaft is too hard—probably a chrome-vanadium alloy—and must be annealed. In this case, go to Step 2.

2. Make up the three aluminum heat sinks of either of the two styles shown in Figure 9-64. Drill the center hole in each heat sink the *same* size as the screwdriver shaft so the body of the heat sink will have full contact with the shaft. These heat sinks will prevent the screwdriver handle from melting because of the oxyacetylene heat. Using three separate heat sinks instead of one large one works better in choking off the heat flow in the screwdriver shaft.

3. Install the three heat sinks on the screwdriver shaft, spacing them as shown in Figure 9-64.

4. Heat slightly more than ½ inch of the end of the screwdriver shaft to cherry red, and as soon as the color is reached, plunge the shaft into dry sand. Cover the rest of the shaft and the heat sinks with more sand and let them cool to room temperature.

5. Cut off the old screwdriver tip with a carbide lathe tool while holding the screwdriver shaft in a 5C collet, or remove the tip with an abrasive cutoff wheel. Whatever method you use, be sure to leave a square tip on the screwdriver shaft. In a lathe, center drill and tap the end of the shaft.

6. Use a button-head hex screw to secure the insert cutter.

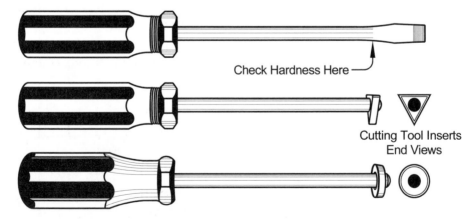

Figure 9-63. Scrapers made from old screwdrivers and lathe cutting tool carbide inserts.

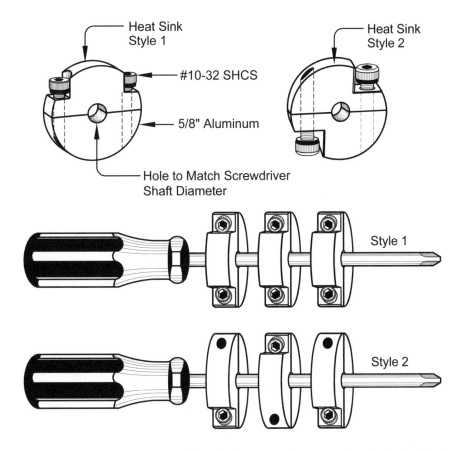

Figure 9-64. Heat sinks on a screwdriver shaft prevent damage to the plastic handle from oxyacetylene torch annealing heat. Pick the heat sink style that is easiest for you to make.

Shop-Made Table Saw Alignment Gage

Contractor-grade table saw blades are supposed to be aligned to within 20 thousandths of an inch of parallel with respect to the saw table miter gage grooves. *Supposed to,* though, does not always mean that they are within that alignment, so saws must all be checked. The simple shop-made alignment gage in Figure 9-65 and a DTI makes this alignment check fast and accurate.

Here are the steps to using this gage:

1. Place the alignment gage in the saw's miter gage groove.
2. Pull back the plunger on the DTI to position the gage so the plunger just touches the saw blade inside its teeth, as in Figure 9-65 (bottom).
3. Zero the DTI gage.
4. Slowly slide the gage—and the DTI—across the saw blade to the other side of the blade, stopping just before reaching the blade tooth.
5. The DTI now reads how out of parallel the blade is.

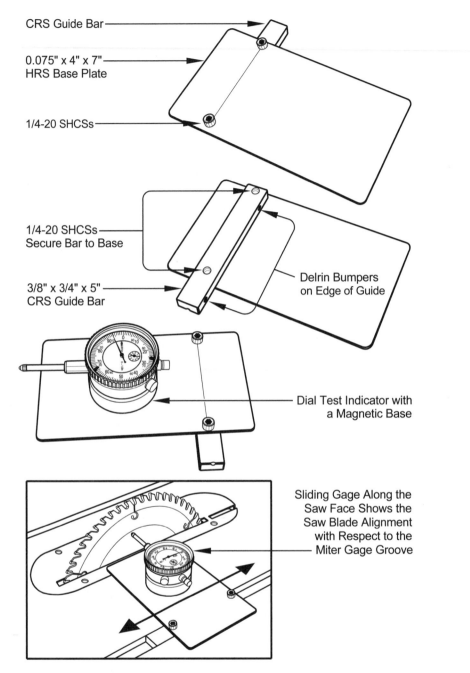

CRS Guide Bar

0.075" x 4" x 7"
HRS Base Plate

1/4-20 SHCSs

1/4-20 SHCSs
Secure Bar to Base

3/8" x 3/4" x 5"
CRS Guide Bar

Delrin Bumpers
on Edge of Guide

Dial Test Indicator with
a Magnetic Base

Sliding Gage Along the
Saw Face Shows the
Saw Blade Alignment
with Respect to the
Miter Gage Groove

Figure 9-65. Table saw alignment gage uses a dial test indicator to
insure that the saw blade is parallel with the miter gage grooves.

6. To return the blade to alignment specification, loosen the bolts holding the
saw bearings—the blade trunnion—and tap it back into place. Remember,
a typical contractors saw requires the saw blade to be no more than 0.020

inches out of alignment when the gage is swept across the width of the saw blade. Use the table saw alignment gage to check when the blade is parallel. Usually the hardest part of this operation is getting access to the bolts holding the trunnion.

7. When the adjustment is complete, apply Locktite to these bolts one by one to secure them.

Because the steel guide bar is slightly narrower than the miter gage groove, two Delrin bumpers, one at each end of the guide bar, are used to remove any slop. The bumpers are held in place by friction and adjusted with a set screw behind each of them. The guide bar should be snug in the saw groove. See Figure 9-66.

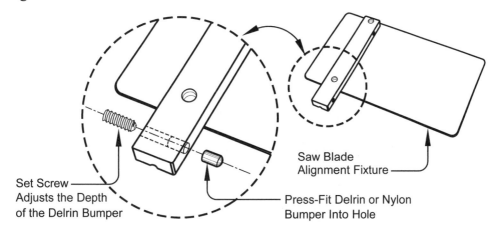

Set Screw
Adjusts the Depth
of the Delrin Bumper

Saw Blade
Alignment Fixture

Press-Fit Delrin or Nylon
Bumper Into Hole

Figure 9-66. Detail of a Delrin bumper on a table saw alignment gage guide bar.

Slide Hammers

Except for car thieves, who use them to pull ignition locks from steering columns, and autobody repairmen, who use them to remove dents in sheet metal, slide hammers are underutilized. These extremely useful tools have two other important uses:

- They break stuck objects loose because the large impulse force they deliver to the work is many times greater than the force a person can apply.

- They deliver this impulse force precisely where it is needed. There is no risk of damaging machinery with a misplaced hammer blow. Slide hammers can deliver this force into tight quarters where there is not room to swing a hammer, and because there is no need to use hand-held chisels and punches, there is no risk of hammering your own hand.

Though there are many different variations, there are only two basic slide hammer designs:

- *Pulling slide hammers* – These are used mainly for pulling out dents or for pulling out stuck roll and dowel pins. Having a strong coupling between the slide hammer and the work is the key to their effectiveness. There are several ways to make this connection:

  - *Chains* or *links* are welded or brazed to Vise-Grip pliers to form a loop which can hook to the tip of the slide hammer as in Figure 9-67.

  - *Wood screws* or *drywall screws,* held by the threaded cap of the slide hammer, securely fasten into the work. See Figure 9-68.

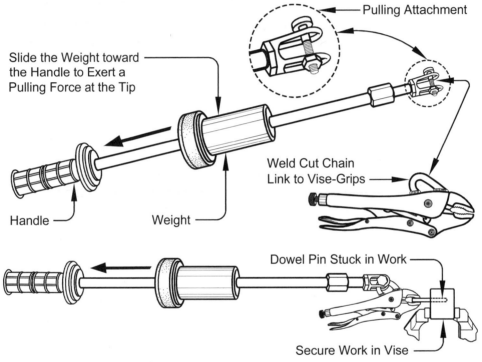

Figure 9-67. Pulling slide hammer with a shop-made adapter for holding Vise-Grip pliers.

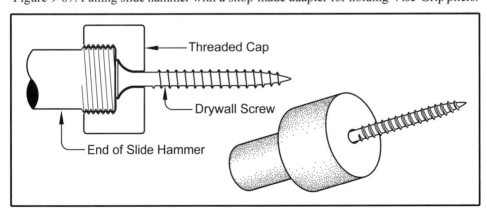

Figure 9-68. Wood screws and drywall screws are fastened to the end of the slide hammer.

- *Welded studs* – Welding a stud or wire directly to the work is an excellent connection method for sheet metal like auto body panels. The hammer grips the stud and later the stud is cut off and ground flat.

- *Hooks* or *rings* on the hammer tip fasten to the work.

• *Pushing slide hammers* – This slide hammer design, seen in Figure 9-69, exerts a pushing force, and is commercially available in a range of sizes from small hammers for sheet metal repairs, to very large hammers for repairing industrial machinery and earth-moving equipment. Wherever large forces are needed for driving pins out of position during repairs, for wedging parts, and for chiseling, pushing slide hammers are just the tool. Most commercial models have a wide range on interchangeable tips and some have accessories for applying bearings and seals.

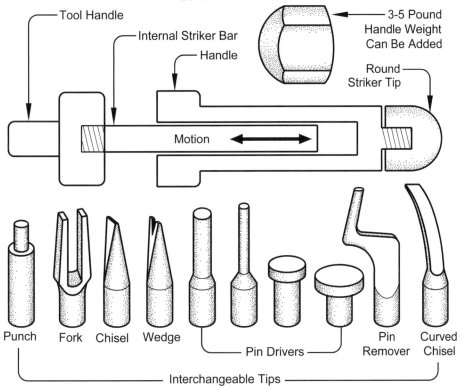

Figure 9-69. A pushing slide hammer and assorted tips that can be shop-made or purchased.

Modifying Vise-Grip Pliers

Vise-Grip pliers can be modified to handle long reaches, Figure 9-70. The welded-on adapters can be simple jaw extensions or pairs of telescoping tubes that can reach inside a part to hold it in place while welding. The two dowel pins in the bottom of Figure 9-70, which sit at 90° to each other, provide smooth, low-friction surfaces for the pliers to pull up on the inside tubing.

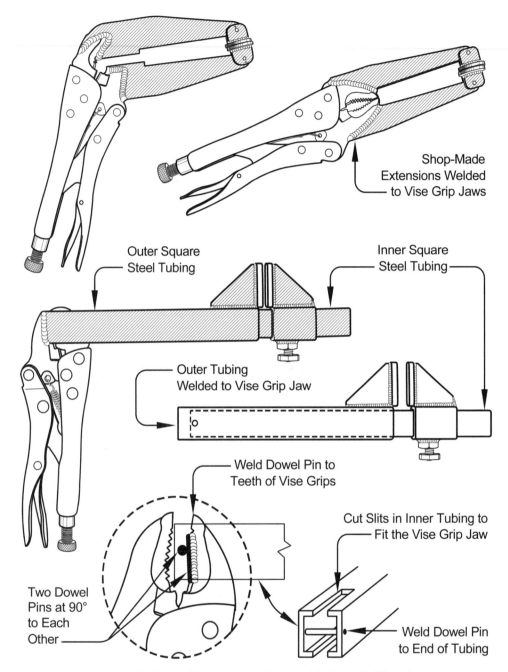

Shop-Made
Extensions Welded
to Vise Grip Jaws

Outer Square
Steel Tubing

Inner Square
Steel Tubing

Outer Tubing
Welded to Vise Grip Jaw

Weld Dowel Pin to
Teeth of Vise Grips

Cut Slits in Inner Tubing to
Fit the Vise Grip Jaw

Two Dowel
Pins at 90°
to Each
Other

Weld Dowel Pin
to End of Tubing

Figure 9-70. Vise-Grip pliers with longer reaches provide better holding for many parts.

Kant Twist Clamps

While we are not suggesting modifying the *Kant Twist clamps* in Figure 9-71, this is a good place to discuss them. Kant Twist clamps are so useful that they belong in every machine and welding shop. Here are their advantages:

- Kant Twist clamps come in a variety of sizes, from 1–12-inch openings, and are strong enough to hold work during milling, drilling and welding. The smallest 1-inch opening clamps have 300 pounds of clamping force, the 3-inch clamps have 1500 pounds of clamping force, and the 12-inch clamps have 6000 pounds of clamping force. More than enough to cover most jobs in the shop.

- Kant Twists are both stronger and weigh less than conventional C-clamps of similar size and can replace them in nearly all applications.

- The cantilevered clamping screws are out of the way of the work, and since the screws are copper plated, welding splatter does not adhere to them. A real plus.

- Their copper-plated swivel jaws always stay parallel, and the jaws rotate to provide four alternative sides: two flat, one single V-groove and one double V-groove to secure the clamp to rods, round stock and wire.

- The most popular Kant Twist frames are steel, but stainless steel frames are available for use in corrosive areas and around surface grinders where magnetic clamps are undesirable.

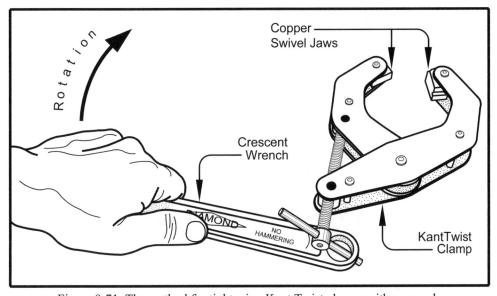

Figure 9-71. The method for tightening Kant Twist clamps with a wrench.

Vise-Grip Clamps

Shops often need clamps that can be applied and removed quickly, yet still apply high clamping forces. Vise-Grip clamps, which are sold in more than a dozen different styles and in many sizes, meet this criteria. The two most useful styles are the locking C-clamp with regular tips, Figure 9-72 (top), and the locking C-clamp with swivel pads, Figure 9-72 (bottom). The swivel-pad version does not damage work by digging into it, but the regular-tip version does dig in, especially on aluminum. But, in their favor, the smaller tips on the regular versions get into tight quarters more easily.

Vise-Grips have upright and inverted positions. The upside down position shown in Figure 9-72 (inset) exposes the screw threads to cutting debris and weld spatter and should be avoided.

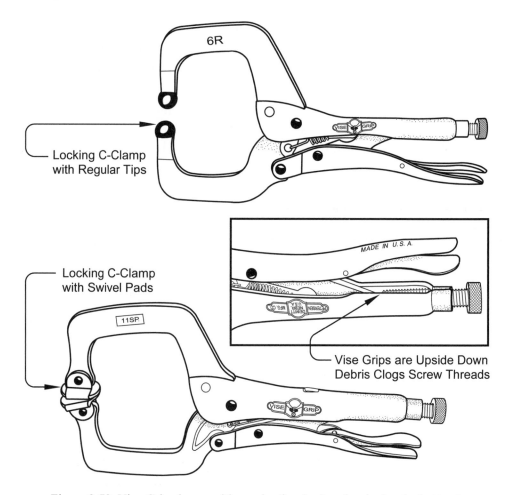

Figure 9-72. Vise-Grip clamps with regular tips (top) and swivel pads (bottom).

Shop-Made Pin Wrench for a Collet Block Nut

The knurled, threaded tightening ring of a 5C collet block has four holes to accommodate a pin wrench. These wrenches are used when large forces will be imposed on the workpiece, such as when held in a milling machine. These wrenches are available commercially, but if you need one immediately, make the pin wrench in Figure 9-73. This unusual pin-wrench design has three advantages:

- It is quick to make—about fifteen minutes—and does not require any complex saw cuts, special materials or tools.

- This wrench is thin enough to seat on the collet block tightening ring. Many commercial wrenches are unable to do this because they have a button-head cap screw sticking out of their sides which bumps the back of the collet block, preventing the wrench from properly aligning.

- It is inexpensive to make.

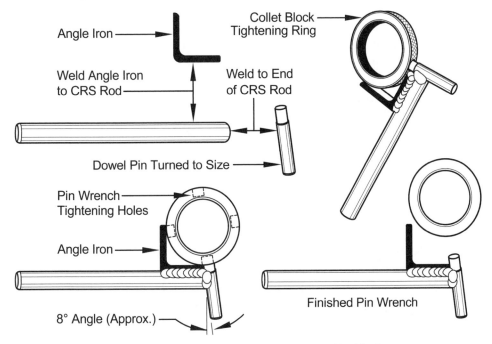

Figure 9-73. A shop-made pin wrench for a collet block nut.

Making a Thread Repair Chisel

Here are two methods to make thread repair chisels:

- If only one chisel is needed, the easiest approach is to grind the chisel on an aluminum oxide grinding wheel of the diameter of the arc needed. Be careful to grind for only a few seconds, then cool the chisel point in water. Do not allow the point to turn blue or it will become annealed.

- The fastest way to make several chisels at once is to anneal the chisels, mill the points to shape in a milling machine, then reharden the chisel points. Here are the steps:

    1. Choose cold chisels with either a square or an octagonal cross section so that they clamp-up in the milling vise with their chisel points horizontal. Chisels with a hexagonal cross-section do not clamp-up properly.

2. Anneal the chisels by heating 2½–3 inches down from the tip a cherry red with an oxyacetylene torch and quickly push the chisels into room temperature dry sand. Heap on more sand so the entire length of the chisels are covered and allow them to cool overnight.

3. The annealed chisels are now easily machined. Make a milling machine cutter from a dowel pin or a CRS round by TIG welding a 60° brazed carbide lathe cutter for threading across the front face of the dowel as in Figure 9-74. Set the carbide cutter to cut a diameter 10–20% larger than the threads to be repaired.

4. Clamp each chisel in the milling vise and use the shop-made 60° brazed carbide lathe cutter to cut the desired arc on the chisel point. The annealed chisel steel will cut easily.

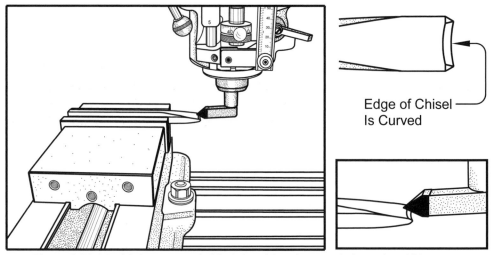

Figure 9-74. Machining a curved chisel tip with a shop-made brazed carbide cutter.

5. Reharden the chisels by heating their first 2½–3 inches red hot and quenching in room temperature oil. The chisel point is now too hard to use and may shatter.

6. Because the chisel point steel will have oxidized during the annealing cycle, clean and polish the chisel point steel so the heat oxidation colors will be visible in Step 8.

7. To temper the chisel, lay it on top of a piece of red-hot steel plate on a fire brick for excellent temperature control. See Figure 9-75 (left).

8. As heat is transferred from the steel plate to the chisel, oxide colors will develop on the polished areas of the chisel point. When the heat oxide area becomes a straw color, remove the chisel from the steel plate and allow the chisel to cool on a zig-zag sheet-metal cooling rack. See Figure 9-75 (right).

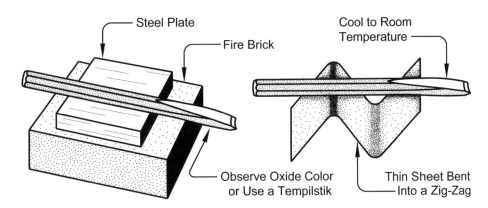

Figure 9-75. Tempering the chisel point by observing its oxide color as heat from the red-hot steel plate enters the chisel (left) and cooling on a zig-zag sheet metal stand (right).

A Shop-Made Air Hose Clamp Wire Applicator

Although stainless-steel worm-screw type hose clamps can secure compressed air lines to their end fittings, these clamps can easily cut open your hand with their sharp edges. An alternative method uses 0.041-inch diameter stainless steel safety wire, fits a wide diameter range of hoses, and leaves no sharp edges. The clamp wire applicator at the top of Figure 9-76 is shop-made, but is also available in commercial versions. This tool has two functions. First, it pulls a stainless steel noose around a hose, and when tight, it turns the noose wires one-half turn over themselves. Here are the steps:

1. Cut a length of stainless steel safety wire about a foot long and form it into a noose. See Figure 9-76 (1).

2. Slip the noose onto the hose and position it over the hose fitting ferrule. If the noose cannot be slipped onto the hose fitting because the hose is too long, the noose can be formed in place over the ferrule. See Figure 9-76 (2).

3. Adjust the wing nut on the hose clamp wire applicator so that the moveable dowel—the dowel through the ¼-20 bolt—is positioned at the cone-end of the applicator. This will provide enough dowel movement so the clamp can pull the wire tight.

4. Position the clamp wire applicator perpendicular to the hose and catch the stainless steel wire of the noose in the nose notch. See Figure 9-76 (3).

5. Run the two pig-tails of the noose over the top of the moveable dowel pin and wrap the remaining lengths of the wire around the dowel pin. See Figure 9-76 (4). Then, tighten the wire noose by turning the wing nut to pull the dowel pin and the stainless steel wire attached to it tight. When properly tightened, the wire noose should begin to dig into the hose. See Figure 9-76 (5).

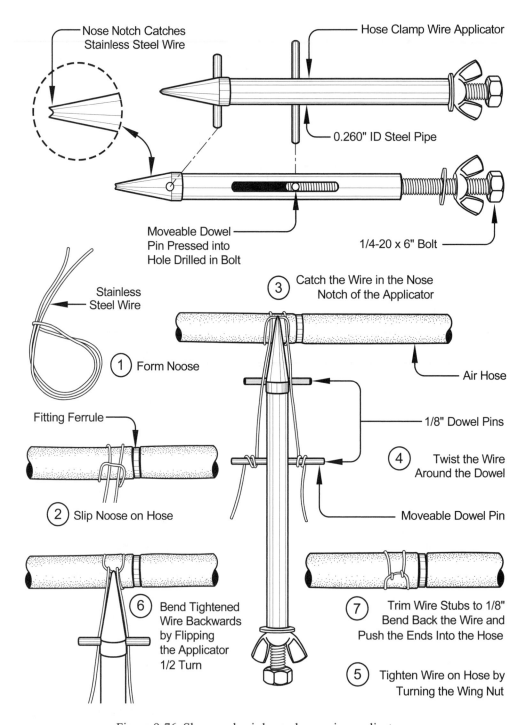

Nose Notch Catches
Stainless Steel Wire

Hose Clamp Wire Applicator

0.260" ID Steel Pipe

Moveable Dowel
Pin Pressed into
Hole Drilled in Bolt

1/4-20 x 6" Bolt

Stainless
Steel Wire

① Form Noose

Fitting Ferrule

② Slip Noose on Hose

③ Catch the Wire in the Nose
Notch of the Applicator

Air Hose

1/8" Dowel Pins

④ Twist the Wire
Around the Dowel

Moveable Dowel Pin

⑥ Bend Tightened
Wire Backwards
by Flipping
the Applicator
1/2 Turn

⑦ Trim Wire Stubs to 1/8"
Bend Back the Wire and
Push the Ends Into the Hose

⑤ Tighten Wire on Hose by
Turning the Wing Nut

Figure 9-76. Shop-made air hose clamp wire applicator.

6. Flip over the clamp applicator one-half turn to lock the noose in place. See Figure 9-76 (6).

7. Cut off the stainless steel wire stubs to about ⅛-inch long, as in Figure 9-76 (7), then use a pair of long-nose pliers to bend the wire ends towards the hose. Finally, press these wire ends into the hose to keep them from snagging on your hands.

Shop-Made Fixture for Welding Single-Lip Milling Cutters

Here is the fixture to make the single-lip cutter shown in Chapter 8 – Milling Machines, Figure 8-57. This fixture makes it easy to weld up a batch of cutters in perfect alignment. See Figure 9-77.

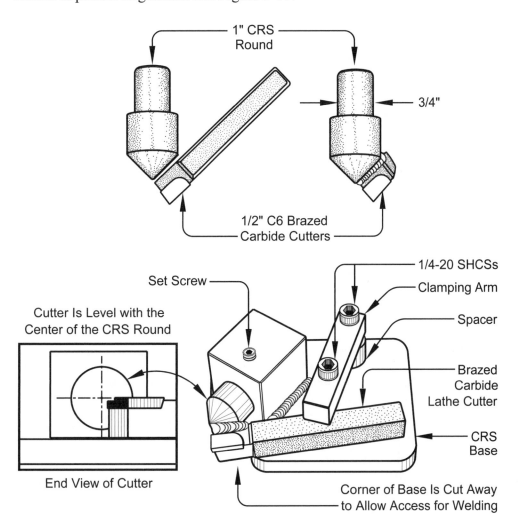

Figure 9-77. Single-lip cutters (top) and the fixture for TIG welding them (bottom).

Section VI – Mechanical Components

Turn-Screw Tightening Handle

Many shop-made tools require high-strength turn-screw tightening handles. Figure 9-78 shows a fixture for making these turn screws which precisely aligns a CRS rod across the top of a SHCS. This is so the rod can be TIG welded or silver brazed to the top of the SHCS. Be sure to remove the blackening finish from the top of the screw head before attempting to silver braze. Use a belt or disc grinder to reach bare steel on the SHCS. The large hole in the fixture provides a space for the torch flame and clearance for the screw head. Figure 9-87 shows a turn-screw tightening handle in use.

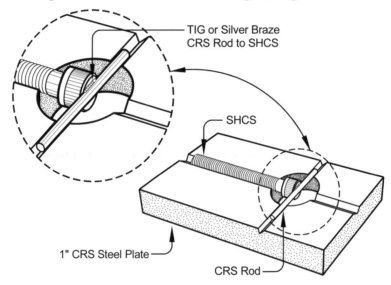

Figure 9-78. Fixture for welding or brazing a rod onto a SHCS to form a turn-screw tightening handle. Use this fixture on a steel table.

Emergency V-Belt Repair Link

Figure 9-79 shows a simple and inexpensive commercial emergency V-belt repair link. A few of these handy devices belong in every shop. These links work on car and truck fan belts, power steering and air conditioning belts, on milling machine belts and on many other machines that use belts. Though one of these links can get you out of a tight spot, remember that these repair links are just a temporary fix. To use one, follow these steps:

1. Trim both failed ends of the V-belt so they are square. Almost any knife or cutter will do the job.

2. Using the repair link as a template, drill a hole in one end of the V-belt for the clamping screw. In a pinch, an awl or ice pick can be used to make the hole.

3. Install the emergency link in the V-belt and pull up the screw. Then, again using the link as a template, drill the hole in the other end of the belt.

4. Finally, install the repair link and pull up the other screw.

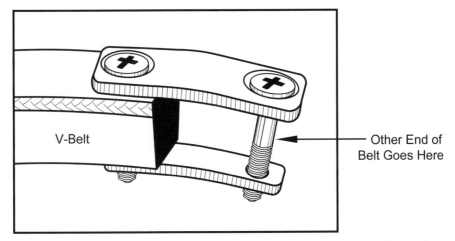

Figure 9-79. An emergency repair link performs a temporary fix in a broken V-belt.

Hose Clamps

Hose clamps always come in handy in the shop, but sometimes they are not long enough. When an extra-long hose clamp is needed, say for clamping a flexible duct to a sheet metal duct, two or more clamps may be joined to extend them. But, be aware that not all hose clamps of the same size are compatible. With different manufacturers, the widths and grooves of the worm screws differ slightly and cannot be joined. See Figure 9-80.

Hose clamps are not just for hoses, they can be used for:

*   Pulling up cylinders of rolled stock for welding, soldering or riveting.

*   Compressing piston rings for installation.

*   Securing brackets to pipes and tubes without drilling, tapping or welding.

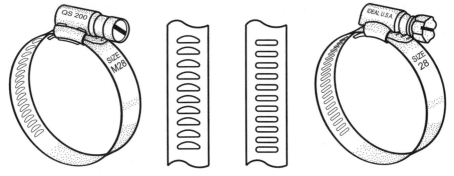

Figure 9-80. Stainless steel hose clamps of the same size may have different thread grooves and cannot be joined to accommodate larger diameters.

O-Rings

O-rings are one-piece donut-shaped, molded elastomeric seals used to prevent fluid leakage between mechanical parts. They are inexpensive, reliable and effective. The two most popular applications are sealing rotating pump shafts and sealing the pistons on hydraulic cylinders. Most O-rings are made of natural or synthetic rubber, but are also offered in fifteen different rubber-based compounds and seven thermoplastic materials. For special applications, O-rings are sometimes made of metals such as indium, copper and nickel.

As mechanical components go, O-rings are newcomers, patented in 1937 by Niels Christensen, a 72-year-old Danish-born American machinist.

The dimensions of O-rings are specified by their ID and cross-sectional diameter, material hardness/durometer, and material composition. See Figure 9-81 (left).

In the USA, O-ring dimensions are often specified by *O-Ring dash numbers* (ANSI/SAE AS568A) which run from -001 ($^1/_{32}$-inch diameter by $^1/_{32}$-inch cross-sectional diameter) on the small end of the scale, through -475 (26.5 inches diameter by 0.25 inches cross-sectional diameter) on the large end of the scale. There are also metric O-ring sizing systems.

O-rings are intentionally oversized—typically 15–20% larger than the groove they fit into—to insure that they deform when installed, causing stresses at the contact point. See Figure 9-81 (right). The stresses at the contact point create the fluid seal, and as long as the fluid pressure does not exceed the contact stress on the O-ring, the fluid seal is maintained.

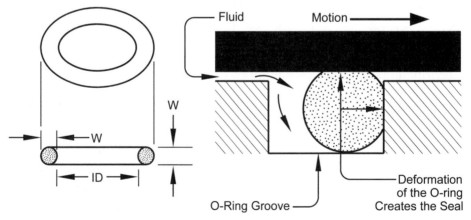

Figure 9-81. O-rings are specified by their ID and cross-sectional diameter.

Several factors are important when choosing O-ring materials and designs:

- Chemical compatibility of the O-ring material with the fluid to be sealed.

- High or low temperatures seen by the O-ring.
- Mechanical factors such as vibration, abrasion and movement.

There are many other uses for O-rings too:

- They can be used on tweezers to hold them closed.
- They make good bumpers to prevent damage to tools and stock.
- They can be used to make small drive belts, pulley rims, check valve seals, spacers and vibration isolators.

Industrial tool distributors sell O-ring cord stock, O-ring adhesives and splicing fixtures so you can make your own. Having the ability to make your own O-rings is a great way to get equipment running quickly.

Stand-off & Spacer Design

Undercutting the center area of a stand-off spacer or equipment foot allows it to be pulled up tight. And, on an uneven surface, this stand-off design helps prevent the equipment from rocking. See Figure 9-82.

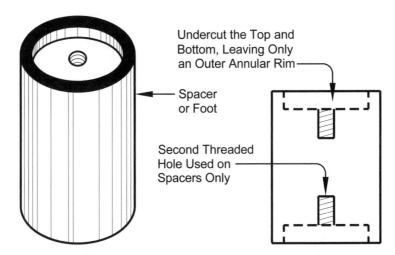

Figure 9-82. Undercutting the center of a stand-off spacer reduces its tendency to rock.

Bending Piano Wire

For sharp bends in piano wire, start by heating the bend point with oxyacetylene or MAAP gas to red, then use the pliers in Figure 9-59 to make the bend. Finish by reheating the wire to red and plunging it into water. This quenching rehardens the wire. For gradual, sweeping bends, use a series of many small bends applied without heat.

Threads in Tubing

To quickly put threads in tubing, use a threaded plug which can be commercially purchased or shop-made. See Figure 9-83.

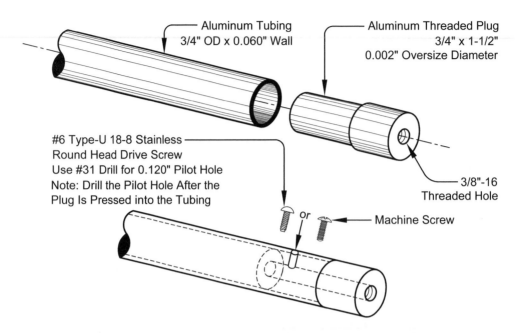

Figure 9-83. Adding threads to a piece of tubing with the addition of a threaded plug.
A screw holds the threaded plug in place.

T-Nuts for Wood

These fasteners are designed for putting steel threads into wood. To install
one, drill a hole in the wood the size of the T-nut barrel, counterbore to
conceal the head of the nut, then hammer the T-nut into place as shown in
Figure 9-84. These nuts are strong, quick to install, and make a finished job.

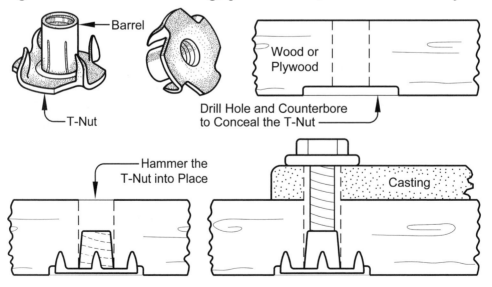

Figure 9-84. T-nuts are a fast and strong way to put threads in wood.

To remove these nuts for reuse, simply screw a fastener into the threads of the T-nut and tap the end of the fastener until both come out. For light loads, T-nuts also work as levelers as shown in Figure 9-85. For T-nut sizes and dimensions, see Table 9-2.

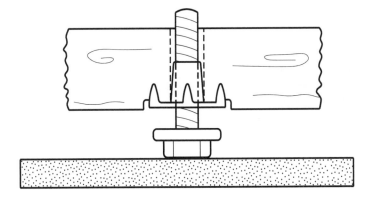

Figure 9-85. T-nuts also make good levelers on shelves, cabinets and tables.

Thread Size	Base Diameter (in.)	Barrel Height (in.)
#8-32	$^5/_8$	$^1/_4$
#9-24	$^3/_4$	$^5/_{16}$
#9-32	$^3/_4$	$^5/_{16}$
$^1/_4$-20	$^3/_4$	$^5/_{16}$
$^5/_{16}$-18	$^7/_8$	$^3/_8$
$^3/_8$-16	1	$^7/_{16}$

Table 9-2. T-Nut sizes and dimensions.

Using Piano Wire for Measuring Straight Edges

When there is a need to check the straightness of a very long workpiece, say 40 feet or more, tightly stretched piano wire is often used. Piano wire, though, is very hard and has high tensile strength, so it is difficult to secure and pull tight. See Figure 9-86 for two different tensioning methods.

The arrangement in Figure 9-87 shows a typical method to check the straightness of long steel bars when the bars are straightened in a hydraulic press. First, vertical supports about 8 inches tall are welded to the ends of the bar being straightened, then the piano wire is stretched between the supports and tensioned by one of the methods shown in Figure 9-86. Next, measurements are taken between the bar and the piano wire to determine where corrective bending forces must be applied. Because the piano wire stretches, it can be left in place during the press cycle and remain undamaged.

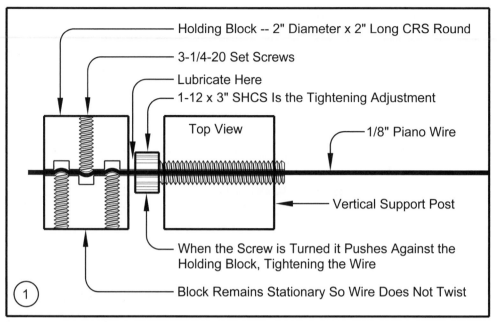

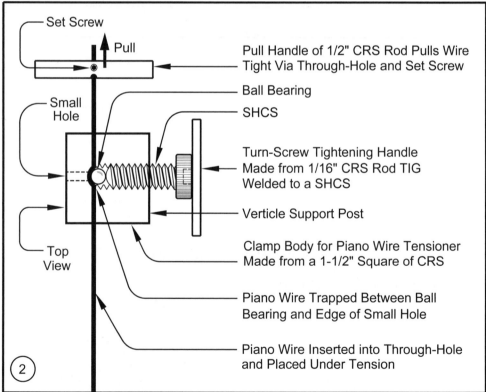

Figure 9-86. Two ways to stretch piano wire. Method 1 (top) shows a technique for securing and tightening the wire that uses set screws in a holding block to tension the wire. Method 2 (bottom) uses a pull handle and a turn-screw tightening handle.

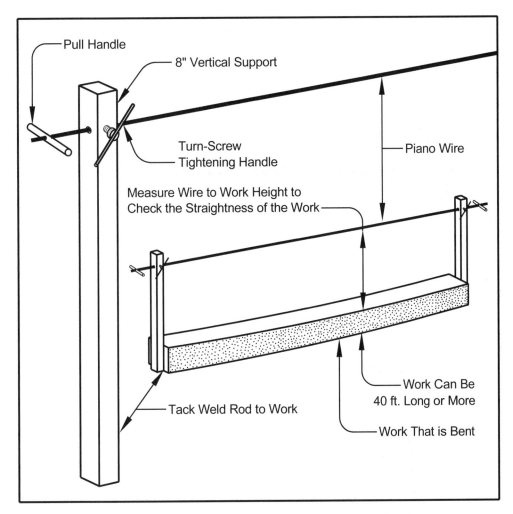

Figure 9-87. Using piano wire to check the straightness of long work.
Note the use of the turn-screw tightening handle.

Section VII – Design Tips

Designs for Resisting Torsion

Diagonal bracing stiffeners are much more effective than longitudinal vertical stiffeners in resisting torsional forces. Figure 9-88 shows two steel bases which support large machines. The base on the left is made of 1-inch steel plate and the one on the right is made of ⅜-inch steel plate. The two bases have about equal resistance to twisting, but the diagonally reinforced design has the advantage of a 60% weight savings, a 78% reduction in welding, and a total manufacturing cost savings of 54% over the longitudinally reinforced design.

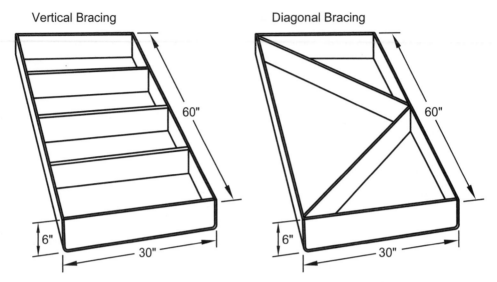

Figure 9-88. Both the base fabricated of 1-inch steel plate (left) and the base fabricated of ⅜-inch steel plate (right) have the same resistance to torsion, but the diagonal bracing of the right-hand base saves weight, welding time, and steel cost.

Cleats in a Plate

When a cable must be attached to a plate to secure or lift the plate without welding on additional hooks or rings to the plate, Figure 9-89 shows how a C-shaped cut-out can be used. This method allows plates to be stacked flat against each other during storage because there are no lift rings sticking out. It also avoids the additional time and cost of both welding and hardware.

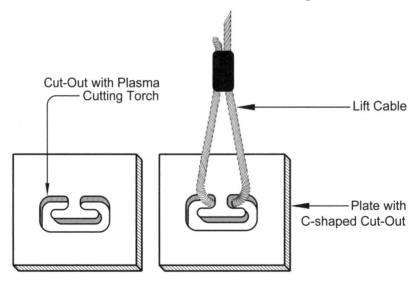

Figure 9-89. A C-shaped cut-out in a plate provides a way to attach a lift cable without using fasteners.

Shop-Made Clamp to Hold a Rod

Figure 9-90 shows how a metal bar can be positioned and clamped anywhere along a rod. This fixture works particularly well when the rod is smoothly ground steel like O-1 stock. The hole in the clamp bar is drilled and reamed to fit the rod. While this arrangement makes a good mount for experimental equipment set-ups, it also works well for holding a rod or thin tubing in place for machining.

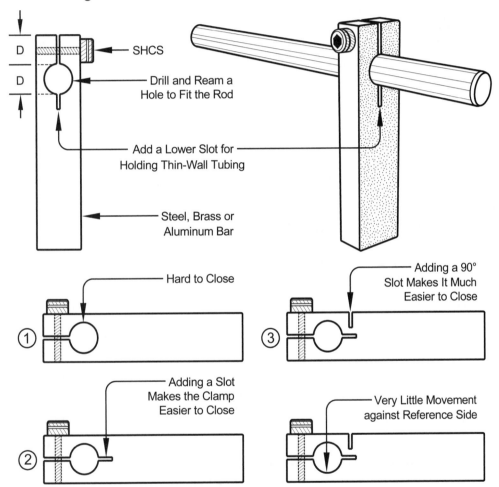

Figure 9-90. A method of clamping a bar to a rod or thin-walled tubing (top),
and three ways to make the clamp hole (bottom).

Accurately Positioning Small Tubing

The medical device industry requires a lot of very fine and accurate machining. Here is an example of a medical packaging machine part which needs a threaded assembly to hold hypodermic tubing. This device has two requirements:

- The hypodermic tubing must be coaxial with the threaded base assembly.

- The tubing must have a liquid-tight seal.

Figure 9-91 shows the solution to this problem. Here is how it's done:

1. Drill and ream a hole in the stainless steel nozzle fitting with a slip fit for the hypodermic tubing. This hole will align the tubing with the stainless steel nozzle fitting.

2. Counterbore the hole drilled in Step 1 with a larger hole, say 6–7 thousandths of an inch larger, so the hypodermic tubing can be silver brazed or silver soldered to form a liquid seal. This larger hole is needed to admit the solder or braze metal.

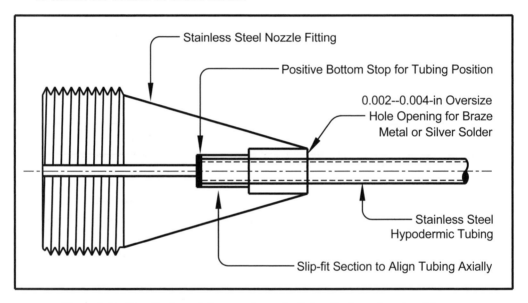

Figure 9-91. Detail of a stainless steel nozzle fitting for hypodermic tubing.

Wire Frames

When making temporary prototypes where great rigidity is not needed and only light loads need to be supported, the wire frame technique in Figure 9-92 may be the answer. Wire frames can be made in almost any shape and go together quickly. They can be soldered, brazed or welded.

There are two types of wire frame joints:

- *Sliding joints* for rapid adjustment are easy to make. On the low-budget end, coat hanger wire can be used, but brazing rod would be stiffer, look better, and be nicer to work with. These joints are not attached to the wire frame itself.

- *Non-sliding joints* hold the wire frame together without allowing movement.

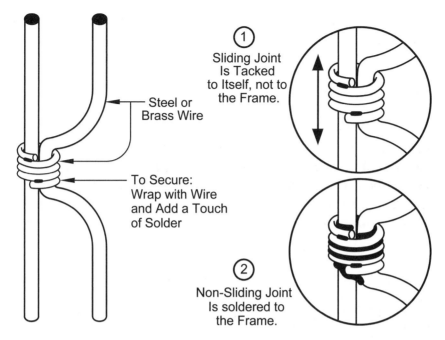

Figure 9-92. Two methods of securing a wire frame:
one with wrapped joints (top) and one with soldered joints (bottom).

Pop Rivets & Corrugated Box Stock Mock-Ups

Where quick mock-ups are needed and forces on them are low, but higher than on a wire frame skeleton, pop rivets and corrugated box stock should be considered. See Figure 9-93.

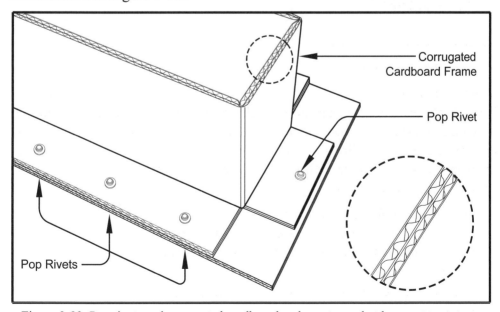

Figure 9-93. Pop rivets and corrugated cardboard make a strong, but low-cost prototype.

Corrugated cardboard prototypes can be quite strong, are easy to build and modify, and low in cost. Score all bends in the cardboard stock with a mat knife to insure neat, sharp corners. To secure pieces together, use pop-rivets or hot glue. Foam core panels can also be used with pop rivets, just as the cardboard, but foam core will accept paint better than corrugated cardboard.

Types of Balancing

There are two types of balancing processes for rotating components:

- *Static balancing* is performed by placing a part on level knife edges and observing the parts' tendency to roll along the edges because of imbalance. See Figure 9-94 (top). By adding balance weights to where the part is too light, or removing material by drilling small holes where the part is too heavy, the part is brought into static balance as in Figure 9-94 (middle). This balancing process works well for "thin" parts, those where most of the mass lies close to one plane. The balancing equipment is simple to put together and the process is quick and requires little skill. Static balancing, however, fails for "thick" parts, those where the part's mass is distributed *along* its rotational axis, not clustered in a single plane. Figure 9-94 (bottom left) shows a part in static balance, but out of dynamic balance, because when this part spins, it will generate vibration. The faster the rotation, the more the vibration. Static balance will not remove this imbalance and in fact, it will not even reveal its existence.

- *Dynamic balancing* requires a machine which spins the parts and senses where weight must be added or taken away. A part dynamically balanced is also statically balanced. However, if the two discs in Figure 9-94 (bottom left) are pushed together on the shaft as in Figure 9-94 (bottom right), because the mass of the parts is nearly all in one plane, the part will be very close to statically and dynamically balanced.

  There is a more subtle issue at work here, too. The forces on the part at high rotational speeds may result in their distortion and bending, which causes imbalance not seen at lower speeds. Additionally, these forces may induce resonant vibrations in both the part and its axle. When parts are dynamically balanced at their operating RPM, both of these problems are avoided.

  Engines, turbines, pumps, electric motors, flywheels, pulleys, wheels, tires, crankshafts, aircraft propellers, gears and all rotating components must be dynamically balanced when run at high speeds. Failure to balance these parts leads to vibration, noise, bearing wear, and eventually—metal fatigue failure.

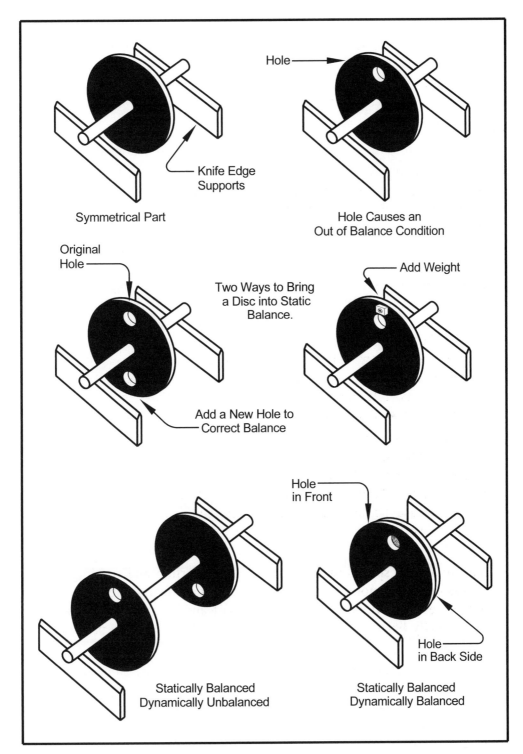

Figure 9-94. Static vs. dynamic balancing.

Index

Credits

Albrecht Inc., Figure 5-16 (right).

Bryce Fastener Inc., Figures 9-41, 9-43.

Clausing Industrial, Inc., Figures 7-8, 7-9, 7-66.

Cooper Industries, Inc., Figures 4-1, 4-14.

Criterion Machine Works, Figures 8-70, 8-71, 8-72, 8-76, 8-77, 8-78, 8-79.

Prof. Robert J. DeVoe, PE, Figures 5-17, 7-60, 7-111, 9-44.

The Do-All Company, Figure 6-3.

Form Roll Die Corporation, Figure 7-98 (F, G & H).

Hardinge Inc. (Bridgeport Milling Machines), Figures 8-4, 8-89.

Jacobs Chuck Manufacturing Company, Figures 5-18, 5-19, 5-20.

James F. Lincoln Arc Welding Foundation, *Design of Weldments* by Omar W. Blodgett, Figure 9-88.

Mitee-Bite Products Company, Figure 8-50.

The M.K. Morse Company, 6-5, 6-6, 6-7, 6-8, 6-9, 6-10, 6-11, 6-12.

David Randal, Figures 1-4, 1-5, 1-12, 1-24, 1-30, 4-16, 4-17, 4-18, 4-19, 4-21, 4-22, 4-24, 4-25, 4-26, 4-27, 4-28, 4-30, 4-31, 4-34, 4-41, 4-42, 4-55, 5-22, 5-23, 5-27, 5-28, 5-29, 5-30, 5-33, 5-34, 5-35, 5-36, 5-38, 5-43, 5-44, 5-46, 6-4, 6-13, 6-16, 6-17, 6-18, 6-19, 6-21, 6-22, 6-23, 6-24, 7-17, 7-18, 7-20, 7-22, 7-23, 7-24, 7-25, 7-26, 7-30, 7-39, 7-57, 7-62, 7-72, 7-82, 7-83, 7-84, 7-90, 7-101, 7-105, 7-109, 7-112, 8-33, 8-57, 8-63, 8-64, 8-69, 8-80, 8-82, 8-83, 8-85, 8-88, 8-92, 8-94, 9-97, 8-98, 8-99, 8-100, 8-102, 8-103, 8-106, 8-107, 9-2, 9-4, 9-5, 9-9, 9-10, 9-11, 9-12, 9-13, 9-14, 9-16, 9-17, 9-18, 9-21, 9-23, 9-24, 9-25, 9-29, 9-31, 9-32, 9-38, 9-39, 9-46, 9-47, 9-48, 9-49, 9-52, 9-53, 9-54, 9-55, 9-57, 9-59, 9-60 ,9-63, 9-64, 9-67, 9-70, 9-73, 9-74, 9-76, 9-77, 9-78, 9-82, 9-86, 9-87, 9-90, 9-91.

Sherline Products, Inc., Figures 7-3, 7-18 (left), 7-37, 7-39, 7-40.

The L.S. Starrett Company, Figures 1-3, 1-22 (left), 1-27, Graph 2-1.

Usines Métallurgiques de Vallorbe SA, Figures 4-4, 4-5, 4-6, 4-8, 4-9, Table 4-1.

Bernard Wasinger, Figures 1-9, 4-56.